Penguin Books
DESERT SIEGE

Chester Wilmot was born in the Melbourne suburb of Brighton in 1911 and later graduated from the University of Melbourne. He became a war correspondent during the Second World War, working first for the ABC in Greece, Syria, Libya and New Guinea, and later covering the whole of western Europe for the BBC. He was noted for his remarkable ability to research and distil information, for the clarity of his despatches, and for his spirited, sometimes controversial, style. After the war he became a broadcaster, journalist and military historian. He published two books, of which *Tobruk* (first published in 1944) was the first. The second, *The Struggle for Europe*, was published in 1952: an authoritative study of Europe in the Second World War, it took him six years to write and was universally acclaimed. In 1954, at the peak of his career, Wilmot died in a plane crash.

Sir Edward Dunlop (1907–1993), AC, CMG, OBE, KCSJ, MS, FRCS, FRACS, LLD(Hon.), DSc. Punjabi (Hon.), FACS, FIC, was born in 1907 near Shepparton in rural Victoria. 'Weary', as he was known, graduated in medicine and surgery just before the outbreak of the Second World War. He served with the AIF in the Middle East, Europe and the Pacific during the war. Captured in Java by the Japanese in 1942, he survived more than three and a half years in some of the most notorious Japanese prison camps; his devotion to his men and his inspirational leadership are legendary. After his return to Melbourne in 1945 Sir Edward continued to practise as a surgeon and was actively involved in community service in Australia and abroad. He was knighted in 1969. *The War Diaries of Weary Dunlop*, his exceptional account of prison-camp life, was published in 1986.

OTHER TITLES IN THIS SERIES

The Coast Watchers by Eric Feldt
Behind Bamboo by Rohan Rivett
We Were the Rats by Lawson Glassop
No Moon Tonight by Don Charlwood
Australia's Pearl Harbour: Darwin 1942 by Douglas Lockwood
Green Armour by Osmar White
The Twenty Thousand Thieves by Eric Lambert
The Ridge and the River by T. A. G. Hungerford
Fear Drive My Feet by Peter Ryan
The Naked Island by Russell Braddon
Into the Smother by Ray Parkin

AUSTRALIAN WAR CLASSICS
PRESENTED BY E. E. (WEARY) DUNLOP

DESERT SIEGE
CHESTER WILMOT

PENGUIN BOOKS

Penguin Books

Penguin Group (Australia)
250 Camberwell Road, Camberwell, Victoria 3124, Australia
Penguin Books Ltd
80 Strand, London WC2R 0RL, England
Penguin Group (USA) Inc.
375 Hudson Street, New York, New York 10014, USA
Penguin Books, a division of Pearson Canada
10 Alcorn Avenue, Toronto, Ontario, Canada M4V 3B2
Penguin Group (NZ)
cnr Airborne and Rosedale Roads, Albany, Auckland 1310, New Zealand
Penguin Books (South Africa) (Pty) Ltd
24 Sturdee Avenue, Rosebank, Johannesburg 2196, South Africa
Penguin Books India (P) Ltd
11, Community Centre, Panchsheel Park, New Delhi 110 017, India

Originally published as *Tobruk 1941*
First published in Australia by Angus & Robertson 1944
First published by Penguin Books Australia 1993
This edition published by Penguin Books Australia Ltd 2003

3 5 7 9 10 8 6 4

Copyright © Chester Wilmot 1944

The moral right of the author has been asserted

All rights reserved. Without limiting the rights under copyright reserved above, no part of this publication may be reproduced, stored in or introduced into a retrieval system, or transmitted, in any form or by any means (electronic, mechanical, photocopying, recording or otherwise), without the prior written permission of both the copyright owner and the above publisher of this book.

Cover photograph   Australian War Memorial negative number 010995
British, Australian, New Zealand and Enemy troops wounded in the 8th army's breakthrough being transported to the hospital ship *Somersetshire* anchored at the entrance to Tobruk Harbour, 1941-11-24.
Photographer: G. Silk

Printed and bound in Australia by McPherson's Printing Group, Maryborough, Victoria

National Library of Australia
Cataloguing-in-Publication data:

Wilmot, Chester, 1911–1954.
Desert seige : Tobruk, 1941.

Includes index.
ISBN 0 14 300172 8.

1. Tobruk, Battles of, 1941–1942. 2. World War, 1939–1945 –
Campaigns – Libya. 3. World War, 1939–1945 –
Participation, Australian. I. Title.

940.5423

www.penguin.com.au

TO
GENERAL MORSHEAD
AND HIS MEN

Foreword

IT affords me pride and pleasure to write the Foreword to this classic of the Second World War, since the distinguished author and war correspondent Chester Wilmot was a cherished friend during our shared years at the University of Melbourne. In recording so vividly and accurately the momentous days of Tobruk's changing fortunes, and Australia's gallant contribution to its defence, Wilmot richly deserves a revival of interest in his work. As a war correspondent, too, his despatches and writings were noted for their cool detachment and admirable professionalism. His tragic death in a postwar air disaster, at the relatively young age of 42, was a great loss to Australia.

All of us who served, however briefly and in whatsoever capacity, during the long siege of the desert town of Tobruk in 1941 will be stirred by this masterly record of events within that grim fortress. The long, bitter, unforgettable fight took place amid fierce heat by day, which contrasted sharply with the freezing nights. The defenders endured savage thirst and choking dust storms, with only a monotonous and limited food ration to sustain their sand-encrusted bodies. Wastage and desert sores were prevalent.

General Sir Archibald Wavell's early thrust into Libya from December 1940, against largely Italian resistance, employed the 6th Australian Division and British troops, stiffened by the 7th Armoured Division. The resolute force had a spectacular success in smashing its way from the eastern Mediterranean to Bengazi via the coastal towns of Sollum, Bardia and Tobruk. Their triumph was reversed, however, with the advent of General Erwin Rommel leading the powerful 'Afrika Korps' of elite German troops. Wavell's available strength was greatly weakened by the diversion of troops to the disastrous campaign in Greece and Crete. Almost trapped by the encircling Axis forces, the inexperienced 9th Australian Division, together with some fine British units, made a confused retreat to Tobruk.

The hastily organised defence of the fortress inflicted a surprising defeat upon the Axis troops, despite the Allies' greatly inferior armoured vehicles being opposed to previously invincible German tanks. The long siege then began in which Lieutenant-General Sir Leslie Morshead strengthened the already formidable defences of Tobruk and initiated probing, fighting patrols that dominated the 'no man's land' about the fortress. In this regard this book stirs in me a further deep interest because of my personal contact and friendship with Morshead, a remarkable man, and with many of the officers and men who served so gallantly in that embattled Libyan fortress at a critical phase of the war.

The entire area was subject to aerial bombardment and attack from heavy guns. One further fierce attack by the Axis forces on the outer fortifications established a salient into the fortress area in May, and achieved the capture of the strategically valuable rise known as Hill 209, before desperate defence stabilised the situation. The siege was marked by an epic aggressive defence, some aspects of which recall the Gallipoli campaign. The British and Australian navies, who ran the gauntlet of overwhelming Axis air domination, cannot be praised too highly. Destroyers, lighters and small ships, largely under cover of darkness, maintained essential reinforcements and supplies and evacuated serious casualties. The harbour was also within range of powerful long-range guns, such as 'Bardia Bill' which fired shells from a position some 15 kilometres away on the Bardia road.

Lord Haw Haw's propaganda broadcasts to the "Rats of Tobruk" led to the cognomen "Tobruk Rat" being adopted proudly by the garrison defenders as if it were a badge of honour. As I have commented elsewhere, this proud brotherhood of veterans has the enduring quality of those depicted in Shakespeare's *Henry V*, who gathered in remembrance to clasp hands upon St Crispin's Day, saying:

> And Crispin Crispian shall ne'er go by,
> From this day to the ending of the world,
> But we in it shall be remembered —
> We few, we happy few, we band of brothers . . .

I commend this book as an uplifting, well-told account of great gallantry and fortitude in the face of harsh adversity.

E. E. DUNLOP.

CONTENTS

	FOREWORD BY E. E. ("WEARY") DUNLOP	vii
	LIST OF MAPS	xi
	PREFACE	xiii
I.	BEFORE ZERO	1
II.	BREAK-THROUGH	18
III.	THE THRUST TO THE TOWN	33
IV.	THE ROUND-UP	46
V.	THE TOWN WE TOOK	54
VI.	TOBRUK DERBY	63
VII.	THE FORTRESS AND ITS GARRISON	84
VIII.	THE EASTER BATTLE	91
IX.	TOBRUK COMMANDER	109
X.	OFFENSIVE DEFENCE	115
XI.	BATTLE OF THE SALIENT	128
XII.	ROMMEL CHANGES HIS TUNE	154
XIII.	WOULDN'T IT?	168
XIV.	HOLDING THE SALIENT	182
XV.	SALIENT SCENES	207
XVI.	THE BATTLE FOR NO-MAN'S-LAND	218
XVII.	"WE NEVER SAY 'NO' "	242
XVIII.	SMASHING THE STUKA PARADE	251
XIX.	KEEPING THE HARBOUR OPEN	265
XX.	SO LONG TOBRUK	280
XXI.	WHAT A RELIEF	290
	EPILOGUE	311
	APPENDIX I. TOBRUK GARRISON	319
	APPENDIX II. HONOURS AND AWARDS	322
	APPENDIX III. THE MAIN EVENTS OF 1941	326
	INDEX	331

LIST OF MAPS

	PAGE
THE CAPTURE OF TOBRUK—THE BREAK-THROUGH, JANUARY 21ST, 1941	23
THE CAPTURE OF TOBRUK—LAST PHASE, JANUARY 21ST-22ND, 1941	33
THE "TOBRUK DERBY"—ROMMEL'S ADVANCE INTO CYRENAICA, APRIL 1ST-9TH, 1941	75
THE EASTER BATTLE, APRIL 14TH, 1941	99
BATTLE OF THE SALIENT—PHASES I AND II, THE GERMAN ATTACK, APRIL 30TH-MAY 1ST, 1941	135
BATTLE OF THE SALIENT—PHASE III. THE GARRISON'S COUNTER-ATTACKS, EVENING, MAY 1ST, 1941	143
BRITISH ATTEMPT TO RELIEVE TOBRUK, JUNE 15TH-17TH, 1941	162
2/23RD's ATTACK ON NORTHERN FLANK OF THE SALIENT, MAY 17TH, 1941	186
THE SALIENT SECTOR SHOWING GROUND REGAINED BY THE GARRISON, MAY-JUNE, 1941	194
THE RELIEF OF TOBRUK—PHASE I. THE EIGHTH ARMY ATTACKS, NOVEMBER 18TH-22ND, 1941	295
THE RELIEF OF TOBRUK—PHASE II. THE EIGHTH ARMY LINKS UP WITH TOBRUK GARRISON, NOVEMBER 23RD-29TH, 1941	303
THE RELIEF OF TOBRUK—PHASE III. ENEMY CUTS EIGHTH ARMY'S LINK WITH TOBRUK, BUT FAILS TO RELIEVE BARDIA, NOVEMBER 30TH-DECEMBER 10TH, 1941	307

Preface

THE Libyan Desert is one of the great natural defensive barriers of the world. From September 1940 to November 1942 it was the chief bulwark of the defence of Egypt. The battle for the Suez Canal was fought in this desert and throughout 1941 the hub of that battle was Tobruk. Its capture by General Wavell's Anglo-Australian forces in January of that year determined the immediate fate of Cyrenaica. Without first taking Tobruk Wavell could never have gone on to Bengazi.

The holding of Tobruk by Australian, British, Indian and later Polish troops from April 10th to December 10th 1941 was fatal to whatever hopes Rommel had of Egyptian conquest that year. Without first taking Tobruk he could not push on far towards Suez. In November 1941, when General Auchinleck launched his counter-offensive, the Tobruk garrison played a crucial part in Rommel's defeat. It is not too much to say that without the capture and holding of Tobruk in 1941, Cyrenaica could not have been conquered by Wavell; Rommel could not have been checked on the frontier of Egypt and Libya from April to November, nor could he have been driven back beyond Bengazi before the end of the year.

To-day when the myth of German invincibility has been finally dispelled on the battlefields of Russia and North Africa, we may be inclined to forget that in April 1941 the Germans were still unchecked on land. The German forces that Rommel brought against Tobruk came fresh from triumphs that had already carried the swastika from Poland to the Pyrenees, from Norway to North Africa. Until then the German blitzkrieg tactics had never been countered. No force or fortress had withstood the Nazi assault. During the first eighteen months of the war the Allied armies suffered one severe defeat after another. Then came the siege of Tobruk, and during the next eight months, when the German armies in the Balkans and Russia were still carrying all before them, Tobruk alone held out unconquered.

This book tells—so far as is possible in wartime—the story of the fighting at and around Tobruk during 1941. It is not a personal story, nor is it a full military history. It is an attempt to record what one man was able to learn of what took place. It deals not only with events but with the men responsible for them—how they lived as well as how they fought. Wherever possible it is told in their own words.

The extent of my indebtedness to officers and men of the A.I.F. is evident on almost every page. The skeleton of the book was pieced together from official A.I.F. and enemy documents. My own observations provide some of the flesh but most of it comes from the eye-witness stories of the men themselves. I am most grateful to those who have made available personal papers, given me first-hand accounts of many incidents and actions or have checked portions of the manuscript. They are too numerous for me to list them here but I do thank them all.

Much of this material was gathered while I was a member of the Australian Broadcasting Commission's Field Unit in the Middle East with the 6th Australian Division during the original capture of Tobruk, with the 9th Division during three months —August, September, October—of the siege and with the British forces that set out to relieve Tobruk in May and November. Wherever possible documentary sources and eye-witness accounts have been cross-checked, but the full story of Tobruk can only be written when all the documents—British and Axis—are available.

Because of the lack of first-hand material I have not attempted to give an account of what happened when Rommel eventually captured Tobruk in 1942. But it is clear that there is no valid comparison between the situation in 1941 and that in 1942. In the latter year Tobruk was attacked by Axis forces, which had already proved strong enough to rout the entire Eighth Army. The garrison was stormed by far stronger forces than Rommel used in 1941 and, moreover, these were not distracted by any British intervention from the frontier. If the Axis attack of June 1942 could have been delivered in April 1941, it is very doubtful whether General Morshead's garrison could have withstood it. After the war, no doubt military scientists will find it most profitable to make a comparative study of the attacks of the two years, but this book deals only with the events of 1941.

For the opportunity to see something of these events I am much indebted to the field commanders concerned—General Mackay and General Morshead—and to the Australian Broadcasting Commission, which gave me as well permission to draw

PREFACE

on dispatches I sent it from the Middle East. I am most grateful also to the official historian of the 1st A.I.F. (Dr C. E. W. Bean) and to his successor (Gavin Long), both of whom gave me valuable advice and assistance; to Colonel L. E. Vail, who checked the proofs; to Sergeant H. B. Paterson, A.I.F., for permission to publish his verses, which appear in Chapter XII; to Corporal Jim Emery, A.I.F., who drew the special relief map; to Noel O'Connor, who designed the jacket; and above all to H. M. Scales whose unflagging aid in the revision and checking of the manuscript was invaluable.

My thanks are due as well to the Department of Information and to the A.I.F.'s Military History Section for permission to reproduce photographs taken by their official cameramen Frank Hurley, George Silk, Damien Parer and the late Lieutenant Tom Fisher. I appreciate particularly the opportunity of reproducing those taken by Tom Fisher, for in both the Middle East and New Guinea he gathered a fine collection of documentary photographs for the A.I.F. His death as a result of enemy air action near Buna in 1942 was widely mourned.

A few words of explanation may be necessary on the vexed question of the use of the term "British". Where I have spoken at large of our forces as opposed to the enemy's, "British" embraces all the Imperial, Dominion and Allied troops. But wherever I have spoken of particular forces I have used it—lacking any suitable alternative—to refer only to those of the United Kindom. This obviously does not imply that Australians regard themselves as any less British than the people of the British Isles.

Because this book is written primarily for Australians and because I was attached to the A.I.F. in the field, I have been mainly concerned with the part it played in the operations described. But every Digger is fully aware of his debt to the Tommies and Scotties who fought beside the A.I.F., and if more first-hand material of their exploits had been available to me it would have been included.

It is as well that we should remember—in these days of our strength and success—what we owe to those who, when we were still weak, checked the run of defeats and gained the first British victories on land in the Second World War. This book has been written as a reminder to us and as a tribute to them.

CHESTER WILMOT.

Sydney,
   October 1943.

CHAPTER I

Before Zero

"Ask, *and it shall be given unto you; seek, and ye shall find; knock, and it shall be opened unto you."*

These words, first quoted by Saint Matthew, were quoted again by Winston Churchill in his Christmas signal to General Sir Archibald Wavell in December 1940. With his genius for weighing the political significance of military events, Churchill knew that the Army of the Nile, then pausing on the frontier of Libya after its victory at Sidi Barrani, *must* go on.

It was only six months since Dunkirk. That dark night might have been long drawn-out if the R.A.F. fighter pilots in the Battle for Britain had not scattered the then-unbroken clouds of defeat and let in the dawn. Yet it was a grey dawn of foreboding storm-clouds, from which the Axis lightning might strike any time—at Britain, at Suez.

The first shaft of light came in through the back door. Hunted from the Eastern Mediterranean by Admiral Sir Andrew Cunningham's fleet, the Italian Navy took shelter behind Taranto Harbour's guns. But on the night of November 11th, 1940 the Fleet Air Arm reached out to the Italian lair, sank a battleship and two cruisers, and left two battleships beached. For twenty-four hours Cunningham trailed his coat on Mussolini's doorstep, but the Italian Navy stayed inside. With Cunningham commanding the sea, Wavell could attack on land with greater hope of victory.

Before Christmas the Middle East sun was beginning to show above the horizon. Two-thirds of Mussolini's Tenth Army, which had been poised to strike for Suez, had been captured at Sidi Barrani or shut up in Bardia. For the time being the threat to Egypt was scotched. With Bardia taken, Wavell's immediate military objective would be gained. Mussolini could not strike again with the small Italian forces still at large in Cyrenaica, and Cunningham's ships would see to it that he was not swiftly reinforced. Wavell had little to gain for the defence of Suez in going beyond Bardia and thus adding to the strain on his over-taxed resources of men and material, already in action on three continents from Malta to Aden, from the Sudan to Albania.

Taking a world view, however, Churchill knew that the Army of the Nile could not stop. The Italians, reeling under the blow of Sidi Barrani, must be driven to the ropes. Part of Mussolini's Empire must be conquered under his very nose; the destruction of his Army must go on till his humiliation was complete. With the Greeks pursuing the Italians into Albania, the British could not afford to call a halt on the Libyan border.

Nor were the British people in a mood for halting. After the defeats and sufferings of the past year it was not enough to beat off the enemy attack on Suez. They wanted to see their own troops sweep through Axis territory, as the Germans had swept through Europe. If the British people were to go on "taking it" through 1941, as they had during the latter part of 1940, they needed the stimulus of a striking victory. Men and women working in the bombed factories of Britain looked for a sign that the arms they had endured so much to fashion really were the tools of victory. America, still torn by dissension, must be shown that the cause she was asked to support was far from being lost.

More important, a strong threat must be established to the Axis in North Africa before spring brought back "invasion weather" to the English Channel. Before then German attention must be turned to the Mediterranean and away from Britain. Knowing all this, Churchill might well say to his Middle East Commander-in-Chief—as he did—"Knock, and it shall be opened unto you."

At noon on January 5th, 1941, Italian resistance at Bardia ended. By dawn next morning Wavell's vanguard was knocking at the door of Tobruk. But whether or not Mussolini's Libyan Empire would be opened to him depended on what happened at that doorway.

Wavell's desert commander was Lieutenant-General Richard O'Connor—a wisp of a man, with a bold spirit and a shrewd brain. O'Connor knew—as Rommel found out later—that no force which by-passed Tobruk could advance far beyond it. The "Imperial Army of the Nile", which was really little more than O'Connor's 13th Corps, had not enough motor transport to maintain its two divisions further than a hundred miles from the nearest port or railhead. Using the Sollum harbour and Bardia's water supply O'Connor's forces could attack Tobruk,

BEFORE ZERO

but they could not advance the next stage to Derna until they had access to the water and harbour of Tobruk. There was certainly not the transport to supply one force containing Tobruk and another continuing westward.

Mussolini's Libyan Commander-in-Chief, Marshal Rodolfo Graziani, still had enough troops to give serious opposition to O'Connor's advance. At Tobruk and Derna he had two infantry divisions and an armoured force with 120 new medium tanks. He had more medium tanks than O'Connor. He had twice as many guns. In his 13th Corps O'Connor had only the 7th British Armoured Division, the 6th Australian Infantry Division, and a small reserve of British infantry, artillery, machine-guns and heavy "I" tanks.[1] He had fewer men, but these had a clear advantage in training, skill and spirit, and in addition the British had command of the sea and superiority in the air.

Nevertheless, O'Connor could not risk the inevitably heavy losses of an immediate assault on Tobruk, for the Italians had prepared it as their main fortress for the defence of Cyrenaica. After Bardia it took a fortnight to gather the necessary forces and supplies for the next attack. Preparations, however, were delayed more by the weather than by the Italians.

Every few days during this fortnight sandstorms clogged the British supply lines. Swirling dust blotted out everything and brought work and traffic almost to a standstill. I was caught in one of these storms on January 15th on the Sidi Barrani-Tobruk road. It was thicker than the worst London fog. You could not see a man ten yards in front of you, and even the sun was browned out.

In Sollum harbour that day, troops unloading supply ships could barely see to work. On the road up the cliff behind them, a captured 10-ton truck missed a sharp turn and plunged into space. Over the beds of the hospital in Bardia, the storm spread an extra blanket. Along the road between Bardia and Tobruk one of the few vehicles which tried to move, got off the tarmac and blew up on a thermos bomb. Around Gambut drome thirty-eight miles east of Tobruk, reconnaissance aircraft, which should have been taking photographs or spotting for the artillery, were grounded. In the wadis near Gambut, ordnance engineers had to

---

[1] These tanks, known officially as "Infantry" or "I" tanks and popularly as "Matildas", because of the skirt which protects their bogies and tracks, were the British reply to the pillbox. Mounting a 2-pounder and a machine-gun and protected by 3-inch armour, they had proved themselves almost invulnerable to enemy fire at Sidi Barrani and Bardia and had been a key factor in crushing enemy infantry resistance.

lash tarpaulins over the precious "I" tanks they had been overhauling, and stop work. On the bare plateau outside Tobruk, Australian and British troops huddled in trucks with anti-gas goggles over their eyes, handkerchiefs across their noses and mouths, or lay in slit-trenches with blankets over their heads while the scourging sand steadily silted in. Preparations for the attack came almost to a halt.

The sandstorm died at dusk. Next morning was bright and clear and the road was packed with traffic making up for lost time. On the shell-torn road between Sollum and Bardia we overtook a long convoy of Italian Diesels driven by dusty, unshaven Diggers. The trucks still bore their Italian markings, but the Australians had given them new numbers—"Wop 69", "Wop 73", and new names—"Dago Dragon", "Spaghetti Sue", "Benito's Bus". Without the hundreds of vehicles captured at Sidi Barrani and Bardia, the speed of the advance through Cyrenaica could never have been maintained.

Inside the Bardia defences, a "Mobile Bath and Decontamination Unit" had set up showers at an Italian water-point beside the road. A convoy had stopped to let some grimy gunners have their last shower until Tobruk fell. At the water-point two huge captured water-trucks were filling up. Near by a military policeman was questioning westbound drivers—"Got any water? Fill your tins or take two from here. Up there the boys are on half a gallon a day for everything."

A mile out of Bardia a blue enamel sign said TOBRUCH 119 KM. Underneath it was a warning—KEEP TO THE ROAD: BEWARE THERMOS BOMBS.[2] Four or five trucks had been blown up already by these bombs, which Italian aircraft had scattered alongside the road.

For the first fifteen miles the road was either pock-marked by shelling or broken by enemy demolition. From there onwards it was a smooth, black highway, stretching like a liquorice strap across the desert. A motley collection of British and captured vehicles streamed westward. Ten-ton Italian Diesels ground laboriously on under 12- and 15-ton loads; staff cars, light trucks and empty ambulances sped past; dust-laden dispatch riders on Italian motor-bikes wove their way in and out among the traffic fast and slow, overtaking everything. Along a desert track, clear of thermos bombs, a few Matildas and some reconditioned

---

[2] Thermos bombs are so called because they look like a thermos flask. They do not go off when dropped, but explode on the next impact or heavy vibration.

Italian tanks rolled slowly towards Tobruk, husbanding their tracks and engines. The road was an ideal strafing target, but the R.A.F. ruled the skies. From time to time Hurricanes on road patrol roared past just above the telegraph poles.

Nothing checked the westbound traffic until it came to a barricade across the road and a sign—

If you lika da spaghetti—KEEP GOING. Next stop TOBRUK—27 Kms.

Fifteen miles to the town, but only four to the fortified perimeter. From this road block, however, you could see nothing of the defences. Even a couple of miles closer all that could be picked up was the outline of barbed wire etched against the skyline. On every side the flat and featureless desert swept away to the horizon. Every yard of the level plateau was covered by Italian machine-guns, firing from concrete posts, flush with the ground and invisible even from a few hundred yards. They were hard to get at and hard to see, but nothing restricted their fire, nothing blocked their view except darkness or duststorm. For the attacker there was no cover. He could be seen a mile or more from the defences and could be covered by fire all the way in.

That was Tobruk's strength. It was not a natural fortress. Its defences had been hewn from the uncompromising desert at tremendous cost. The Italians had fortified this piece of wasteland because here there is a harbour and a few springs of moderately pure water—the only good harbour between Bengazi and Alexandria; the only good water supply between Derna and Mersa Matruh.

The harbour is the heart of the Fortress. The defences built to protect it run in a rough semicircle across the desert from the coast eight miles east of the harbour to the coast again nine miles west of it. This fortified semicircle makes a perimeter thirty miles long, enclosing an area roughly the size of Adelaide and its suburbs. The harbour is not large—only two and a quarter miles long and a mile wide—but it is safe and fairly deep. Its northern shore is protected by a high tongue-shaped promontory, on the slopes of which the Italians built the garrison town of Tobruk—a cluster of little white houses, big concrete barracks and other naval and military installations covering an area about half a mile by a mile.

Between the high coastal cliffs and the perimeter the desert plateau rises in three steps—each step leading to a flat shelf a mile or two wide before the next escarpment carries the plateau another fifty to a hundred feet higher. The edge of these escarpments is broken by a series of rough wadis, useful for concealing artillery and headquarters.

The coastal cliffs are also broken by wadis and several of these, with their reliable wells and occasional clump of thirsty palms, might almost pass for oases. These are the least unpleasant places in the Fortress, for in addition they open on to sheltered beaches of white sand. Elsewhere there is a wasteland of rock and bare, brown earth bound together by stubby, thorny camel-bush. It is a hard, cruel and parched land and even the ten inches of rain, which reputedly fall each year, often leave the desert two or three miles inland bone dry. There nothing lays the dust or gives shade from the fierce summer sun or shelter from the winter's bitter wind.

Around the 30-mile perimeter the Italians by January 1941 had drilled and blasted a fairly strong defensive system. First there was a double wire fence—five feet high. Outside this they had begun to dig an anti-tank ditch. Where it was finished, it was twenty feet wide and twelve feet deep and in most places it had been cut out of solid rock. In the southern sector, however, for four miles east of the El Adem road the ditch was uncompleted and very shallow. In the western sector there was no ditch at all, although a deep wadi running five miles inland was incorporated in the defences and provided a natural tank trap. Where the ditch was unfinished or non-existent, the Italians had laid minefields, but they had made the mistake of laying these as much as 150 yards in front of the wire. To stop engineers coming forward at night and disarming the mines, however, they had put down a belt of "booby-traps" in front of the minefields.

The perimeter was covered by two lines of strongpoints—128 in all. The forward series were right on the wire, 600 to 800 yards apart. Some 500 yards behind them ran a second series which covered the gaps between the forward posts. All posts were protected by individual barbed-wire fences, and each of the forward ones was surrounded by a circular anti-tank ditch as well.

The posts were not linked by any connecting trenches, but could support each other with fire which was linked to cover the barbed wire and the anti-tank trench or minefields and to sweep the plateau for hundreds of yards into no-man's-land.

BEFORE ZERO

The front was also covered by field and medium guns emplaced several miles behind the perimeter.

Each strongpoint had two or three machine-guns and an anti-tank or light field gun. Some had a mortar as well and certain key posts had twice this fire power. The weapons were emplaced in circular pits, each roughly four feet deep and six feet wide, about twenty yards apart and connected by deep trenches. Opening off these were bomb- and shell-proof ammunition chambers, command posts and cramped sleeping quarters for about twenty men.

Although the posts were concreted, they were not pillboxes. Concrete, which should have been used to roof the fire positions, had been put into the floors and sides of the pits and trenches. The posts, like those at Bardia, were more funk-holes than fighting trenches. They had insufficient fire positions, and those that there were, had no overhead cover for the troops who manned them. But there was full protection for those who stayed below.

The defence of Tobruk was organized in part by the elusive General Bergonzoli, nicknamed "Electric Beard" by his troops when they were "non-intervening" in Spain. Already he had escaped the Australian clutches once at Bardia, where he had been in command until the last night. Then, realizing the position was hopeless, he and a few of his staff had walked out through the British lines and after five days had reached Tobruk.

There he found 72-year-old General Petasso Manella in command of a garrison of 25,000,[3] strong in artillery but weak in infantry. His main force was the 61st Division under General Della Mura, but its six battalions (plus two odd battalions from other divisions) were barely sufficient to man the 30-mile perimeter. At Bardia Bergonzoli had found that even with twenty-two battalions he could not hold a 17-mile line. Maybe this explains why he put himself and his celebrated beard on the last plane to leave Tobruk before the attack.[4]

Because of weakness in infantry, Manella was relying on artillery to check any break-through. He had plenty of guns for this purpose—140 field and 68 medium and heavy pieces. In

---
[3] Of these, about 10,000 were anti-aircraft or coast artillery gunners, lines of communication troops and naval personnel.

[4] He evaded the Australians at Derna too, but was finally caught in the last round-up by the 7th Armoured Division at Beda Fomm, south of Bengazi.

addition there were 36 heavy A.A. and a dozen coast defence guns (including a 12-inch naval monster) which could be turned against attacking ground troops. However, he did not have men enough to establish defence in depth to protect these guns if a break-through should be made. Behind the shell formed by the outer perimeter he had only a few strongpoints covering the main gun positions and road junctions. To strengthen the defence of these areas, a number of light and medium tanks had been dug in as pillboxes and in front of them were booby-traps and minefields. Lacking defence in depth, the enemy needed a strong mobile reserve of tanks and infantry to counter-attack. But for this task he had only twenty-three medium tanks and one infantry battalion. With all these weaknesses, the Tobruk Fortress was still strong enough to make its capture costly, unless the attack were thoroughly prepared.

The Italian garrison in Tobruk would have been in a reasonably strong position if Mussolini's forces farther west had done anything to help it beyond dropping leaflets exhorting it to hold out. The Italian Navy made no attempt to bring relief or even to interfere with the British warships, which supported O'Connor's preparations with naval bombardment. After Bardia the Italian Air Force yielded the skies to the R.A.F. which bombed Tobruk as it wished. The attackers thus had unrestricted aerial observation; the defenders had none.

Even the remaining ground forces in Cyrenaica—the 60th Infantry Division and General Babini's 120 medium tanks—remained inactive between Derna and Mechili.[5] They made no effort to keep open the garrison's landward way of escape to Derna or to draw off any of O'Connor's forces. The Tobruk garrison was left to its fate. Against it Wavell was free to concentrate all the land, sea and air power he had available in Libya and off its coasts.

As at Bardia, O'Connor delegated the task of planning and carrying out the attack to Major-General Iven Mackay and his 6th Australian Division, plus supporting British troops. As at Bardia, O'Connor decided that the British should keep the ring with the 7th Armoured Division and the Navy, and provide a powerful left lead with tanks, bombers and artillery, while Australian infantry was to be the strong right, which would break through the enemy defence and deliver the knock-out.

---

[5] When Rommel eventually attacked Tobruk, he was never able to concentrate his full strength against it because of the diversion provided by the British forces on the frontier.

For the Tobruk attack, Mackay's forces were weaker in "I" tanks, but stronger in other supporting arms than they had been at Bardia. There they had twenty-six "I" tanks of the 7th Royal Tank Regiment; but ten of these were now out of action through mechanical trouble. Private enterprise, however, on the part of "A" Squadron of the 6th Divisional Cavalry Regiment added to the tank strength. (The rest of the regiment was besieging the Italians at Giarabub.) It salvaged fifteen Italian mediums from Sidi Barrani and Bardia. It also doubled its normal establishment of carriers so that its O.C. (Major Denzil Macarthur Onslow) had one "squadron" of tanks and two of carriers. Even with these captures, there were insufficient tanks to give the infantry as much support as at Bardia, and there were only enough "I" tanks to assist one infantry brigade in the opening phase of the attack.

Mackay had the following force available:

Australian:
    16th Infantry Brigade—2/1st, 2/2nd, 2/3rd Battalions.
    17th Infantry Brigade—2/5th, 2/6th, 2/7th Battalions.
    19th Infantry Brigade—2/4th, 2/8th, 2/11th Battalions.
    2/1st, 2/2nd and one battery of the 2/3rd Field Regiments.
    16th and one troop of the 17th Anti-tank Companies.
    2/1st, 2/2nd, and 2/8th Field Companies.
    "A" squadron plus two scratch "squadrons" of 6th Divisional Cavalry.

ritish:
    7th Royal Tank Regiment, 1st Royal Northumberland Fusiliers (M.Gs). 1st Battalion, Cheshire Regiment (M.Gs).
    104th Royal Horse Artillery Regiment; one battery of 4th R.H.A.; 51st Field Regiment; 7th Medium Regiment; one battery of 64th Medium Regiment; two batteries of 3rd R.H.A. (anti-tank). The other battery of 4th R.H.A. and most of the guns of 1st R.H.A. were also available to support the Armoured Division's demonstration.

The general plan was for the armoured division in the west and south-west, and the 17th Australian Brigade in the east, to make a demonstration, while the main attack was launched from the south. To soften up the garrison and support these diversions, the Navy and the R.A.F. were to bombard vital areas inside the perimeter during the night immediately preceding the direct assault. Then before dawn, under cover of a heavy barrage, the 16th Australian Brigade was to seize a small bridgehead on the perimeter about three miles east of the El Adem road. With "I" tank and artillery support, this brigade was then to roll up the perimeter and over-run the field guns immediately behind it on either side of the bridgehead towards the El Adem road on the left and the Bardia road on the right. At the end of this phase, with eight miles of the perimeter captured, the way would be open for a deep thrust to the junction of the El Adem and Bardia roads (hereafter to be called the "El Adem crossroads") and onwards into the heart of the defences. This deep thrust was to be made by the 19th Australian Brigade, supported by Macarthur Onslow's carriers and captured tanks, and by strong artillery concentrations.

It was expected that at the end of these two phases the 17th Brigade would have swung in from the east and established itself along the Bardia road ready to drive north to the sea; the 19th Brigade would be beyond the El Adem crossroads, commanding the high ground of the main escarpment and in a position to attack generally west-north-west, while the 16th Brigade—now holding the line of the El Adem road—could roll up the western perimeter.

These were the planned objectives for the first day, but individual Brigadiers were given freedom to exploit their success and it was hoped that by nightfall the most advanced troops would hold the last escarpment overlooking the town and harbour. Mackay's problem was not *whether* he could take Tobruk, but *how cheaply* and *how quickly*. Speed in overcoming resistance, once the perimeter had been breached, was most necessary to scotch any counter-attack and to prevent the enemy demolishing the port installations and water pumping and distilling plants, which were the main prizes of the battle.

In broad outline the plan was simple, but the most detailed and complex organization was needed to carry out the closely timed programme smoothly and swiftly. Important preliminary problems had to be solved. First, patrols had to test the enemy defences and plot the minefields, booby-traps, anti-tank ditch and barbed wire in the sector where the bridgehead was to be established. Bright moonlight made this patrolling hazardous, for the enemy was very jumpy. He did not patrol far out beyond his wire, but covered the front with heavy fire on the slightest provocation. One particularly sensitive area became known as "Jittery Corner" and the Diggers pictured Italians sitting beside a heap of machine-gun belts with orders to reel them off before dawn.

The point for the actual break-through was selected only after prolonged reconnaissance. Infantry and engineer patrols early located the shallow section of the anti-tank ditch east of the El

BEFORE ZERO

Adem road, but the various patrol reports were so conflicting that Mackay eventually sent two lieutenants from his Engineer H.Q.—G. Beckingsale and P. R. Gilmour—to survey the area between Posts 55 and 57, which seemed most suitable. On the night of January 15th-16th these two sapper officers spent more than seven hours with compass and tape, checking bearings and measuring distances until they had accurately plotted the positions of the ditch, minefields and booby-traps. As a result of their work the point of penetration was finally chosen.

Engineers of the 2/1st Field Company—commanded by Major Alec Torr—continued this good work by finding the way through the enemy's defensive screen. Two of them, Lieutenant B. Dawson and Sergeant E. J. Johnston, located parts of the ditch that were only two feet deep and had sides so soft that they could be dug in to make ramps for vehicles and tanks. The fields of mines and booby-traps were thoroughly explored by Lieutenant S. B. Cann and Sergeant V. E. Nash. They found that the traps were mounted on small posts eighteen inches above the ground and consisted of canisters filled with explosive and fragments of metal. From the trigger on each booby-trap a trip-line of tough twine ran ankle-high to the post of the next trap, fifteen yards away. Cann and Nash found, however, that by slipping a nail into the slot, from which the Italians had removed the "safety pin", they could neutralize the trap. They taught their men to find these by walking slowly forward with a thin stick held out before them pointing groundwards until the stick touched the trip-line. Then they could follow this along, "delouse" the trap and cut the twine.

In the minefield they discovered a double row of mines laid as close as stepping stones, but just as easy to delouse as the booby-traps. There was nothing to prevent them lifting the lids of the long green boxes, which housed the mines, and removing percussion caps and detonators. With the same thoroughness the enemy barbed wire was explored by Lieutenant W. A. Davey and Sergeant R. Williams. Back in the field company's lines sappers then built models of the defences, and test demolitions were carried out on the wire with "home-made" Bangalore torpedoes, consisting of high explosive packed into 12-foot lengths of 3-inch water-pipe. (At Bardia two Bangalores placed side by side had blown 25-foot gaps in the Italian wire despite its great strength.) Meanwhile, the rank and file practised delousing specimen mines and booby-traps brought back by Cann and Nash.

The second problem was to keep the enemy artillery quiet—especially during the second phase, when the "I" tanks would not be available to help the 19th Brigade. Fortunately the 6th Division's artillery commander, Brigadier E. F. Herring, had 140 field and 26 medium guns to support the attack.[6] The gunners' main task during the first phase was to silence all enemy weapons in the area where the bridgehead was to be established, and then to put down concentrations in front of the battalions as they pushed east and west along, and inside, the perimeter. Roughly half the guns were allotted to these tasks. The remainder were to silence enemy batteries, especially those which could shell the bridgehead area.

In the second phase the path of the 19th Brigade's advance was to be covered by a creeping barrage, and more than a hundred guns were simultaneously to blast the enemy batteries, so that the infantry would not run into point-blank artillery fire as the 17th Brigade had done at Bardia. If the 19th Brigade's deep thrust was going to succeed the enemy guns must be silenced.

The barrages on the perimeter posts and the known infantry positions provided no great problem. At Bardia the Australian infantry had followed in as close as 150 yards behind the barrage and overwhelmed the posts before the Italians had recovered from the shelling.

The counter-battery tasks were not so simple. The enemy battery positions had first to be found and precisely plotted. Captured maps and the R.A.F.'s command of the air made this possible, for excellent maps of the Tobruk defences and details of the garrison were found at Bardia. Even at Sidi Barrani the Italians had with them maps of Tobruk that showed minefields, anti-tank obstacles and battery positions. These positions, as marked on the captured maps, were confirmed by air photographs, and by reconnaissance planes which observed the batteries in action. Once the pilots had "fixed" a battery position they kept close watch to make sure that it was not moved without their knowledge or that it was not a dummy. These reconnaissances were carried out in slow, vulnerable Lysanders, which regularly "stooged around" spotting for half an hour or so at 4000 to 6000 feet in the face of strong ack-ack fire; and yet on only two out of forty-six reconnaissances was a plane hit.

---

[6] There were 116 25-pounders; 12 18-pounders; 12 4.5-inch howitzers; 16 4.5-inch guns (last war 60-pounders converted to fire a heavier, longer shell further); 2 60-pounders and 8 6-inch howitzers.

Having located the enemy batteries, Herring needed to find out what area each was given to shell, and especially what guns could fire on the proposed break-through area, so that all his counter-battery effort could be concentrated on these at the start. Some of this information came from the pilots but most from "flash-spotting". (For flash-spotting, men were posted at a number of positions near the perimeter to watch for the flashes of enemy guns. When they saw a flash each took a compass bearing on the point from which the flash came and noted the time. Simultaneously other observers noted where the shells fell. When all the observers compared their readings they could locate the batteries and thus tell which were most active, and what were their individual areas of fire.) The next phase was to check the accuracy of our fire by ranging on the enemy batteries. This too called for aerial spotting because only one enemy gun position could be seen from the ground. The Italians had much better observation because they had erected many pole and tower O.Ps.

The gunners had one final problem. They were mostly in positions near the Bardia road, but in order to support the proposed attack they had to move their guns to an area south of the break-through point. To avoid revealing the direction of the attack, however, they could not fire from their new positions until zero hour. This meant that the gunners had to lay their guns on the initial targets by survey and mathematical calculation without any check by ranging.

The organizing brains behind the artillery plan were Brigadier Herring, a really great commander, and his very able staff officer, Major George O'Brien, a regular gunner. Herring served with the British Army in the Great War, at the outbreak of which he was a Rhodes Scholar at Oxford. As an artillery officer in France and Macedonia he won a D.S.O. and an M.C. Between the two wars he rose to be one of Australia's leading King's Counsel. This background helped him considerably in Libya. More than half his gunners were British and at first some regular British artillery commanders were reluctant to serve under an Australian "civilian soldier". But Herring has a quiet, easy manner and his last war service had given him an understanding of the British to which they were quick to respond. After Bardia and Tobruk those officers who had been most sceptical were his strongest champions. In building up the artillery plan Herring brought to bear the same thorough, relentless logic and attention to detail with which he had so often built up a legal argument.

The artillery support that his gunners could give left little doubt that the 16th Brigade would establish the bridgehead and clean up its share of the perimeter, just as it had done at Bardia. Its success there had been the result of thorough training during the previous eleven months in Palestine and Egypt under the command of Brigadier Arthur Allen.

A Sydney accountant in private life, Allen began his career of active service in 1914 a a platoon commander in the 13th Battalion, but typhoid fever stopped him getting to Gallipoli. Within three years, however he was commanding the 48th Battalion in France at the age of twenty-four. He gained then a reputation, which his men in this war strongly endorse, of being fair and fearless. He is now one of the most experienced soldiers in Australia. In the Syrian campaign, when he gained command of the 7th Division, he, like Mackay before him, achieved the distinction of having commanded in battle everything from a platoon to a division.

Although at forty-seven his last-war nickname, "Tubby", was even more appropriate, he was still hard and active. He proved this later in New Guinea by marching with his troops for five days through the back-breaking Owen Stanley Range. His strength in training or in planning an operation was his thoroughness and his capacity for inspiring men to great efforts. Allen was fortunate in having as his right-hand man, Major Ian Campbell—probably the most brilliant of all the younger staff officers in the A.I.F. and a commanding personality. He, as his Brigadier was the first to insist, played a very big part in the splendid planning of the assaults at Bardia and Tobruk.[7]

For the second phase of the attack which called for speed, drive and daring, General Mackay could not have found a more suitable man than Brigadier H. C. H. Robertson, a Staff Corps officer who commanded the 19th Brigade. Those who have served under or with him rank him second to none as an audacious, brilliant, hard-driving leader. He is, moreover, as able in the training camp as in the field. He showed this later in 1941 when he built up the A.I.F. Reinforcement Depot in Palestine from little more than a drafting camp to a first-class training centre, which General Auchinleck took as a model for all Middle East forces.

He possesses undoubted brilliance—a fact of which he is not

---

[7] Campbell's subsequent capture in Crete was a severe blow to the A.I.F. He then commanded the 2/1st Battalion, which held Retimo aerodrome so long as its ammunition lasted.

unaware. His eagerness to exercise his talents in a wider field and his sharp intolerance of the shortcomings of others, have made him a target for criticism, and it is unfortunate that these traits have tended to blind his critics to his real ability. In the task of making soldiers and leading them he may be right in thinking there is no place for the gloved hand and the soft tongue. Certainly his methods have produced outstanding results. Mackay appreciated his qualities and gave him a free hand to plan Phase II of the attack.

Describing his plan to me later the Brigadier said:

> I believed that the Italians could be defeated by speed and that, if my brigade could penetrate fast enough, we could strike at the heart of the Tobruk defences before the enemy could organize an effective counter-attack. I set myself to get to the El Adem crossroads by the middle of the morning so that the artillery could move inside the perimeter about midday and be ready to support a further advance early in the afternoon. In that case I considered we might capture the H.Q. of the Tobruk Fortress before dark.
>
> This meant that my brigade had to pass through the perimeter gap while the 16th Brigade's attack was still in progress and would have to move at a hundred yards a minute during the approach march and the attack. That would involve covering twelve miles in four hours—and fighting the last three of them. The success of this plan depended on the 16th Brigade carrying out its programme to time, the artillery silencing the enemy batteries and my troops keeping up the stiff pace. I felt confident they could do this because in training them I had concentrated on mobility, speed and hardness, and before the battle every man was told what he had to do and was impressed with the importance of speed.

The 16th Brigade's plans for the break-through involved most careful reconnaissance of the bridgehead area, but because of bright moonlight and booby-traps this was extremely dangerous. The point which had been chosen for the initial break-through could be easily picked on the map, but on the featureless ground at night it was difficult to find. Nor was it easy in the open desert to fix a start-line for the infantry advance.

The problem was solved at Tobruk, as at Bardia, by the resource and daring of Major Ian Campbell. Aerial photographs and maps showed that between Posts 55 and 57 the anti-tank ditch ran first south-east and then turned sharply north-east. If this elbow could be found there would be a certain reference point from which to start. On the night of January 18th-19th Captain R. W. Knights, Allen's new Brigade Major, and Captain F. G. Hassett and Lieutenant H. O. Bamford of the 2/3rd Battalion were wounded by booby-traps in trying to locate this point. On the night of January 19th-20th, Campbell, recalled from Divisional H.Q., went out himself, crawled through the booby-trap field and found the turn in the ditch. From there he moved due south on a compass bearing for a thousand yards and thus established the position for the start-line. It was then marked by pegging a light-coloured hessian tape to the ground. The stage was set for Mackay's forces to make the assault, led by engineers of the 2/1st Field Company and infantry of the 2/3rd Battalion.

The final problem was to fool the Italians as to the date and direction of the attack. Zero hour was eventually fixed for 5.40 a.m. on Tuesday, January 21st. On the previous Friday, Saturday and Sunday nights, the Navy, the R.A.F. and Herring's artillery carried out the same bombardment programme as they did on Monday night—the eve of the attack. They directed their fire on to the town, the inner defences and the eastern and western perimeter. Every night during the previous week patrols exploded Bangalore torpedoes in the enemy wire and shot up posts from close quarters in sectors other than that chosen for the break-through.

South of this sector on the Sunday and Monday, there was nothing to attract the attention of any inquisitive pilot. He would have seen most of the guns, tanks, carriers and trucks still concentrated in the Bardia road area. They did not move until the Monday night and the noise they made was covered by bombing and shelling. Nevertheless, it was no easy task to assemble unobserved in a small area of open desert eight infantry battalions, five artillery regiments, more than fifty tanks and carriers and hundreds of vehicles.

By the afternoon of the 20th everything was ready. The assaulting infantry was "stripped for action". To give them speed and freedom, respirators were dumped; ground-sheets and greatcoats shed. Shrunken haversacks contained only a dixie, a tin of bully, four packets of biscuits and a few personal odds and ends. Pouches bulged with at least a hundred rounds of .303 ammunition and two or three grenades. In some battalions each man carried four empty sandbags—to be filled, if necessary, from the desert. At dusk they had a hot meal and a swig of rum, and turned in for a few hours' sleep before the battle. They missed their greatcoats and, though their leather jerkins helped to keep out the biting Libyan cold, they were glad even at the bottom of a slit trench of the four blankets, specially provided for this night's rest.

And as they slept British warships stole in to bombard the Tobruk garrison into sleeplessness and to distract the Italians' attention from the desert outside, which had suddenly come to life as night fell. There, field and medium guns bumped over camel-thorn hummocks to battle positions beside ready-stacked ammunition. Tanks, carriers and trucks rumbled across the desert to the concentration areas, two miles south of the start-line. By midnight they were all in position and the Navy turned out to sea again—its first task over. Back in Egypt aircraftsmen fuelled and bombed-up Wellingtons and Blenheims, which were to begin the bombing offensive at 3.30 in the morning.

From inside the perimeter came occasionally the nervous chatter of Italian machine-guns and the sullen roar of routine gun-fire, but among the Diggers and Tommies lying in wait on the desert all was quiet. The orders said "No lights—no smoking—no talking."

But there was bright electric light, smoking and talking, the buzz of field telephones and the rattle of typewriters back at Mackay's headquarters, where staff officers and clerks were checking last-minute details. They worked on undisturbed for H.Q. was housed in two ancient Roman cisterns hollowed, like catacombs, out of the cavernous limestone plateau.

In one of these cisterns earlier in the evening I talked with an A.I.F. staff officer about the attack. "If it goes to timetable," he said, "it'll be over in two days. It all depends on that first hour or so. If we take them by surprise, it'll be all right. If not, well—it may be a stiff go. To-morrow morning'll show us. They're very quiet to-night. Maybe they don't know; maybe they do."

CHAPTER II

Break-through

THEIR only weapons were a thin willowy stick, a pair of scissors, a pocket full of nails and a revolver. Yet they were the advance guard of the 16,000 Australian and British troops who assembled on the dark face of the desert on the night of January 20th, 1941, ready to attack Tobruk before dawn. On the steady nerves and fingers of these men with strange weapons, the waiting infantry relied to clear the maze of booby-traps, which screened the Italian defences.

They were thirty-three members of the 2/1st Field Company, led by Lieutenant S. B. Cann. Several hours before moonrise they moved out into no-man's-land to the accompaniment of jibes from infantry, who little realized how important those thin willowy sticks were. A stinging wind swept across the desert and the sappers were thankful for their army-issue jerkins and long woollen underwear, and for "rum-primed" water-bottles, which were some compensation for the greatcoats they had left behind. To lessen risk of detection they wore woollen Balaclavas instead of tin hats and their shiny leather jerkins were turned inside out.

For more than three hours the sappers felt their way round among the booby-traps, working as fast as half-numb fingers and the all-too-close enemy patrols would let them. If they were not to be discovered, they had to finish delousing the necessary 2000-yard gap in the belt of traps in front of Posts 55 and 57 before the moon rose at 1.15 a.m. But, as it climbed over the horizon, some sappers were still lying on their stomachs, feeling for booby-traps, while an Italian patrol passed only seventy yards away. It was over an hour before these sappers managed to crawl back undetected.

In the concentration area, three miles south of the perimeter, the booby-trap parties finally rejoined the rest of the 2/1st Field Company, and the 2/3rd Battalion. At 2.30 a.m. the troops had a meal, brought up from unit kitchens in hot boxes, and got ready to move. The Navy's preliminary bombardment had ended at midnight, but soon the R.A.F. was pounding the inner Tobruk defences. To the distant music of their own bombs the troops marched to the start-line 1000 yards south of Posts 55 and 57. They were glad to be on the move at last, for the strain of waiting without talking or smoking was worse than going in to attack. They were as eager for the first bark of the barrage as a sprinter for the starter's gun. Company by company they took up their positions on the taped start-line. One last check on equipment and orders and they were ready.

About 5.30 there was a lull in the bombing and stillness once more settled on the desert. Back behind the assembly area at a British 6-inch howitzer position, I watched the gunners gulp their last mouthfuls of bully-beef stew and tea as they stood by their guns. The "hows" were ready, loaded and laid. There was no sound except the voice of a signaller speaking from a shallow dug-out behind the gun-pits to an officer at the observation post—a low mound in the desert a mile or more from the perimeter. At the entrance to the dug-out the troop commander was peering at his luminous watch, set like all other watches for the battle by the B.B.C. time signal. Megaphone in hand, he waited to give the order. The last few silent minutes dragged by ... 5.38, ... 5.39, ... 5.40—"*Fire!*"

His voice was lost in the roar of the four howitzers as they spoke together. Breeches flew open, were loaded and slammed shut. The guns settled down to a slow, rhythmic pounding almost as regular as the beat of a pump. Soon they stood in a dust-cloud of their own making.

The leading troops were already on the move. From the sea to the north of them, from the land to the south, east and west of them, came the thunder of the heaviest bombardment the Middle East had known. Out to sea stood more than twenty warships, including three 15-inch battleships; firing from the desert were 166 guns. Sixty of them put down a box barrage on and around the five posts that the 2/3rd were to attack first. Meantime the other hundred guns concentrated on three tasks: neutralizing the posts nearest to 55 and 57; silencing the most dangerous batteries beyond these posts; and shelling the Bardia road and western sectors to provide a diversion.

The desert across which the troops advanced was so flat that they could see the flash of their own guns firing behind them and of their own shells bursting in front. From their new positions the gunners had not fired even ranging rounds, but the infantry soon knew that the artillery was right on its targets. As the troops moved towards the wire very little enemy fire met them and much of what there was went well over their heads. But as the 2/3rd got near the anti-tank ditch one chance salvo landed in the middle of Major J. N. Abbot's "C" Company, killing or wounding an officer and twenty men.

With the infantry went some engineers with Bangalore torpedoes. Other sappers followed behind to clear the minefield, which lay between the belt of deloused booby-traps and the anti-tank ditch. The minefield did not check the infantry. The mines were not set to explode under a man's weight and the Diggers picked their way safely through. At 5.55 a.m. they reached the anti-tank ditch and took cover there for ten minutes while our gunners concentrated their fury on Posts 55 and 57.

As the troops lay there more than a ton of high explosive burst on and around each of these posts every minute. This was the climax of the 25-minute bombardment in which 5000 shells had plastered an area a few hundred yards square. They had left many scars but few craters in the stony ground which made the shell splinters spread farther, and magnified the blast. For the Australians in the ditch the noise was deafening, but in the concrete dug-outs, where the Italians lay, the detonations reverberated like a succession of thunder-claps, leaving the garrisons dazed.

During all this the C.O. of the 2/3rd (Lieutenant-Colonel V. T. England) was in the ditch with the attacking companies, but, when Brigadier "Tubby" Allen joined them, England said, "Isn't this a bit far forward for Brigade H.Q.?" "I came up to dodge the shelling," replied the Brigadier.

At 6.5 a.m. the barrage lifted from the two forward posts, and engineers raced to the wire—which was anything from twenty to fifty yards from the ditch—dragging their long Bangalore torpedoes. Some were hit. A shell landed among a pioneer detachment of the 2/3rd wounding all but one man, Private R. A. McBain. Undaunted, McBain dragged a Bangalore to the wire alone and scrambled back into the anti-tank ditch as it went off. Meantime at four other points along a 400-yard section of the wire other engineers had done the same, but, through some mischance, not all the torpedoes exploded. Knowing that the wire must be blown at all costs, sappers dashed forward again with new torpedoes and by 6.15 five clear gaps were open for the infantry. But it was still a race against time. In the half-hour of darkness that remained the two leading companies had to take three forward and two supporting posts, covering a front of over a mile.

Through gaps to the right went Abbot's depleted company, to capture Posts 57, 58 and 59. The platoon that attacked 57 was on top of the post before the Italians had recovered from the barrage, but darkness and the smoke and dust raised by the shelling made it hard to find the other posts. In the confusion Sergeant L. L. Stone's platoon was about to open fire on some shadowy figures, when one of them dashed forward using language which was unmistakably Australian. Lieutenant D. E. Williams's platoon had lost its way. Momentarily disregarding the enemy fire, Stone took time off to apologize. "Don't worry," said Williams, "I put it down to excessive zeal." And he led his men off to take Post 56.

On the other flank "D" Company, commanded by Captain R. W. F. McDonald, had a hard fight, which was won only just in time. The platoon that went for Post 54 became lost in the darkness and somewhat disorganized under heavy fire. The situation was saved by the prompt action of McDonald who rallied the men and led them in to take the post.

Meantime it was touch-and-go whether Lieutenant J. E. Macdonald's platoon took Post 55. There the enemy had six machine-guns and a light field piece, and even though the Australians attacked from the rear, they came under heavy fire. As they rushed the post all but Macdonald, a sergeant and one man crashed through the flimsy camouflage covering the anti-tank ditch that encircled the post. Macdonald was wounded, but he continued on, pitching hand grenades towards the Italian machine-gun pits. The man beside him was killed and he himself was wounded again, yet he kept the post quiet while his sergeant rallied the platoon for a final attack. Only two of the garrison of twenty-two were captured unwounded.

By 6.40 the two attacking companies had taken the five posts, which were their initial objective, and "B" Company of the 2/3rd was holding the edge of the escarpment a thousand yards north of 54 and 56, to check any counter-attack from that quarter. The bridgehead was established a mile wide and a mile deep.

By this time too the engineers had cleared the minefield for several hundred yards on either side of the gap and had dug-in the sides of the anti-tank ditch to make crossings for the "I" tanks, carriers and vehicles which were already streaming towards the perimeter. In the grey dawn light, as the first column of prisoners moved back, they passed the leading British "I" tanks and the 2 1st Battalion on their way in to exploit the advantage already won. The first critical phase was over. The danger that the attacking companies might not clear a bridgehead before daylight, and that the supporting battalions might be caught in the open by an alert enemy during their approach march, had been averted.

Herring's gunners had done their job well. The Italians had been slow to realize that anything special was afoot and by the time they did bring their guns into action many of ours had been switched from the barrage supporting the breakthrough to concentrations on Italian battery positions. Many of the enemy guns that had been intended to cover the area of the break-through had been neutralized; but others, including coast defence and ack-ack guns, were now swung round to shell the area across which the British and Australian troops were advancing northward. The 2/1st Battalion (commanded by Lieutenant-Colonel K. W. Eather) had some anxious moments getting through the gap. Before they reached the wire coast defence guns were landing big stuff behind them, while ahead salvoes from enemy field guns were coming down along the anti-tank ditch. Luckily the Australians managed to hurry through during a brief lull.

As soon as the first six tanks reached the gap, three of them swung right to lead the 2/1st in rolling up the perimeter posts to the east as far as the Bardia road. The other three turned left to help the 2/3rd do the same thing with the posts to the west, between the bridgehead and the El Adem road. Both were to be supported by artillery concentrations moving ahead of them and switching from post to post. As these two battalions started widening the gap, nine more tanks followed through in front of the 2/2nd Battalion. Its task—with the help of these tanks—was to deal with the batteries inside the perimeter on the northern flank of the 2/1st and 2/3rd Battalions.

This worked out almost exactly to plan, except that, after over-running nine posts in the first two miles of their push westward, the 2/3rd were then held up by stubborn opposition from Posts 45 and 42, half a mile short of the El Adem road. Until then the going had been fairly easy. The general tactics were that tanks and infantry followed as closely as possible behind the barrage, and those posts which were not silenced by shelling were kept quiet by tanks, while infantry moved in with bayonet and grenade to enforce surrender. What fight was

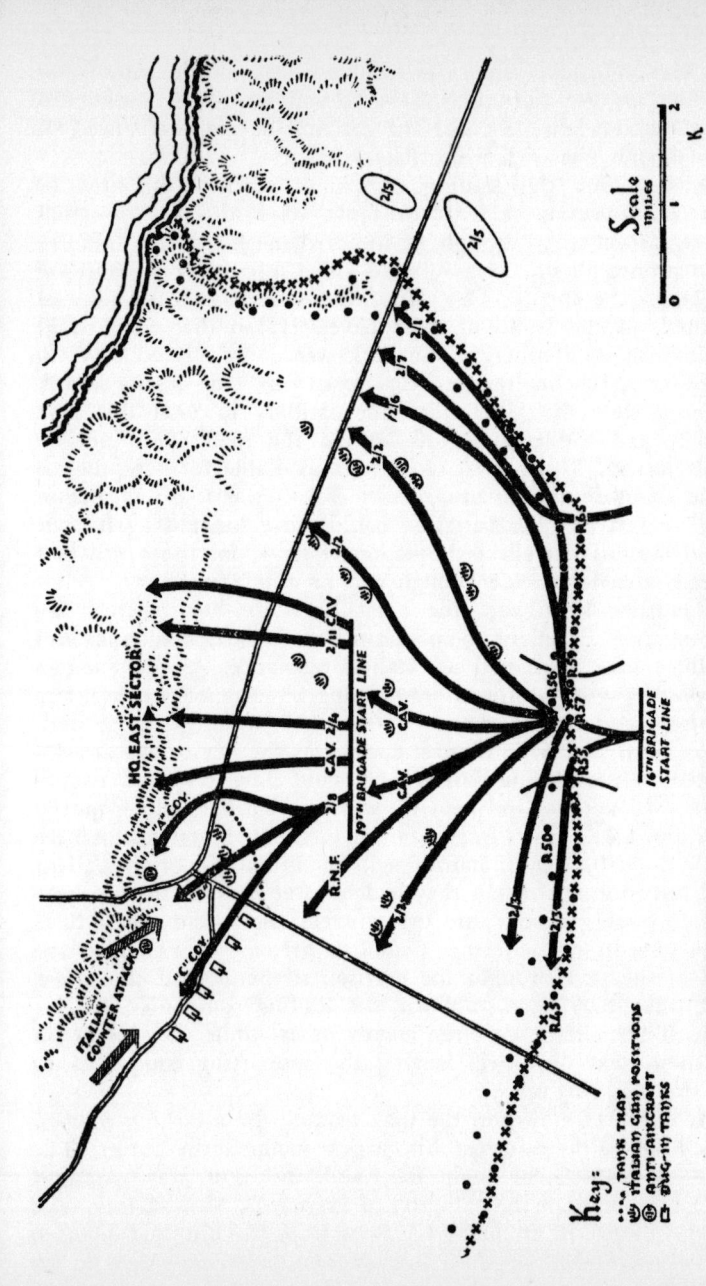

THE CAPTURE OF TOBRUK—THE BREAK-THROUGH, JANUARY 21st, 1941

left in the Italians after the bombardment was in most cases subdued by the sight of the tanks and bayonets. Some even surrendered when they saw the garrison of the post ahead of them march out with white flags.

By the time the leading companies reached the area of Post 45, however, their three tanks were all out of action through mechanical trouble or minor damage and the infantry were pinned down on a forward slope, providing a tempting target for the enemy. The white patches which the troops had stitched on the backs of their haversacks so that they could distinguish each other in the dark were now all too clear to the enemy. His fire was not easy to silence. One disabled tank was too close to 45 to allow the artillery to shell this post heavily and the enemy guns beyond the road could not be easily located. Until fresh tanks were available further progress could be made only at unnecessary cost. It was 1.30 p.m. before they arrived and the battalion could move forward again, but the delay did not affect the action at large, for the 2/3rd had already cleared a wide enough gap on this flank.

Meantime by 9 a.m. the 2/1st Battalion had reached the Bardia road. Excellent co-operation between artillery, tanks and infantry had smothered all Italian resistance. As the enemy's supporting gun positions were being simultaneously over-run by the 2/2nd Battalion and "I" tanks, his infantry in the perimeter posts had little chance. Speed was the key to the attack's success, but only first-class troops could have captured twenty Italian strongposts and kept up with the barrage, which moved four and a half miles in two hours. Without the tanks this pace could never have been maintained. The infantry, more impatient and less squeamish than they had been at Bardia, did not hesitate to pitch grenades into the concrete dug-outs if the Italians were slow in surrendering. Usually a grenade thrown into one end of the post brought the garrison streaming out the other. But when they were stubborn, the leading companies did not wait. They merely kept the enemy quiet, while they swept on to their next objective, leaving the supporting companies to do the mopping-up.

At one post, however, the tank leading the attacking platoon was disabled by a direct hit, which jammed the turret. The Italians maintained their fire, and the post was captured primarily through the gallantry of Private D. M. McGinty, who went forward alone, firing his Bren from the hip, and silenced the enemy machine-guns. One or two posts were left to be mopped up by the 2/6th Battalion, which was following along in support, and for a time the rear of the 2/1st came under fire from these. Luckily this fire was inaccurate and there was no serious hitch until the leading companies reached the Bardia road shortly before 9 a.m.

By this time the guns that had been supporting the 2/1st had been switched to help the 19th Brigade's attack, and when Captain J. H. Hodge led his company across the road they came under heavy machine-gun fire. They took the four nearest posts but could make no impression on the next two, and for over an hour were pinned down in the anti-tank ditch north of the road. They were not extricated until 10.30 when a company of the 2/7th Battalion attacked the obstructive posts from the flank. (The 2/7th had entered the perimeter at Post 65, about half-way between the bridgehead and the Bardia road, as soon as the 2/1st and 2/6th had passed. It had now come up to relieve the 2/1st, and the 2/6th had moved farther west to relieve the 2/2nd.)

Well before this the 2/2nd Battalion had cleaned up the battery positions between the Bardia and El Adem roads immediately behind the sections of the perimeter over-run by the 2/1st and 2/3rd. These positions fanned out in three lines behind the bridgehead. Three companies of the 2/2nd, each supported by three "I" tanks and twenty-four guns, had been detailed to attack these three lines of batteries.

It was a daring plan, for the companies were in effect deep patrols operating behind enemy lines, which were simultaneously being attacked by other battalions. This plan had been tried at Bardia, but had not been an unqualified success, primarily because a number of enemy guns had not been silenced by our artillery or else not located at all until the infantry came under their point-blank fire. If it were going to succeed at Tobruk, our shelling of the enemy batteries had to be accurate and severe and the infantry had to follow in behind the barrage so closely that the enemy could be overwhelmed before he brought his guns into action. So that his battalion would know its role perfectly, the C.O. of the 2/2nd, Lieutenant-Colonel F. O. Chilton, before the battle had the detailed plan explained to each man on a sand table model.

The result was a sweeping success. Advancing behind a 44-gun barrage the two companies on the right captured ten battery positions, each containing either four or six guns, and advanced more than two and a half miles in an hour and a half. The company on the left was equally successful. In each case, however, long before the infantry gained its first objective the tanks were lost in the dust and half-light of the early morning, but they roamed well ahead shooting up everything they saw.

The Italian gun positions had few infantry to protect them and most of their gunners were still too dazed by our shelling to offer much resistance to the Diggers, who appeared unexpectedly out of the dust-clouds the shells had raised. Some of the guns—and particularly an ack-ack battery firing shrapnel over open sights—were troublesome, and in dealing with these the infantry made up for the lack of tanks, by fire from mortars mounted on carriers.[1] Throughout the attack Chilton's greatest problem was to keep contact with his widely-scattered companies. He was able to do this primarily because the capture of Bardia had given the 6th Division a much-needed haul of motor-cycles for its dispatch riders.

While the 16th Brigade was rolling up the perimeter posts and their supporting field guns on either flank of the bridgehead, the area immediately north of it was cleared by a mixed force of carriers of the 6th Divisional Cavalry, machine-gunners of the Northumberland Fusiliers and anti-tank guns of the 3rd Royal Horse Artillery. By 8 a.m. this force had over-run several Italian battery positions and penetrated two and a quarter miles inside the perimeter. There it reached the line that the 19th Brigade had chosen as the start of its deep northward thrust—the second phase of the attack.

Before 8.30 the transport of the attacking battalions was moving inside the perimeter. I nosed my utility truck into one column heading for Post 65 where the 2/7th Battalion had gone through about two miles east of the bridgehead. Near the perimeter a military policeman rattled past on a motor-bike shouting to drivers, "Keep moving—don't bunch up and don't get off the marked track. There's still mines about." The danger from bunching was slight because the Italians had not yet found this gap, and in addition our shelling made their fire ragged. A few strays landed about five hundred yards away and threw up tall, thin columns of dust, which rose in the still morning air like brown poplars.

In front of Post 65 sappers had cleared a track through the

---

[1] This was probably the first time carriers had been used for such a purpose, but in spite of their success, it was a year before this practice was adopted generally.

minefield and thrown a narrow wooden bridge over the deep anti-tank ditch. The bridge was as busy as Pitt Street, Sydney, at 5 p.m. The vehicles moved forward—tailboard to radiator—enveloped in dust. Military police shouted themselves hoarse as they urged the drivers on. Beside the ditch were chalked signboards—KEEP MOVING: NO PARKING. Other signs—CAUTION MINES—were hung on the flimsy wire fence, which marked off the enemy minefields. As cars, ambulances, and trucks moved by the Australian newsreel man, Damien Parer,[2] was filming them. The sight of the trucks of the photographic and broadcasting units parked together prompted one policeman to comment to another, "Blimey Bert, propaganda goes ter war!"

Inside the perimeter I turned west towards the sector where the 2/3rd had broken through, and came to a post that was still resisting. The 2/1st Battalion had over-run this area, but when the post held out they went on, leaving the 2/6th to mop it up. Machine-gun fire and hand grenades had failed to shift the Italians from their underground shelter. As I got there the Diggers were "rabbiting". They lit some crude oil at one end of the trench and three Italian officers and thirty-four men bobbed out the other.

Farther on outside the wire well over a thousand prisoners, shepherded by four Diggers, shuffled through the dust. Bardia had shown the troops that large escorts were not needed. One brigade there had finally instructed its battalions—"Prisoners will *not* be sent back in lots of less than one thousand."

At Post 57 the 16th Brigade had its battle headquarters, but the first thing I saw was four engineers heating Italian coffee on a captured primus and breakfasting on Italian tinned stew. This was typical of the general air of normality—the battle might have been fifty miles away. A postal orderly was dealing out mail that had come up on a ration truck. In a machine-gun pit an officer with a map on his knees was talking on the phone. Up the steps from a concrete dug-out came two Diggers, their arms filled with Italian uniforms, dixies and other junk. They were turning the dug-out into the Brigade Signals Office. Near the entrance Brigadier Allen was talking to two liaison officers. They finished pencilling instructions in their notebooks and hurried off to rejoin their battalions.

---

[2] For the Bardia Battle Parer had been aboard one of the bombarding warships and he was now filming his first land action. He soon earned a name as one of the finest and gamest of war photographers.

By 8.30 the stage was set for the second act. In the critical hour and three-quarters since daylight, eight infantry battalions, more than fifty tanks and carriers and a dozen anti-tank guns had moved in through one narrow bridgehead. The attack had gained such momentum that the Italians would have little hope of stopping it unless they could organize rapidly a strong counter-attack.

Brigadier Robertson, however, had planned his advance to defeat just such a move. To secure a deep penetration he drew up his battalions in arrowhead formation, with the flanks covered by the captured tanks, and carriers of the 6th Divisional Cavalry. The 2/4th, in the centre, was to head due north and capture the eastern sector H.Q., located in a wadi about a mile north of the Bardia road, while the 2/11th cleared wadis on the right and linked up with the 2/6th Battalion along the Bardia road. Simultaneously the 2/8th was to capture the strongly defended junction of the El Adem crossroads.

With forty 25-pounders shelling this road junction and another forty putting down a creeping barrage in front of the tanks and infantry, the 19th Brigade attack began at 8.40 a.m. The barrage lifted at a hundred yards a minute, but the infantry maintained parade ground pace to keep up with it. The troops had been so impressed with the need for speed, that at times the 2/4th almost ran into the barrage and the leading companies of the 2/8th forged ahead of the tanks.

For the first mile, from the start-line to the Bardia road, the artillery blotted out all opposition in the path of the 2/4th, but then they came under heavy machine-gun fire from positions near the road junction. However, Vickers guns on the supporting carriers soon silenced this fire and the 2/4th advanced two and a half miles and captured the sector H.Q. in less than an hour.

On its right flank Lieutenant-Colonel T. S. Louch's 2/11th kept pace. On the left the 2/8th struck little opposition from the crossroads area until the barrage lifted from there to the gun positions farther north. Then the 2/8th came under close range machine-gun and artillery fire from what was virtually an inner perimeter, circling the road junction and running west towards Fort Pilastrino.

The Italians had not completed these defences but they were quite formidable. Behind mines, barbed wire and stone walls, they had a number of machine-gun emplacements, some con-

creted, others protected by sandbags or rocks. On the ground
in front of these were aerial bombs, explodable by trip-wires,
and behind them were four 6-inch naval guns and an anti-
aircraft battery. In addition there was a double line of tanks
dug in as pillboxes—seven mediums in the angle between the
two roads and another twenty-two medium and fifteen light
tanks west of the El Adem road.

Fire from these defences was answered by the cavalry's carriers
and one tank—for, in spite of all the cavalry's good work, only
seven captured tanks survived the approach march and only
one of these reached the road junction, all the others falling
out with mechanical trouble. However, under cover of fire
from the carriers and this one tank, the infantry got right to
the Italian positions with comparatively few casualties. But,
even so, dealing with the dug-in tanks was no easy task. Against
those south-east of the road junction, the C.O. of the 2/8th
(Lieutenant-Colonel J. W. Mitchell[3]) sent his "B" Company
commanded by Captain C. J. A. Coombes. Two other companies
were sent round the flanks to envelop the position. Captain Don
Campbell's "C" Company pushed across the El Adem road to
tackle the line of tanks to the west, while "A" Company, under
Major H. H. McDonald, crossed the Bardia road east of the
Italian position to strike at the guns north of the road junction.

The tactics of the different platoons in dealing with the
dug-in tanks varied, but they had the common virtue of courage,
blended with cheek. In some cases fire from anti-tank rifles[4]
penetrated the tank and dislodged the crew. If these tactics
failed a couple of men worked forward close enough to put a
burst from a Bren through any hole in the tank's armour. As
a final resort one or two men rushed the tank, climbed on top,
opened the lid of the turret and dropped a hand grenade
inside.

The hero of one of these attacks was Sergeant Jim Burgess.
Dashing forward through heavy machine-gun fire, he reached
a tank and climbed on top of it, grenade in hand, ready to

---

[3] Mitchell gained command of the 8th Battalion in the 1st A.I.F. at the
age of twenty-six. He was the only commander of a 1st A.I.F. Battalion to
receive command of the same battalion in the 2nd A.I.F.

[4] The Boyes anti-tank rifle, which in these days was the infantier's chief
defence against tanks, is a heavy, long-barrelled rifle, firing a ½-inch armour-
piercing shot. It was carried by one man and could penetrate a light tank
and, at very close range, even an Italian medium.

drop it inside with the pin removed.[5] But as he tried to open the turret lid he was severely hit by a machine-gun burst from another tank. As he toppled back, he struggled to put the pin back in the grenade so that it would not explode among his men, who were waiting in the lee of the tank. He succeeded, fell and died.

Gradually, by attacking the tanks from the flank so that they came under the fire of only one or two at a time, the 2/8th silenced every one. Their task was made difficult, however, by the stubbornness with which the Italian machine-gun posts held out. These were finally cleaned up with bayonet and grenade, but this took time, for in some posts the Italians lay low while the first infantry went through, and then fired on the following troops.

Meantime "A" Company had had a stiff fight to take the guns north of the Bardia road. The Italians had the crest of the road covered by machine-guns and the infantry were pinned down south of it, until a squadron of carriers led by Lieutenant E. C. Hennessy came up, hull-down behind the raised bank of the road. As nearly all the carriers mounted both a Bren and a Vickers gun, they were able to blanket the enemy positions with fire while the infantry dashed forward.

Even so the infantry were not able to close on the Italians until Hennessy led his carriers round in a wide sweep to attack simultaneously from the enemy's eastern flank. Hennessy managed to carry out this manoeuvre even though his carriers were a perfect target for the enemy artillery, while they were momentarily silhouetted against the skyline as they crossed the road. Then with a dozen Vickers and Brens covering them the infantry soon over-ran the Italian positions and captured seven hundred prisoners.

By midday the positions of the attacking battalions were as follows: on the Bardia road (from the perimeter inwards), the 2/7th, 2/6th, 2/11th, 2/4th and the 2/8th—the last-named being at the crossroads. On the general line of the El Adem road, 2/3rd, one company of the 2/2nd, two companies of the Northumberland Fusiliers. The 2/1st and the rest of the 2/2nd were marching across-country from the positions they had captured on the Bardia road to new positions on the El Adem road.

---

[5] The British hand-grenade or Mills bomb has a lever which is kept in place by a split pin. Even though the pin is removed the grenade will not explode until four or seven seconds (according to the setting of the fuse) after the lever has been released on leaving the thrower's hand.

BREAK-THROUGH

The 19th Brigade had now gained all its objectives and Brigadier Robertson had his headquarters near the El Adem crossroads. He was eager to push on as soon as the eighty-four guns allotted to him had moved up within range. The eastern half of the defences had crumbled, but most of the garrison was still holding out in the western sector, the commander of which, General Della Mura, had his reserve of tanks and infantry intact. During the morning he had tried to organize a counter-attack, but had been hindered by lack of information about the fighting in the eastern sector and by the R.A.F.'s persistent bombing. At about one o'clock, however, R.A.F. Lysanders, which had been cruising round spotting for the guns and bombers all morning, sent urgent radio warnings that the Italians around Fort Pilastrino, four miles west-north-west of the El Adem crossroads, were massing for attack.

CHAPTER III

The Thrust to the Town

NEWS of the impending counter-attack from the west did not deflect Brigadier Robertson from his determination to continue his drive northwards and capture the Tobruk Fortress H.Q. before dark. A commander less bold, less self-confident, might well have stood his ground at the El Adem crossroads awaiting the attack, or have sent his main strength forward to meet it. But both these courses were foreign to Robertson's fighting temperament. Thanks to the delay that the R.A.F.'s bombing had imposed on Della Mura's preparations, and the speed with which Robertson had pushed his brigade through to the El Adem crossroads, the Australian advance could go on.

At his Battle H.Q. (a staff car, an office van, and a couple of signal trucks near the crossroads) early in the afternoon Robertson explained his plan to a group of British, Australian and American correspondents. "My troops have already reached their planned objective," he said, "but I intend to push on north and west this afternoon. I want to capture the headquarters of the Tobruk garrison to-day. So far as I know it's in an old Roman fort—Solaro—about three miles nor'-nor'-west of here. My attack begins at two o'clock. That's the earliest the artillery can get up. I'm sending the 4th Battalion against Solaro, and I've ordered it to go on, if possible, and cut the Derna road at Airente—another old Roman fort. If they do that they'll have driven a wedge between the town and the western sector. I'm protecting their right flank by sending the 11th Battalion north to the south shore of the harbour, and I'm sending the 8th westward along the top of the escarpment to Fort Pilastrino. The Italians are trying to organize a counter-attack with tanks there. I want to stop that.

"If we capture Solaro and Pilastrino to-night we should have all the Italian generals in the bag. I hope to bring my tally to six. I captured one major-general in the last war and I've now got two in this campaign. But I'm going to have a new job

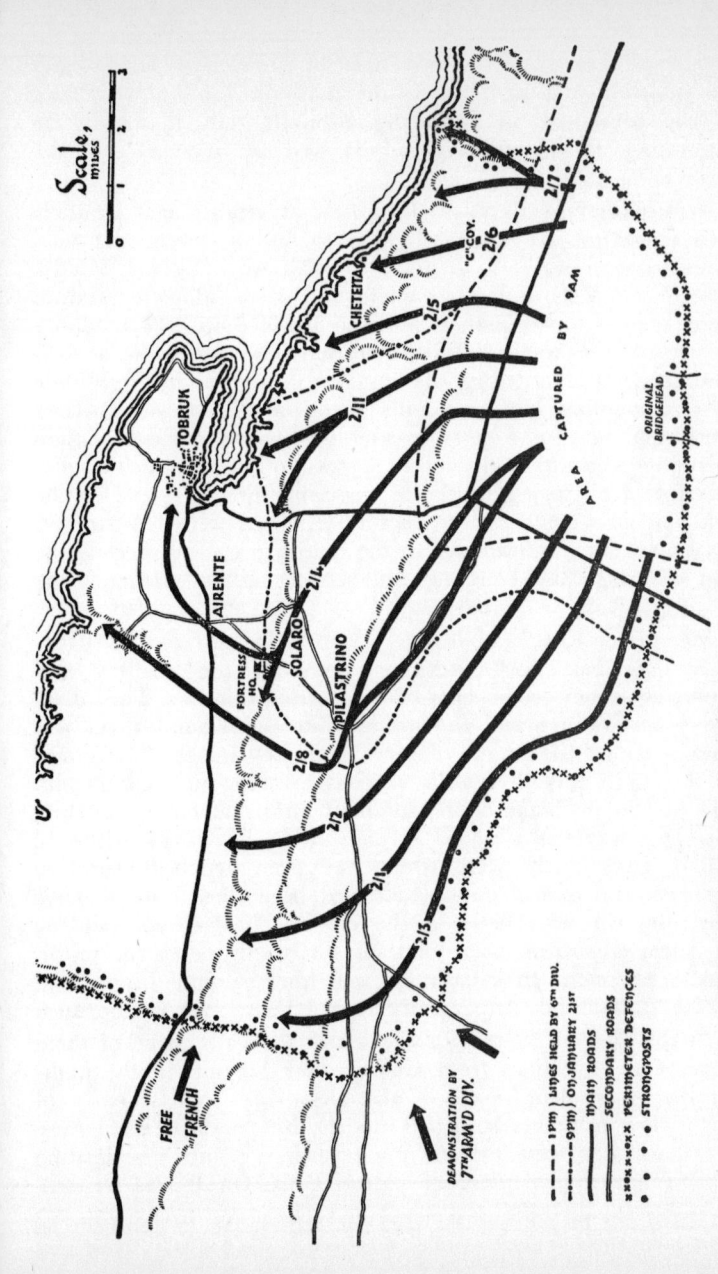

THE CAPTURE OF TOBRUK—LAST PHASE, JANUARY 21ST-22ND, 1941

to-morrow—accepting the surrender of the Italian cruiser *San Giorgio*, which is aground in the harbour. I'm not very sure of the procedure in capturing admirals, but it should be interesting. If the attack goes very well we may get into the town to-night."

British correspondents—so long held at arm's length by their own senior officers—were delighted to find a commander who would and could talk. It took a year's work by the Middle East Public Relations Department and a special memorandum from Wavell to all British units to break down the tendency to regard the war correspondent as first cousin to a fifth columnist. At least during the first year of the war in the Middle East, Australian correspondents with the A.I.F. were trusted more, told more and given greater freedom of movement than correspondents attached to other forces. To our British colleagues therefore Robertson's frankness was something new and in the next few days comments by "a sunburnt, red-headed Australian Brigadier" hit the headlines of the British press—not because he had said something startling, but because he had said anything at all.

Meantime R.A.F. spotting planes hovered unconcernedly above the battlefield, picking targets for the artillery and reporting enemy movements to the waiting infantry. They drew heavy ack-ack fire and the bright blue sky around them was soon speckled with puffs of black and grey smoke. The desert to the south was alive with vehicles bringing up ammunition and fuel in the wake of the infantry, guns and tanks. Heading the other way was a ragged column of the morning's prisoners. Italian guns in the west, which had been switched round to fire east, and coastal guns which had been turned south, were searching the area between the original bridgehead and the El Adem crossroads. Some of their shells fell among the unfortunate prisoners. In a flash the marching column disappeared as the Italians not unnaturally buried themselves in the dust.

As the Diggers waited for the attack to begin, some of them ferreted stray Italians from sangars[1] and dug-outs in the wadis on the escarpment north of the crossroads. Soon a party of twenty-five prisoners straggled up the hill towards the correspondents, who were looking for a vantage point. The leading Italian held out a piece of paper to us. On it was written,

---

[1] Where the ground was too hard for digging, the Italians built up stone breastworks or sangars, which they used as fire positions. These were usually six feet by four with an all-round wall two to three feet high.

THE THRUST TO THE TOWN

"Itie soldati. Please direct to Tom Blamey's prison camp." The writer was a little astray in his geography, for Lieutenant-General Sir Thomas Blamey's headquarters were then in Palestine and he and his Corps H.Q. were not called upon to take part in the drive through Cyrenaica. However, we pointed to the road and they tramped off towards the vast prisoner-of-war cage, which the Italians had built near the El Adem crossroads to house British prisoners.

While waiting for the attack to begin Edward Ward of the B.B.C., Dick McMillan of United Press, and several other correspondents, including myself, were exploring one of the wadis when we heard a noise from a small stone hut. McMillan drew back the curtain covering the doorway and there, seated at a table sipping their after-luncheon coffee, were thirteen Italian officers. At the sight of McMillan their hands automatically went up. "We are ready to go," said one, and they filed out carrying their ready-packed bags with them. They needed no escort and we put them on the road leading southwards. It would be unfair to the troops who had to fight for their prisoners not to point out that these were officers of the ordnance branch, which in the Italian Army appears to be hardly a combatant force.

This was certainly no indication of the enemy resistance still to come, as the 2/8th Battalion soon found in their drive to Pilastrino, which began at 2 p.m. At once they struck trouble. West of the crossroads were a number of buildings and the large wire-fenced prisoners' cage. While consolidating there about midday, the 2/8th had come under heavy machine-gun and mortar fire from the wadis that scarred the face of the escarpment to the north-west.

As Coombes's company, in the centre, moved out to deal with this and clear a start-line for the afternoon attack, three medium tanks lumbered out of a wadi and rammed a carrier that was leading the attack. The crew was captured and the tanks continued on. They were soon disabled, however, by anti-tank rifle fire directed at their tracks and the crews were either captured or silenced in the now conventional style with grenades.

Nevertheless, Coombes's company, and McDonald's on the right, were still held up by fire from the wadis. If the battalion had had the full issue of carriers and mortars, they could soon have silenced this. But instead of fourteen mortars, the 2/8th had two, and one of these had been patched up with Italian spare parts. They had only two of their ten carriers. (This was

fairly typical of the equipment position in the 6th Division—
apart from the 16th Brigade. Consequently the troops were
bitterly scornful of Army Minister Spender's reported statement
that they were "the best-equipped in the world".) Because of
this shortage in supporting weapons, these two companies were
checked until the guns could give them covering fire. Then the
wadis were soon scoured and among the prisoners the Diggers
discovered General Umberto Barberis, who had eluded the
2/4th when they over-ran the eastern sector H.Q. during the
morning.

Meantime, Campbell's company on the left had gone more
than a mile and a half west of the El Adem road. On the way
it had cleaned up thirty-seven dug-in tanks, but this had been
costly. At about 2.30 it was still heavily engaged and all available men from H.Q. Company were sent to reinforce it. From
the roof of a building near the crossroads, Colonel Mitchell and
his Intelligence Officer (Lieutenant Allan Fleming) could see
the Italian counter-attack developing, and it was clear that
Campbell's company would have to bear the main shock. After
the battle Fleming told me:

> We saw several hundred Italians moving towards us from Pilastrino, led
> by more than a dozen medium tanks covered by a barrage. The barrage
> lifted—either by design or because our guns got on to theirs. The Italian
> infantry seemed to waver but the tanks kept moving towards our left
> company. The colonel sent the reserve company—under Jack Smith—to help
> them and ordered the two companies on the right to press on as fast as
> they could. But before any of them arrived Campbell's company had taken
> the first brunt of the attack by seven of the enemy tanks, and for a while
> they had a sticky time.

Campbell was fatally wounded and Major A. S. Key of H.Q.
Company took over command when things were at their worst.
He told me later how the situation was eventually restored:

> As the tanks came on we couldn't check them because we had no 2-pounders
> and most of the men with anti-tank rifles were hit before the tanks got
> close enough for our weapons to do much damage. The forward platoon
> was over-run and several men were forced to surrender. The rest of us
> took cover in sangars and shallow trenches, and fired at the tanks whenever
> we could. In several cases, men played hide and seek with a tank, sheltering
> behind sangars, moving as it moved, to keep clear of its fire, and then
> taking a quick shot with a Boyes rifle. The tanks came up so close that
> we disabled several—even though they were M13s.[2]

In this kind of fighting, however, the enemy had every
advantage and the forward troops suffered heavily. In "C"
Company four officers out of five were killed or wounded and

---
[2] The M13 was the latest medium tank Italy had produced.

THE THRUST TO THE TOWN

the casualties among the men were also heavy. But help arrived in time when the two companies on the right came into the battle and prevented the Italian infantry from taking advantage of their tanks' success.

The tanks, too, were soon dealt with, even though another half dozen came up. A sergeant appeared from nowhere trailing a captured anti-tank gun and with one of his first shots knocked out an M13. About the same time the Boyes rifles scored telling hits on three others, and two anti-tank guns of the 3rd Royal Horse Artillery arrived and accounted for two more. To clinch the victory, two "I" tanks appeared in the distance. On seeing them the Italian tanks withdrew leaving six knocked out on the battlefield.

As they pulled back, the Diggers followed and attacked the Italian infantry who had been sheltering behind low stone walls. In Fleming's words: "With wild yells and fixed bayonets, the troops went for the sangars from which rifles, machine-guns and small mortars were still firing. Some of the enemy were bayoneted; the rest crumbled and so did the counter-attack."

This, however, did not end the battalion's difficulties. They were advancing along the crest of the escarpment and by now they had drawn fire from field guns on their front and both flanks. To make matters worse, at this juncture some of the guns that had been supporting them were switched to help the 16th Brigade, and communication with their remaining guns broke down. The battalion was left without any artillery support.

The advance of the 2/4th to Solaro, however, stopped some of the shelling from the north and the commander of one "I" tank, seeing that the counter-attack was broken, swung away to the south to deal with the troublesome guns there. Nevertheless, it was an hour before the shelling abated sufficiently for the infantry to continue.

As they neared Pilastrino in the late afternoon, they came under severe fire from mortars and machine-guns, which the setting sun made it difficult to locate. Still more trouble came from four heavy A.A. guns using shrapnel at a range of about half a mile. Fortunately, just when it seemed that the advance would again be checked, an officer of the R.H.A. arrived in a carrier and asked Mitchell how he could help.

Pointing towards Pilastrino Mitchell said, "Get those bloody guns." Within ten minutes, to the relief of the troops, one salvo of shells was followed by a terrific explosion, which—to quote Fleming again—

> . . . sent a column of smoke and debris three hundred feet into the air and dulled all other sounds. It came from the area of the A.A. battery. Later we found our shells had hit a magazine and the guns had been lifted from their concrete emplacements and left twisted wrecks.
>
> With the A.A. battery silenced, progress was quicker, even though the troops had to fight their way through heavily wired machine-gun posts. By dusk we were within striking distance of the fort. Spasmodic scrapping continued after dark, but by 9.30 p.m. we had our H.Q. in Fort Pilastrino, which proved to be little more than a collection of barracks buildings surrounded by a solid stone wall.

The 2/8th had reason to be proud of their day's work. They had marched more than fifteen miles and from 9 a.m. until after dark had been engaged in hard and almost continuous fighting. They had captured the two main strongpoints inside the perimeter, rolled up the enemy's reserve line and smashed his main counter-attacking force. Their casualties—more than a hundred killed or wounded[3]—were twice as heavy as those of any other battalion; but in view of what they had accomplished it is remarkable that their losses were not double that number.

By taking the full brunt of the counter-attack, the 2/8th made it easier for the 2/4th in their attack on Solaro, and beyond. The success of this drive was largely due to the stirring leadership of the 2/4th's C.O., Lieutenant-Colonel I. N. Dougherty. Riding in the battalion's only carrier, he covered many miles during the afternoon, controlling, directing and urging on his troops as they became more and more spread out in pursuit of the enemy.

From the crest of the escarpment which overlooked Solaro, Ward and I watched the 2/4th attack. As the guns of the 104th R.H.A. and the 2/3rd Field Regiment put down a screen of shell-fire on Solaro and on enemy batteries beyond and beside it, great dust-spouts shot up around the pile of rubble that the map flattered with the name "fort". Soon even Solaro's tall observation tower was blotted out by the rising cloud of dust and smoke.

Under cover of this fire the 2/4th advanced steadily across the flat, west of the main Tobruk road. They had marched more than twelve miles during the morning, but they still kept to their amazing pace of nearly a hundred yards a minute. They might have been marching along a road instead of over

---

[3] Four officers and 19 other ranks were killed, 5 officers and 76 other ranks wounded.

THE THRUST TO THE TOWN

a desert surface that was alternately rock, sand and camel-thorn. The machine-gun fire that came from Solaro did not worry them, for they were well dispersed in extended line. As we looked down from the escarpment, the desert seemed to be covered with moving dots. Several Italian tanks appeared from the west, but these were driven off by two of the R.H.A.'s anti-tank guns, mounted on trucks, which were travelling with the leading companies.

Then an ack-ack battery on a rise east of Solaro turned its guns on them. Moving from one to the other in his carrier, Dougherty ordered his leading companies to keep going, switched some of the 104th's guns on to the Italian battery and under their fire sent in his right reserve company to capture it. This they did, and by four o'clock the two leading companies (commanded by Captain H. S. Conkey and Captain C. B. N. Rolfe) had taken possession of the low knoll on which Solaro stands. They had met only light machine-gun fire over the last stage and most of the garrison had fled westward before the Australians arrived. In the words of one Digger, "When we got 'ere, there was nothin'; not even loot."

Nor was there any sign of the prize Dougherty sought so keenly—the Tobruk Fortress H.Q.—though there were tunnels beneath the ruins which might have housed it. They were empty, so Dougherty urged his men westward in the hope of finding the headquarters before dark. By six o'clock Rolfe's company was half a mile beyond the Pilastrino-Tobruk road and fully occupied in trying to cut off Italians fleeing to the west; but still there was no trace of the headquarters. Enemy guns from the west, south-west and north were now shelling the Solaro area heavily and Italians in machine-gun posts on the right, where the Pilastrino-Tobruk road cut through an escarpment, were fighting back strongly.

Captain J. McCarty's company was sent to deal with them and, as Dougherty followed in his carrier, he was met by an excited runner from the leading platoon who said they had captured the posts and a general. Dougherty told me of the incident later:

> I went down the road and through the cutting and found myself among a throng of Italians, of various ranks, who were being rounded up by my lads. Soon a naval officer, speaking perfect English, was brought to me, and then an Egyptian, who was an officer of the Italian Army, and could speak reasonably good English. There was also a priest, dressed in the gaudiest raiment imaginable, who looked at me with a supercilious air.
>
> I was presented with our captive general, and was assured by the

English-speaking officer, that he was Petasso Manella, the commander of Tobruk. He was an old man, dignified, quiet and very tired. He had fought beside the Allies in the last war.

I was told we had another general, commander of the Tobruk artillery. There were scores of other officers, senior and junior. In all we had captured about 1600 prisoners in the last hour. By this time it was too late to go on to Airente, and, as we had captured the Tobruk H.Q., I decided to take our chief prisoners back to Brigade.

The only available vehicle was a captured gun tractor. In this the two generals, Manella's chief-of-staff, the English-speaking naval officer, myself and an armed escort, drove off. Our prisoners feared that I might take them over a minefield, but we reached Brigade H.Q. safely. As we drove back, pillars of flame leapt heavenwards from the fuel and ammunition dumps which the Italians were demolishing in the west. But when Manella was paraded to Brigadier Robertson he stated that the Italians had their orders to fight to a finish and that he would not surrender the garrison of Tobruk.

This decision was already out of his hands, as the fires and explosions in the west indicated. There had been similar evidence from the town in the late afternoon. By 4 p.m. the leading companies of the 2/11th had reached the last escarpment overlooking the town without much fighting. They had run into some enemy machine-gun fire, but when the Italians saw they could not stop the advance, they began waving white flags, while the Diggers were still several hundred yards away.

The Australians at Tobruk and Bardia were bitter about this. They had seen their mates hit and they wanted to get their own back. I heard one of them spit out this comment: "They keep firin' till they see they can't stop you. Then they toss in the towel. Every Itie I've seen had a white hankie all ready to wave when we made it too hot. That's O.K. for them, but when your mates've copped it, you want to get stuck into the bastards."

The mere sight of the 2/11th coming over the last escarpment above the harbour was quite enough for some of the troops in the town. As we drove down the road behind the infantry, two 10-ton lorries came out slowly from Tobruk, packed with Italians driving to surrender with white flags fluttering. They were "bailed up" by Major Gordon Hayman, a 6th Division ordnance officer, who had brought a couple of men forward in search of captured transport. He brandished a Bardia souvenir which he called a "repeating shot-gun", and the leading truck disgorged twenty smiling Italians, each equipped with white handkerchief, water-bottle, blanket and a small bundle of belongings. It was a friendly party. Hayman's men had trouble in starting one truck; the Italian driver hopped

THE THRUST TO THE TOWN

up and started it for them. But when the Diggers drove the trucks off empty, the Italians' faces fell as they saw they were being left to walk.

From the escarpment we looked down on the harbour and town. On the south shore two beached victims of the R.A.F. were blazing—the 15,000-ton liner *Marco Polo,* and a smaller freighter, *Liguria.* A thick plume of black smoke rose from a tanker at a jetty near the town. Farther along the northern shore lay the Italian cruiser *San Giorgio.* She had been there since the third day of the war, when the R.A.F. damaged her so badly that she had to be beached. Since then she had been patched up to serve as an anti-aircraft ship.

Earlier in the day she had turned her guns inland and shelled our troops and these shells had particularly worried a squadron of the cavalry, under Lieutenant Tom Mills, which had reached the edge of the last escarpment before 11 a.m. His carriers had been driven back by fire from *San Giorgio* and from ack-ack and coastal guns. The cruiser was now silent, but a coastal battery on the hill behind the town was still very active. Our guns were searching for it, but couldn't get the range, and the Italians were making the most of their last chance.

In the town itself every few minutes a new explosion and trail of smoke told of more sabotage. But at the water's edge half a mile from us the two invaluable water distilling plants were intact. One platoon of the 2/11th had been ordered to fight its way through and save the plants at all costs. They had surprised the enemy in the middle of a meal and, having captured 250 prisoners, had polished off the steak and green peas the Italians had prepared for themselves. This was a very minor incident in the day's fighting, but the capture of these plants undamaged had a significance that no one fully appreciated until Tobruk became besieged.

During the night Italian guns in the west kept up spasmodic fire, while demolition parties continued their work. The Australian and British troops for the most part rested after their day's fighting and marching. But patrols from the 2/8th and 2/3rd gained some small successes. The 2/8th brought in the remaining Italian general—Della Mura, the western sector commander. The 2/3rd captured two more posts.

Next to the 2/8th, the 2/3rd had the hardest fighting at Tobruk. As we saw earlier, their westward drive along the perimeter was held up about 9 a.m. when they were still half a mile short of the El Adem road. There they were stopped for four and a half hours, until at last another troop of "I" tanks came up, commanded by Captain Philip Gardner, of the 7th R.T.R., who later won a V.C. in the second Libyan campaign.

With these tanks, and thirty-six British 25-pounders, plus some Vickers guns of the Northumberland Fusiliers to support them, the 2/3rd attacked at 1.30 p.m. "D" Company on the left quickly over-ran the three posts east of the El Adem road which had held them up all the morning. Leap-frogging through, "A" Company—now commanded by its sergeant-major, Warrant-Officer Bruce MacDougal—went on to capture two posts west of the road. The tanks then withdrew to refuel, but the infantry continued on, and by 3 p.m. four more posts were in their hands.

From the next two posts, however, and from several battery positions behind them, came such heavy fire that Colonel England decided not to push on, especially as he did not know what was the position on his right flank. The 2/8th Battalion was still fighting hard on the ridge leading to Pilastrino and the 2/1st and 2/2nd Battalions were not yet in position to cover the gap between the 2/8th and the 2/3rd in force.

The 2/3rd soon found that they could not stay undisturbed where they were. Several Italian machine-gun posts kept firing and Sergeant L. L. Stone's platoon was sent to deal with them. On the way it came under heavy but inaccurate fire from a number of field pieces and machine-guns in a strongpoint behind the forward posts. But when the Italians saw the Diggers steadily coming on they put up white flags. More than five hundred trooped out leaving eighteen field guns and many machine-guns as booty for Stone and his twenty-five men. The Australians then dealt with the machine-guns that had been worrying the forward troops and collected another thousand prisoners—most of them, however, lines of communication personnel, who were being used as infantry. After dark another patrol, led by Sergeant L. M. Long, captured two perimeter posts (34 and 35) which had been resisting strongly at dusk.

The 2/3rd had a quiet night. They deserved it. They had had some hard fighting making the bridgehead, and the Italians in the perimeter posts had generally fought better than at Bardia. In spite of this, the battalion had remarkably light casualties—seven killed and forty-six (including five officers) wounded. These losses would have been much heavier but for the excellent co-operation between the Australian infantry and the British tanks and artillery.

By chance Ward and I found ourselves near the 2/3rd's positions not long after dark. As we drove back along the road from the town to the El Adem crossroads we overtook a column of prisoners, straggling along the tarmac. An Australian sergeant hopped on the running-board and said, "Would you drive us along a bit? I want to head these bloody weaners off down the road to Bardia."

We drove blindly on for several miles. The prisoners had taken the wrong turn and we ended up at the point where the El Adem road crossed the perimeter. The sergeant had a nice job ahead of him—turning the Italians back to the other road—for the column was nearly four miles long. The leading prisoners were bunched up against the road-block and the weight of the moving column was behind them. They were starting a clamour, calling out "Acqua" and chattering excitedly among themselves. They were scared, for the Australian front was only about a mile west of the road and from that direction came occasional bursts of machine-gun and artillery fire. Burning dumps made the western sky an angry red and every now and then the desert was lit by brilliant flashes as more petrol or ammunition went up.

By this time our truck was wedged tightly against the barricade with prisoners milling round, many of them clamouring for a lift. One of them bobbed up beside me with a roll of notes as "passage money" but we hunted him away. If they had wanted to, these prisoners could have made plenty of trouble. Scattered beside the road were hundreds of rifles and stacks of ammunition and hand grenades. Guarding the Italians, there were no more than a dozen Diggers.

"B——d if I know 'ow we can shift 'em," said the sergeant, "but I've got to get 'em back somehow."

"We'll be here all night," said Ward, "unless one of their own officers can get them moving. I'll see what I can do." He found an officer, who could speak French. In a few minutes the Italian was standing on a petrol drum yelling at the mob. With much excited bleating the Italians passed the word along the line and soon they were moving back the way they had come.

As we were about to drive off, an Italian pushed through the crowd to our truck, shouting excitedly—"Wounded soldiers. Please take Red Cross—Strada Bardia." We followed him to a dug-out where three badly wounded Italians lay. With shouts from the bearers and groans from the wounded, these were eventually settled in the truck and we turned back towards the crossroads where Australians and Italians were carrying on a joint dressing station in a little white stone building. We unloaded our patients there and turned east down the Bardia road. We had to find our camp outside the perimeter, write our dispatches and record them before the second day's fighting began.

Long before dawn on Wednesday, January 22nd, it was obvious the battle was over. But there were still enough guns and men in the town itself to make its capture expensive if they cared to fight, and especially if *San Giorgio* were to make a last gesture. During the Tuesday night, however, the crew had set her alight and taken refuge ashore; most of the ack-ack and coastal guns had been blown up as well; oil and ammunition dumps had been fired. By dawn a heavy pall of smoke hung over the town and harbour.

For the day's mopping up Mackay told the 17th Brigade to clear the wadis between the Bardia road and the sea near the eastern perimeter. The 19th Brigade was sent to occupy the town and the headland behind it, and the 16th to clean up the western sector.

While the 2/4th Battalion was getting ready to advance north and then east into the town, Brigadier Robertson sent two troops of carriers under Lieutenant E. C. Hennessy and Sergeant G. Mills on reconnaissance along the bitumen road that ran round the western end of the harbour and into the town. They had no trouble until Mills's carrier came to a road-block made of sandbags on the outskirts of the town. With the help of two Italians whom he found sheltering under a nearby culvert, Mills and his crew pulled down the sandbags, while the other carriers covered them. From one carrier a Digger spotted an Italian farther up the street about to open fire on Mills, and with a burst from a Bren made him change his mind. Mills had no Vickers gun on his carrier and so let Hennessy go first.

"As we drove through," said Hennessy later, "a truck loaded with Italians was moving back into the town. A couple of bursts from my Vickers stopped it and the occupants were taken prisoner. As the carriers moved towards the centre of the town an immaculately clad Italian officer came to meet us and eventually made me understand that he had been sent to lead us to the naval H.Q., where the admiral was waiting to surrender. There the admiral handed me his sword, but I told him to keep it and sent a carrier back for Brigadier Robertson. Pending his

THE THRUST TO THE TOWN

arrival our blokes consumed a goodly quantity of excellent champagne."

Robertson had anticipated some such collapse, and he and Macarthur Onslow were on the road overlooking the harbour when the carrier came back to report. At once a procession of four or five vehicles, including the Brigadier's car, filed into the town. One of these carried three Australian correspondents, Gavin Long, John Hetherington and Reg. Glennie.[4] With Robertson was Brigadier L. J. Morshead, who little knew then how closely his fate in the next eight months would be bound up with that of Tobruk. Morshead's brigade had been diverted to Britain in the middle of 1940 and it had only recently arrived in Egypt. Keen as ever to be up with the fighting, he had joined Mackay's forces as an observer. It was fortunate that he did, for he gained direct knowledge of the ground and defences, which was invaluable when he was called upon to command the Tobruk Fortress three months later.

At the door of the naval H.Q. a nervous Italian officer was waiting to take Robertson to a room where Admiral Massimiliano Vietina, commander of the naval garrison, was standing surrounded by a group of senior officers. The building was filled with smoke from documents smouldering in rooms and offices. An Italian naval officer, who acted as interpreter, told Robertson that the Admiral and 1500 officers and men were ready to surrender. In reply Robertson demanded to be told if there were any mines or booby-traps in the town. With his penetrating eye fixed on the Admiral himself, Robertson warned him that if one Australian should be killed, an Italian would pay for it. The Admiral replied that all mines and traps had been "sprung" and added—what was evident from the loud explosions outside—that his men were still "springing" the ammunition dumps.

As soon as Robertson's interview with the flustered Admiral was over, Macarthur Onslow went into the courtyard and fired half a dozen Very lights into the sky as a signal that the town was in our hands. But the real token of the fall of Tobruk was the hoisting to the head of the flag-pole outside the Admiral's headquarters of a Digger's slouch hat.

---

[4] Unfortunately at this important time, Edward Ward of the B.B.C. and I were many miles away trying to find a plane to take our recorded descriptions of the first day's fighting to Cairo. For the account of what happened in Tobruk on this morning, I am indebted to Gavin Long and Macarthur Onslow.

CHAPTER IV

The Round-up

TWENTY-NINE hours after the first Australian troops broke through the Italian perimeter Tobruk town fell. But the speed with which the Anglo-Australian forces overwhelmed the garrison and the comparatively few men lost[1] in doing so might suggest that the Italians put up merely a token resistance. Any such suggestion would be unjust to commanders and troops alike. The Italians collapsed because they were outgeneralled and out-fought. They were crushed mainly by the speed and boldness of the plan and action. The blows struck were so directed and co-ordinated that at most of the Italian positions the battle was lost before they realized it had begun. But where they did gain enough respite to gather strength they fought stubbornly, as the 2/3rd and 2/8th Battalions know. Bold, resolute commanders and determined, well-trained troops win their battles cheaply. There is a dangerous heresy from the last war that small casualties mean poor opposition; they may just as well mean first-class soldiering, as they did in the capture of Tobruk.

The blow delivered by Mackay's forces on the first day was so severe that enemy resistance on the second collapsed. While Robertson was accepting the admiral's surrender in the town, the battle was still being nominally fought in the eastern and western sectors of the perimeter, but in these it was only a matter of rounding up the already well-beaten Italians.

In the west the 16th Brigade had a long march collecting prisoners. Barely a shot was fired and the only problem was to move fast enough to forestall further destruction of guns and stores. The Italians had done their sabotage as well as they could. Nearly all petrol dumps and vehicles had been set alight, but there was so much ammunition that they could not destroy more than a fraction of it. About half the field and ack-ack guns

---

[1] The Australian casualties were: Killed or died of wounds—41; wounded —205; missing—2; total—248.

had been either blown up or put out of action by the removal of breech-blocks and other vital parts. In many cases, however, these were found buried in the sand near by and the guns were salvaged.

For the most part the surrender was "well organized" and in more than one instance a full battalion marched in waving white flags or handkerchiefs with its colonel in the lead. At many perimeter posts the 2/3rd found the garrisons packed ready to leave. Near the Derna road the Diggers discovered that Free French marines, attached to the 7th Armoured Division, had made a diversionary attack the day before and had now captured the remaining perimeter posts. The battle in the western sector was over.

In the east, the 17th Brigade had rougher country to scour but met no greater opposition. It was expected that a nest of coast defence guns at Fort Cheteita would show fight, but when Captain J. G. Rowan with "C" Company of the 2/6th Battalion advanced to attack it the Italians ran up the white flag. To the Australians' amazement, forty officers and four hundred men (about a third of them naval personnel) streamed out. Their fort had been armed with four 6-inch and six 3-inch naval guns and two A.A. guns, but most of them had been destroyed before the Australians got there.

On the eastern perimeter one company of the 2/7th, under Captain J. R. Savige, had a wearying job clambering over rough wadis to collect their prisoners. Finally only two posts remained, but they were situated on a high point on the far side of a wadi 350 feet deep, and the Diggers were in no mood for further foot-slogging. In halting French, aided by a few signs, Savige told the Italian sector commander to get in touch with the two posts and order their garrisons to come in. These orders were conveyed by telephone and soon the last Italians were in the bag—a literal example of "having your enemy's number".

The 17th Brigade, commanded by Brigadier S. G. Savige,[2] after its hard fighting and quite considerable casualties at Bardia, had not been called upon to do anything spectacular at Tobruk. For the most part its battalions had the thankless task of

---

[2] Brigadier Savige—in civil life a Melbourne business man—was awarded the D.S.O. and the M.C. for his gallantry in the Great War. He served with the A.I.F. in the 24th Battalion and on the staff of the 6th Brigade before he went to Mesopotamia and Persia as one of the hand-picked officers sent to "Dunsterforce" in 1917. In this war after serving in Libya, Greece and Syria, Savige returned to Australia, was promoted Major-General and led the 3rd Division with distinction in New Guinea.

following in the wake of other brigades, mopping up and collecting prisoners. However, it had played a valuable part in the early daylight hours of the first day by providing a spirited diversion and drawing much of the enemy's fire on to the 2/5th and 2/7th Battalions, which were in positions astride and south of the Bardia road. After this, its battalions had a walking war. The 2/6th, for example, marched sixteen miles on the first day and fifteen on the second, and barely fired a shot.

This experience drew a pointed comment from one Digger who had joined the battalion as a reinforcement after Bardia and had been regaled by the "old hands" with stories (based on fact) of the fighting the 2/6th had had there in taking certain posts. After two days almost unopposed foot-slogging at Tobruk this Digger turned to some of the yarn-spinners and said, "Fightin'? Call this fightin'? Gawd . . . the police in Tel-Aviv give us a better fight than this."

The 17th Brigade, however, was spared hard fighting because of the excellence of Mackay's plan and the admirable way in which the troops chosen for the spearheads carried it out. The net result was that Tobruk yielded a haul of prisoners and war material which would have been considered colossal if it had not followed on the mass captures of Sidi Barrani and Bardia. A comparison of the prisoners, guns and tanks, taken in the four major battles of the campaign is illuminating. The figures were:

	Sidi Barrani	Bardia	Tobruk	Beda Fomm[3]
Men	38,000	45,000	25,000	20,000
Field and Medium Guns	214	223	208	110
Medium Tanks	28	13	23	120
Vehicles	1,000	700	200	600

(No accurate figures are available for A.A. or anti-tank guns for all these actions, but more than fifty of each were captured at Sidi Barrani, Bardia and at Tobruk. Figures are given only for medium tanks, for the Italian light tank was useless in action except when dug-in as a pillbox. As to the prisoners, more than 7000 of the Italians captured at both Bardia and Tobruk were A.A. or coast defence troops. At Tobruk another 3000 were naval personnel. Altogether in the campaign Mussolini lost eight Italian infantry divisions, the nucleus of one armoured division and two native Libyan divisions—virtually eleven in all. General O'Connor's 13th Corps on the other hand never included much

---

[3] Beda Fomm was the brilliant action, in which the British 7th Armoured Division cut off and captured the remnants of Graziani's army south of Bengazi early in February 1941.

more than two divisions, for when the 6th Australian Division joined the 7th Armoured Division, the 4th Indian Division went to Eritrea.)

The main factor, I believe, in achieving the victory at Tobruk so quickly and with so few casualties, was the superb work of the British and Australian gunners. Thanks primarily to the fearless reconnaissance pilots of the R.A.F., the Italian batteries were accurately pin-pointed, but even the most confident gunner could hardly have expected his shelling to be as accurate and effective as it proved to be. The evidence of the shell-scarred ground proved that at seventeen out of the twenty principal battery positions, the enemy could not have got near his guns during our bombardment.

In spite of this, the Italian artillery fought better than their infantry; but it was thwarted by the speed of the attack. Those gunners who could observe the advancing infantry, were generally over-run before they had recovered from our shelling. Those who had no direct observation did not know where to fire. As a rule, by the time the Italians switched their guns to deal with any particular threat, our infantry had advanced so far that the enemy shells landed well behind them.

Enemy attempts to deal with our guns were similarly ineffective because they did not find our new positions. Most of our batteries that fired from their old positions were heavily shelled for a while, but some guns of the 2/3rd Field Regiment, which had expected trouble, got none. Later, a captured map showed that the Italian battery detailed to shell this position had been knocked out by our guns before it could do any damage.

The way he solved the artillery problems at Tobruk and Bardia marked Herring as an outstanding commander, and it was no surprise that he later succeeded to the command of the 6th Division, when Mackay became C-in-C., Home Forces in Australia. In 1942, taking command in the Northern Territory when Australia was in danger of invasion, Herring rallied the inexperienced Darwin garrison into a strong fighting force chiefly by the strength of his own personality. In New Guinea, as Corps Commander during the Buna campaign, he proved himself a leader whose patience, thoroughness and capacity to take the long and broad view would carry him far. After conducting two strenuous and successful campaigns in New Guinea, however, he retired from active service on receiving the appointment of Chief Justice of Victoria early in 1944.

Because of the artillery's excellent work the "I" tanks did not play such an important part at Tobruk as they had done at Sidi Barrani and Bardia. The difficult and daring advance by the 19th Brigade—unsupported by "I" tanks—could not have been so successful if Herring's guns had not dealt so effectively with enemy batteries. Nevertheless, the moral effect of the tanks was substantial. The enemy knew by this time that his anti-tank shells bounced off the heavy armour of the "I" tank and that only a chance hit in some vulnerable part could even disable one. By the first afternoon the appearance of an "I" tank was often sufficient to crack the opposition.

The 6th Divisional Cavalry's enterprising experiment with the captured tanks was not a great success. In spite of the crews' hard work, most of these tanks broke down before they reached the real fighting. The cavalry's ingenuity also produced several dummy tanks by building wooden frames over light trucks. Two of these "tanks" at one stage found themselves heading straight into an Italian gun position. It was too late to turn back; they kept going and discovered that the Italian guns were also made of wood.

The daring work of Macarthur Onslow's carriers did much to compensate for the shortage of tanks. He is probably the ablest of the young commanders produced by the 2nd A.I.F. and made his mark from the very first days of this campaign. Throughout the battles of Bardia and Tobruk, he moved all day in his carrier within a few hundred yards of the barrage. He was the eyes of the attackers, searching out enemy strongpoints and battery positions, warning the tanks or calling up his own carriers to deal with them. Major R. K. Anderson,[4] Robertson's Brigade Major, said to me after Tobruk, "Macarthur Onslow himself is worth a squadron of cavalry." And this was hardly an over-statement.

Standing high in his carrier—scorning a steel helmet even after a bullet had drilled a hole in the lobe of his black beret at Bardia—he could be seen by the forward troops moving in and out of the dust-clouds ahead, pausing sometimes to use his field-glasses, sometimes his camera.

Macarthur Onslow brought originality and ingenuity to mechanized cavalry problems and he evolved in Libya some strikingly successful tactics for his carriers. First he gave them greatly increased fire-power. Almost every one mounted a Vickers gun, an

---

[4] Major Anderson died of wounds received while commanding 2/32nd Battalion during the siege of Tobruk.

anti-tank rifle and either a Bren or a tommy gun. For better cooling, the water jacket of each Vickers was connected to the radiator system of its carrier and thus could maintain exceptionally long bursts of fire.

In telling me of the Tobruk fighting afterwards, Macarthur Onslow said: "The fact that the carriers could maintain such a volume of fire while moving was largely responsible for minimizing our infantry casualties. Right through the advance the Vickers guns were kept firing at any and every object that remotely resembled enemy defences. With all this lead zipping about the Italians were in no frame of mind to put their heads up and see what was going on.

"Mills's squadron," he continued, "was very successful in dealing with enemy strongpoints. He had three troops—each of four carriers. Two troops would open fire with streamlined ammunition on their objective from a range of 1800 to 2000 yards, while the third troop moved in some 500 or 600 yards and opened fire from the enemy's flank. As soon as it was in action one of the other troops would follow in and take up a position at about the same range. Then the third would leapfrog through to within 1000 yards of the enemy. In this way the tremendous fire of eight Vickers guns was kept on the objective at all times and from different angles. Almost invariably the enemy found their gun positions untenable and either retired or surrendered."

At Tobruk, by these and similar tactics, Macarthur Onslow's carriers captured fourteen enemy battery positions and strongpoints. The key to their success was his leadership. An infectious enthusiasm is the secret of his power of command, but the quality above all others that wins the loyalty and affection of his men is his complete freedom from pretence.

By their speed and stamina the infantry clinched the advantages won by the guns, tanks and carriers. In the 19th Brigade's attack, for example, the Diggers kept up with a barrage which lifted 100 yards a minute. They made their own task easier because they could maintain a pace that bewildered the enemy.

Basically, however, Tobruk was a victory for planning and perfect co-ordination of land, naval and air forces and of British and Australian troops. It was as much a British as it was an Australian victory, for neither could have achieved success without the other. But in planning the actual assault General Mackay and his two chief staff officers, Colonel F. H. Berryman and Colonel G. A. Vasey, bore the chief responsibility.

Anyone casually meeting quiet-mannered Iven Gifford Mackay might not at first recognize in him the man whom the official historian of the 1st A.I.F. (Dr C. E. W. Bean) ranked among its first half dozen "fighting generals par excellence". He was never a fiery leader but rather a man impelled by a high sense of duty. Twenty years as a University lecturer and school headmaster have made this characteristic even more marked than it was when he first led men into battle on Gallipoli. There he gained special distinction as a company commander in the attack on Lone Pine, and, as Bean says, "fought for a night and a day in front of his men". Courageous and conscientious leadership gained him the D.S.O. at Pozières, command of the 4th Battalion at the age of thirty-four and of the 1st Brigade at thirty-six.

As the 6th Division's commander his strength lay in the thoroughness he demanded both in training and planning operations. Typical of this was his refusal to launch the attack on Tobruk until his artillery had available 500 rounds per gun, and until he was completely satisfied with the reconnaissance of the Italian defences. He left nothing to chance when the lives of his men were at stake.

His natural reticence prevented him from being a popular figure among the troops, but they respected him for the high personal standards he set himself and demanded of his officers. He was widely known as "Mr Chips", primarily because he brought traces of the headmaster's manner with him into the A.I.F. But this rather didactic approach was valuable for the division in its formative days, for every general must have in him something of the headmaster. His brigade commanders and senior staff officers were men of strong personality and such personalities frequently clash. Not the least of Mackay's achievements was the way he welded them into a team, and used the abilities of each to the best advantage. He certainly commanded the division himself but he was wise in making full use of his right- and left-hand men—Berryman and Vasey.[5]

If it had not been for the rule preventing Duntroon graduates from rising above the rank of major in the 1st A.I.F., both Berryman and Vasey would no doubt have then gained greater distinction than they did. In the 2nd A.I.F., however, they soon stood out as brilliant staff officers and later as fine commanders. In many ways they are alike, though they are very different in

---

[5] Berryman was Mackay's "G.1." (General Staff Officer Grade 1, i.e., chief-of-staff); Vasey was Assistant Adjutant and Quartermaster-General.

THE ROUND-UP

temperament. Both are highly efficient themselves and intolerant of inefficiency in others. Both are bold, hard-working, hard-driving. In Syria Berryman, then a Brigadier, seeing some of his troops hesitating in an attack on an enemy position, led them in himself. In Greece, Vasey, then also a Brigadier, being advised by one of his forward battalions that German tanks had broken through its front replied, "All the better, now you can shoot 'em up the backside. That's their weak spot."

The most noticeable difference between them is in build and manner. Berryman is short, spare, wiry; Vasey is tall, lithe and well built. In speech, Berryman is incisive, and sometimes terse. Vasey, blunt colourful and hard-swearing, is widely known as "Bloody George", because of his propensity for lurid language without consideration of time, place or person. Famous, too, is the operational order he gave to his brigade when it took up what was thought to be a "do-or-die" position in Greece: "Here we bloody-well are; and here we bloody-well stay"—an order which his Brigade Major redrafted to read: "The 19th Aust. Inf. Bde. will hold its present positions, come what may."

At Bardia and Tobruk, Berryman and Vasey made a first class team. Berryman gave point and substance to Mackay's broad plan. The audacity of the tactics sprang mainly from Berryman and his efficient staff work was a prime factor in their smooth working. Supply problems, which—as ever—limited the cloth from which the tactical pattern had to be cut, were admirably handled by Vasey. In the face of a plan so well conceived, organized and carried out, the Italians in Tobruk did not stand much chance.

Now with the Tobruk harbour and water supply at its back O'Connor's 13th Corps could press on to the destruction of the last remnants of Graziani's fleeing forces. Tobruk had not been as long or as hard a fight as the battles of Sidi Barrani and Bardia, but for a force bent on conquering Cyrenaica and destroying an enemy army, it was just as important. With the fall of Tobruk nothing could save Derna and Bengazi. The current of war swept on from Tobruk, but it was soon to sweep back.

CHAPTER V

The Town We Took

THE morning after the battle ended, smoke from smouldering dumps and ships still drifted over the town and harbour of Tobruk, though the front had already jumped a hundred miles westward to the heights above Derna. Before continuing their advance the Australian and British troops who had stormed Tobruk could rest, swim and look around. Only a few were supposed to have access to the town, but several hundred spirited themselves inside.

Driving in that morning, we turned up Via Mussolini, already renamed "Pitt Street", and past "Albergo Tobruch", which now bore the sign "Young and Jackson's". Down the road swaggered a party of Diggers, Italian national and regimental pennants flying from their bayonets, gay Fascist badges, cockades and ribbons stuck in their hats or pinned to their jackets. Their pockets bulged with miscellaneous souvenirs—monogrammed ashtrays and cutlery from "Albergo Tobruch", knick-knacks from officers' houses, revolvers, Fascist badges, sashes, swords, whistles and knives from Italian ordnance stores. They reminded me of an incident that occurred earlier in the campaign. A Digger who was escorting some prisoners had acquired an Italian captain's insignia and badges of rank. I asked him how he got them and he said, "I swapped 'em—for a coupla fags; for 'arf a bloody packet, I coulda been a blasted general."

Further down the road I saw some Australians with a pile of Italian paper money and it soon became fashionable to light a cigarette with 50 or 100 lire or to post an autographed note back to Australia. Useless in Tobruk, these same notes were real money in Bengazi as the troops ruefully discovered a few weeks later. Through the streets troops were driving anything that moved, little Fiats, big Lancias, captured motor-cycles and Diesel trucks. Some of these and a number of British trucks were drawn up in front of the Italian Navy and Army stores, where there was all the food the troops wanted—and they lost no time in supplementing their rations.

The comparatively few military police on hand had an unenviable task keeping high spirits in check. I saw no riotous looting, but there was some thoughtless damaging of property and much pointless souveniring of things that the troops threw away as soon as they were on the move again. Unfortunately some military equipment, transport in particular, was heedlessly destroyed or damaged. But so far as I saw, the men mainly responsible for this did not come from the fighting units. They were part of the irresponsible element, which has always been found in the A.I.F. It would be idle to pretend that it does not exist, but it is small and it is regrettable that a section of the Australian press has tended to glorify this element and to represent it as typical of the A.I.F. This misrepresentation has adversely affected the reputation of the force overseas and its fighting efficiency. While this is so, it should be remembered that the adventurous spirit, which leads to exuberance such as we saw in Tobruk this day, is the very quality which gives the best Australian troops their initiative and dash in battle.

In Tobruk that morning one man who had seen something of the 6th Division's Provosts in action was Edward Ward, the B.B.C. observer. He and I had spent the previous day chasing from one airfield to another between Tobruk and Sollum trying to find a plane to take our recordings of the first day's battle back to Cairo. At last we caught one, but it was dark before we got back to H.Q., 6th Division. Ward, however, decided to hitchhike into Tobruk town.

He had no trouble in getting a lift from two Diggers in a passing car, but he soon found that they regarded him with some suspicion. They examined his papers and then began cross-examining him as to his recent movements. Ward asked them what the game was and one Digger who was sitting behind him replied: "We happen to be military police and I've got a Smith and Wesson .45 two inches behind your back. We don't know who you are and those papers of yours don't mean a thing to us."

"That's all right," said Ward, "this'll make a fine story for me."

"It'll make a fine story if you're dinkum, but if you aren't it'll be just too bad. Anyway we're taking you to H.Q."

When they finally reached Tobruk the two provosts turned Ward over to the O.C. of the company garrisoning the town. His identity was soon established and the two M.Ps went off apparently satisfied. Ward was more than satisfied for the incident provided an amusing story for his next broadcast. A sensitive censor in Cairo, however, did not see the funny side. He banned the broadcast because, he said, it ridiculed the provosts who had made "an honest mistake".

Neither the censor nor Ward then knew what the two M.Ps told me later. When I asked them what their idea was in arresting a perfectly good B.B.C. correspondent, one of them replied: "That was all right. We knew he was on the level right from the jump, but we wanted an excuse to get into the town to look around, so we picked him up. As an excuse he was pretty good."

For the troops who had been out in the desert for over a month, there was plenty to see in the town. In peacetime the Italians had done their best to make it livable, and as desert garrison towns go it must have ranked high. Tobruk is built on the rocky headland which forms the northern shore of the harbour and extends about a mile along the waterfront and half a mile inshore. Its normal peacetime population was a garrison of some 10,000 Italian and native troops, and 1000 Italian civil servants and shopkeepers. There were a further 9000 Arab civilians, the majority of whom lived in a native village half a mile north of the Italian town. Before the war nearly all troops were quartered outside, but the senior officers and civilians, many of whom had their families with them, lived in comfortable houses in the town itself. These were mostly grouped in a dozen streets around the Piazza Vittorio Emmanuele, and architecturally these and the military buildings showed signs of Fascist regimentation. They were almost entirely constructed of brick or stone covered with white plaster, relieved only by blue or green wooden shutters.

The town boasted a "Grand Hotel" and two other inns; a restaurant-cabaret, known as "The Lido", where Italian officers had dined and danced or watched a film on the piazza overlooking the harbour. Its bank and town hall—symbols of commercial and civic respectability—were good buildings. There was a fine school—named, inevitably, after Mussolini; a handsome church; a mosque and a first-rate hospital. Dominating all was the huge three-storied, concrete naval headquarters standing on a bluff above the harbour. It was only three-parts finished but was well built and later withstood a direct hit by a 500-pound German bomb.

By the waterfront stood an electric power station, a couple of big godowns, and a huge cool-store which kept fresh the garrison's meat. At considerable cost the Italians had also tunnelled into the slope of the headland to make a number of bomb-proof air-raid shelters, and storage places for fuel, ammunition and vital supplies.

We had expected to find little more than a rubble heap after our bombing and shelling, and Italian sabotage. But the remarkable thing was not how much was destroyed, but how much was still intact. Evidently the speed with which the attack succeeded had prevented the Italians from carrying out much of their planned demolitions. Some of these attempts had misfired; in other cases the charges were found ready for blowing. The enemy had tried very clumsily to set alight the main power station, but an Australian naval officer (Lieutenant Arnold Green, Liaison Officer attached to 13th Corps H.Q.) was attracted by smoke drifting from the building, and put the fire out before any serious damage had been done.

From the top of the naval building on January 23rd I studied the main prize of the battle—the harbour. One pier had been completely demolished by R.A.F. bombs, but the Italian attempt to wreck the other main jetty had resulted in nothing more than a small gap on one side. Lying sunk or beached were a dozen victims of R.A.F. bombing, but fortunately none blocked the channel. Obligingly the Italians had left undamaged six auxiliary schooners, twenty large pontoons, a couple of dozen lighters and several fast launches. With these available the demolition of the main jetty and of the two main cranes did not much matter. Within three days minesweepers had cleared the channel and the port was once more in operation.

The Italian gunners had carried out their demolitions better than the sailors. Of the twelve main coast defence guns only two were intact. There was nothing but a huge crater where "Tobruk Tom", the 12-inch naval gun, had been emplaced. Its crew had blown up the ammunition dump, housed in a tunnel beneath the gun position. Most of the anti-aircraft guns had also been destroyed, but there were twenty 105-mm. and twelve 149-mm. guns undamaged in an ordnance store—brand new. These were a boon to the Greeks, to whom they were soon shipped together with a mass of other captured war material.

The vital Tobruk water supply plant was intact, though, of course, the pipeline by which the Italians had brought water more than a hundred miles from Derna was cut. The two distilleries, however, which delivered 20,000 gallons a day and the sub-artesian wells which could provide a further 20,000 were untouched. It may well be that the Italians were reluctant to destroy the water resources lest they—as prisoners—should be the first to suffer from any shortage. The normal ration budgeted for in the desert was one gallon per man per day for all purposes, cooking, drinking and washing, though the troops frequently had to carry on with as little as half a gallon. Even with the Tobruk supplies they now had very little more than this.

The Italians, however, had left substantial stores of Chianti, cognac, aniseed brandy and a mineral water named Recoaro. The Chianti was good but the brandy was fiery and the aniseed worse. The Recoaro was excellent and the Italians had shipped hundreds of thousands of cases of it from Italy. Apparently this was the only water their officers drank and it was occasionally issued to the men. They had even carried thousands of cases of Recoaro with them when they advanced to Sidi Barrani, and I saw Recoaro bottles strewn from their forward camps almost back to El Agheila. In Tobruk there was one huge iron shed packed with cases of it and almost every mess in General O'Connor's forces was soon well supplied.

Tobruk was stocked with enough tinned food for a garrison of 25,000 for two months—a windfall for our troops who had been existing on little but bully-beef, biscuits, butter, jam and tea. The Italian tinned fruit and vegetables were as good as Australia's best. In one store in Tobruk there were vast supplies of tinned cherries, strawberries, pears, apricots, beans, peas, and carrots, and these were soon being issued along with regular British rations. Most welcome of all were square 2-gallon tins of pulped tomatoes and great boxes of spaghetti; but packets of powdered garlic had few takers. Even the cool-store was well stocked with meat, and in one dump there were several hundred tons of flour which went straight to our field bakeries.

There was little stock in the Tobruk shops, for most of the civilian owners were evidently evacuated immediately after the Sidi Barrani battle. The date stamps in the bank were still set for December 15th. Nearly all the Tobruk shops had been run under government monopoly. They were generally poorly stocked, but they did carry some surprising items. In one, for instance, there were a dozen Singer sewing-machines, several good radios, and typewriters. Peacetime stock must have been more extensive, judging by what I saw in officers' houses. One colonel's home might have been lifted intact from a modern suburb in Rome, with all the requisites of bourgeois comfort —radio, electric stove, refrigerator, hot water system, a tiled bathroom, a kitchen bright with chromium fittings, a cellar stocked with good Italian wines.

In the colonel's wardrobe were half a dozen gaudy uniforms, with tight waists, silk-linings, bright trimmings and velvet collars. In other houses I saw even more elaborate wardrobes complete with dress sword, jack-boots, tasselled sashes, satin-lined swagger capes, and officers' "dressing-tables" stocked with perfume, powder and heavily scented hair oil. The Colonel's family had apparently been with him—at least until the outbreak of war; for one room was littered with children's toys and books. Over everything now lay a coating of dust, broken glass and fallen plaster, shaken down by bombing. In one room a splinter from an R.A.F. bomb had gone through the window and buried itself in the wall a foot or two over the head of a bed. Above the splinter the colonel had scribbled his signature, the date, and in large letters *"Viva il Duce"*.

It is not surprising that the Italian houses were well equipped, for Tobruk was an important peacetime garrison. In most British or American garrison towns of similar importance you would find much the same standard of comfort in officers' billets. There would be the traditional mess and ceremonial uniforms and the gay trappings, with which any army likes to surround itself in peacetime. But the British and Australians shed these accessories in the desert in time of war. They lived hard and travelled light. When necessary they existed on a tin of bully-beef, two packets of biscuits and a bottle of salty water per day; they slept on the hard dust-swept ground and carried only shorts and shirts and simple battle-dress. They adapted themselves to the desert's hard conditions and by doing so gained freedom of action. The desert was their sea. Over it they privateered and struck—equipped as lightly as could be for personal comfort, as heavily as could be for the job of discomfiting the enemy.

The Italian policy was the direct opposite. They feared the desert and set out to make themselves comfortable in spite of it. When they advanced to Sidi Barrani in September 1940 they were followed by trucks carrying crates of Recoaro water and flagons of Chianti, tinned delicacies and even fresh rolls brought up from Bardia wrapped in cellophane. They brought their dandies' uniforms, flash accoutrements and boxes of clothes as grand as those we found in Tobruk. I saw all these things lying in the sand at the Italian camps the British over-ran near Sidi Barrani in December 1940.

The Italians were not prepared to accept or adapt themselves to the rigours the desert inflicts on those who fight across its wastes. In the battle against it they squandered time, effort and transport that would have been better employed in the real fight.

This difference in the attitude of the British and Italians to the desert was symptomatic of their fundamentally different attitude to the war. The Tommies and Diggers knew that war was a serious, hard and brutal business. They had no illusions—but they were prepared to endure hardship and reverse because the things they were fighting for mattered to them personally. They needed no fancy rations to maintain their spirits; no glittering uniforms to keep up their confidence.

But to the Italians such luxurious trappings were natural and necessary. They were an essential part of the illusion Mussolini had fostered in the hope of inspiring them with a warlike spirit and an Imperial ambition. In his speeches and propaganda he had glamorized war and sought to sell them the idea that it was a grand adventure, with power, plunder and glory as the prizes. To bolster their faint hearts he had told them that the young, virile Fascist legions had only to march and the jaded, effete British would collapse. It was fitting that the Duce's conquering army should live well and carry with it into the desert the panoply of victorious heroes so that they could make a proper show when they goose-stepped through the streets of Alexandria and Cairo.

They soon found that there was no glory or glamour for them in desert warfare, only danger and hardship. Over this their spirit could not triumph in spite of Graziani's pampering. When the prospect of power and plunder turned into the reality of defeat and disgrace at the hands of the enemy they had been taught to despise, their illusion was shattered.

Another blow to the spirit of the Italians in Tobruk came from the Duce himself. When the bulk of his great army was routed and captured at Sidi Barrani and Bardia he explained away the disaster by declaring that the British had gathered an irresistible weight of men and metal. At Bardia they had used, according to Rome Radio, "hordes of blood-thirsty Australians"—three divisions of them, plus two British armoured divisions. In justifying himself to his own people with this gross exaggeration Mussolini had put a shot in the heart of his forces in Tobruk.

They had little left to die for. No doubt they wanted the same things from life as the Diggers and the Tommies—peace, freedom, security. But they must have realized that Mussolini and his Fascists were not fighting for these; that Fascism was nothing but a false front. Italians with whom I talked found it hard to believe that the Australians were volunteers. They understood their own position. They had been sent to Libya to win glory for Mussolini. They presumed that the Tommies were there merely to defend British Imperial interests. But why were the Australian volunteers there?

The ordinary Digger would have found it rather hard to tell you. If you had ever persuaded him to talk he would not have spoken of defending freedom, or removing injustice, or of saving the Empire. He might have said, "Oh, I wanted a bit of fun;" or else, "I dunno, I was fed up with my job;" or perhaps, "Well, all my cobbers were joining up and so I went along too." Not much more than that. These would not be the real answers. Men may join up for fun or for a change, but if these were the only reasons, they would not go into action and fight through with bayonet and grenade when machine-gun bullets kick the dust around their feet and they see the man next to them go down. If you could get the ordinary Australian to say what he really feels, it might be something like this:

"Well, I came away because I believe in a fair go and I wanted to be with my mates; because I like to be able to say to a copper, 'That's all right, copper, you got nothin' on me;' because I want to say what I like when we're having a beer at the pub; because I want to do what I like with the few quid I've got in the bank; and because women and kids are being bombed in London and shot in Prague, and someday this might happen at home if we don't do something about it." It was because they felt that the battle was being fought for things like these, which mattered directly to them, that the Mallee farmer and the Kalgoorlie miner, the Bendigo bank-clerk and the Sydney solicitor made the soldiers of Tobruk just as they had made those of Gallipoli.

At Tobruk, as at Bardia, the 2nd A.I.F. showed that it had inherited the traditions and qualities of the original Anzacs. But the battle that was just over was a small test of the new A.I.F's spirit and soldierly worth by comparison with those that were to be fought later on this same battlefield.

In the Piazza Vittorio Emmanuele on the morning after

Tobruk fell, I was talking with Lieutenant-Colonel Arthur Godfrey, C.O., 2/6th Battalion. As a bunch of Italian prisoners were marched away, he said, "That's about the last of the 25,000. If we'd had 25,000 Australians inside these defences not even the Germans would have got us out in six months." He little knew that within a few weeks he would be with the 9th Division inside Tobruk commanding one of the brigades whose job it was to make these words good.

CHAPTER VI

Tobruk Derby

ON December 6th, 1940, when the men of the British 7th Armoured Division stocked their tanks with food and ammunition, and strapped bed-rolls outside, they thought they were going on a four-day raid behind the Italian positions at Sidi Barrani. Two months later they finished their "four-day raid" 500 miles farther west at El Agheila on the border of Tripolitania.

By the time Wavell's forces reached the end of their pursuit, 175 miles south of Bengazi, they were at the end of their tether. They were tired; over-worked transport was on its last wheels; tanks were on their last tracks. They had advanced as far as this only by impressing hundreds of captured Italian lorries. A regiment of armoured cars, two battalions of infantry, three batteries of artillery and one squadron of tanks were all that reached El Agheila in mid-February. Even a month later the forward troops were little stronger. With a supply line stretching 900 miles back to the Nile Valley, no larger force could be maintained. The supply problem would have been much easier if more use could have been made of Bengazi harbour, but by now the Luftwaffe was operating from Tripolitania in strength and the R.A.F. had insufficient aircraft to keep that port open. Even if the forces near El Agheila had been twice as strong they could not have broken through the narrow bottleneck between the salt marshes and the sea. In any case, it would have been a grave mistake to have attempted a further push westwards to Tripoli when it was known that Hitler was about to attack in the Balkans.

It is widely believed, however, that if there had been no expedition to Greece, Wavell could have held Cyrenaica, and could also have gone on to Tripoli and swept the Axis from North Africa two years before the Allies eventually did. This view springs from either wishful thinking or ignorance. I believe that even if Wavell had had available all the troops and equipment which went to Greece, the Axis could still have retaken most of Cyrenaica before the middle of 1941.

Two main considerations governed warfare in the Libyan-Egyptian Desert: supply, and the balance of "mobile striking power"—a term which may be used to cover the combined power of tanks, anti-tank guns and field artillery working together as a common force. The chief geographical factor influencing tactics in this desert is that, except at El Alamein near Alexandria and at El Agheila on the border of Tripolitania, there are no defensive positions that cannot be outflanked. At both these places secure flanks are provided by narrow bottlenecks—between the Mediterranean and the Qattara Depression in one case, and the Great Sand Sea in the other. Everywhere else there is an open desert flank, the cause of constant anxiety to the commander who has not superiority in mobile striking power. Even the most gallant infantry cannot hold fixed positions in this desert when once enemy armoured forces have outflanked them. Then, if they are not to be cut off, they must withdraw and keep on withdrawing until wear and tear or supply difficulties reduce the enemy's superiority in armoured and mobile forces to such an extent that he loses control of the open desert flank. Their only alternative is to establish themselves behind a fortified perimeter covering a water-point and harbour like that at Tobruk.

In view of all this, the two Australian and New Zealand divisions that were the backbone of the force in Greece could hardly have stopped, though they might have delayed, Rommel's drive through Cyrenaica. The only place west of Tobruk where infantry lacking in tank support could have held Rommel was in the El Agheila bottleneck. But it would have taken more than a division to stop him here, and the Middle East could not have maintained a force of this size at El Agheila before the end of April. Rommel attacked at the end of March.

At that time, even with the tanks which went to Greece, it is doubtful if Wavell could have gained the armoured superiority necessary to hold any position with an open desert flank west of Tobruk. In March he had only two armoured divisions in the Middle East. Of these the 7th, after eight months' action in the desert, was back in the Nile Valley resting and refitting. Three-quarters of its tanks were worn out and new ones had not yet arrived. The 2nd Armoured Division had just come from Britain with new tanks, but most of these and one of its two armoured brigades went to Greece.

Even if these tanks could have been sent to the desert, the

Germans would still have had a two to one advantage in armour. Moreover, the British cruiser tank was hardly a match for the Mark III (medium) and the Mark IV (heavy) German tanks, which Rommel brought with him; the inferiority of British anti-tank weapons was an even greater weakness. The strongest armoured force Wavell could have put in the field in Western Cyrenaica in March or April would have been one weak and inexperienced division.

The basic fact is that Wavell was called upon to do too much with too little. If there had been no Greek expedition, he would still have needed to take some steps to meet the German threat on his northern flank. He would have had to reinforce both Crete and Cyprus and he would probably have needed also to crush growing Axis power in Iraq and Syria several months earlier than he eventually did. In March he could not have put into Western Cyrenaica a sufficient proportion of the troops who went to Greece to match the strength Rommel had amassed.

By early March Rommel already had in Tripoli his highly trained, hand-picked Afrika Korps, consisting of the 15th Armoured Division and the 5th Light Motorized Division (which was virtually a light armoured division then and was soon turned into the 21st Armoured Division). He had nearly 300 German tanks, half of them Mark IIIs and Mark IVs, plus considerable supporting field and anti-tank artillery, and motorized infantry. Moreover, the Luftwaffe had in Libya alone a far greater number of aircraft than the R.A.F. could have mustered in all the Middle East. In addition, Rommel had brought the six best divisions that he could pick from Mussolini's Army. One of these, the 132nd Ariete, was armoured. In the face of this strength the British and Australian forces in Cyrenaica could never have gone on; actually they soon had to come back.

The new Axis commander, Lieutenant-General Erwin Rommel, was a Nazi product—a self-made general upon whom the professional soldiers of the Reichswehr looked askance. Born in 1891, the son of a Bavarian schoolmaster, he had proved a tough soldier in the Great War. In 1915 he won the highest Prussian decoration when a small detachment of mountain troops, led by him, forced a French battalion to retire. He joined the Nazi party in 1923 and became the leader of one of Hitler's S.S. basher-gangs. Later he rose to be the head of the Führer's personal bodyguard. When Hitler began to expand the Reichswehr in 1934, Rommel returned to the Army and at once became interested in tanks. A colonel at the time of the invasion of Poland, he was soon promoted major-general and commanded the 7th Armoured Division in the attack on Belgium and France. There he played an important part in the break-through to the Channel, and this led to his being given the task of commanding and training the Afrika Korps.

At G.H.Q., Cairo, in March neither Rommel's intentions nor strength were properly appreciated. Wavell later stated publicly that he had made a miscalculation about Rommel's Libyan offensive. He said that he did not think that the enemy could counter-attack before May at the earliest and by then he had hoped to have tanks enough to put another armoured division in the field.

It is strange, however, that both General Wavell's G.H.Q. and Lieutenant-General Sir Philip Neame's Cyrenaica Command H.Q. ("Cyrcom" for short) should have taken so long to appreciate the rising German menace in Cyrenaica. From mid-February dozens of German planes were operating daily over Bengazi and El Agheila. Before the end of that month the most advanced Australian brigade (Brigadier S. G. Savige's 17th) reported the presence of German armoured cars and troops near El Agheila, and R.A.F. reconnaissance discovered unusually large convoys heading east along the road from Tripoli.

Nevertheless the "Cairo Military Spokesman" on March 1st scouted the idea that the Germans had anything but small patrols in the El Agheila area, adding that "their main force undoubtedly lies in Western Libya". The general opinion at G.H.Q. and at "Cyrcom" was that, even if large German forces had reached Tripoli, they could not be ready to attack seriously before summer heat "ended the campaigning season" in May. It would surely take them several months to gather their equipment and to become acclimatized and trained for desert warfare.

It was not then known that Rommel had given his Afrika Korps special desert training in Germany. On a sandy peninsula in the Baltic, he had found terrain which approximated that in Libya and there had worked out tactical and maintenance problems. The troops had lived and worked in over-heated barracks and artificial sandstorms, and on strictly rationed water and limited food. After this "hot-house" training they were ready for desert action when they stepped off the ships at Tripoli.

That was evident from the speed with which the Germans appeared at El Agheila. From Intelligence sources in Tripoli and Tunisia came warnings of the size and intention of the Axis forces, but G.H.Q. and "Cyrcom" were still reluctant to believe that dangerously large forces could have slipped through without the Navy knowing.

The Royal Navy, however, had been too busy elsewhere in February and March to maintain the close patrol that had restricted reinforcements to Tripoli in the last months of 1940. Since January the Luftwaffe, operating in force and almost unopposed from Sicily and Tripoli, had greatly increased the difficulty of intercepting Axis convoys, primarily because the British could not maintain the same air reconnaissance. Moreover, Admiral Cunningham's ships and crews were strained dangerously close to their limit. They were fetching and carrying as well as fighting and patrolling. From mid-February to mid-March they were fully occupied ferrying and escorting troops and equipment to Greece. The ships were seldom in port longer than it took to refuel, re-victual and re-ammunition. They barely had time to carry out minimum maintenance. It was certainly no reflection on the Navy that Rommel shipped his force to Africa.

Much of the shipping sneaked through with the connivance of Vichy France. Axis ships, flying the tricolour, sailed from the South of France to French North Africa and then hugged the coast to Tripoli inside the 3-mile limit. The importance of this route was not realized until too late. In April, however, Cunningham was able to deliver two severe blows at Axis shipping in "mid-Med" and Tripoli harbour.

On April 16th the Admiralty announced that British naval forces had sunk every one of a convoy of five supply ships and three destroyers bound for Tripoli. On April 21st a battlefleet stood off Tripoli and rained 553 tons of shells into shipping in the harbour and into vital targets ashore. Simultaneously the R.A.F. and the Fleet Air Arm bombed the harbour. Three supply ships were sunk; three others and a destroyer were left burning fiercely after fifty minutes of the fiercest bombardment of the war. These blows seriously disrupted Rommel's supply system, but by this time he was already striking at Tobruk and on the Egyptian frontier.

The British withdrawal, which preceded these attacks, was known to the troops either as the "Tobruk Derby" or the "Bengazi-Tobruk Handicap". Rommel actually launched his offensive at the end of March, but for a month his Air Force had been preparing the way. By mid-February JU87s (Stukas) and JU88s (medium bombers) had made Bengazi harbour almost too hot to use. ME110s were strafing the Bengazi-El Agheila road so severely that it became known as "Messerschmitt Alley". It was nothing to see a swarm of twenty Messerschmitts machine-gunning the road from a hundred feet, and soon supply columns could move freely only at night.

Operating from Benina aerodrome near Bengazi and from Agedabia, seventy-five miles east of El Agheila, Hurricanes of the R.A.A.F.'s No. 3 Squadron did their best to check the German air attacks. But this lone squadron could not give adequate cover to the forward troops and supply lines as well as to Bengazi harbour, and the R.A.F. could spare no others to help it. The Luftwaffe had fighter superiority of at least five to one, but it usually made its attack at times when the Hurricanes had come down to refuel. The result was that in four weeks, though the squadron broke up many German attacks, it shot down only fifteen planes for certain.

On March 8th, the 6th Australian Division was relieved in Libya by the newly-formed 9th Divison under Major-General L. J. Morshead. The 9th Division had been originally formed from the troops who were diverted to Britain when Italy came into the war. It consisted then of the 18th Brigade, and a new brigade (the 25th) formed in Britain. When these brigades reached Egypt in January 1941, the 24th was added to them to complete the 9th Division. Before the 1st Australian Corps left for Greece, however, the 18th and 25th Brigades were transferred to the 7th Division, and two of its brigades—the 20th and 26th—became part of the 9th.

G.H.Q. thought so little of the possibility of an Axis counter-offensive that Morshead was told that his division would merely act as garrison troops and would have time to complete its training and equipping before going into action. At this time its units had hardly passed the stage of elementary training and they were very short of essential equipment such as Bren guns, mortars and anti-tank weapons. The division had very little signal equipment and less than half of its transport. Its field regiments had no guns, its cavalry no carriers, and so only the three infantry brigades and some divisional troops were moved to Cyrenaica.

Consequently only one brigade, the 20th, was sent forward to support the British 3rd Armoured Brigade, which was covering the eastern end of the El Agheila bottleneck. The 20th was commanded by Brigadier John Murray, a big, genial Irishman who loves a fight. He is personally easy-going but brooks no slackness among his troops and even before Tobruk his brigade was marked out as one of the best-trained in the 2nd A.I.F. His dogged temperament made him well suited for the defensive tasks that lay ahead. He had shown himself a strong leader in the Great War when he won the D.S.O. and M.C. and rose to be second-in-command of the 53rd Battalion.

The 3rd Armoured Brigade that Murray's 20th was to support was pitifully weak in tanks, and Morshead and his "G.1." (Colonel C. E. M. Lloyd) realized at once that the El Agheila position could not be held against the attack which the Germans were obviously mounting. They said so in a report to "Cyrcom", suggesting further that the Germans would attack with an armoured division supported by Italians, and would cut across the desert to Mechili and outflank the Anglo-Australian forces in Western Cyrenaica.

Morshead consequently urged Neame to withdraw the 20th Brigade from the El Agheila area, arguing that, with little transport and limited weapons and supporting artillery, it would only be an embarrassment to the British armoured forces when the attack came. Neame disagreed, but on March 17th the Chief of the British General Staff (General Sir John Dill) and General Wavell met Morshead at Beda Fomm. Wavell did not share the Australian concern, but he and Dill agreed that it was wise to withdraw the 20th Brigade. The only people not pleased with this move were the Diggers themselves. As one of their officers wrote later: "All that night we travelled by truck back along the black road which we had thought was to lead us to Tripoli . . . We had not come to Libya to run away. We wanted to stay and fight. We did not know where we were going nor why, but running made us afraid."

On March 23rd the 20th Brigade took up positions east and north-east of Bengazi. The 9th Division was to defend the escarpment that runs from Er Regima—thirty miles east of Bengazi—northwards through Tocra to the coast. To hold this 62-mile front Morshead had only the three battalions of the 20th Brigade and one of the 26th, with another on the way up. The remaining brigade, the 24th, was training in the Tobruk-Gazala area. In support he had only one British field regiment (the 51st) with sixteen guns. This front, so thinly held, could have withstood no serious German attack. It had a dangerously open flank, for there was only the one weak armoured brigade to stop the Germans cutting across the desert south of Er Regima and heading for Mechili. This was the natural route for them to take, since it had been pioneered by the British tanks early in February when they had crossed the desert to Beda Fomm and cut off the last of Graziani's forces fleeing from Bengazi.

This danger was fully appreciated by Morshead. The El Agheila front was now being held by the 2nd Armoured Division, commanded by Major-General M. D. Gambier-Parry. It contained only a Support Group and the three armoured regiments of the 3rd Brigade equipped with worn-out or captured tanks. The 3rd Hussars had obsolete light tanks, suitable only for reconnaissance; the 6th R.T.R. had Italian M13s salvaged from the Beda Fomm battlefield; the 5th R.T.R. had once had fifty aged cruisers but already had lost thirty of them through mechanical trouble which developed on the way forward.

In these circumstances it is not surprising that the advanced British elements were driven from El Agheila on March 24th, and that a week later the 3rd Armoured Brigade was badly mauled by German tanks at Mersa Brega. On April 2nd it was attacked again at Agedabia, 100 miles south of Bengazi, and lost most of its remaining tanks in an unequal battle. Rommel gained unmistakable armoured superiority and there was little chance of holding him in the open desert. Nevertheless, Morshead's fears were not shared by Neame, who still hoped that the Germans would be satisfied with the recapture of Bengazi and would not go for Mechili. It was decided that the remainder of the 3rd Armoured Brigade would cover the open desert flank while the Australians attempted to check any advance beyond Bengazi by holding their positions along the Er Regima-Tocra escarpment.

The Australians dug in and waited for the Germans to come. Below them on the plain lay white-walled Bengazi with its avenues of gums and wattles, now blanketed with black smoke as engineers blew up everything the enemy might value. The last of the R.A.A.F.'s Hurricanes rose from Benina and headed eastwards, but on this escarpment the Diggers hoped that they would stand and fight.

Meantime "Cyrcom", on April 3rd, did not know what was happening on the crucial desert flank. Communications with the 3rd Armoured Brigade, which was shadowing the German advance guard, had broken down. Nazi aircraft, concentrating their attacks on its wireless trucks, had knocked most of them out. Air reconnaissance reported an armoured column at Msus— a third of the way to Mechili. At first it was said to be German;

then British; no one could be sure. What few orders reached the
2nd Armoured Division were conflicting. It was told to move along
the coast to Bengazi; then it was ordered to Msus. Result: the
3rd Armoured Brigade reached Msus on the night of the 3rd-4th
but the Support Group withdrew through Bengazi.

It needed a cool head and a firm hand to prevent the withdrawal becoming a rout. This was provided by the arrival of
Lieutenant-General Sir Richard O'Connor, the successful commander of the first Libyan offensive. He was sent by Wavell to
"Cyrcom", but did not take command; he acted only in an
advisory capacity. At "Cyrcom" that morning there was still
considerable support for the theory that Rommel was only
interested in Bengazi. This was particularly the view of Gambier-
Parry, who said that he was in no way alarmed at the situation
and that Bengazi was the enemy's final objective for the present
at least. On O'Connor's advice, however, it was decided to withdraw the 3rd Armoured Brigade across the desert to Mechili
and the 9th Division through the Gebel Akdar—the "Green
Mountains"—to Derna. Meantime the 20th Brigade was to hold
at Er Regima and cover the withdrawal.

By midday on April 4th the only Australians barring the
German path on the Er Regima escarpment were the 2/13th
Battalion (commanded by Lieutenant-Colonel F. A. Burrows).
They were told that they must hold the pass until seven that
evening because no transport could be sent before then. The
Australian positions were not strong. The escarpment rose
sharply for about 400 feet above the Bengazi plain, but there
were several passes leading to the plateau above. Through the
easiest of these ran the road and narrow-gauge railway to Barce
—forty-five miles north. The face of the escarpment and the
wadis was bare, shaly rock. Unable to dig trenches, the troops
built themselves sangars which would withstand machine-gun
fire, but could be easily blown in by a tank shell. The Italinas
had dug an anti-tank ditch, but it was on the top of the plateau,
designed to stop any tank advance from the east.

Burrows had only three rifle companies of the 2/13th (the
fourth was at Barce doing guard duty), four 4.5-inch howitzers
and two captured Italian anti-tank guns with which to hold
this escarpment, and these were spread out on a 9-mile front.
His "D" Company was astride the main pass; four miles away
on its left was "B" Company guarding a flanking wadi; "A"
Company was in reserve. Burrows was advised that more field,
anti-tank and Vickers guns would be sent to him, but by early

afternoon on the 4th there was no sign of these. There was, however, sign of the enemy. About 2 p.m. vehicles were seen near Benina airfield, six miles west of the pass, and in their exposed and extended positions along the escarpment the 2/13th got ready for the first clash between the A.I.F. and the Germans in this war.

By 3.30 there were several hundred vehicles round Benina and Captain E. A. Handley, O.C. of "D" Company, reported that about 2000 lorried infantry and a dozen tanks were moving slowly towards the escarpment. There, Royal Engineers had laid a minefield and had also mined a section of the road, but when the road was now blown most of the mines also exploded by sympathetic detonation.

About 4.30 the German advance guard of armoured cars and light tanks came within range of the howitzers and two Italian long-range mortars that the 2/13th were using, having none of their own. The mortar crews scored an early success, landing a bomb on the turret of a light tank and putting it out of action. As the mortar and artillery fire became hotter, the tanks and armoured cars withdrew.

Half an hour later came the real German attack. Sixteen tanks approached line abreast, in two waves, with thirty or forty lorries laden with troops behind them. As they advanced towards the main pass, four armoured cars swung to the right, guided by an Arab who flashed a petrol tin in the late afternoon sun at the mouth of a wadi that was neither mined nor covered by our infantry. These armoured cars succeeded in climbing the escarpment, but the old Italian anti-tank ditch stopped them from getting behind the troops in the pass.

Meantime, Handley's company was heavily engaged with the main enemy force. The minefield, having already been blown up, was no barrier to the tanks' advance, and the fire from the four British howitzers was not enough to stop them. As the tanks reached the bottom of the pass, the Australians in sangars on the escarpment-face came under heavy fire from machine-guns and 37-mm. and 75-mm. cannon. The shells smashed through the stone walls of the sangars, but the Diggers fought back with Brens and their solitary anti-tank rifle, even though their fire was ineffective.

Several tanks drove up the road but at one point engineers had prepared it for blowing. As the leading tank reached there Handley fired the charge; the road went up taking the tank with it, but the explosion was so violent that it blew down the neighbouring sangars, and the forward platoon had to withdraw to the top of the pass. Undeterred by the fate of the leading tank, the next two worked round the blown road and continued through the pass, firing at the infantry as they went but not stopping to clean them up. The Australians held on, waiting for the German infantry and hoping that the guns would deal with the tanks.

At the foot of the escarpment the German infantry jumped from their lorries amid steady fire from artillery, small arms and mortars. The crew of one mortar kept this up so constantly that the weapon almost shook to pieces. Eventually it could only be fired with one man gripping the barrel and another lying flat across the base-plate to steady it. But the crew kept it in action and eventually the Germans were dissuaded from pressing their direct attack up the pass. Their infantry sheered off and worked round the flanks of Handley's company.

His men clung to their positions as long as they could, and fought a yard-by-yard withdrawal. One platoon was nearly enveloped, but its commander (Sergeant Roy Simmonds) held on and sent a runner back to ask Handley if he might "withdraw a little as the position is precarious". Unfortunately the platoon stayed so long that only five men out of thirty got back.

Finally Handley's company was forced to retire behind the anti-tank ditch at the top of the pass. There it held on and the reserve company was sent to stop the enemy's outflanking movement on the right, while "B" Company was withdrawn to cover the left flank. Meantime the two tanks that had come up the pass were checked by the anti-tank ditch. They cruised up and down behind it, blazing away and searching for a crossing.

Just as they seemed likely to get through, four 18-pounders of the 51st Field Regiment came down the road from Barce. They swung off into action positions, but two of them were knocked out by the tanks before they fired a shot. The others destroyed one tank, but they too were silenced by the second. The second tank was disabled by Boyes rifle fire and a lone Digger (Private S. Eland) dashed forward with a Bren and forced the crew to surrender.

With their tanks silenced, the German infantry were held in check chiefly by the howitzers, and, as darkness fell, the main body of Germans paused to consolidate west of the anti-tank ditch. It was fortunate that they did so, for the howitzers by then had run out of ammunition. Under cover of darkness the 2/13th continued to withdraw, only to find that Germans were behind them and had machine-guns covering the road. From there, however, the enemy was driven back at bayonet point, and the road was cleared.

It was nearly 11 p.m. before the transport arrived, but the Germans did not press on in the dark and the laden trucks headed north for Barce without interference. These trucks carried eighty-two men less than the trucks that had brought the battalion there. It was unfortunate that the action had to end in withdrawal, but the 2/13th and the British gunners had done all that was asked of them. They had given the rest of the force time to get away.

All through that night on the way to Barce and beyond, "fifty miles of road was choked with fleeing vehicles and men," wrote one member of the 2/17th Battalion later. "When speed was all that mattered, the best that could be achieved was ten miles an hour. It was dark and, in spite of the crush, very lonely on the road. In the early hours of the morning Barce was ablaze. . . . The Senussi were looting the town. . . . The night was urgent and full of fear. We scrambled into new positions and looked down on Barce as we had looked down on Bengazi. Fear left us . . . this time we would fight."

That was their hope, but everything depended on what happened on the desert flank. No one at "Cyrcom" next day, April 5th, was sure what was happening. It was out of touch with the 3rd Armoured Brigade, but there was a large column heading eastwards for Mechili—ours or theirs? That afternoon the R.A.F. reported it was British and on the morning of April 6th Neame met Morshead and told him that a line was to be held on the escarpment overlooking Barce.

An hour after Neame left, O'Connor rang from "Cyrcom" to say that the Germans had shelled Mechili that morning and were there in force. Morshead at once suggested that the 9th Division should withdraw to Gazala, thirty miles west of Tobruk. As Neame had not returned to "Cyrcom", however, O'Connor was reluctant to reverse Neame's orders, and thought it wiser in any case not to move until dark, because of the probability of Axis air attack. Morshead persuaded him that this risk had to be taken. There was not a moment to lose for the 9th Division was in grave danger of envelopment. The Germans at Mechili were only forty-eight miles *south* of Derna; most of the 20th and 26th Australian Brigades were more than a hundred miles *west* of Derna. Rommel had a first-class chance of cutting off the whole force by a bold thrust north to Derna

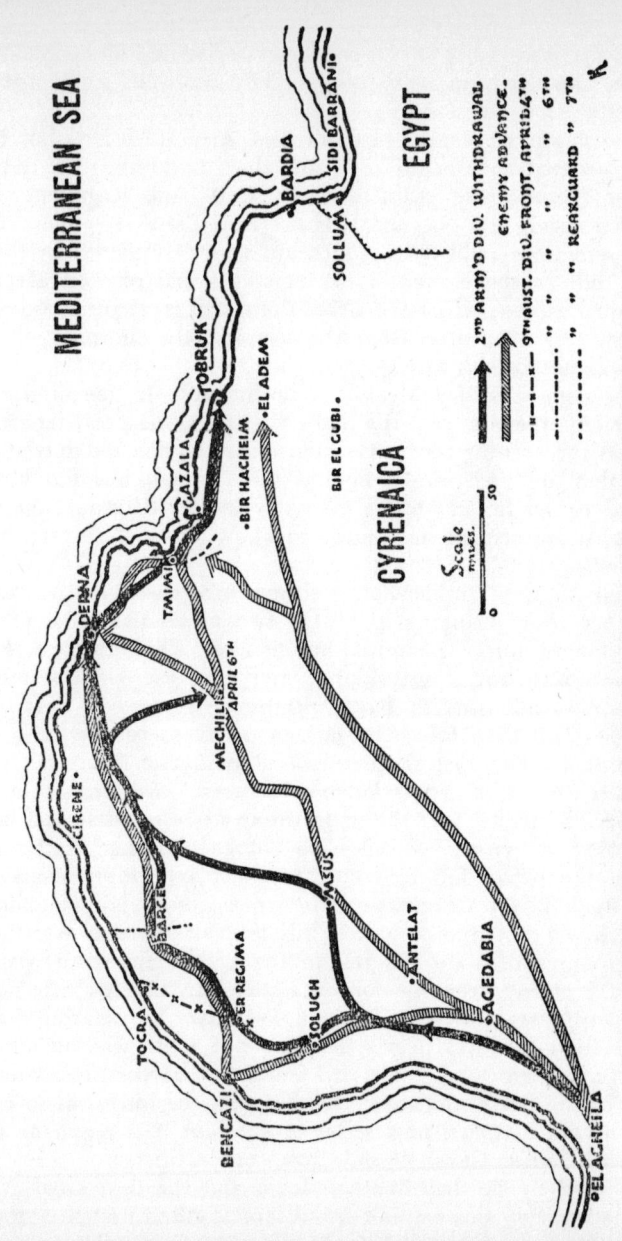

THE "TOBRUK DERBY"—ROMMEL'S ADVANCE IN CYRENAICA, APRIL 1st-9th, 1941

or to the coast road at Tmimi—sixty miles due east. The fate of the 9th Division now hung chiefly on what happened at Mechili.

The rump of Gambier-Parry's 2nd Armoured Division had been ordered to Mechili to guard that flank; the 3rd Indian Motor Brigade, the 3rd Australian Anti-Tank Regiment (less two batteries) and the 3rd R.H.A. (Anti-Tank) Regiment had been sent from Tobruk to rendezvous with Gambier-Parry there. The Indians and the anti-tank regiments had reached Mechili on April 4th expecting the British tanks to meet them, but the column that appeared from the west on the morning of the 6th was not British but German.

The enemy shelled Mechili that morning. In the afternoon he placed troops astride the main tracks leading north and east and in the evening sent a German officer to demand surrender. The demand was refused but, as the German was not blindfolded before he was brought to the Indian Brigade H.Q., he probably learned all he wanted to know about the strength of the force.

That night Gambier-Parry slipped in through the loose enemy cordon, bringing his H.Q., two tanks and some of his unarmoured units. Apparently no one knew where the rest of his division was, but it was found later that the 3rd Armoured Brigade, which was to have withdrawn across the desert to Mechili, had been forced by lack of petrol to cut north to the main road. The fuel shortage was due to two disasters. Near Msus a convoy of trucks laden with petrol had been shot up by German planes and the main dump at Msus itself had been destroyed in error. The officer in charge of it had orders not to let the petrol fall into enemy hands and, mistaking some British tanks for German, had blown up thousands of gallons.

This was not known at Mechili and all through April 7th the troops waited for the rest of the 2nd Armoured Division, and the enemy drew his cordon tighter. In the late afternoon the perimeter formed by the Anglo-Indian forces around the old Italian fort was heavily shelled, but there was no attack. At 1.30 next morning, however, Lieutenant-Colonel E. E. Munro, C.O. of the 3rd Anti-Tanks, was told that the force was to fight its way out at dawn in a series of columns. His regiment and the 18th Indian Cavalry would form one of these.

Cloaked by the half-light of dawn and the dust swirled up by the vehicles, this column struck out south-east with weapons firing from lurching trucks. The enemy fired back into the dust-cloud they raised. No one knew where they were going; each vehicle followed the dust-trail ahead until it had run through the belt of enemy fire. The bulk of this column broke out, and so did another, including most of the 3rd R.H.A., but Gambier-Parry and his H.Q. together with Munro and 108 men of the 3rd Anti-Tank Regiment did not. Most of them were taken prisoner after a sharp engagement, in which one Australian gun, commanded by Sergeant R. L. F. Kelly, put out of action six German tanks before it and its crew were knocked out by a direct hit.

Soon the Nazi swastika was flying over the ruins of Fort Mechili, but this strange mix-up did achieve something. The two days the Germans paused there were those on which the 9th Division got back to Gazala. It was in great peril, however, for there was not enough transport to move all the troops at once, and the desert flank was dangerously open. As soon as it was known that the Germans were at Mechili the 2/13th was ordered to withdraw to Martuba, fifteen miles south-east of Derna, and to cover the track leading in from Mechili. The 2/48th was sent to Tmimi to block the track from Mechili that joined the coast road there.

About dark on April 6th the 2/13th reached Martuba, travelling in huge Italian Diesel trucks packed so tight that some men even travelled on the roofs. It reached there just in time to check the advance elements of a German reconnaissance column that came up the road from Mechili. There was no time or opportunity to dig-in in the hard rock, so the Australians took up positions among the ruins of old stone houses that flanked the road leading through the Martuba oasis. When the Germans found the oasis was held, they became cautious and did not attempt to cut through to the main road.

The troops withdrawing past Derna had the choice of two routes. One led through the town itself and the other by-passed it by making a short cut straight across the desert. To avoid congestion on the coast road that descended and climbed two very steep cliffs, some units were ordered to take the desert track, which was also considerably shorter. For this last reason O'Connor and Neame decided to take this route, as they hurried eastwards. Somewhere along that track on the night of the 6th they were evidently warned that Germans were astride it near Martuba, so they turned down a side track leading to Derna. Bumping along in the darkness the driver of the general's big blue sedan saw the two trucks ahead of him stop short. He stopped too. Someone brandished a tommy gun; someone else spoke in German. The generals were in the bag. They did not know it then, but they had been captured by a German officer and three men.[1]

Part of the 9th Divisional H.Q. nearly went the same way. One of its convoys—including the office trucks of the Intelligence, Operations and Cipher sections, complete with files, codes, and records—was challenged by a German who shoved a tommy gun into the face of the leading driver. The German rapped out an order but the unruffled Digger said, "I don't get yer lingo, mate, go round the other side and talk to the boss." The German did. He ordered the officer from the front seat and the other passengers from the back of the truck. They all got out, except one—Lieutenant L. K. Shave. He lay doggo until the German moved to the next truck. Then Shave followed him, shot him, rallied the party, and drove off into the night. It had been a daring piece of bluff on the German's part, for the man with the tommy gun had held up the convoy alone.

During the night forty-one members of the 2/8th Field Ambulance were also ambushed and captured on this desert track. Soon after dawn the Germans got their largest haul, when eighteen of their tanks surprised Lieutenant-Colonel R. F. Marlan and the H.Q. of his 2/15th Battalion, as well as part of the 8th Light A.A. Battery, which had stopped for breakfast. Four A.A. guns tried to fight the Germans off, but when two of them were knocked out and the enemy worked round both flanks the position became hopeless. The whole party was captured—the 2/15th having eight officers and about 175 men taken prisoner, and the 8th Light A.A. Battery losing an officer and 40 other ranks.

The losses might easily have been much more severe. As it was, the remaining units were clear of Derna soon after dawn on April 7th, and the 2/13th pulled out from Martuba at noon. As they left, however, they saw German tanks closing in on the oasis from the desert side. By this time another enemy column was threatening the coast road near Tmimi—sixty miles west of Tobruk—but a covering force, under Brigadier R. W. Tovell[2] (Commander 26th Brigade) held it off while units

---

[1] This officer was later captured at Tobruk and told this story.

[2] Brigadier Ray Tovell, a Melbourne chartered accountant, enlisted as a private in the 1st A.I.F., but rose to be Brigade Major of the 4th Brigade by 1917 and well deserved the D.S.O. he was awarded that year. Orthodox but not rigid in outlook, and affable in manner, he proved a competent and popular commander.

farther west passed through. That night the 9th Division's rearguard reached Gazala. Next morning, under cover of a heavy duststorm, the troops pulled back to Acroma, only five miles from the Tobruk perimeter.

Just before they turned off the road they passed a landmark which told them that Tobruk was not far away. It was one of the little white roadhouses the Italians had built every twenty miles or so along the coast road. This one the Diggers all remembered, for it was distinguished by a huge sign. At first sight that morning the sign must have seemed a mirage, for it showed a foaming glass and a bottle of Australian beer, and carried the inscription: "KEEP GOING—fill up in town. A good drink but bloody hard to get." It drew from many tired and thirsty troops who drove past a chorus of "You're telling us!"

The troops who reached Acroma that morning owed much to the Air Force. They could never have withdrawn so swiftly or so successfully if it had not been for the R.A.A.F.'s No. 3 Squadron, commanded by Squadron-Leader Peter Jeffrey, and (in the last few days) the R.A.F.'s No. 73 Squadron. Every day for more than a week the pilots of No. 3 kept their Hurricanes in the air from dawn till dark, coming down only for fuel and ammunition. They patrolled the roads; fought off German aircraft; strafed enemy troops, tanks and transport. By doing so they checked his moves and speeded up our own. The Luftwaffe appeared in force only twice during the withdrawal and each time it was severely defeated by No. 3 Squadron, which shot down twenty-one enemy planes in a week. After losing ten of these in one scrap the Germans kept clear of the Hurricanes.

This fighting withdrawal was as much a strain on the ground crews as on the pilots. By day they serviced aircraft; by night they moved in lumbering waggons to new dromes so as to be ready at dawn to service the Hurricanes. In six days No. 3 Squadron had seven moves. One of these was delayed until enemy tanks were only a few miles away. The night the 2/13th pulled out from Er Regima, the squadron was at a landing ground only fifteen miles away. Well after dark Jeffrey received orders to move back immediately. He sent his ground crews out that night, but the pilots could not move till dawn. Even then they were lucky to get one of their planes away. It had blown out a tyre, but its pilot (Flying-Officer Peter Turnbull) packed the tyre with grass and a blanket and made it fit for the take-off. But for these pilots and those of No. 73 Squadron the Luftwaffe could have turned its full weight against the roads packed with transport, and escape might have become impossible.

The duststorm on the 8th, which covered the Australians' withdrawal to Acroma, delayed the German advance and gave the hard-pressed commanders time to take stock. That day outside Tobruk the 26th and 20th Brigades dug rough defensive positions. Two other Australian brigades (the 24th and 18th) were manning part of the old Tobruk perimeter. (The 18th Brigade—part of the 7th Division—had been rushed up from Alexandria by road and sea.) At El Adem, sixteen miles south, Brigadier W. E. H. Gott had the 7th Armoured Division's Support Group.[3] The only other troops between Rommel and the Nile were the 22nd Guards Brigade (motorized infantry) at Matruh and a Polish brigade at Alexandria. There was no news from Mechili, but it was clear that the 2nd Armoured Division was finished. All these forces combined did not have thirty tanks. Heading east across Cyrenaica Rommel had nearly 300.

Without an adequate armoured force and supporting artillery —especially anti-tank guns—no stand could be made in the open desert. The British and Australian troops had either to withdraw inside Tobruk or pull right back to the frontier. There was in Cyrenaica, however, no commander who could make that decision, Neame and O'Connor having been captured, but it was already clear that any withdrawal beyond Tobruk would be almost impossible because there was not sufficient transport to move even a third of the troops. In anticipation of a stand being made at Tobruk, the area commander, Colonel T. P. Cook, was strenuously organizing the defence of the Fortress, but no final decision as to the holding of it had been made when news was received that General Wavell and Major-General J. D. Lavarack (G.O.C. 7th Australian Division) were coming up from Cairo.

In a fierce duststorm on the morning of April 8th a Lockheed Lodestar, carrying Wavell and Lavarack, landed on the Tobruk drome. The two previous days in Cairo had been a time of difficult and anxious decision. At a crucial conference on the 6th, General Wavell, General Sir John Dill, Mr Anthony Eden, Admiral Cunningham and Air Chief Marshal Sir Arthur Longmore (Air Officer Commanding-in-Chief, R.A.F., M.E.) had

---

[3] An armoured division's Support Group then consisted of two motorized infantry battalions, a field regiment, an anti-tank battery, an A.A. battery, some engineers, signals and medical personnel, and a group H.Q.

decided that if possible Tobruk should be held. Following this, Wavell determined that the balance of the 7th Australian Division should go to Matruh instead of to Greece and that Lavarack should succeed Neame as commander in Cyrenaica and go to Tobruk at once.

In a battered house in Tobruk on the 8th, Wavell and Lavarack met Morshead, Lloyd and the senior surviving officer of "Cyrcom" (Brigadier G. Harding). Harding outlined the position and asked whether they were to hold Tobruk. Wavell did not reply at once. He took out his eye-glass, polished it, and asked for a map. He studied this for a few minutes and then announced that Lavarack was to take command in Cyrenaica and that a stand was to be made at Tobruk. "There is nothing," he said to Lavarack, "between you and Cairo."

Then he took three sheets of notepaper and pencilled for Lavarack these brief, broad, and none-too-optimistic instructions:

1. You will take over command of all troops in Cyrenaica. Certain reinforcements have already been notified as being sent you. You will be informed of any others which it is decided to send.

2. Your main task will be to hold the enemy's advance at Tobruk, in order to give time for the assembly of reinforcements, especially of armoured troops, for the defence of Egypt.

3. To gain time for the assembly of the required reinforcements it may be necessary to hold Tobruk for about two months.

4. Should you consider after reviewing the situation and in the light of the strength deployed by the enemy that it is not possible to maintain your position at Tobruk for this length of time, you will report your views when a decision will be taken by G.H.Q.

5. You will in any case prepare a plan for withdrawal from Tobruk, by land and by sea, should withdrawal become necessary.

6. Your defence will be as mobile as possible and you will take any opportunity of hindering the enemy's concentration by offensive action.

After lunch Wavell left for Cairo. Next day he was in Greece taking the load of further great decisions on his willing shoulders. During that first year of war in the Middle East he had a tremendous burden to carry. He was short of men, weapons, tanks and aircraft. His command extended from the Indian Ocean to the mid-Mediterranean, from Central Africa to the Central Balkans. Few generals can have had such a vast and varied command. Yet by plane he kept in close personal touch with all fronts. His great strength lay in his capacity for prompt decision, his grasp of broad essentials, his determination and his calm. It is true that he made some miscalculations, and these were chiefly the result of a tendency to underestimate the speed of enemy preparations and moves. Later he frankly admitted this[4]—and in admitting it revealed an important element in his greatness.

When he left Tobruk that afternoon Wavell still hoped the Axis advance might be held along the general line—Tobruk-El Adem and that landward communication with Egypt would not be cut. Nominally he had left some discretion to Lavarack as to whether Tobruk could be held, in the light of the strength Rommel mustered, but in fact further withdrawal was out of the question, because of the shortage of transport.

That afternoon Lavarack made a quick reconnaissance of the Italian defences, arranged for Morshead to bring the rest of the 9th Division inside the perimeter the following night, and organized staffs from scattered units to take command of artillery, tanks, and ack-ack defences. There was still no word from Gambier-Parry, but Germans were reported to be coming down the road from Derna and across the desert from Mechili in force and concentrating south-west of Acroma. The holding of Tobruk had now changed from a strategic desirability to a tactical necessity. There was no alternative but to stand and fight.

None welcomed this more than the troops. For a week they had been retreating almost without a fight, yielding to some unseen, undefined pressure. They did not know why they had withdrawn and they were bewildered and bitter, because reverse had been inflicted on them through no fault of their own.

What they felt was well summed up in the words of two Diggers. One of them, Corporal G. H. Fearnside of the 2/13th, wrote in his diary: "By the time we got to Tobruk our nerves were ragged. All the way back from Regima we'd steeled ourselves to action which never came and every soldier knows that the waiting before the attack is worst."

Another Digger—Sergeant F. H. Legg of the 2/48th Battalion—wrote much the same thing: "We came to Tobruk in pretty poor shape. For eight days and nights we'd been out in the desert on the move (chiefly in the wrong direction) and always on the verge of action but always denied the opportunity of 'having a go'. We'd experienced our first taste of bombing and shelling. We'd had our first casualties, but most of us hadn't struck a blow."

---

[4] I was able to appreciate the quality of his frankness at an interview he granted me shortly before he left for India, when he spent more than an hour discussing a broadcast script and outlining the background of his Middle East campaigns.

This feeling of bitterness produced among the troops an itching for retaliation; an urgent desire to show that this withdrawal was not typical of the 9th Division, and that the 9th was at least as good as any other Australian division. As one Tobruk officer put it: "We couldn't let it be said that the 9th had lost what the 6th had won."

CHAPTER VII

The Fortress and its Garrison

ON April 8th the Khamsin, that fury which periodically scourges the drifting surface of the desert into blinding duststorms, wreaked its will. All through that day and the next the troops at Tobruk cursed the dust, little knowing that it was a blessing in disguise. In the battle against time the storm caused more delay and dislocation to the enemy's preparations for attack than to those of the garrison for defence. In Tobruk urgent tasks fully occupied both Lavarack and Morshead. The 9th Division had withdrawn in good order with comparatively few losses—less than 500 killed or captured—but its units had never even trained together, and it had no field artillery of its own. British artillery regiments were now allotted to it, but these and its own units had to be rallied into a co-ordinated fighting formation and established in battle position. This took the full attention of Morshead and his staff.

Lavarack made Morshead responsible for the defence of the Tobruk perimeter, but kept under his own direct command the 18th Brigade, and Gott's Support Group at El Adem. Gott was ordered to delay as long as possible any Axis attempt to sweep past Tobruk and cut the Bardia road, but when he could no longer hold the enemy he was to retire to the frontier. There linking up with the 22nd Guards Brigade, he was to harass the Germans and Italians and draw off from Tobruk as much of their force as he could.

The immediate problem was how to dispose the forces inside Tobruk. Because of the comparatively few infantry available— only four brigades—Wavell had suggested that the Tobruk garrison should take up a shorter line than that of the Italian-built defences on the 30-mile outer perimeter and should hold an inner perimeter, about fifteen miles long, which was shown on some Italian maps. The weakness in the Italian defence had been that so much of their infantry was tied up holding the outer line of posts that all too few were left to provide either defence in depth or an adequate reserve for counter-attack. These weaknesses had to be overcome, for Rommel could not be prevented from breaking through the perimeter at any one point. Tobruk could be held only by a defence that had depth and mobility.

Reconnaissance of the defences with Morshead and the brigade commanders on the morning of April 9th, however, convinced Lavarack that the old Italian perimeter was the only possible line. There was in fact no inner perimeter and, even though the outer defences were not strong, they were continuous and had a series of posts covering a barbed-wire fence and either an anti-tank ditch or minefield. The Italian minefield had been disarmed around most of the perimeter, but it was not a long job to lay new mines or rearm those which were still in position. The posts were well sited for observation and had good fields of fire, though they were too far apart to stop enemy infiltration. Moreover, if any shorter line were held, enemy field guns could shell the harbour and possibly make it unusable.

To meet these problems, the perimeter was manned by only seven of the garrison's thirteen infantry battalions,[1] and each of these seven had a reserve company in a dug and wired position half a mile behind the concrete posts. This meant that perimeter companies usually held a front of over a mile, which was considerably more than the average battalion front in France in the Great War.

The defence system made up of the perimeter posts and the reserve company positions became known as the "Red Line". It was held not by numbers, but by fire-power. Concrete posts, which the Italians had garrisoned with twenty-five—and even as many as fifty—men were now held by ten or fifteen Australians, but their fire was very much increased by the use of captured weapons. One typical post that I saw was held by fourteen men. They had a 47-mm. Italian anti-tank gun, three machine-guns (two of them captured), an anti-tank rifle and a tommy gun. There was scope for all these weapons, because of the flatness of the desert, but to make room for them Morshead ordered the preparation of new fire positions in the concrete posts. Where posts were too far apart, new positions were dug between them.

---

[1] The four infantry brigades eventually had three battalions each. The additional "battalion" was the 18th Indian Cavalry Regiment. Later the 2/1st Pioneer Battalion was also used in the line, and, under Lieutenant-Colonel Arnold Brown, carried out its infantry role excellently.

In this way the garrison used fewer men and yet could put down heavier fire than the Italians had done.

About two miles behind the Red Line, the garrison eventually constructed a second defence system, which became known as the "Blue Line". This consisted of a continuous minefield covered by barbed wire and by fire from anti-tank and machine-guns located in a series of dug, wired and mined strongposts, each held by a platoon, roughly every 500 yards. Each of the forward brigades had two battalions in the Red Line and one in the Blue Line.

The main job of the battalions in the Blue Line was to stop any deep penetration by forces which broke through the perimeter. They provided a counter-attacking reserve within their brigade area and local protection for the field guns behind them. In particular they covered the reserve minefields with fire, so as to prevent enemy sappers clearing a passage for tanks.

To provide depth in the defence against tanks, minefields were eventually laid in both the main lines, as well as in the area between them, and behind the Blue Line. In the end there were minefields everywhere. Even the engineers could hardly keep track of them all, and the garrison lost a number of trucks on its own mines. The anti-tank guns were similarly distributed through the Red and Blue lines. (The garrison ultimately had 113 anti-tank guns, half of them captured; fourteen disabled tanks were also dug in for anti-tank defence.) Thus these lines comprised a series of inter-dependent posts, each one covering its front and the posts on either side, and designed to deal with frontal attacks and also with those from flank or rear. These defences formed not two thin lines held by men, but a deep belt held by fire. This belt did not end at the Blue Line. Behind it again were the field guns—nearly a hundred of them if we count the captured Italian pieces, but all too few to cover a 30-mile front. They were, however, the core of the anti-tank defence, for most of them were 25-pounders, which are deadly weapons against tanks at close range.

Still farther back was the mobile reserve for counter-attack. This consisted of a motorized infantry brigade with its three battalions so placed that one was at each of the three main crossroads—the El Adem crossroads, Pilastrino, and Airente (the junction of the Derna and Pilastrino roads); twenty-four anti-tank guns mounted on the backs of 30-cwt. trucks; and last but not least, the tank reserve. On April 10th this was pitifully small; the garrison had only four "I" tanks and twenty-three

THE FORTRESS AND ITS GARRISON

cruisers, plus twenty obsolete light tanks, which were useless in any armoured battle.

The other mobile element in the defence was a fast-moving force of armoured cars, light tanks and Bren carriers, organized for action against troops landed by parachute or from the sea. Finally, there were the anti-aircraft batteries—mostly concentrated round the harbour. Their primary role, of course, was to deal with aircraft, but almost every ack-ack gun-position carried some armour-piercing ammunition and had an anti-tank task. Thus, even if some tanks did manage to get through the outer belts of minefields and fire from anti-tank and field guns, they would still have to silence the ack-ack guns before they could reach the harbour and the town. Tobruk's greatest weakness was in its coastal defences. The garrison had neither the men nor the weapons for adequate protection of the beaches, and the only guns available to deal with a sea-borne attack were two well-worn Italian 149-mm. coastal guns and half a dozen pieces of light artillery suitable only for beach defence. The real defence of Tobruk's twenty miles of coastline was the Royal Navy, but even it could never have stopped small raiding parties sneaking along the coast by night.

At the outset Morshead called his commanders together and said: "There'll be no Dunkirk here. If we should have to get out, we shall fight our way out. There is to be no surrender and no retreat." He impressed on every man that, no matter where he was or what his job might be, he was first and foremost a fighter; that, if the enemy were to break through, no section post, no gun position was to yield a yard. Should the enemy get past the Red Line the men there were to hold their posts and rely on those in the Blue Line and the mobile reserve to deal with any penetration. If odd tanks or stray parties of infantry managed to pierce the Blue Line or evade the mobile reserve, then cooks, clerks, batmen—all who could handle a weapon—were to tackle them. This was Tobruk's strength when the British and Australians held it. The Italian defence had been a superficially strong outer shell. Once that was pierced, the fortress was cracked wide open. But the Anglo-Australian defence was a nest of cells—cells of minefields and guns manned by men who were ordered to stand and fight and who did. Tobruk was organized as a fortress from the perimeter to the sea.

This elaborate defensive system took months to complete, but the troops, knowing that at last they were to fight, worked magnificently to repair the Italian defences and make new ones. Nevertheless, it was a motley collection of units that gathered inside Tobruk on April 9th and 10th. Apart from the British gunners and tankmen, few had seen any action, and the garrison contained a large number of miscellaneous units, many of which were completely disorganized after the withdrawal.

The final count showed more than 40,000 men inside the perimeter. On April 12th there were some 5000 Axis prisoners, and 35,307 British, Australians and Indians, but many of these were not front-line troops. There were far more Ordnance, Army Service Corps and medical personnel than the garrison needed; five British engineer companies, which had been working on roads and installations throughout Cyrenaica; hundreds of Air Force ground staff, and a number of stragglers. Fortunately the fighting units had reached Tobruk in good order, and they were now joined by two urgently-needed regiments of Royal Horse Artillery, which were rushed up from Egypt.

Before the end of April some 12,000 troops and airmen and more than 7000 prisoners of war were withdrawn from Tobruk by sea and the final streamlined garrison—stripped down to essential personnel—from early May to late August averaged little more than 23,000, and fell as low as 22,026 in July. Of these nearly 15,000 were Australians and about 500 were Indians. The rest came from Great Britain and she has probably never been served by finer troops.

The main Australian formations[2] were the three infantry brigades of the 9th Division, the 20th, 24th and 26th, and the 18th Brigade of the 7th Division. Of these the 18th was at first kept in reserve and the others disposed in the Red and Blue lines as follows: western sector, 26th Brigade; southern or El Adem sector, 20th Brigade; eastern or Bardia road sector, 24th Brigade. In the west near the sea, the 18th Indian Cavalry was soon brought in to provide another front-line battalion, and a similar position in the east was held by three scratch companies raised from surplus Army Service Corps personnel. They were most valuable throughout the defence, but particularly at this stage, for the 24th Brigade had only two battalions. (Its other battalion, the 2/32nd, arrived on May 4th.) The A.S.C. later provided much-needed reinforcements for infantry battalions in the hottest sector of the Tobruk front. As a reward, those who fought as infantry were given the right to

---

[2] For further details of the numbers and units in Tobruk see Appendix I.

keep and carry the bayonets they had won in the field. They value this highly, for bayonets are not issued to the A.S.C.

In addition to these infantry brigades, the A.I.F. provided all the field companies (engineers), two-thirds of the anti-tank gunners, an A.A. battery and later a field regiment. The Tobruk hospital, the casualty clearing station and the field ambulances were also Australian. Nearly all the field and ack-ack gunners, a third of the anti-tank gunners, all the tank crews and the Vickers gun battalion, were British. There was thus a convenient division of labour between the Diggers and the Tommies. It is broadly true that while the perimeter was occupied almost exclusively by Australians, the bulk of the supporting weapons were manned by British troops. This was an ideal combination. The dash and daring needed by the front-line troops—particularly in their patrolling—was provided by the Australians. The steadiness and dogged reliability, required especially of the field and ack-ack gunners, came from the British.

The complete understanding between Digger and Tommy gave an inspiring unity to the garrison. From April until the end of August, Australians comprised two-thirds of the garrison, but in spite of this it is doubtful if they played a more important part than did the British. When the defence began the Australians had seen virtually no action—many were raw troops. But the British—and especially the gunners of the R.H.A. and the 51st Field Regiment, the tankmen and the Royal Northumberland Fusiliers, who had fought through the first Libyan campaign in support of the 6th Australian Division—provided a hard-bitten core of experience. What their steadiness meant to the garrison in the early days can hardly be over-stressed.

The Australians were quick to appreciate this and no other Middle East front saw co-operation so close or understanding so complete. The Diggers and Tommies went through the fire together and learned to know and respect each other's worth. Australian troops gained the limelight at Tobruk mainly because they had the more spectacular tasks. Theirs were the infantry patrols that carried out the dramatic raids on enemy positions; but just as important as these was the staunch, unobtrusive work done by the British gunners who beat off the German tanks and Stukas.

The spirit and comradeship which became Tobruk's great strength were forged in battle. But when the various units first sorted themselves out and were drafted to action stations on April 10th, no one could tell how they would stand the test.

Everything was against them. The Australians—at any rate—were short of training, equipment and experience; most of them and many of the British troops had just come through a week of dispiriting, bewildering withdrawal. Almost overnight commanders of units and arms, who had never even met before, had to work out co-ordinated plans. There was no time for detailed preparation; much had to depend on what individuals could improvise. The defences were far from strong; the weapons far from adequate. Compared with the enemy, the garrison had but a handful of tanks and aircraft.

They had been carried back to Tobruk on the ebb-tide of defeat, which had swept unchecked from Narvik and Dunkirk; the enemy came against them on the flood-tide of victory, which had already engulfed half Europe. The new German Army with its Blitzkrieg technique and its mass of tanks and dive-bombers had, until this time, appeared invincible. Knowing all this, these men might well have quailed, but the very urgency of their common peril welded them together and fired them with a unity of purpose that only a grave crisis could have developed so swiftly. Yet more important for them than the danger to Suez or themselves was the fact that their reputation in the eyes of their fellows was at stake. They had come to fight; they now had a chance to fight—and fight they would.

CHAPTER VIII

The Easter Battle

THIRTY-SIX hours after the last of the garrison withdrew inside the perimeter, the Germans began probing for weak spots preparatory to launching the concentrated attack that became known as the "Easter Battle". Those thirty-six hours were invaluable. Throughout a hot, dusty day and night sappers laid a minefield around most of the perimeter, while infantry repaired barbed wire and shovelled sand out of the half-filled anti-tank ditch and concrete posts. Transport drivers toiled ceaselessly carrying ammunition, food and water to forward posts and artillery positions. Gunners dug-in their 25-pounders and camouflaged them as best they could. Signallers ran out several hundred miles of wire linking the scattered units. It was a period of hard work, hasty improvisation and urgent "scrounging".

The infantry were perilously short of essential weapons, such as Bren guns and mortars. In time they made up for this by salvaging captured Italian weapons, but not many of these were ready for action when the first attacks came. Weak also in anti-tank artillery, the infantry recovered Italian field guns, which had been lying abandoned since the capture of Tobruk, and set them in position for anti-tank defence. Few of these had sights or instruments, but they were soon giving valuable support to the regular guns and became known as the "bush artillery". The anti-tank defences were considerably strengthened by the last-minute arrival from Mechili on April 10th of the survivors from the 3rd Australian Anti-Tank Regiment and the 3rd R.H.A. They brought with them forty urgently needed guns but the garrison still had not enough to give adequate defence against Rommel's great tank strength.

This was specially so in view of the inadequate minefields. Because of the scarcity of British mines, Italian ones had to be used, and there was no time to load them with booby-traps which could stop enemy sappers delousing them. This was done later, but in the first few days these mines were as easy for he

Germans to delouse as they had been for the Australians. There was no reserve minefield, and work on the Blue Line had not begun when the first attacks were made. The signal position was still serious. With companies holding such vast fronts, telephone communication between forward posts and Company H.Q. was all-important, but the Italian phones, wire and switchboards, which later gave Tobruk an excellent signals service, had not then been salvaged.

During April 9th and 10th, however, Rommel was no more ready for attack than Tobruk was for defence, and the garrison gained time to put at least the outer defences in order. It seems that Rommel had originally intended to go only as far as Bengazi and to consolidate there before launching his main attack on Cyrenaica; and that he pushed straight on across the desert merely because he found that the British armoured forces were so weak.

Consequently, by the time his vanguard got to Tobruk, he had over-reached himself and had to pause for a few days while the slower-moving elements caught up. Their advance, as we have seen, was delayed by a "dust blizzard", under cover of which the last Australian units withdrew inside the perimeter on the night of April 9th-10th. About noon on the 10th the dust cleared and the 2/28th Battalion, then holding part of the western perimeter, saw enemy tanks and trucks coming down the road from Derna and across the desert to the south of it. Sappers promptly blew up the Derna road bridge just outside the perimeter and "bush artillery" manned by infantry of the 2/28th struck the first blow for the garrison.

One of the gunners, Sergeant E. D. Rule, said later that when the battalion reached Tobruk it acquired eight Italian 75s and two 105s and dug them in about 500 yards behind the forward posts, near the Derna road, primarily for defence against tanks. A British artillery sergeant gave the carrier platoon a few gunnery lessons and by April 10th they were set for action.

"On this morning," Rule said, "our Transport Officer was in command of the guns and, when the first enemy vehicles appeared, Battalion H.Q. said he could engage them. The guns had no sights but we got direction by squinting down the barrel, and range by trial and error. As it happened, a British artillery colonel was there and he gave expert advice. Our gun drill wasn't very good and our fire orders would have shocked the R.H.A., but we got the shells away. When the vehicles were about 500 yards out, the T.O. called, 'All ready boys, let 'er go.'

THE EASTER BATTLE

The first shell fell short. 'Cock 'em up a bit, boys,' said the colonel. We did, and the second shot fell dead between the two leading vehicles. We kept on firing and they disappeared in a cloud of dust—and stayed out of range for the rest of the day."

Soon afterwards, near the Derna road, another "bush artillery battery" and some guns of the 51st Field Regiment had a more prolonged encounter, which ended in the destruction of two enemy armoured cars and seven vehicles. The Axis column withdrew, but not before its artillery had knocked out two guns and two Bren carriers.

Apart from spasmodic shelling and the occasional appearance of enemy vehicles in the distance, the garrison continued work on the defences undisturbed. But R.A.F. reconnaissance planes brought back unmistakable warning of the enemy's intention. Early on the 10th pilots reported 700 enemy vehicles on the road between Gazala and Tobruk; by nightfall the leading vehicles were discovered only seven miles west of El Adem.

Before noon on the 11th—which was Good Friday—the Germans had by-passed Tobruk; four tanks and some lorried infantry had cut the Bardia road and a column of 300 vehicles was moving east between Tobruk and El Adem. Gott's Support Group had to pull back towards the frontier. Tobruk was cut off.

On Good Friday afternoon the Axis forces staged a demonstration against Tobruk; it was half reconnaissance and half attack. They made their move against the southern sector of the defences, where Murray's 20th Brigade was holding a $10\frac{1}{2}$ mile front astride the El Adem road, with the 2/17th on the right, the 2/13th on the left and the 2/15th in reserve. The forward troops were still seriously short of weapons. The 2/17th, for instance, had only the normal establishment of one Bren gun per section and one anti-tank rifle per platoon. They had no anti-tank guns or 2-inch mortars forward and only one 3-inch mortar in the battalion. Captured weapons—so necessary to give them the fire-power to cover their 5-mile front—had not yet been issued.

In the middle of the afternoon the O.C. of the 2/17th's left company (Major J. W. Balfe) saw enemy infantry, estimated at about a battalion, advancing out of the desert haze some 1500 yards from the perimeter. He called for artillery fire and, as shells began falling round the infantry, they went to ground. Enemy tanks appeared; the infantry rallied and advanced with them straight for Balfe's company's front. Our artillery intensified its fire and the infantry went down again, but the tanks continued on.

Balfe later gave me this account of the engagement that followed:

About seventy tanks came right up to the anti-tank ditch and opened fire on our forward posts. They advanced in three waves of about twenty and one of ten. Some of them were big German Mark IVs, mounting a 75-mm. gun. Others were Italian M13s and there were a lot of Italian light tanks too. The ditch here wasn't any real obstacle to them, the minefield had only been hastily rearmed, and we hadn't one anti-tank gun forward. We fired on them with anti-tank rifles, Brens and rifles and they didn't attempt to come through, but blazed away at us and then sheered off east towards the 2/13th's front.

Before this about a battalion of infantry had advanced in close formation on that front as well. As these came on, an officer of the 1st R.H.A., who was directing his guns from a perimeter post, waited until the enemy was less than a mile from the wire. Then he ordered "twenty-five rounds gun-fire" from his four 25-pounders. This sharp greeting stopped the infantry, but about twenty tanks (no doubt one of the waves of tanks which Balfe saw) that had been moving up behind them advanced through the barrage as far as the anti-tank ditch. Then they moved eastwards along the perimeter shelling the forward posts. Near the El Adem road they ran into fire from two Italian 47-mm. anti-tank guns, manned by the 2/13th's mortar platoon. One M13 was knocked out and several others hit. The rest sheered off and swung south. One Italian light tank was even disabled by intense small arms fire, and its crew was captured near the junction of the road and the perimeter.

As the tanks withdrew eleven cruisers of the 1st R.T.R. engaged them from inside the wire. When the last wave of ten tanks appeared the cruisers tackled them too. In thirty minutes of long-range sparring they knocked out one M13 and the artillery destroyed a German Mark IV. Three other Italian "lights" were disposed of during the general skirmish, bringing the Axis losses to seven. Two British tanks were lost, and since the garrison had only twenty-three cruisers it could ill afford to lose them.

After the Axis tank demonstration the infantry began to move forward once more. According to Balfe:

About 700 of them advanced almost shoulder to shoulder. The R.H.A. let them have it again, but, even though some of the shells fell right among them, they still came on. In later months our patrols in no-man's-land found scores of German graves, marked by crosses dated April 11th. When

THE EASTER BATTLE

the infantry were about 500 yards out we opened up, but in the posts that could reach them we had only two Brens, two anti-tank rifles and a couple of dozen ordinary rifles. The Jerries went to ground at first, but gradually moved forward in bounds under cover of their machine-guns. It was nearly dusk by this time and they managed to reach the anti-tank ditch. From there they mortared nearby posts heavily. We hadn't any mortars with which to reply and our artillery couldn't shell the ditch without risk of hitting our own posts.

About ten o'clock we got three mortars and with these kept their machine-guns quiet, while two platoons of the reserve company counter-attacked. But before they reached the ditch, the Germans had withdrawn. We sent two fighting patrols to follow them, but both were driven back by heavy machine-gun fire, which continued sporadically throughout the night.

Meantime there was even more significant activity on the 2/13th Battalion's front. In the moonlight several enemy tanks came up to the anti-tank ditch, evidently looking for a shallow crossing. They could not find one, and withdrew. In the ditch shortly afterwards a 2/13th patrol disturbed what was evidently a party of pioneers, sent to blow the wire and make a tank crossing. The Germans cleared out, abandoning tools, explosives, Bangalore torpedoes, and a pack radio transmitter. Had this enemy party established a bridgehead, German tanks would no doubt have attacked at dawn. Anticipating this from the events of Good Friday and from R.A.F. reconnaissance, Lavarack during the night deployed the reserve tanks and infantry to meet any attack on the El Adem sector. None came but the enemy gave the garrison time for a useful dress-rehearsal.

Next morning—Saturday, April 12th—Balfe's company found that the Germans who had withdrawn from the ditch the night before were dug in about 400 yards out on a 1200-yard front. Sniping from there, the enemy hindered the installation of seven anti-tank guns, which reached the perimeter posts about 9 a.m.

These guns arrived just in time, for the advanced screen of Germans was clearly covering preparations for a major attack. Dust-clouds rose from a slight hollow where the enemy was assembling tanks, guns and lorried infantry about 3000 yards out. Three Blenheims bombed one concentration of tanks and transport and the R.H.A. shelled others very heavily and no attack developed that day. After the gunners had landed 500 shells in ninety minutes among one group of sixty vehicles, half a dozen ambulances appeared and picked up the casualties. During the afternoon, in response to an urgent request from Lavarack, half a dozen bombers attacked a concentration of about sixty tanks near the El Adem road.

Later twelve tanks approached the wire, but were driven off

by the newly installed anti-tank guns. In the evening more vehicles were seen, some of them towing field pieces, and Balfe directed a moonlight shoot, in which the 1st R.H.A. fired more than 400 rounds. When the dust and smoke cleared there was not a vehicle to be seen. Apart from occasional shelling and machine-gun and mortar fire the rest of the night was quiet, though patrols sent out from the forward posts could not advance far into no-man's-land.

During that day enemy planes had been more active in reconnaissance and bombing. Twice they attacked the guns of the 1st R.H.A. and fifteen Stukas with strong escort went for the harbour. They were engaged by ack-ack batteries and by the half-dozen surviving Hurricanes of No. 73 Squadron—the only fighters operating from inside the Fortress. Three enemy planes were shot down.

In addition to dropping bombs the enemy scattered pamphlets far and wide. These said:

> The General Officer Commanding the German forces in Libya hereby requests that the British troops occupying Tobruk surrender their arms. Single soldiers waving white handkerchiefs are not fired on. Strong German forces have already surrounded Tobruk and it is useless to try and escape. Remember Mekili. Our dive-bombers and Stukas are awaiting your ships which are lying in Tobruk.

The request went unheeded. "No doubt," said the Tobruk H.Q. operational summary, "owing to the prevailing dust and the necessity to ration water for essential purposes there were no white handkerchiefs available." Advising G.H.Q. Cairo of this in its daily situation report, "Cyrcom" said: "Leaflets dropped calling on tps to surrender stop answer ——" The answer consisted of two "unprintable" letters of the alphabet which, though hardly military symbols, expressed the garrison's reply in the Diggers' own language.

On Easter Sunday morning, April 13th, the enemy was still busier, though a duststorm cloaked his activities. "We saw staff cars and motor-cycles pulled up apparently near a battle H.Q. and we had a crack at them," said Balfe later. "At the extreme range of 2000 yards our anti-tank gunners hit two motor-cycles and a staff car. But the Germans continued to bring up vehicles and during the morning their artillery began shelling our forward posts. At noon a 'recce' plane circled round our company area at about 2000 feet. Late in the afternoon, after a brief bombardment, enemy tanks and infantry again advanced towards the perimeter, but were again stopped by our artillery.

THE EASTER BATTLE

Everything indicated, however, that a major assault was coming and that it would be on my company's front."

By Easter Sunday afternoon the enemy had gathered a considerable force for this attack. Fortunately Gott's Support Group had drawn off some Axis troops to the frontier and these had already occupied Bardia and were threatening Sollum. Even so, the R.A.F. in the previous two days had reported more than 200 tanks either near El Adem or on their way to Acroma. On the Sunday afternoon, in spite of bad visibility, pilots had spotted 300 vehicles, including a large number of tanks, astride the El Adem road, four or five miles south of the perimeter. Rommel then had outside Tobruk most of the 5th Light Motorized Division—with well over a hundred German tanks of the 5th Regiment; part of the 132nd Ariete Armoured Division with about the same number of Italian tanks; one motorized and one infantry division, both Italian. These last two straddled the Derna and Bardia roads, but the bulk of the other two had been assembled north of El Adem for attack on Tobruk.

The enemy had substantial superiority in tanks and aircraft, but the half-hearted, abortive moves he had made during the week-end had given the garrison experience, self-confidence—and warning. The troops had been able to take stock and they fully appreciated the significance of the message Wavell sent Morshead that Easter Sunday.

Enemy advance means your isolation by land for time being. Defence Egypt now depends largely on your holding enemy on your front . . . Am glad that I have at this crisis such stout-hearted and magnificent troops in Tobruk. I know I can count on you to hold Tobruk to end. My best wishes to you all.

The attack came that night. By eleven o'clock, after an hour's heavy mortar and machine-gun fire on the forward posts of Balfe's company, the enemy was seen moving through the wire east of Post 33. About thirty Germans established themselves just inside the wire, and brought up two light field guns, some mortars and eight machine-guns. Small arms fire could not shift them and it was strongly answered from both inside and outside the wire. The position was serious. If this party stayed there, it could cover a bridgehead and hold the gate open for the tanks.

The platoon commander in Post 33 was a 23-year-old Sydney Lieutenant, Austin Mackell. He was short, slight, quiet and seemed to the rough and ready Diggers under him little more than a schoolboy. But the prompt and determined action he took was that of a seasoned and gallant leader. He knew the enemy must be dislodged, and without hesitation took a corporal and five men to drive them back at bayonet point.

This is the story of their attack as he told it later—after much persuasion:

About a quarter to twelve we set out, Corporal Jack Edmondson, five men and myself—with fixed bayonets and two grenades apiece. The Germans were dug in about a hundred yards to the east of our post, but we headed northwards away from it, and swung round in a three-quarter circle so as to take them in the flank.

As we left the post there was spasmodic fire. Then they saw us running and seemed to turn all their guns on us. We didn't waste any time. After a 200-yard sprint we went to ground for breath; got up again, running till we were about fifty yards from them. Then we went to ground for another breather, and as we lay there, pulled the pins out of our grenades. Apparently the Germans had been able to see us all the way, and they kept up their fire. But it had been reduced a lot because the men we'd left in the post had been firing to cover us. They did a grand job, for they drew much of the enemy fire on themselves.

We'd arranged with them that, as we got up for the final charge, we'd shout and they would stop firing and start shouting, too. The plan worked. We charged and yelled, but for a moment or two the Germans turned everything onto us. It's amazing that we weren't all hit. As we ran we threw our grenades and when they burst the German fire stopped. But already Jack Edmondson had been seriously wounded by a burst from a machine-gun that had got him in the stomach, and he'd also been hit in the neck. Still he ran on, and before the Germans could open up again we were into them.

They left their guns and scattered. In their panic some actually ran slap into the barbed wire behind them and another party that was coming through the gap turned and fled. We went for them with the bayonet. In spite of his wounds Edmondson was magnificent. As the Germans scattered, he chased them and killed at least two. By this time I was in difficulties wrestling with one German on the ground while another was coming straight for me with a pistol. I called out—"Jack"—and from about fifteen yards away Edmondson ran to help me and bayoneted both Germans. He then went on and bayoneted at least one more.

Mackell scrambled to his feet at once, grabbed his rifle, bayoneted one German, but broke his bayonet in doing so. Then he used his rifle as a club. Meantime Edmondson and the others had killed at least a dozen Germans and taken one prisoner. The rest fled leaving their weapons behind them. They had sat resolutely enough behind their machine-guns while the Australians charged, but had cracked at the sight of the bayonet.

Edmondson had continued fighting till he could no longer stand. His mates helped him back to the post, but he died early next morning. Jack Edmondson's death was a sad blow to his battalion, for he had already made his mark as a man and a leader of men. He was only twenty-six, but considerable experience on his father's grazing property near Liverpool, New South Wales, had made him older than his years. His heroism did

THE EASTER BATTLE 99

not go unrecognized. He was posthumously awarded the V.C.—
the first won by any member of the 2nd A.I.F.

After seeing his men safely back to his own post, Mackell
reported the result of the attack to Balfe's H.Q. Speaking from
there to his C.O. (Lieutenant-Colonel J. W. Crawford) he said
with expressive brevity—"We've been into 'em, and they're
running like ———".

Crawford had already sent two fighting patrols out under
Lieutenants W. B. A. Geikie and C. G. Pitman. They had driven

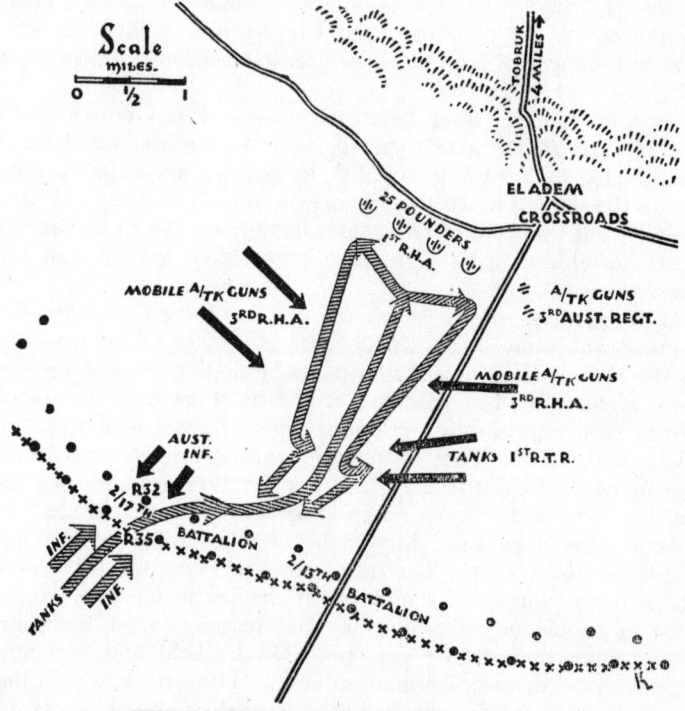

THE EASTER BATTLE, APRIL 14TH, 1941

back small parties of Germans and had each brought in a
prisoner from the 8th German Machine-gun Battalion as well as
reports of extensive enemy movement right along Balfe's front.
Crawford now moved his reserve company (under Captain C. H.
Wilson) to a position just behind Post 32 ready for a strong
counter-attack at dawn.

The offensive action taken by the 2/17th's patrols, however, had disorganized the enemy's schedule. Mackell's charge had routed the German advance guard and it was a couple of hours before they sent forward another force strong enough to hold the gap near 33. About 2.15 a.m. some 200 German infantry moved through the wire and soon established a bridgehead extending several hundred yards inside. At 2.30 Balfe sent up a Very light calling for artillery fire on the ditch, wire and forward posts around 33. Two regiments of the R.H.A. shelled the area heavily; the posts fired everything they had, but this time the Germans could not be dislodged, though they had many casualties. In the moonlight the Diggers in the forward posts saw ambulances picking up wounded some distance outside the wire.

At 5.20—half an hour before dawn—the first German tanks moved through the gaps their engineers had made, and headed straight for Balfe's Company H.Q. at Post 32, about half a mile inside the wire. The British gunners were still shelling the area heavily, but the forward companies had orders not to attract the tanks' attention, to let them pass if necessary, and to wait for the enemy infantry.

Consequently, the Australians lay low, even though the leading tank came within thirty yards of Post 32 before it swung to the right and, with a dozen tanks behind it, headed for the town eight miles away. Behind each tank there were groups of fifteen to twenty machine-gunners, some of them riding on the backs of the tanks. They dropped off inside the perimeter, their job being to hold the bridgehead while the tanks pushed on north-east towards the El Adem crossroads, 4½ miles inside.

Soon after 5.45 a.m. thirty-eight German tanks of the 5th Tank Regiment's 2nd Battalion were forming up for attack about three-quarters of a mile inside the perimeter wire. Meantime, a couple of miles outside, that regiment's 1st Battalion was moving towards the gap, preceded by field and anti-tank guns and additional German infantry. The attack was going exactly to the plan that had so often shattered defences in Europe. For the 5th Regiment, which had fought in Poland and France, this would be another "push-over". The break-through had been made; now the deep armoured thrust, and then the exploitation by further armoured and mechanized troops who would pour through the gap, fan out behind the defences and roll them up.

As the 2nd Battalion's tanks assembled for attack, the dust-cloud they raised could be picked out in the fading moonlight and gathering dawn by the gunners of the 1st R.H.A., whose 25-pounders were behind the embryonic Blue Line about a mile south-west of the El Adem crossroads. At once they switched their fire from the gap to the tanks and increased it as these moved forward. The Germans also came under fire from several of the 3rd R.H.A.'s anti-tank guns, which were dug in behind the forward posts, but it was still too dark for the guns to engage the tanks effectively.

The Germans, however, were already impressed by the British fire. One of their tank officers (Lieutenant Schorm, of the 5th Tank Regiment) wrote later in his diary: "Slowly, much too slowly, the column moves forward. In this way the enemy has time to prepare resistance. In proportion as darkness lifts the enemy strikes harder. Destructive fire starts up in front of us now. Five batteries rain their shells on us."

By this time the German tanks were two miles inside the wire and British guns on either side of the El Adem road were putting down a steady barrage in their path, but they replied with machine-guns and their 75- and 37-mm. cannon. "The air was lit with tracer shells and bullets until it looked like Blackpool illuminations," according to Sergeant-Major Reg Batten, who was commanding one of the 1st R.H.A.'s guns. Later he said:

Their tracers put us right on to them, but so long as they were a mile or so away we couldn't stop them because they were so well dispersed. They kept their machine-guns going as they moved, but when the Mark IVs used their big "75", they stopped, took deliberate aim at our flashes and then came on again. They seemed to work to a plan. Some fired while the others kept moving. The bulk of their tanks headed straight for the gap between two troops of our guns, but two Mark IVs tried to go round our flank, past the gun where I was.

As they came up within half a mile we engaged them over open sights. At about 600 yards we hit one and then swung the gun to deal with the other. Our first round fell short, but we saw sparks fly as splinters[1] struck the side of the tank. We were about to fire again when a 75-mm. shell hit us square on the shield. The gun was knocked out and all the crew, except myself, were either killed or wounded. I managed to fire the round that was still in the gun and the tanks turned tail and withdrew. It's a good thing they didn't know that we couldn't fire again and that no other gun near by could have tackled them if they'd kept going. But they turned back and later the tank we'd hit lost its track.

No other tanks got even as far as these. As the main force

---

[1] Because they had no A.P. (solid armour-piercing ammunition), which the 25-pounders generally use when engaging tanks at close range, the R.H.A. were using H.E. (high explosive shells). With A.P. it could have done much greater damage.

tried to thrust its way through the line of guns it was stopped short by the barrage. The British gunners had never engaged tanks directly over open sights before but they did not falter. One troop of four guns fired more than a hundred rounds per gun in twenty minutes, as the Germans kept attacking in a determined effort to silence the British fire and smash through. But they had little chance of knocking out guns dug in almost flush with the ground.

At a point-blank range of five to six hundred yards the 25-pounders were irresistible. Seven tanks were knocked out—one, a 22-tonner, which was simultaneously hit by two shells, had its massive turret blown clean off. Leaving several tanks blazing on the battlefield, the survivors swung eastwards and tried to get round the field batteries, but they came under fire from two guns of the 3rd Australian Anti-tank Regiment as they got near the El Adem road. (These two guns claim to have knocked out four enemy tanks in this area, but there seems to be some duplication between their claims and those of 1st R.H.A.) Several more enemy tanks were hit, but managed to struggle back.

Thwarted and battered, the German tanks retired beyond the open sights range of the 25-pounders and the anti-tank guns in the Blue Line. But as they went the 3rd R.H.A.'s mobile anti-tank guns attacked them from both flanks. These guns, mounted on the backs of 30-cwt. trucks, had no protective armour, but this did not deter their crews. They employed what they later described as "mosquito tactics". At one stage three guns engaged three heavy German tanks. Heading their trucks straight for these, the drivers raced across the desert at break-spring speed till they were within half a mile of the tanks; there they swung round, fired half a dozen shells from their 2-pounders and then raced out again. At first the tanks were taken by surprise, but on going in for the second and later attacks the trucks ran into heavy machine-gun and shell fire. Several were hit, but none was put out of action. One had a remarkable escape. A German armour-piercing shell went right through the reserve petrol tank under the driver's seat without setting the truck on fire. By attacks like these the enemy was harried as he withdrew and several of his tanks were hit.

Before 7 a.m. about a mile south of the Blue Line the Germans rallied and tried to form up for another mass attack, but the British gunners continued to shell them. The tanks were helpless without the anti-tank and field guns and the 8th M.G.

Battalion, all of which should have followed them; but there was no sign of these supporting arms. Actually they were still trying to get through, in the face of tactics they had never before encountered. As we have seen, the Diggers in the perimeter posts had not engaged the tanks. Apparently the Germans expected the Australians would give in as soon as the tanks had gone past; some of them had even called on the Diggers to surrender, shouting out that the tanks had broken through and Tobruk had fallen. The answers they received were hardly printable. Once the tanks had moved on, however, the troops in the perimeter posts opened fire on the infantry with everything they had. Some Germans had got through in the darkness, but the rest were now forced to take refuge in the anti-tank ditch outside the wire.

At dawn when the Germans began bringing up anti-tank and field guns Balfe's men held their fire. "As it got light," said Balfe "we saw them dragging three anti-tank guns towards the gap. We let them come on till they were within fifty yards of my H.Q. Then we sniped the crews and, though they did fire back, we eventually killed every man. The Germans next brought up some heavy, long-barrelled guns[2] to the anti-tank ditch, but we knocked out their crews before they had fired a round. The same thing happened to a 75-mm. field gun. Nothing got past us after daylight."

Meantime heavy shelling of the area outside the wire well south of the bridgehead was disorganizing German attempts to get further reinforcements forward, and the few hundred infantry of the 8th M.G. Battalion, who had slipped through the perimeter posts in the darkness, were soon dealt with. Some of them had taken refuge from the British shelling in shallow wadis on the sloping ground behind the forward posts, but one party had established itself with half a dozen machine-guns in a ruined house a few hundred yards north of Post 32. At 6.30 a.m. Colonel Crawford sent two platoons to clean up this area.

They drove some of the enemy back through the wire and then dealt with those in the ruined house. The attack was made by two sections, led by Sergeant R. M. McElroy, who told me later that, while the other sections gave them covering fire, his men went in with the bayonet. This fire kept most of the German machine-guns quiet and McElroy's party was able

---

[2] These guns were actually 88-mm. anti-aircraft guns, which the Germans were using in an anti-tank role, even at this stage. See Chapter XII.

to advance in dead ground until they were within fifty yards of the house. Then they charged, under cover of a hail of grenades. "As these burst," McElroy said afterwards, "the Germans practically stopped firing. Some came running out to surrender; some did not. We got at them with the bayonet. Eighteen were killed and eighteen captured. Few escaped."

Because of these operations, no guns or infantry came forward to support the German tanks, and by 7 o'clock they were being attacked from all sides by artillery, anti-tank guns and finally British tanks. Long before the first German tanks got through the wire Morshead had taken steps to deal with them. The enemy had made no attempt to conceal the point and direction of his thrust, and during the night, when it became clear that he meant business, the mobile reserve of tanks and anti-tank guns had been moved into position to meet the attack. By dawn two groups of cruiser tanks—half a dozen in each—were disposed to the east of the El Adem road, so that they could attack the enemy's flank with the early morning sun behind them. They had been ordered to let the enemy armour first batter itself against the field and anti-tank guns, and then to fall on it from the flank. The plan worked well and now, while the Germans tried to re-form for another advance, they came under heavier fire than ever. The British tanks then moved in to attack. From the Germans' eastern flank five cruisers of the 1st R.T.R., commanded by Major A. E. Benzie, opened fire on them at about 1800 yards. Although they were out-numbered five or six to one, the British closed in to a range of less than half a mile, firing into the mass of milling tanks, which replied strongly. Benzie's tank was disabled by two direct hits. "I ordered the crew to get out and just as they did so, it was hit again and caught fire," said Benzie in telling me the story later. "I hopped on the back of my second-in-command's tank and he continued to engage the Germans with me hanging on to the turret, until his tank was hit too.

"My other tanks kept fighting. During the battle it was almost impossible to tell what was happening. All I could see was round after round of tracer going into the cloud of dust and smoke where their tanks were. But we could tell we had them on the run, and as we followed up, there were four German tanks abandoned on the battlefield."

By this time the combined British fire plus the failure of his own infantry and guns to appear had been too much for the enemy. As the British tanks, now reinforced by four Matildas,

THE EASTER BATTLE

continued their attack, the Germans turned and raced for the perimeter. Evidently they fled in some panic, if the description of the battle written by Schorm, the tank officer already quoted, is any guide. He wrote:

Our heavy tanks fire for all they are worth, just as we do, but the enemy, with his superior force and all the tactical advantages of his own territory, makes heavy gaps in our ranks. We are right in the middle of it with no prospect of getting out. From both flanks armour-piercing shells whizz by at 100 metres a second . . . On the radio—"Right turn!"—"Left turn!"—"Retire!" Now we come slap into the 1st Battalion which is following us. Some of our tanks are already on fire. The crews call for doctors who alight to help in this witches' cauldron. English anti-tank units fall upon us with their guns firing into our midst. My driver, in the thick of it, says: "The engines are no longer running properly, brakes not acting, transmission working only with great difficulty."

We bear off to the right. Anti-tank guns 900 metres distance in the hollow, and a tank. Behind that in the next dip, 1200 metres away, another tank.

Italian fighter planes come into the fray above us. Two of them crash in our midst. Our optical instruments are spoiled by the dust; nevertheless I register several unmistakable hits. A few anti-tank guns are silenced; some enemy tanks are burning. Just then we are hit and the radio is smashed to bits. Now our communications are cut off. What is more, our ammunition is giving out. I follow the battalion commander.

Our attack is fading out. From every side the superior forces of the enemy shoot at us. "Retire." We take a wounded man and two others on board and other tanks do the same . . .

With its last strength my tank follows the others which we lose from time to time in dust-clouds. But we have to press on towards the south. It is the only way through. Suppose we don't find it? Suppose the engines won't do any more?

Close in on our right and left flanks the English tanks shoot into our midst. We are struck in the tracks which creak and groan. At last the gap is in sight. Everything hastens towards it. English anti-tank guns shoot into the mass. Our own anti-tank and 88-mm. anti-aircraft guns are almost deserted. The crews are lying silent beside them. Italian artillery which was to have protected our left flank is equally deserted. We go on. Now comes the gap. Now the ditch. The driver cannot see a thing for the dust, nor I either; we drive by instinct. The tank almost gets stuck in the ditch but manages to extricate itself after a great struggle. With their last reserves of power the crew get out of range and we return to camp. I examine the damage to the tank. My men extract an armour-piercing shell from the right-hand auxiliary petrol tank. The auxiliary tank—three centimetres of armour plate—is cut clean through; the petrol had run out without igniting. We were lucky to escape alive.

As the German tanks fled through the narrow gap, they had to run the gauntlet of British anti-tank guns dug in near the perimeter. Shells fell and whizzed all around them and six more were destroyed, bringing the total knocked out by artillery, tanks, and anti-tank guns to seventeen.

By 7.30 a.m. the Germans were struggling madly through the

wire in complete rout. In a vivid description of their exit Balfe said:

> There was terrible confusion at the only gap as tanks and infantry pushed their way through it. The crossing was badly churned up and the tanks raised clouds of dust as they went. In addition, there was the smoke of two tanks blazing just outside the wire.
>
> Into this cloud of dust and smoke we fired anti-tank weapons, Brens, rifles, and mortars, and the gunners sent hundreds of shells. We shot up a lot of infantry as they tried to get past, and many, who took refuge in the anti-tank ditch, were later captured. It was all I could do to stop the troops following them outside the wire. The Germans were a rabble, but the crews of three tanks did keep their heads. They stopped at the anti-tank ditch and hitched on behind them the big guns, whose crews had been killed. They dragged these about 1000 yards, but by then we had directed our artillery on to them. They unhitched the guns and went for their lives. That was the last we saw of the tanks, but it took us several hours to clean up small parties of infantry who hadn't been able to get away.

This mopping-up had been going on since dawn, as we have seen, but it was the middle of the morning before the last of the Germans were gathered in. One particularly troublesome party of nearly a hundred established itself in a wadi behind Post 28. It was not silenced until Captain C. H. Wilson led part of the 2/17th's "B" Company against it in a bayonet charge. Some Germans were killed, seventy-five were captured and a few got away, though they were probably picked up later by the patrols from the 2/15th and the Indian Cavalry who collected nearly a hundred more bewildered Germans during the morning.

While the battle was raging between the guns and the tanks there had also been heavy scrapping in the air. Shortly after dawn German and Italian fighters had joined in the battle striving to knock out Tobruk's few remaining Hurricanes. One Hurricane and two Italian fighters had spun to earth in sheets of fire in the midst of the German tanks, and added their flames to the "witches' cauldron".

At 7.30, just when the German tanks were making their retreat through the wire, forty Stukas and Messerschmitts attacked the harbour and ack-ack guns. The Hurricanes shot down six; the ack-ack got four. Apparently the Germans had estimated that by this time their tanks would have been approaching the town and the Stuka attack was intended to be the final blow!

In addition to the 12 planes, the Germans left inside the defences 17 tanks, 110 men killed and 254 taken prisoner. But they must have had many more casualties outside the perimeter in the preliminary encounters and in the disorganized retreat, and possibly a number of the tanks that were hit never fought again. Schorm's company, which had led the attack, lost ten tanks and five 75-mm. guns which had been sent up to support it. "It went badly," he wrote, "for the anti-tank units and the light and heavy A.A., but especially for the 8th Machine-Gun Battalion. It is practically wiped out." The garrison's casualties were incredibly few: 20 killed, 60 wounded, 12 missing; two tanks and one 25-pounder gun knocked out; two aircraft shot down.

The Germans were shocked at their defeat. Captured diaries show what they thought. The commander of one troop of tanks wrote: "We simply cannot understand how we ever managed to get out. It is the general opinion that this was the most severely fought battle of the war. The survivors call this day 'Hell of Tobruk' . . . 38 tanks went into action, 17 were knocked out and many more were put temporarily out of action."

In their diaries the Germans made various excuses for their failure. The commander of the tank battalion which led the attack wrote:

The information distributed before the action told us that the enemy was about to withdraw, his artillery was weak and his morale had become very low. We had been led to believe that the enemy would retire immediately on the approach of German tanks. Before the beginning of the third attack[3] the regiment had not the slightest idea of the well-designed and executed defences of the enemy nor of a single battery position nor of the terrific number of anti-tank guns. Also it was not known that he had heavy tanks. The regiment went into battle with firm confidence and iron determination to break through the enemy and take Tobruk. Only the vastly superior enemy, the frightful loss and the lack of any supporting weapons, caused the regiment to fail in its task.

The prisoners were equally bewildered and bitter. They had expected that the attack would be a walkover and the 8th Machine-gunners had even brought their battalion office truck, complete with files, right to the wire expecting to drive it straight into Tobruk. Characteristic of the prisoners' comments was that of a German doctor, who had served throughout the campaigns in Europe. "I cannot understand you Australians," he said. "In Poland, France and Belgium once the tanks got through the soldiers took it for granted that they were beaten. But you are like demons. The tanks break through and your infantry still keep fighting."

That was a prime cause of the garrison's success. When the tanks broke through, the Australian infantry held their ground

---

[3] The one on April 14th.

and their fire until the German infantry and gunners appeared. The result was that the tanks were left to advance without the support they had expected. The further they advanced, the more intense became the fire which they encountered but could not answer. They were defeated by defence in depth. Checked by frontal fire from the 25-pounders, they found their flanks assailed by tanks and mobile anti-tank guns before they could re-form for another attack.

After the battle Lavarack issued a Special Order of the Day, in which he briefly summed up the causes of the enemy rout. He said:

> I wish to congratulate all ranks of the garrison of TOBRUK FORTRESS on the stern and determined resistance offered to the enemy's attacks with tanks, infantry and aircraft to-day.
> Refusal by all infantry posts to give up their ground, a prompt counter-attack by reserves of the 20th Bde, skilful shooting by our artillery and anti-tank guns, combined with a rapid counter-stroke by our tanks, stopped the enemy's advance and drove him from the perimeter in disorder. At the same time the R.A.F. and our A.A. defences dealt severely with the enemy in the air.
> Stern determination, prompt action and close co-operation by all arms ensured the enemy's defeat, and we can now feel more certain than ever of our ability to hold TOBRUK in the face of any attacks the enemy can stage.
> Every one can feel justly proud of the way the enemy has been dealt with. Well done TOBRUK!

This Order of the Day was actually Lavarack's farewell message to Tobruk. As the Fortress was no longer in touch with the frontier, the place for the desert headquarters was Egypt. Consequently that night Lavarack handed over complete command to Morshead and "Cyrcom" H.Q. was transferred to Maaten Baguish, twenty miles east of Mersa Matruh. There it was absorbed by "Western Desert Force H.Q.", which was soon commanded by Lieutenant-General N. M. Beresford Peirse. He had led the 4th Indian Division in the desert the year before, when the Italians were checked and defeated at Sidi Barrani, and he knew the ground and the problems. This appointment, however, was in no way a reflection on Lavarack, as Wavell made clear. Lavarack, one of the finest military brains Australia has produced, was soon appointed to command the 1st Australian Corps in Syria, and what Wavell thought of his work at Tobruk was expressed in the signal he sent to him after the Easter Battle: "Most grateful your invaluable services in stabilizing situation in Cyrenaica."

CHAPTER IX

Tobruk Commander

On April 25th, 1915 when the 1st A.I.F. landed on Gallipoli, a "dark, dapper, little schoolmaster" was second-in-command of a company of the 2nd Battalion. According to the *Official History of Australia in the War of 1914-18* this young captain was in the forefront of the battle to gain a foothold on the ridges above Anzac Cove and, in the bitter fight that afternoon to hold the hill the Anzacs named "Baby 700", he took command of a platoon that fought to the last. He was one of the very few surviving officers in this sector at the end of that costly day.

It is as well that he lived through it, for one year later the captain had become a lieutenant-colonel, commanding the 33rd A.I.F. Battalion at the age of twenty-six. Now he is Lieutenant-General Sir Leslie James Morshead. He well earned both his knighthood and his lieutenant-generalcy by his gallant conduct of the defence of Tobruk Fortress which he commanded from the Easter week-end until October 23rd when the G.O.C. 70th British Division, Major-General R. M. Scobie, took over from him.

Morshead is a citizen-soldier in the Monash tradition. Although between the two wars he was a business man, who rose to be Sydney manager of the Orient Line, his peacetime soldiering was no mere hobby; it was an all-absorbing spare-time interest. Even when he went to Britain on holiday in 1937 he spent much of his time visiting British Army Training Schools and attending manoeuvres. He was thus able to keep in touch with developments during a period of great change in Army thinking; his mind remained youthfully receptive to new ideas. Youthful, too, in appearance, at fifty-one he looked nearly ten years younger, and set himself the same rigorous standard of fitness that he demanded of his troops.

In his history of the first A.I.F., Dr Bean has a graphic character sketch of Morshead whom he then described as:

A battalion commander marked beyond most others as a fighting leader in whom the traditions of the British Army had been bottled from his childhood like tight-corked champagne; the nearest approach to a martinet among all the young Australian colonels, but able to distinguish the valuable from the worthless in the old Army practice . . . he had turned out a battalion which any one acquainted with the whole force recognized, even before Messines, as one of the very best.

And Bean's estimate is as true now as when it was written.

Right through his military career Morshead has been a fighter. After six months on Gallipoli, he was wounded and invalided back to Australia. At home he was soon given command of the 33rd Battalion, formed it, trained it, took it to France and commanded it right through with rare distinction, particularly at Messines, Passchendaele and Villers-Bretonneux. By the end of the war he had been wounded twice and mentioned in dispatches six times, and he wore the ribbons of the C.M.G., the D.S.O., and the Légion d'Honneur.

He did not return to teaching, but even to-day in civilian clothes he might pass for a schoolmaster. He is still something of a martinet, as Bean observed; precise, meticulous and straight to the point, he is now known to his troops as "Ming the Merciless", because he is never content with anything but the best and is a strict disciplinarian. He is, however, just as critical of himself as of his men. One day, speaking to me of the fighting early in May, he said: "I didn't handle my tanks well. I should have kept them concentrated and used them all together. I didn't know as much about handling tanks then as I do now." Another time, discussing something I had written about one of his battalions, he said: "You're making excuses for them. Don't excuse them: they didn't do well."

Much of this self-criticism was explained by his own modesty. No persuasion of mine could induce him to record a broadcast, although every other senior A.I.F. commander had done so and he freely allowed his brigadiers and other members of the garrison to record broadcasts about operations. He helped correspondents to obtain a first-hand and accurate picture of events, but insisted that the importance of Tobruk and the difficulties of operations and living should not be exaggerated. He wanted his men to get their due, but no more. He read nearly all dispatches by correspondents before they were sent to Cairo, and read them very carefully—even to the extent of suggesting grammatical alterations. He disliked slang and one time suggested that a Digger in a broadcast should talk about "men" not "chaps" and about "devitalizing" minefields and not "delousing" them.

I can see him now coming out of his office with a script of mine in one hand, pencil in the other, glasses on the bridge of his nose, and saying to me: "Just a moment, Mr Wilmot. There's one thing here that's not quite right." He fixed me with a stern look; we might have been in the classroom—and perhaps we were.

Morshead is no airy military theorist; he is a hard, practical commander. A stickler for accuracy, he gives close attention to detail, though he never loses himself in it. Before making a decision he likes to master all the facts, study all the implications and see his final position clearly and exactly. This characteristic proved valuable at Tobruk, where several times a precipitate decision might have been costly. Morshead had the courage and patience to "wait and see" and then to decide. He is not a man of swift, bold or spectacular decision, but once he has made up his mind on the right course of action he sticks to it.

It is popularly believed that the Australian soldier chafes under strict discipline, but Morshead has always held that without it there is nothing to bind the strong individuality of the Australian soldiers into an organized fighting force. His troops have responded to discipline because they have proved its value in battle. Captured diaries showed that after the attack of April 14th the Germans were amazed at the discipline of the men who fearlessly stood their ground after the tanks broke through.

Although holding Tobruk was a defensive task, it was actually held by offensive tactics. From the first days Morshead ordered active patrolling of no-man's-land and regular raiding of enemy posts. In his own words, "I determined we should make no-man's-land *our* land". I remember his being incensed on one occasion by an Australian newspaper headline, which read: "Tobruk can take it." "That's one of the most dangerous phrases coined in this war," he said. "We're not here to 'take it', we're here to 'give it'." Because he instilled these principles into his men, they kept the initiative and gained a moral ascendency over the enemy which they never lost.

He inspired everyone in Tobruk with the firm conviction that there could be no yielding; that if every man fought without flinching the garrison was invincible. When the Germans forced a salient in May and made it extremely difficult to hold the original perimeter on either side of it, some of his advisers suggested withdrawing from the Red Line to the Blue Line in this sector. "I couldn't listen to these counsels of fear," Mors head told me. "We will never yield a yard unless they take it from us." Nor was he content to see the enemy remain in possession of any ground we had once held. Any other spirit might have lost Tobruk.

Tobruk might also have been lost if the General had not been so thorough in supervising in detail the strengthening of the defences and the building up of reserve supplies. He was unrelenting when he had to deal with anyone who, he was convinced, had let him down. One senior staff officer was packed off to Palestine for a mistake which, in less serious circumstances, might have brought only a rebuke. He would tolerate no inefficiency, no slackness. He could demand this of his staff and his troops because he demanded it of himself. Both in Tobruk and out of it he lived austerely. The troops admired him because they knew that he had been through it as they had, and that before he was thirty he had commanded an infantry battalion in the line for three years.

They knew that he did not direct the defence from the security of the deep tunnels in the escarpment near the Pilastrino road, which housed his H.Q. He regularly visited all parts of the perimeter, and examined for himself the positions in the Salient. He was most critical of the amount of work which had been done on these posts and his criticism struck home because he spoke from personal observation.

The possible hostility of his troops would never deter him from any course he believed necessary. In Tobruk as the stalemate dragged on and boredom increased, so did gambling. Troops were frittering away their savings at two-up schools of doubtful probity. Morshead banned two-up and took severe disciplinary action against those who disregarded the order. The ban was most unpopular, but the troops respected the man who issued it.

Between the two World Wars Morshead rose to command an infantry brigade in the A.M.F., and when the 6th Division was formed he was one of the original brigade commanders. But his brigade (the 18th) went to Britain, and there he was able to work with those who had learned much from the fighting in France before Dunkirk.

In January 1941 he arrived in the Middle East with his brigade in time to be an observer at the capture of Tobruk. Six weeks later he was appointed to command the 9th Division, which was to garrison Cyrenaica, and complete its training and equipment. But, as we have seen, he had barely moved his men there before he had to extricate them from a most perilous situation. His quality as a divisional commander was established at once. At the very outset his division would probably have suffered crippling losses had it not been for his foresight in anticipating Rommel's outflanking move; his tenacity in battling against Neame and going beyond him to Wavell regarding the withdrawal of the 20th Brigade from the El Agheila area; and his excellent control and direction of his troops during the withdrawal.

Back in Tobruk, from the beginning of the siege, he was responsible for the defence of the perimeter, and after the Easter Battle, when "Cyrcom" H.Q. moved to the Western Desert, he was in complete command of the Fortress. Thus from being a brigade commander in March he found himself virtually a corps commander in April. Though still only a Major-General he had under him more than a division and a half plus a number of Fortress troops, R.A.F. and naval personnel. From commanding 2500 Australian soldiers, he had risen in a few weeks to command 25,000 British, Australians and Indians; soldiers, sailors and airmen. But Morshead made his task easier for himself by building up a first class staff.[1]

As his "G.1" he had one of the ablest staff officers and most colourful characters in the A.I.F., Colonel C. E. M. Lloyd, universally known as "Gaffer". Big and bluff, Lloyd has a manner that is a strange mixture of bluntness and friendliness. His initial bluntness springs from a dislike of humbug and a desire to come straight to the point; but those who stand up to him and have something to say find him most approachable. He is no respecter of persons and is essentially a realist who sees a job to be done and goes about it in the most direct way.

His capacity lies in his ability to make an immediate decision, his readiness to shoulder responsibility and the fact that he never becomes ruffled. Although a permanent soldier, Lloyd found time to graduate in Law at Sydney University. This, and his keen interest in non-military affairs, have given him a breadth of outlook that life in the Regular Army tends to discourage. These qualities have made him an outstanding staff

---

[1] The principal officers of this staff were: Chief of Staff (G.1.), Colonel C. E. M. Lloyd; Chief Administrative Officer (Assistant Adjutant and Quartermaster-General, to quote his official title), Colonel A. P. O. White, and later Colonel B. W. Pulver. Other branches and services were commanded as follows: Engineers, Colonel J. Mann; Medical Services, Colonel H. G. Furnell; Signals, Lieutenant-Colonel D. N. Veron; A.S.C., Lieutenant-Colonel J. A. Watson; Ordnance, Lieutenant-Colonel A. L. Noton.

officer and he fully deserved his promotion between 1940 and 1943 from Major to Major-General. This rise carried him from a second-grade staff appointment on 6th Divisional H.Q. to the key administrative post of Adjutant-General of the Australian Military Forces. When he became a general he was the youngest officer of that rank in the Australian forces, and the first of those, too young for service in the last war, to attain it.

The thorough staff work that Morshead demanded was an important factor in his success as a leader. At Tobruk he made his name as a fighting commander in defensive warfare, renowned for his determination, thoroughness and guts. A year later at El Alamein he was to be greeted by Churchill with the warm tribute—"Well done, Morshead! You've stemmed the tide again." He showed there that he was—if anything—even more able and successful in command of an attacking force. His troops have complete faith in him. In Tobruk he won their respect and admiration; to-day they worship him. In Morshead Australia has found another fine citizen soldier—a man with a profound sincerity, honesty and strength of purpose and with more experience now as a fighting commander in this war and the last than any other Australian. In April 1941, however, this reputation was still in the making.

CHAPTER X

Offensive Defence

THE Easter Battle was a severe shock to the Germans, but it was by no means a crippling defeat. The German units involved suffered heavily, but the losses were light in relation to the total Axis strength in Cyrenaica. Because of the speed with which the garrison had snapped off the spearhead of the attack, the bulk of the forces that the enemy had intended to send against the Fortress that Easter Monday had not been brought into action. Tobruk was still in great danger, especially as fresh German and Italian forces were arriving outside the perimeter every day. The garrison, on the other hand, had little chance of being reinforced. In view of the German threat to the frontier and Egypt all Wavell could send immediately was eight new "I" tanks.

Wavell could, however, force Rommel to divert German troops from Tobruk to the frontier. On April 13th they had captured Sollum and Halfaya Pass, but Brigadier Gott's force, backed by a most effective bombardment from H.M.A.S. *Stuart* and a British destroyer and gunboat, had stopped them going farther into Egypt. Before Rommel could consolidate his gains, Gott struck back. He had been reinforced by the 22nd Guards Brigade and a few tanks, and on April 15th he sent a mobile column around the enemy's open desert flank to attack Capuzzo, while other columns went for Halfaya and Sollum. This combination of direct attack and outflanking movement forced the Axis troops from those positions though they held Capuzzo. Five nights later British commandos raided Bardia and caused some damage and great consternation.

Rommel's reply was to switch a large number of tanks from Tobruk and to consolidate his position on the frontier before he renewed his assault on the garrison. Rommel had two tank regiments in Libya—the 5th and the 8th—each originally with about 150 tanks. After the Easter Battle it seems that the 5th rested and refitted, while one battalion of the 8th Regiment went to the frontier. Its other battalion was evidently still on its way up from Bengazi. The Easter Battle had shown that he would need at least a hundred German tanks, plus a heavy concentration of artillery, if he were to have a chance of breaking through the Tobruk defences. But such a force represented nearly half the tanks he then had in the Tobruk-Sollum area. He could not afford to concentrate so many against Morshead's garrison until he felt safe from attack on the frontier and had been reinforced by the remaining tanks of the 15th Armoured Division, which were already moving up from Bengazi.

He must have realized too that the next attack on Tobruk would need to be much more carefully prepared. The Germans had obviously been over-confident when they attacked at Easter and had not troubled about such detailed preparations as Mackay's forces had made the previous January. He had made a deliberate attack, but the Germans had evidently believed that a strong immediate thrust would bring swift success. Mackay had gained the advantage of surprise as to both place and time of attack. Once the bridgehead had been made, the Anglo-Australian forces had not pushed recklessly through the narrow gap and bolted for the town. They had widened it and established secure flanks before attempting deep penetration. They had been supported by thorough artillery bombardment, because they had taken care to locate all enemy batteries and amass the guns and ammunition necessary to silence them. Colonel Pohnhardt, C.O. of the 8th M.G. Battalion, who had led the German attack at Easter, had failed to take these precautions. Moreover, he was so confident that he drove in through the gap behind the tanks in a staff car; it was knocked out by an anti-tank shell and he was killed.

Warned by this set-back, Rommel now prepared for a thorough-going attack on the Fortress. This time there would be no mistake. Meanwhile, his German forces recovered from the Easter Battle and dealt with the threat from the frontier. He left it largely to the Italians to maintain the pressure on Tobruk.

Thwarted in the south, the enemy turned his attention to the western sector of the perimeter, which was being held by Tovell's 26th Brigade, with the 2/24th Battalion on the right; the 2/48th on the left and the 2/23rd in reserve. Prisoners' statements and captured diaries suggest that the Germans had intended the Italians to attack in the west on the Easter Monday while they made the main assault from the south. This plan went astray, apparently because the German operation order did not reach the Italian H.Q. in time to be translated and acted upon. There was no attack in the west on the 14th, but next day the Italians tried to make amends.

During the morning of April 15th several hundred infantry approached the 2/48th's front, but when the 51st Field Regiment began to shell them some fled and others took refuge in a wadi about three-quarters of a mile west of the perimeter. While the gunners encouraged the refugees to lie low, a patrol of 22 men of the 2/48th, led by Lieutenant Claude Jenkins, rounded up an Italian officer and 74 men.

Meanwhile another force—estimated at more than a battalion—had approached the wire farther north where the 2/48th linked up with the 2/24th. Advancing bunched together, they provided a perfect target for the British gunners and later patrols found evidence that the gunners had made the most of their chance. The Italians were held up for about an hour, but then the guns had to stop firing through lack of ammunition; the Italians rallied and came on. Several hundred got through the wire between two posts which were nearly a mile apart, but fire soon pinned them down. Patrols gathered in 111 Italians, and the bodies of 30 victims of mortar fire were found in a nearby wadi next morning.

In spite of these costly rebuffs, the Italians continued to probe the front next day, April 16th, but their attacks were ill-planned and half-hearted, and merely yielded another big bag of prisoners. The day's round-up began early, when a small patrol from the 2/24th went out along the Derna road and brought six Italian officers and 63 men back for breakfast. A little later Lieutenant A. Wardle and 26 men of the 2/48th found 98 Italians in a wadi a mile outside the perimeter. They shot one and the others surrendered, but the day's biggest haul was yet to come.

Late in the afternoon another patrol reported that an enemy battalion had advanced down the road from Acroma and was deploying for attack a mile and a half west of the perimeter. As the British gunners got on to them, the Italians scattered in confusion. It was then seen that they were being followed, or possibly driven into action, by twelve tanks. The gunners soon dispersed these and put down a barrage behind the Italian infantry to stop them from withdrawing, while three carriers under Lieutenant O. H. Isaksson went out to reconnoitre.

In one carrier was Private R. G. Daniells, who told me later that they were sent merely to "see what the Ities were up to". He said:

As we drove out they put up a few shots, but we kept our Brens and anti-tank rifles spraying them. When we got near they stopped firing. One carrier went round each flank and one ran straight through the middle of them. We fired over their heads; they dropped their rifles and machine-guns, waved white handkerchiefs, and put up their hands. As we drove through, they began marching towards our wire, leaving all their gear on the ground. When we got to the back of the mob we turned our carriers and drove the Ities in like sheep. The first of them had just reached the perimeter when some tanks came up behind and had a go at us with H.E. They landed a few in the middle of the prisoners, who bolted inside the wire.

It seems certain that the tanks were German and that the crews were deliberately showing contempt for their allies. They were soon driven off, however, by the 25-pounders. About 570 prisoners were brought in by the carriers and another 150 were rounded up by Lieutenant A. E. Brocksopp and 15 men. The 2/48th's total for the day was 26 officers and 777 men captured, at a cost of one man killed and one wounded. The prisoners turned out to be almost the entire 1st Battalion of the 62nd Trento Regiment, including their colonel. He was so delighted with his reception and so infuriated at having been fired on by German tanks that he helped Tobruk H.Q. draft a leaflet appealing to other Italians to follow his example.

The leaflet, which was scattered next day over enemy lines by the R.A.F., read:

SOLDIERS OF ITALY!
For you and your companions the day of peace and happiness is close at hand. In all Africa your comrades have given up the battle. In Abyssinia the war is over; the Ambassador from the Duke D'Aosta has already made preliminary peace terms with British G.H.Q.
Yesterday thousands of your countrymen were taken prisoner at Tobruk. It is quite useless to make any further sacrifices of this kind. All Italian soldiers who have been captured by the British have been treated in the finest manner.
So make an end of this before your losses become considerably larger.

The Italians made no general response to this appeal, but the tally of prisoners continued to mount, even though their next attack on April 17th was much better planned. Their objective was an important rise across which the western perimeter defences ran. It was known as Hill 209 or Ras El Medauuar, and was the most valuable feature in this sector. It rose in a gentle slope only a hundred feet above the surrounding desert, but it commanded that for several miles.

The enemy attack opened late in the morning with heavy

OFFENSIVE DEFENCE

machine-gun and mortar fire from well-concealed positions, into which small parties of Italians had smuggled themselves during the night. Then enemy artillery plastered Hill 209, and tanks and troop-carrying vehicles appeared from behind another rise, named Carrier Hill, half a mile west of 209.

British artillery shelled them, but about a battalion debussed and moved towards the perimeter led by twelve tanks. Several of these were German, but the rest were Italian mediums and lights. They headed for the positions on 209, held by Lieutenant D. Bryant's platoon. His story of the action was this:

The tanks came on through the shelling and forced their way over a broken down part of the wire. One Italian "light" blew up on the minefield, and two more were knocked out by our anti-tank rifles before they got very far. The rest continued on and we couldn't stop them. One party of four or five tanks shot up our sangars on 209 and over-ran the 51st Regiment's O.P., wounding its C.O. (Colonel Douglas). Then a medium tank went for one of the concrete posts, crashed through the wire and fell into the circular anti-tank ditch. Before the troops could deal with it, the tank reversed and cleared out trailing a coil of concertina wire.

While some weapons were turned against the tanks, others kept the Italian infantry pinned down half a mile outside the wire. When these tanks found they could not subdue the posts and that their infantry could not advance, they withdrew. The remainder had careered on eastwards to the 2/48th's reserve company position a mile inside. There was no minefield to stop them and they charged through the flimsy barbed wire and over the shallow weapon-pits and trenches, where one man even had the epaulette torn from his shoulder by a tank track.

The troops fired everything they had but only knocked out a single light tank. The rest pushed on another mile until they came to a stone wall the Italians had built as a tank obstacle. By this time the gunners were pasting them heavily; they turned back to the perimeter, but another was disabled on the way out and its crew captured. Under cross-examination these prisoners admitted that they had been sent to capture and hold 209, confident, in spite of the Easter Battle, that once the tanks got through the wire the defending infantry would surrender. Warned by enemy interest in this sector, Morshead had already ordered engineers to lay a minefield two miles long inside the perimeter and parallel with it, half a mile behind Hill 209. Work on this and the Blue Line positions a mile farther in was now intensified.

For the next four days there was a lull in enemy activity except in the air. Formations of up to forty dive-bombers attacked the harbour and ack-ack guns at least once a day. The gunners brought down four on April 19th and hit back so vigorously that eight new "I" tanks were safely unloaded on the 21st. But these were nothing compared with what Rommel gained by the arrival outside Tobruk of the rest of his 15th Armoured Division.

During the lull in ground fighting, the enemy brought up a number of artillery batteries and began building a chain of defensive positions several thousand yards outside the western perimeter extending from north of the Derna road to south of Carrier Hill. Behind this hill Australian patrols discovered a number of field guns, tanks and infantry.

When the Italians originally built the perimeter fortifications they did not take in this hill. That oversight weakened the western defences considerably, for behind it an enemy could mass unobserved for an attack on 209. Unfortunately the garrison had not enough men or weapons to hold Carrier Hill, but Tovell determined to clear the area beyond it, and simultaneously to raid enemy positions astride the Derna road. He wanted to destroy several batteries that were harassing the forward posts and to keep up the ascendancy that the offensive defence of the Easter Battle and subsequent patrol clashes had won. On April 22nd, therefore, the 2/48th and 2/23rd Battalions carried out two bold daylight raids.

The raid on Carrier Hill was made by ninety men of the 2/48th, supported by three "I" tanks of the 7th R.T.R. and with mobile anti-tank guns and carriers to protect the flanks. The plan was for the tanks and infantry to sweep round Carrier Hill, attack the Italians from the rear, and drive them back to the perimeter. The raid was led by a short, slight, red-headed Adelaide school-teacher, Captain Bill Forbes. His men had already gained useful experience in the patrols that had mopped up so many Italians the week before; this time the prize was bigger.

At dawn on the 22nd, Forbes's raiding party moved out more than a mile westward, skirting the southern slope of Carrier Hill. Overhead a Lysander cruised about to drown the noise of the tanks. They were intended to lead the infantry but they went so fast that they were soon lost in the morning mist. Forbes did not see them again until the raid was over. This did not worry the Diggers. Forbes led them west of Carrier Hill and then swung north moving along a shallow wadi, while the carriers covered his left flank. One of Forbes's platoon commanders, Lieutenant D. G. Kimber, describing the raid, said:

> The enemy hadn't spotted us at this stage and his guns were still shelling 209 as we came up behind them. To our left was a transport park, and the carriers dealt with that while we went on. We came over a slight rise, marching spread out in line abreast with Forbes well in front. We were about 500 yards from the Italians when they saw us. As they opened up with mortars, M.Gs and anti-tank guns, Forbes waved to us to keep going. Their fire was heavy but it was all over the place. By coming at them from the rear we'd surprised them and in their panic they shot wildly. Then the carriers came up on our left and drove straight into the Italian positions with every gun going.

Leading them was Sergeant L. W. C. Batty, whose carrier over-ran one gun-position and went on to deal with another, but was stopped by an anti-tank shell. Batty was wounded, but his gunner, R. G. Daniells, kept nearby Italians quiet. When he too was hit, the driver, J. L. Spavin, engaged them until the infantry arrived. To continue Kimber's account:

> We covered the last few hundred yards firing our Brens and rifles from the hip. By the time we were fifty yards from their nearest sangars every Italian was well out of sight and not one weapon was firing on my platoon. In the first sangar I came to there were three Dagoes—with their heads buried in a corner and their tails sticking up in the air. After that it was just a matter of gathering up prisoners and dropping hand grenades in the breeches of the guns we couldn't move.

They brought back 16 Italian officers and 354 men; a number of anti-tank and machine-guns; several vehicles and motor-bikes. Having been ordered to return within two hours, Forbes could not stay to collect or even complete the destruction of all the booty. Sights and instruments, however, were removed from guns that had to be left and these were soon being used by the hitherto "sightless" Bush Artillery. Primarily because of Forbes's bold handling of the raid, the Australian casualties were slight—two killed and seven wounded.

The troops who attacked on the Derna road, however, had a harder fight and far heavier casualties. Here the 2/23rd sent out two raiding parties—each of two officers and forty-four other ranks. The enemy held a strong position astride the road, and the plan was for one party to outflank this position north of the road while the other worked round it on the south side. Then both were to turn in towards the road, join forces and roll up the position from the rear.

The northern party under Captain Rupert Rattray advanced at dawn up a wadi that led westward from the perimeter. They struck no opposition in the first mile, but then came under intense machine-gun fire from enemy sangars at the head of the wadi. They moved for cover into a small side wadi on the right, but the enemy immediately searched this with mortar-bombs and shells. Rattray said later:

> We couldn't stay there and we couldn't attack straight up the main wadi, so we decided to move against them across the top of the plateau. When they saw us come over the skyline, they turned their guns on us, but while one section gave covering fire, the other dashed in with the bayonet, pitching hand grenades ahead of them. As they got to the sangars the Italians brought out white handkerchiefs. We took nineteen prisoners and about as many more were killed by grenades and M.G. fire. Meantime the reserve section had collected another twenty-one prisoners at the head of the side wadi.
>
> We had intended to push southwards from here along the enemy line, but now we were coming under heavy fire from both flanks and the ground ahead was bare and flat. It would have meant throwing away good lives to go on, so we came back with our forty prisoners.

The fight was long and bitter, south of the road, where the Italians had one A.A.-anti-tank battery with two batteries of field guns behind it. All were well protected by machine-gun posts. The enemy, however, held his fire until Lieutenant R. W. James and the two leading sections were less than 500 yards away. Then ack-ack guns, mortars and artillery caught James and his men on a forward slope and kept them there. Seeing their acute danger, the patrol leader, Lieutenant J. A. Hutchinson, hurried the other two sections round to take the Italians in the flank and split their fire. He led his troops forward in short rushes, and four carriers came up to support them.

At last his leading troops got near enough to charge and—to quote Hutchinson himself:

> The combined effect of the bayonet, grenades and carriers was too much for the Italians. They ran out of their stone sangars with their hands up, and I don't think they stopped until they reached the perimeter 3000 yards away.
>
> This gave us our first objective—the ack-ack battery. But most of James's two sections had been either killed or wounded and the rest of us now came under point-blank fire from artillery batteries and infantry 300 yards farther west. These guns were our second objective and, although we now had less than half our original strength, we decided to push on in the hope of linking up with Rattray's patrol. Working forward along a wadi, we got to within fifty yards of the nearest gun-position. With Lance-Corporal W. Crummey, I made a dash for the gun and the crew abandoned it, but Crummey was hit and fell. A grenade he was holding ready to throw exploded, killing him and wounding me in the leg so badly that I could not move.

Sergeant J. W. Barnard and the ten men Hutchinson had left in the wadi tried to get forward to the next gun-position with supporting fire from four carriers. But Barnard was already

badly wounded, two of the carriers were hit and set ablaze
and any further advance became impossible in the face of the
scorching fire the enemy was putting down. Thinking Hutchinson had been killed, Barnard decided to withdraw protected
by his remaining carriers. When they too were hit, the crews
dismounted and gave covering fire with their Brens from the
ground.[1] Withdrawal was not easy. The enemy fire grew more
intense and the ground offered no cover to the retiring troops.
Nevertheless Bren carriers made several trips from the perimeter
forward to pick up wounded. They also brought back captured
weapons and Barnard's party destroyed those they could not
take with them.

Of Hutchinson's patrol 80 per cent had become casualties
by the time they reached the perimeter after a 4-hour fight.
The losses for the two parties were—one killed, twenty-three
missing (most of them in fact killed), twenty-two wounded. But
even though it was costly and had not succeeded in cleaning
up the entire enemy position, the raid was justly described by
Morshead as "an epic worthy of the finest traditions of the
A.I.F." Eighty-seven prisoners had been taken and as many
more killed or wounded. One prisoner, captured later, stated
that out of his company of more than a hundred only ten were
left after the battle. Shaken by the strength and daring of the
Australian attack, the enemy at once reinforced the Derna road
positions.

Two days after this the Italians made a belated attempt to
restore their confidence. At dawn Kimber's platoon on Hill 209
came under fire from a force that had established itself in the
wire between two perimeter posts. According to Kimber, there
was a fierce machine-gun duel for about a quarter of an hour;
"then their white flags came up; we sent out a patrol, gathered
in 107 Italians and buried nearly 40." Later that morning
German infantry appeared on the western sector for the first
time. Machine-gun fire stopped them 300 yards from the wire
and a 2/48th patrol chased them back. Several were killed and
seven captured. One of these was an officer, who knew enough
English to proclaim with vehemence, "——— Hitler!"

This brought the total of prisoners captured on the 26th
Brigade's front in ten days to more than 1700.[2] But so many

---

[1] After Barnard's party had withdrawn Hutchinson tried to hobble back,
but was taken prisoner. Nearly a year later, however, he was released in an
exchange of prisoners of war.

[2] During eighteen days in the line at this time, the 2/48th Battalion alone
captured 1375 prisoners, for the loss of 15 men killed and 20 wounded.

were a decided embarrassment to the garrison, whose water ration at this time was half a gallon per man per day—eight cupfuls for all purposes. Nevertheless these patrol successes were encouraging. They gave the troops experience and confidence, and delayed the enemy preparations for attack. Lest success should make them over-confident, however, Morshead warned all units to "remember that continued vigilance is necessary and that most of our patrol successes have been against the Italians."

Behind this slightly comic facade provided by Il Duce's heroes, Rommel had been preparing for an all-out attack. Reconnaissance aircraft reported continuous movement along the road from Derna and heavy concentrations of enemy tanks, guns and vehicles around Acroma, five miles west of Hill 209.

The R.A.F., operating from bases inside Egypt, did its best to hinder enemy preparations by bombing and strafing. Although few aircraft were available these raids caused the Germans some concern, as is shown by these extracts from Schorm's diary. For April 16th he wrote: "The airmen get on our nerves. Ten raids or more a day. No A.A., no fighter planes to meet them. We remain on the alert. At night two raids." For April 17th: "The day begins with the usual bombing and shelling.... No German troops up to the present have had such a drubbing as we."

By this time Schorm, who had already fought through the campaigns in Poland and Western Europe, had changed his ideas about the nature of war. In his diary for the 16th he wrote:

The war in Africa is quite different from the war in Europe. It is absolutely individual. Here there are not masses of men and material. Nobody and nothing can be concealed. Whether in battle between opposing land forces or between those of the air or between both it is the same sort of fight, face to face; each side thrusts and counter-thrusts. If the struggle were not so brutal, so entirely without rules, one would be inclined to think of the romantic idea of a knight's tourney.

Meanwhile Rommel's preparations went on, and in anticipation of a new assault Morshead's troops worked day and night to strengthen the defences. By the end of the month captured weapons had been liberally issued to the forward posts; existing minefields had been strengthened and new ones laid; gun-positions had been camouflaged and stocked with ample reserve ammunition; new signal lines and reconditioned Italian phones had given forward posts the means of communication they had lacked. Telegraph poles, which lined the four main Tobruk roads providing prominent finger-posts on a featureless horizon, were cut down so that if enemy tanks should break through they could not be guided by them. The garrison had eight new "I" tanks, but this gain was more than cancelled out by the unavoidable withdrawal on April 26th of the remaining R.A.F. fighters.

In the previous three weeks No. 73 Squadron had lost twenty-seven of its thirty-two Hurricanes, and it would have been suicidal to leave the remaining five in Tobruk. At this time the total British fighter strength in the Western Desert—from Tobruk to Alexandria—was thirteen Hurricanes! All available fighters had been sent to Greece in a desperate attempt to check the German attacks on the roads along which the British and Anzac forces were now fighting their bitter rearguard action. No reinforcements for Libya could be quickly obtained. In a last-minute effort to get Hurricanes from Britain several attempts were made to fly them out, using Gibraltar and Malta as intermediate stopping places. This proved costly. Some lost their way; some were shot down; some crashed in the sea when they ran out of petrol. I was at a fighter drome in the desert in May, when one group of these fighters came in, and pilots told me that of thirty-two that had left Britain only fifteen reached the desert. Because of this critical shortage of fighters, the Germans had complete air supremacy over Tobruk and the frontier from mid-April to mid-May, and British air strength in the Western Desert then was lower than it had been at any time during the war.

While they were in Tobruk, No. 73 Squadron, led by Squadron-Leader Peter Wykeham Barnes, fought an almost continuous battle at odds of anything up to ten to one. They seldom had half a dozen aircraft serviceable, and against this handful of Hurricanes the Germans could send as many as thirty ME109s at any time. From any one of six airfields within twenty-five miles of Tobruk they could launch attacks almost before the Hurricanes were off the ground, and there were never enough British planes to maintain a standing patrol.

The pilots were in action several times a day. As soon as a plane landed, ground personnel refuelled and rearmed it and another pilot took it over. Pilots were shot down, bailed out, and went up to fight again next day. Wykeham Barnes was brought down twice. The second time he landed outside the perimeter but managed to get back safely. Because of their superior numbers the Germans were able to continue fighting until the Hurricanes were out of ammunition and almost out of petrol. Then, as the British pilots made a last-minute dash for the Tobruk drome, German fighters would follow them in for the kill as they landed. They were equally in danger when taking off.

In their final battles, however, they took heavy toll of the enemy. On April 23rd they destroyed four German planes for the loss of two. Next day three Hurricanes brought down eight Germans before they were inevitably overwhelmed. Although the fighters were then withdrawn the R.A.F. maintained, throughout most of the siege, one or two Hurricanes inside Tobruk by housing them in underground hangars. The pilots made daily reconnaissance of enemy positions and brought back valuable information, even though they could stay only long enough for a "quick look".

Having driven out the Hurricanes, the Luftwaffe was able to turn its full fury against the anti-aircraft guns and in the last four days of April its attacks reached a new intensity. On the 27th more than fifty dive-bombers concentrated on the town and the main A.A. positions. Four of the sixteen heavy guns attacked were damaged, but none was knocked out. The gunners found that if they fought the Stukas all the way down, they were comparatively safe.[8]

Next day the harbour and the ack-ack guns were dive-bombed by nine planes in the morning and thirty-five in the afternoon, and another heavy raid was made on the field gun-positions near Pilastrino that evening. On the 29th the sky throbbed with enemy planes almost all day. They concentrated most of their fury on the forward posts near Hill 209 and on the gun-positions west of Pilastrino. In five raids more than 150 aircraft blitzed these areas, while Stukas bombed the harbour again and sank a small merchantman laden with outgoing mail.

In spite of the ferocity of these attacks the ack-ack gunners fought staunchly back. In the last three weeks of April, 677 aircraft took part in 52 raids on the harbour and ack-ack defences, and several hundred more attacked the field guns and perimeter posts. But the guns were never silenced and by the end of the month, in addition to some 30 planes brought down by the R.A.F., the ack-ack had certainly destroyed 37, probably destroyed 16, and damaged 43. Disregarding this evidence of the gunners' invincible spirit and good shooting, Rommel appar-

---
[8] See Chapter XVIII.

OFFENSIVE DEFENCE

ently considered that by April 30th the garrison had been softened up enough for him to attack again.

For the Germans this was the time to strike. The British and Anzac Expeditionary Force had been unceremoniously driven from Greece. Admittedly most of the troops had escaped, but they had lost all weapons except their personal arms. The survivors were either stranded in Crete or back in Egypt somewhat disorganized. The tanks and aircraft, which might have given the British effective striking power in the Western Desert, had all been lost in Greece, where the Germans were now mounting forces for another major thrust.

By April 26th Rommel had re-established himself on the frontier by re-capturing Sollum and Halfaya, from which he could effectively check any British diversion designed to help Tobruk. He could now give undivided attention to crushing its "impudent" resistance. He could employ twice the tanks and aircraft he had used on April 14th; he now had two German armoured divisions instead of one, and three Italian divisions as well. R.A.F. reconnaissance planes brought back daily reports of greater and still greater German concentrations around Acroma. It was clear that Tobruk's hour had come. On one of the last days of the month, an enemy plane was shot down over the Fortress; in it was a map marked with a red arrow, which ran from Acroma through Hill 209 to the very heart of Tobruk.

CHAPTER XI

Battle of the Salient

PHASE I. THE PENETRATION AND THE FIRST THRUST

ALL day long on April 30th dust-clouds billowed up from the desert between Acroma and Hill 209 in a steadily thickening pall. Through the haze Australians in the perimeter posts caught glimpses of enemy infantry debussing from lorries, and of tanks and guns being assembled two miles beyond the perimeter astride the Acroma road. Much the same thing had been happening almost daily for the past fortnight, but this time the dust-clouds were heavier and the enemy forces continued to mass regardless of spasmodic shelling by British guns. During the afternoon the posts near 209 were heavily shelled and dive-bombed. The sun dipped down towards the horizon, glaring an angry red through the curtain of dust. In the evening glow the Stukas struck again.

Roaring down out of that ominous sky at 7.15, twenty-two of them unleashed their fury with bomb and machine-gun on Hill 209 and Australian posts to the north of it. Back and forth they went along the perimeter until their ammunition ran out. As they swung away another twenty came in to strafe 209, and the posts immediately south of it. In fifty minutes of intense attack the two waves of Stukas concentrated their bombs on the barbed wire and their machine-guns on the infantry positions.

The chatter of the last burst had barely died away when, at 8 p.m., the full force of Rommel's artillery was turned against the positions which the 2/24th Battalion was now holding on Hill 209 and to either side of it.

[The 2/24th, commanded by Lieutenant-Colonel Allan Spowers, was holding a $4\frac{1}{2}$-mile front from S11, south through Hill 209 to R10. (The numbers of the posts north of 209 were prefixed by the letter "S"; those south of it by the letter "R".) Three companies ("C", "A", and "D") were manning twenty-two concrete posts on the perimeter, and "B" Company was in reserve, a mile east of 209. On its right the 2/24th had the

2/23rd; on its left the 2/15th, and behind it in the Blue Line, the 2/48th. It was supported by the 51st British Field Regiment, plus Vickers guns of the Northumberland Fusiliers, and anti-tank guns of the 3rd R.H.A. and the 24th and 26th Australian Anti-Tank Companies.]

Under cover of this barrage, the dust it raised and the gathering darkness, infantry of the 2nd German Machine-gun Battalion and sappers of the 33rd Panzer Pioneers advanced to the perimeter, deloused the minefield, and blew gaps in the wire at half a dozen places on either flank of 209. Infantry in the forward posts reported that they were being heavily shelled and machine-gunned—so heavily, it now seems, that their fire was neutralized, while the enemy breached the perimeter defences, and then infiltrated between the widely separated posts and established machine-guns behind them.

As a result of this infiltration, or the shelling, or both, all signal lines between the company on Hill 209 and the 2/24th's H.Q. were cut by 8.30 p.m., and Spowers could get no news of the position there. At nine, however, a flare went up from near 209 and at once the enemy's barrage lifted from the hill, evidently to allow his infantry to attack the posts there. At 9.15 some Germans were a mile inside the perimeter, machine-gunning the 2/24th's reserve company. It was ordered to send out fighting patrols to deal with the infiltrating parties and re-establish contact with the company on 209. These drove some of the enemy back and in one clash captured three Germans and killed several others, but in the darkness they could not find the perimeter posts. Lack of information made action difficult. As Spowers told me later:

Every attempt to find out what was happening failed. When the signal lines were cut, I sent our carrier platoon forward, but it could not find the passage through the tactical minefield that had been laid between our reserve company and 209. Again and again signalmen and runners went out into the shell and machine-gun fire. Some didn't get through; others didn't get back. One man took four and a half hours to cover a mile and three-quarters from his company position to my H.Q., mending the signal line as he went. We sent out patrols, but the men did not know the ground and lost their way in the dark. We could not tell what we were holding, but when the reserve company reported six enemy tanks and a number of infantry east of 209 at 5.15 a.m. it looked as though the posts on the hill had gone.

At dawn a ground mist hung over the desert and the general position was so uncertain that we were reluctant to turn the artillery on to 209. We sent carriers out to make contact, but they were driven back by German tanks. At last about 7.30 the mist began to clear, and from my H.Q., three miles inside the perimeter, I counted forty tanks on the eastern slope of the hill.

Soon after eight o'clock the curtain of mist lifted, revealing that the Germans had established a bridgehead about a mile and a half wide. They had captured seven perimeter posts on or around 209, but as none of the Australians in these escaped, we know little of what happened there during the night. From enemy accounts it seems that the heavy shelling had kept the posts quiet while infantry swarmed in to reduce them one by one. Few of these were manned by more than ten men and, even though some held out till dawn, seven posts were overwhelmed by then. In the early fog, Australians south of 209 saw more than a hundred prisoners being marched off. These men, however, had taken the first sting and momentum out of the attack and had upset the enemy's timetable.

Warned by their experience in the Easter Battle, the Germans had set out to establish a wide bridgehead before attempting to make a deep armoured thrust; they had estimated that, with this established and their tanks and supporting troops assembled inside the perimeter during the night, they could attack at dawn. But the stubborn resistance on 209 and the early mist delayed them and at 7.30 they were still consolidating and bringing in anti-tank and field guns, lorry-borne infantry and tanks. Unfortunately at this time lack of news and the loss of observation posts deterred the British gunners from shelling the forty tanks forming up on 209. These tanks were to make a direct thrust east towards Tobruk, while another forty helped the German infantry to widen the bridgehead and roll up the perimeter posts on either side of it.[1]

In accordance with this plan, shortly after 8 a.m. forty tanks headed east towards the 2/24th's reserve company position, raking it with their machine-guns and cannon as they advanced. When one group of a dozen tanks got near the Acroma road, they came under fire from guns of the 24th Australian Anti-Tank Company.[2] One of these guns, commanded by Corporal F. C. Aston, knocked out a German Mark III, setting it alight, but at once attracted the concentrated fire of eleven others. Two of the crew were wounded but the gun claimed two more tank victims before it was put out of action by direct hits. Two other guns near by suffered a similar fate

---

[1] The captured diary of an officer of the 2nd Battalion of the 5th Tank Regiment contained a full account of the German plans and moves during this day, and I have drawn on it for this and other statements.
[2] This company, commanded by Captain C. H. B. Norman, was specially commended by Morshead for its good work on this day. At Tobruk its casualties amounted to more than 50 per cent of the unit.

BATTLE OF THE SALIENT

and in spite of British shelling the tanks continued their advance until they ran straight into the minefield in front of the 2/24th's reserve company position.

According to its commander, Captain Peter Gebhardt:

> In a few minutes seventeen of them were immobilized—mostly with damaged tracks. They were a wonderful target, but any anti-tank guns within range had been knocked out, and our field guns were too far back to engage them over open sights with A.P. They shelled them with H.E., but couldn't shell too heavily for fear of exploding mines and clearing a passage. We engaged them with our Boyes rifles and Brens but couldn't make any impression. Consequently, during the morning more tanks brought up repair crews, who worked on the disabled tanks under cover of fire from others. Some were towed back and before midday all but five had been repaired or removed. These five operated as pillboxes and stood over our position all day sniping whenever we put our heads up.
>
> Apparently the Germans didn't expect[3] to find a minefield there, for they brought no sappers or infantry with them to clear gaps. When the leading tanks blew up, the rest didn't try to find a way through near us. Apart from those which stayed to cover the disabled ones, they sheered off and turned either back towards the perimeter or southwards along the west side of the minefield.

Those that turned south were shelled as they went and were engaged by several guns of the 26th Anti-Tank Company, which were well placed to fire into the Germans' flank. The gunners claim to have disabled several, and the remaining tanks, finding this fire too hot, headed back towards the perimeter.

One of the tanks that was turned back by the minefield and the shelling was commanded by our old friend, Schorm, who starts off his diary for May 1st with the pronouncement, "We intend to take Tobruk." The note of confidence is less emphatic in these later entries:

> We file through the gap where many of our comrades have fallen. Then we deploy at once. The British artillery fires on us. We attack. Tier upon tier of guns boom out from the triangular fortifications before us. Then things happen suddenly. A frightful crash to the right. Artillery shell hit? No. It must be a mine. I immediately send a wireless message: "See if you can turn round in your own tracks." Back through the artillery fire for 100 metres. Wireless order: "Tanks to retire. The men of the mined tank are all right. Enemy is attacking with tanks, but must be put to flight." Retire carefully. Nine heavy and three light tanks of the company have had to abandon the fight owing to mines. Of course the enemy goes on shooting at us for some time. I move back through the gap with a salvaged tank in tow.

Luckily for the German tanks a duststorm helped to cover their retreat, but they were heavily engaged by the guns of the

---

[3] There had been no tactical minefield behind 209 when the Italian tanks had charged right across this reserve position on April 17th, and so the Germans expected to have a clear run once they got through the perimeter.

51st Field Regiment, which scored a number of direct and indirect hits with high-explosive shells. One of the 51st's forward observation officers claimed that his guns disabled seven tanks during the morning. This may be so, but it was very difficult to tell which tank casualties were caused by mines and which by shells. It seems likely, however, that more than twenty German tanks were at least temporarily disabled by the combined defences during this eastward enemy move. It was unfortunate that, while so many German tanks were sitting shots in the minefield, there were no British tanks or mobile anti-tank guns in position to attack them; Morshead was fully occupied preparing to meet other and more serious threats. It was not yet certain that the thrust at Hill 209 was Rommel's main one. The fact that it had been made with so little attempt at surprise strongly suggested that it was only a blind.

There was already evidence that a diversion, at least, would be made from the south. During the night a patrol of six men of the 2/13th Battalion, led by Corporal G. V. Hewitt, had ambushed and put to flight about fifty Germans who were heading towards the wire near the El Adem road. As they fled, the Germans discarded their equipment, including a quantity of explosives and Bangalore torpedoes, and one of the six prisoners taken revealed that they were moving up to prepare the way for tanks. Before dawn enemy tanks had advanced to within 500 yards of the perimeter and had been driven back by shell-fire, and about 8.30 a.m. twenty of them made a further demonstration in this sector under cover of a smoke screen. Because of this threat and the possibility of another German attack in greater strength from the west, Morshead was reluctant to commit his few tanks until the enemy had definitely shown his hand.

Phase II. Widening the Breach

Rommel's first tank thrust had petered out by 9 a.m., but he was not to be denied, and he still had the bulk of his tanks in reserve. Air reconnaissance soon after dawn reported 400 of them between Acroma and 209. This suggested that Rommel had massed there all the tanks of his two German and one Italian armoured divisions. Another pilot at 9 a.m. could identify only 120 tanks in this area; the other vehicles, he said, were troop carriers. These 120 plus those inside the perimeter and others demonstrating on the El Adem sector made from

BATTLE OF THE SALIENT

180 to 200 in all. This was better news, but it was still very serious, for Morshead's nominal tank strength was 12 Matildas and 19 cruisers, some of which were out of action through mechanical faults. Consequently his tactics were to hold his tanks back until mines and shells had taken their toll of enemy strength. As in the Easter Battle, he had to pin his faith to the artillery.

Rommel also knew this and as soon as his tanks were checked in the minefield he intensified his attack on the British field gunners whose fire was covering it. Twice during the morning he sent thirty Stukas to bomb and strafe them and from behind 209 his artillery shelled them heavily but inaccurately. The guns would not be silenced and all through the morning they pounded 209, drove back delousing parties and shelled any tanks that approached the minefield or tried to move southwards along the perimeter.

This southward thrust became the main German attack when the eastward drive was checked. Since dawn two companies (i.e. squadrons) of German tanks—about forty in all—had supported the Panzer Pioneers and machine-gunners in attacking the posts south of 209. While one tank company moved along inside the line of posts to deal with British anti-tank guns, the other led infantry against the perimeter posts. The general tactics were that four or five tanks sat over each post in turn and drove the garrison below ground, while German infantry moved in for the final assault. At the same time a smaller force of tanks with Italian infantry was fighting its way northward to widen the bridgehead on that flank.

On the southern side of 209, Posts R1 and R2 had been subdued before 7 a.m., but when the tanks began to move south they were stubbornly opposed by four anti-tank guns of the 3rd R.H.A., which were dug in several hundred yards behind the inner line of concrete posts. Anticipating this opposition, the Germans had established machine-gunners well inside the wire and behind the anti-tank positions during the night.

Very few of these anti-tank gunners escaped and one Tommy, Sergeant Bettsworth (of "J" Battery, 3rd R.H.A.), whose gun and truck were dug in behind R8, later told me how his and other positions had been overwhelmed:

We saw the guns north of us shot up one by one as the tanks came down. Eventually they got within range of us and we were having a crack at a tank in front when five more came up on our flank. We swung the gun round to deal with them, and, as we did, German machine-gunners opened fire from behind. All my crew were wounded except the driver, but our truck wasn't hit and we managed to tow the gun back to R9. From there I saw another of our guns disable five German tanks before it was wiped out by the same tactics. Our guns could not do much when attacked from front, flank and rear, but even so it was several hours before all those between 209 and R8 were silenced.

As the tanks advanced along the line of posts, at least a dozen were put out of action by fire from anti-tank guns or anti-tank rifles, but this did not break up the German attacks, and individual posts had little chance against them. The enemy tactics were described to me by Corporal Bob McLeish, who was captured in R4 but eventually escaped from a prison camp near Derna:

When the fog lifted we saw about thirty tanks lined up near R2—half a mile to the west of us. The tanks dispersed, four or five going to each of the posts near by. Infantry followed in parties of about sixty. As they got within range we opened up and they went to ground, but four tanks came on. Their machine-guns kept our heads down and their cannon blasted away our sandbag parapets. The sand got into our MGs and we spent as much time cleaning them as we did firing them, but we sniped at the infantry whenever we got a chance. Our anti-tank rifle put one light tank out of action, but it couldn't check the heavier ones, which came right up to the post. We threw hand grenades at them but these bounced off, and the best we could do was to keep the infantry from getting closer than a hundred yards.

After about an hour of this fighting the tanks withdrew, but about ten o'clock more came back. They drove through the wire and one even cruised up and down over our communication trench dropping stick bombs into it. We held their infantry off most of the morning, but eventually under cover of this attack they got into one end of the post, where the Bren crew had all been wounded. Then the Germans worked along the trench while the rest of us were still firing from the other pits. By this time more than half our chaps—we'd only had fifteen—had been killed or wounded, and the Germans got command of the post before we survivors realized what had happened. Just then our artillery began shelling it heavily and the German tanks must have been driven off. So there we were, Germans and Aussies stuck in the post together with shells falling outside. A Jerry sergeant said, "I don't know who'll be the prisoners—you or us. We'd better wait awhile until the shelling stops." When the shelling stopped more Germans came in and the sergeant said, "You're the prisoners." And we were.

The Germans did not capture R4 until shortly after midday and although they used the same tactics against R6 during the morning it beat off several attacks by infantry and twelve tanks, one of which it disabled. When the tanks failed to reduce this post German infantry dug in behind it and kept it under fire until further tanks and infantry arrived.

According to the German diary already quoted, the Panzer Pioneers. even with tank support, had not enough fire-power to

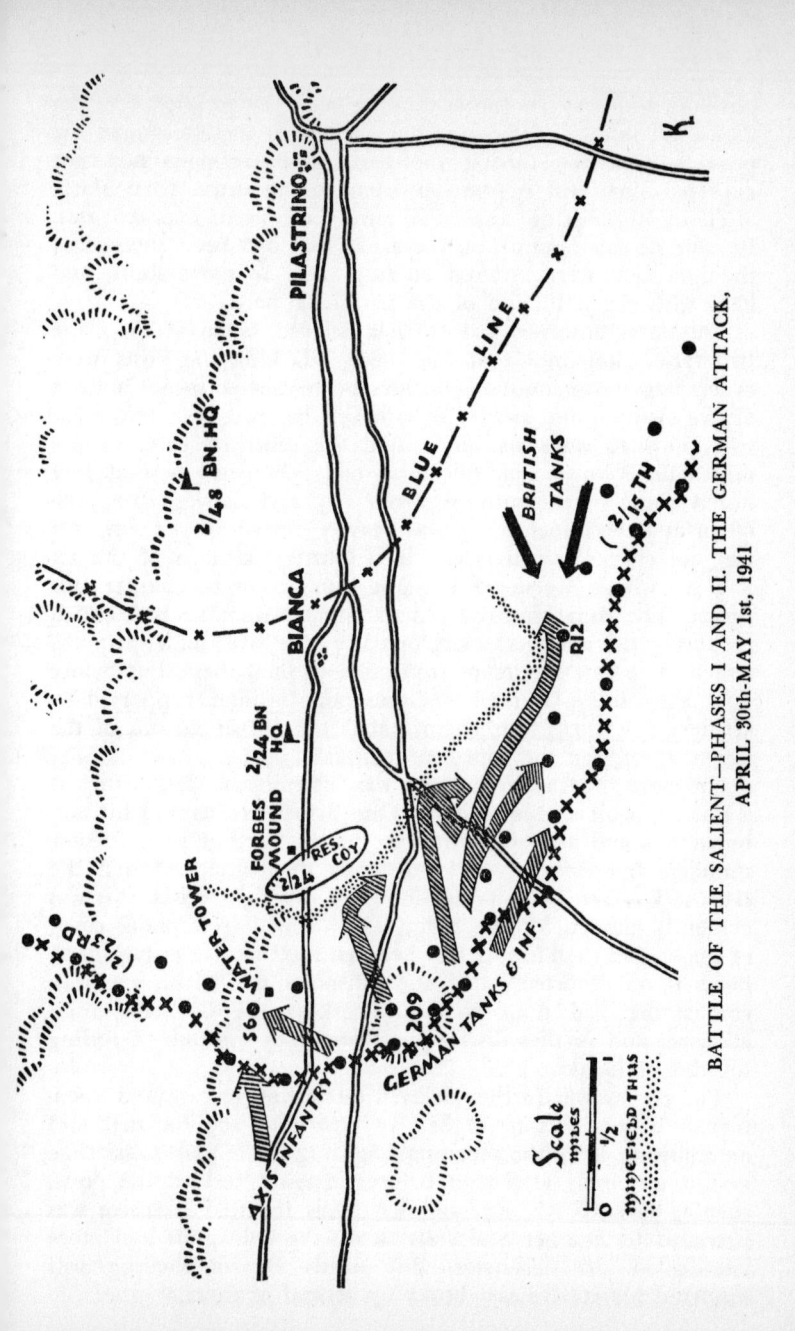

BATTLE OF THE SALIENT—PHASES I AND II. THE GERMAN ATTACK,
APRIL 30th-MAY 1st, 1941

push on, and heavy, accurate shelling made co-operation between tanks and infantry difficult. After the initial success against the posts around 209 during the night, the Germans had not expected such stiff opposition from the infantry, particularly after its supporting anti-tank guns had been knocked out. Because of this opposition, the tanks that had been checked at the minefield were ordered at 10.45 a.m. to move south and help with the reduction of the perimeter posts.

This task, however, was further delayed, when at 11.45 the two tank companies that had been attacking the posts were ordered to move south-east inside the perimeter to aid a force of five medium and twenty light tanks that had been trying for two hours to work its way round the southern flank of the minefield. By 9.30 a.m. this force had penetrated beyond R12 nearly three miles south-east from 209, and between the perimeter and the minefield. It was heavily shelled all the way, but was not checked until it ran into fourteen cruisers of the 1st R.T.R., which Morshead brought into action to counter this thrust. The thin-skinned German "lights" were no real match for the British and were soon forced to take cover under a smoke screen. The 51st Regiment continued to shell them, but before noon some more German mediums came up and, supported by artillery fire, thirty-four enemy tanks now advanced out of the smoke to engage the fourteen cruisers.

For more than an hour there was intermittent skirmishing at a range of half a mile or more. One British cruiser was hit and burnt out and another damaged, but in spite of their greater numbers the Germans did not press their attack. When the cruisers knocked out one medium and two light tanks, this was evidently enough for the enemy and he withdrew under cover of smoke and shell-fire. It had been an inconclusive engagement, but with only fourteen tanks at his disposal, the British squadron commander had done well in checking the German tanks' advance, and further distracting them from the task of rolling up the perimeter.

The enemy was further delayed (according to captured documents) because his tanks had to return to 209 for fuel and ammunition after the morning's fighting. This took some time and it was early afternoon before he again tackled the posts, turning now to R6, R7, and R8. This renewed offensive was preceded by another Stuka attack on the field guns and more strafing of the perimeter. But steady British shelling still hindered his attacks and broke up several of them.

Typical of this phase was the experience of the men in R8 which was told to me by the sergeant in command there, Ernest Thurman:

Soon after one o'clock twenty-four tanks advanced on R8 and R9, but they were slowed down by our anti-tank rifle fire. Riding on the back of some were engineers brought along to delouse minefields. We sniped them with our Brens and they jumped to the ground. We also held up the infantry who were following some distance back, and the tanks came on alone. Two mediums kept going till they were only fifty yards from us, but then they stopped, apparently afraid of a minefield that didn't exist. They raked the top of the post with machine-guns and cannon, and the crews even stood up in their turrets and threw stick bombs into our communication trench. But we still kept firing at both tanks and infantry. We'd take a few pot-shots and then duck before their machine-gun bullets thudded into our sandbags. This duel went on until about four o'clock when our artillery came down on them. Shells thundered round the post and the tanks cleared out towards 209. By this time half a dozen of my men were wounded and our Bren was out of action. As we couldn't have held out against another attack even by infantry, we withdrew to R10. From there we held off another German attack and, by keeping R8 covered with heavy fire, stopped the Germans occupying it.

The shelling, which made the German tanks abandon their attack on R8, broke up other attempts by them to organize a major drive down the line of posts. North of R6 at 3.30 p.m., one Australian counted fifty-three German tanks, but an hour later they had withdrawn to escape the British bombardment. All day, supply and ammunition trucks as well as lorried infantry and guns, which they had brought to the bridgehead, were heavily shelled. German prisoners spoke feelingly of the disorganization and delay this caused. In the late afternoon, while the enemy hesitated, British tanks made another attempt to drive him back.

This British force consisted of three cruisers and five "I" tanks. At 3.30 these had been ordered to move along the perimeter from the south-east and to re-establish control of each post in turn. Soon after 5 p.m. they reported that R6, R8 and R9 had been attacked but were still held by the 2/24th. From R6 they saw about fifteen German tanks near R4 and three more on the wire at R3. The British attacked and lost one cruiser in driving off these three, but while doing so, exposed themselves to a flank attack by the fifteen which advanced from R4. One Matilda was hit and although it was not knocked out all the crew except the driver were killed. The fire from the German tanks and the artillery supporting them was so heavy that the surviving British tanks were forced to withdraw, firing as they went. As they pulled back a new threat developed from fourteen fresh tanks that came up on their right flank. Describing this, Sergeant Stockley, who commanded one of the Matildas, said:

Jerry tanks seemed to attack us from all sides. One cruiser was disabled and the other, because of its light armour, had to withdraw leaving us four to fight it out. They had the advantage of being on lower ground, which made us skyline targets. We were all hit many times, but our heavier armour saved us and we kept the Jerry tanks off until it became hard to tell theirs from ours in the half light. Finally we ran short of ammo. and fuel so we had to break away, but we couldn't keep up our rate of fire and they closed in. Two more of our tanks were knocked out. As we came back one "I" tank tried to tow a crippled cruiser to safety, but it had to be left behind when a chance shell shot away the tow-rope.

This brought the total British casualties in the action to six. Two "I" tanks had been destroyed and two temporarily disabled; two cruisers had also been burnt out. The Germans had had four tanks badly damaged. The British tanks, however, might have had greater success if they had not been used in "penny packets".

It has been proved that it is better to risk all your tanks in one bold action than to fritter them away in several. Throughout May 1st Morshead always kept a third of his tanks in reserve, with the result that in each action the British tanks were more heavily outnumbered than they might have been. Morshead, however, was in a dilemma. Most of his tanks were old and in bad mechanical condition. He did not know which was the enemy's main thrust nor how severe that might prove to be, for aerial reports were conflicting. Consequently during the morning he kept his tank forces divided and disposed to meet a thrust from the west and from the south as well. He was reluctant to counter-attack with them, because they were needed as a final reserve to deal with any deep penetration. He used them in the morning only in a defensive role, when the Germans threatened to outflank the minefield, and he could not then employ all his tanks since he had them dispersed in three groups.

These considerations explain the handling of the tanks in the morning, but they do not account for the failure to mass all the Matildas and cruisers for a major attack in the afternoon, once the tanks had been ordered to restore the position south of 209. At that stage the German tanks were still dispersed attacking the perimeter posts and recovering from their earlier mauling, but the Tobruk tank commander, Colonel H. L. Birks, sent in barely a third of the available tanks and used even those in twos and threes. A bold stroke at this time might have driven the enemy tanks back before his infantry had been able to consolidate its position on the southern flank of 209, and would have greatly assisted the Australian infantry when they counter-attacked at dusk. Morshead himself admits this to be fair criticism. It is, however, very easy to criticize after the event, when all the facts are known.

The British tanks used for this late afternoon attack took severe punishment, but did hold up the enemy's advance until it was too late for him to push on. Even though the British were forced to withdraw, the enemy did not follow them. He was evidently dissuaded from doing so by the heavy bombardment, for which the British tanks called by radio as they broke off the engagement. Instead of pressing their advantage, the German tanks turned back to help their infantry, who were still held up at R6 and R7.

This time the Germans attacked R6 in force. All day they had been exerting strong pressure against it and for several hours two heavy tanks had stood off some seventy-five yards and tried to blast the garrison into submission. Under cover of this fire, enemy infantry had attempted to rush the post but had been repeatedly stopped. Several times the Australian machine-guns had been put out of action, but Corporal A. A. Francis, although wounded twice and working only with a nail file, had got them going again. But, as dusk fell, a battalion of infantry attacked with the support of tanks and flame-throwers.[4] By this time direct hits had knocked out both machine-guns in R6, and half the garrison of fourteen, including its commander (Captain A. C. Bird), had become casualties. Its strength was now so reduced that in the face of this fresh German attack it was forced to surrender at 7.30 p.m.

Simultaneously the Germans attacked R7, but it managed to hold out until the following morning. We know little of what happened in R3 and R5 because the survivors were all captured, but it is known that they were attacked from both inside and outside the wire and that flame-throwers were used against them. While these three posts were holding out they were dive-bombed and machine-gunned by German planes and must have received a severe hammering before they were captured. The strength of their resistance is indicated by the slow enemy pro-

---

[4] Mounted on a light tank chassis, these were more spectacular than effective. They threw out spurts of flame thirty feet long and nine feet high, but were very vulnerable to fire from the Boyes anti-tank rifle. The enemy soon stopped using them.

gress during the day. Between dawn and dark he had advanced barely a mile from 209 and had taken only five posts.

At 7 p.m., soon after the tank battle ended, the commander of the 5th German Tank Regiment was ordered to prepare for a major drive south-east along the perimeter with his 2nd Battalion plus German and Italian infantry and part of the Ariete Armoured Division. If this force could widen the bridgehead beyond the southern end of the minefield, which had blocked the advance that day, the way would be clear for a deep thrust on the morrow. But at 8 p.m., as they were getting ready for this new attack, the Axis tanks were urgently recalled to 209 to meet a counter-attack that Australian infantry had launched half an hour earlier. Without their tanks the Axis infantry could make no further progress and as darkness fell they began to dig in around R7. That evening men of the 2/1st Pioneers were sent to reinforce the posts on this flank and to prepare a switch-line running eastwards to the minefield to stop the fresh thrust that the Germans were expected to make in the morning, if not earlier.

Meantime the enemy advance had been similarly checked on the northern flank of 209. We do not know what happened there in the morning of May 1st because no one escaped from the area he over-ran. By 7.30 a.m. he had gained possession of five strongpoints on Hill 209 and north of it, but it took him all the morning to advance a thousand yards and subdue the next three (S5, S6 and S7). During the afternoon Italian infantry, without tank support, could make little impression on the next three posts—S8, S9 and S10, held by part of the 2/24th's right company. Back in Spowers's H.Q., however, no one knew what had happened to these three posts, for all signal communications with them had broken down. In the late afternoon therefore Tovell ordered the battalion on Spowers's right, the 2/23rd, to re-establish contact with, or, if necessary, control of, these three positions. Captain Ian Malloch's company went out at dusk. Their advance was greeted by mortars and artillery. Bren carriers protecting their flank drew shells from Axis anti-tank guns. They found that S10 was still held by Lieutenant J. S. Rosel and half a dozen men, although it was under heavy fire from positions beyond. These seven had beaten off several enemy attacks and had only a thousand rounds of ammunition left.

While one of Malloch's platoons helped to silence nearby machine-guns, his other two pushed on to S8 and S9. At the former five unwounded survivors were still holding on, though they too were down to their last few hundred rounds. When Lieutenant J. N. Bowden's platoon got near S9 they found the enemy had surrounded it, but after a short hand-to-hand struggle with Italians in the anti-tank ditch around the post they captured thirty-three of them and fought their way through to the relief of Lieutenant J. S. Christie and five men. Christie told them that at dusk, under cover of heavy machine-gun fire from the escarpment near S7, Italian infantry had succeeded in getting up to the anti-tank ditch around S9, but had been pinned down there by small arms fire and grenades. Soon after dark, the position in this area was fully restored and the enemy attempt to widen the bridgehead on the northern flank had been stopped. Everything now depended on the counter-attack that the 2/48th Battalion had launched against 209 from the east.

By dark the Germans had been checked on the perimeter both north and south of 209. They had captured fifteen posts on a 3-mile front but had paid heavily for their gains. They had spared no effort and were baffled by the strength of the resistance and alarmed now at the prospect of counter-attack. Schorm's diary shows this clearly:

It is now late afternoon. Dive-bombers and twin-engined fighters have been attacking the enemy constantly. In spite of this the British repeatedly counter-thrust with tanks. As soon as our planes have gone their artillery starts up furiously. It is beginning to grow dark. Which is friend, which is foe? Shots are being fired all over the place, often on our own troops and on tanks in front, which are on their way back. Suddenly a wireless message—"The British are attacking the gap with infantry."

Phase III. Counter-attack and Stalemate

The infantry counter-attack was made by the 2/48th Battalion. Morshead had intended to launch this attack during the afternoon, but had been distracted by a threat from the south. Consequently it was 4.45 p.m. before the 2/48th's C.O., Lieutenant-Colonel W. J. V. Windeyer, received his final orders to counter-attack westward that evening at 7.15, retake Hill 209, and drive the enemy outside the perimeter. Windeyer asked that the attack be delayed until the following dawn for these reasons: no tanks were available; there was no time for reconnaissance and little for preparation of an adequate artillery programme; and his battalion was widely dispersed on a 5-mile front in the Blue Line. Morshead replied that, in view of the dangerous situation developing on the perimeter south-east of 209, delay might be serious, and that, in spite of the difficulties, the attack must be made that evening. But he added that British tanks would protect Windeyer's left flank by continuing to engage the German tanks.

With only two and a half hours in which to get his troops to their start-line, Windeyer had a difficult task, particularly as this was the first time his men had made a battalion attack, and this task was made the more difficult by enemy aircraft. Attracted by the dust of the transport bringing the 2/10th to take over the 2/48th's section of the Blue Line, they swooped on it just as the battalions were changing over. This and a duststorm caused such delay that the 2/48th were twenty minutes late in reaching the start-line about half a mile west of Bianca. The enemy's complete command of the air gave him ample warning and the Australians were heavily shelled as they debussed. This caused further casualties and delay, and by the time they moved off their artillery barrage had already lifted too far ahead to give them the support that had been planned.

To make matters worse, the troops had little information as to how far the enemy had penetrated and they could not now pick out his positions in the bad light and the dust raised by the wind and shelling. Carriers were sent forward to draw fire from enemy machine-guns in the hope of discovering where these were, but they were driven back by anti-tank fire.

The general line of the attack was down the Acroma road—a dirt track leading due west from Bianca and crossing the perimeter half a mile north of 209. "D" Company was ordered to advance along the right of this road, while "A", on the left, struck direct for 209 along a track that these South Australians had named "Pirie Street". "B" Company of the 2/24th was ordered to move from its reserve position westwards down the Acroma road in conjunction with the 2/48th's advance.

In spite of the shelling, "D" Company advanced more than a mile before it was checked just at dark by severe fire from anti-tank and machine-guns emplaced near S4 and S6. Forced to bear off to the right, it lost contact with the company on its left. The Australians tried to get forward in bounds, but the enemy fire became heavier and they were finally pinned down 250 yards short of the German positions. The company Sergeant-Major (E. A. Noble) told me later that as they advanced the Germans in front of them pulled back, but those on the flanks held their ground. "And so we were soon being shot up from our front and both flanks," he said. "We couldn't use our

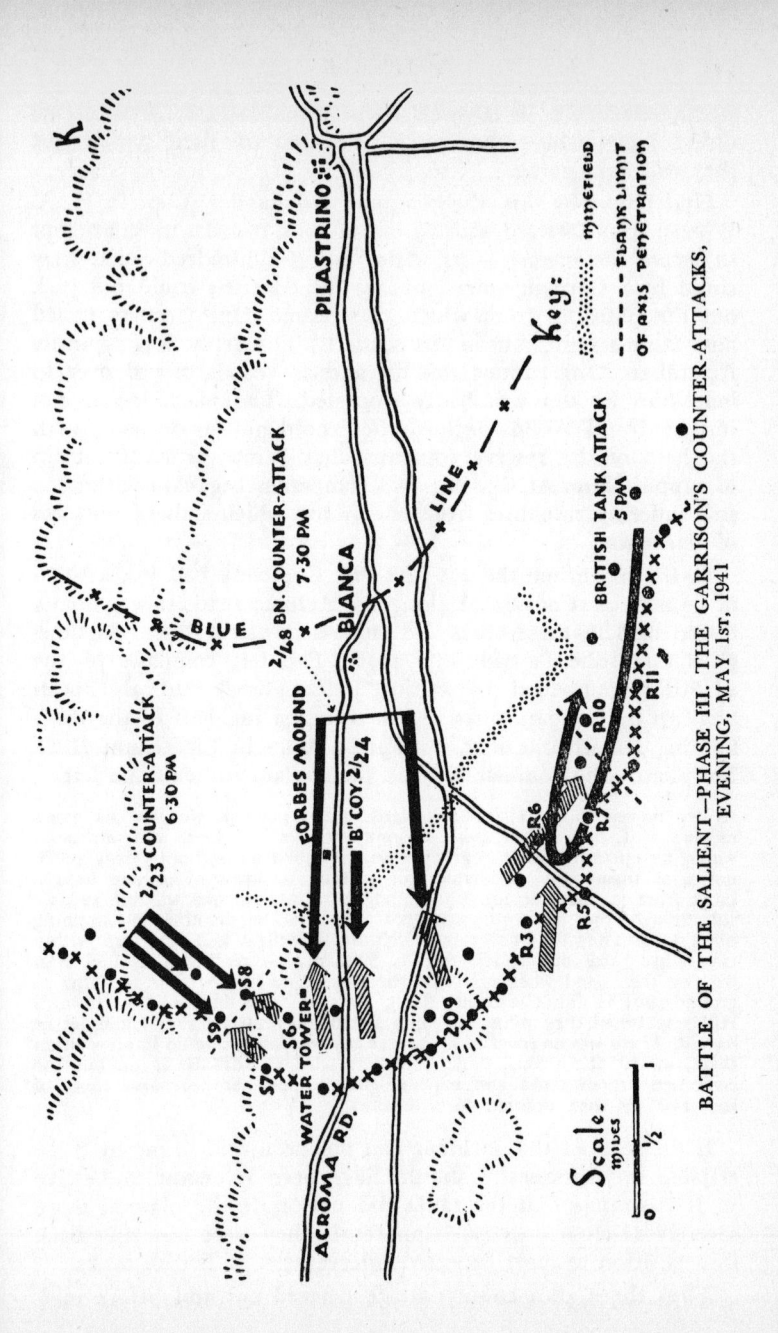

BATTLE OF THE SALIENT—PHASE III. THE GARRISON'S COUNTER-ATTACKS, EVENING, MAY 1st, 1941

Brens effectively to answer their machine-guns, because we didn't know where they were. We fired on their flashes but they still kept going."

Undeterred by this, the company commander (Captain H. A. Woods) crept forward with Noble and two runners in an attempt to locate the enemy posts. After going a hundred yards they could hear German voices, but in the darkness could not pick out the positions from which these came. One German called out, "Come here, Aussie. Surrender!" The reply was typically Australian. One runner was hit and as Woods moved over to help him he too was badly wounded. The machine-gun fire increased and Woods decided they could not go on, even with the help of the reserve company that Windeyer had sent up to support him. At 9.30 the two companies began to withdraw, still suffering casualties from enemy fire which showed no signs of slackening.

In the meantime the 2/24th's "B" Company had lost a third of its men as it advanced along the Acroma road. It was finally forced back by three tanks and more than half a dozen machine-guns established astride the road. The left company of the 2/48th (commanded by Major J. Loughrey) had also been held up by German tanks in the strangest incident in the day's fighting. An account of this was given to me by Lieutenant H. C. Morphett, who commanded the platoon on the extreme left.

> As we moved down Pirie St. towards the minefield, we saw six tanks moving west, half a mile away on our left. We had been told our tanks would be operating in that area so we continued on without taking much notice of them. But when they got within 150 yards of us one fired a burst from its machine-gun right along our line. No one was hit and we still thought they were ours and that they must be shooting at something beyond us. They followed us through the minefield and came up within twenty-five yards of our left section. Suddenly we realized they had Nazi flags on them, and when one tank fired again we lost no time in going to ground. But it didn't continue firing and the tanks filed past us towards Hill 209. When they were 300 yards ahead, they turned round and let us have it. There was no cover at all and as our weapons made no impression on them, we lay there until dark. Then we tried to advance again, but the combined fire of tanks and machine-guns stopped us 500 yards short of 209, and we were ordered to withdraw.

If the story of this incident had not been told to me by three reliable eye-witnesses, I should have been reluctant to believe it. It is strange that the tanks did not strafe the platoon more severely at close quarters. Apparently they were hurrying back into position to meet expected intervention of British tanks.

Thus the 2/48th counter-attack petered out and before midnight the battalion was back at Bianca. It had not achieved its main objective—the recapture of 209—primarily because the assisting fire was insufficient. It had no Vickers gun support and, having lost the advantage of the barrage, its own fire-power was not enough to carry it through. Nevertheless, it had stopped two dangerous German moves. As we saw earlier, the enemy's plan to attack in force southwards along the perimeter at dusk had petered out when his tanks had been rushed back to 209 to ward off the 2/48th's attack.[5] This gave Morshead time to establish fresh anti-tank guns and infantry on the southern flank of the enemy salient. Similarly he was able to consolidate the position on the northern flank.

Most important of all, however, the 2/48th forced the enemy on to the defensive and stopped him sending sappers forward after dark to delouse the minefield that had checked his tanks during the first morning. Late in the afternoon half a dozen German tanks had found a way through the minefield, but they had been withdrawn when the counter-attack was launched. The 2/48th might have achieved even more if, instead of withdrawing to the Blue Line after the attack, it had been ordered to dig in on the east side of the tactical minefield. Its advance had driven the enemy back west of this field, and the ground it had recovered might well have been held. As it was, when dawn broke on May 2nd, there was nothing between the Germans and Bianca, except the minefield, for even the 2/24th's reserve company had been withdrawn from its position near Forbes Mound—a small rise just north of the Acroma road and a mile west of Bianca—named after Captain W. Forbes of the 2/48th.

The way was open and the Germans were expected to attack again at first light on May 2nd. But by then a heavy duststorm blanketed Tobruk, making movement difficult and serious attack unlikely. Small parties of Germans felt their way forward in half-hearted probings, but the enemy made no concerted drive. The storm gave the garrison time to bring up fresh infantry, form a new switch-line to contain the enemy salient and move more field and anti-tank guns to cover it. All day British gunners poured shell after shell into enemy-held areas, while Australian infantry dug new positions and sappers laid new minefields. But even as they fired and worked, they did not know when

---

[5] The 2/48th had 52 casualties in this attack. One officer and 14 men were killed or died of wounds; three officers and 34 other ranks were wounded.

the storm would raise its curtain and reveal the stage set for another German thrust.

May 2nd was a gunners' day even more than May 1st; their heavy fire disorganized any plans the Germans had of renewing the attack when the storm abated. All through the 2nd, very little stood between the Germans in the Salient and the guns that harassed them so persistently, and the enemy's forward troops even crept right to Bianca itself, where the 51st Regiment's observation post was established on a low knoll. The Germans were held up by the only force available there—two Vickers guns of the Northumberland Fusiliers, an Australian anti-tank gun and small arms fire from the artillery observation party. That was all.

From this exposed position on Bianca, Captain Braddock of the 51st directed fire all through May 2nd—and May 3rd also. His guns kept firing in spite of enemy dive-bombing, and of machine-gunning from ground and air. The duststorm on May 2nd hampered the movements of both forces, but in the morning Braddock observed small parties of enemy infantry working their way forward on the Tobruk side of the minefield. They were evidently trying to cover delousing parties, but accurate shelling disturbed them. Nevertheless, they cleared some gaps; but again the gunners blocked the tanks from coming through.

That afternoon in an attempt to silence the artillery, the Germans pushed machine-gunners forward to shoot up the most advanced troop of British guns. But even this did not deter the Tommies. While some kept the guns going, others engaged enemy snipers with rifles and Brens. All day the artillery maintained its fire on enemy working parties, transport and tanks, which could be picked out whenever the storm momentarily cleared. But in the early evening more Germans moved up and the sniping became so severe that during the night the forward guns were withdrawn to alternative positions.

Late on the afternoon of the 2nd there was a heavy air raid on the field artillery and during the night it was spasmodically shelled. At dawn on May 3rd, with the 2/10th manning the northern flank of the Salient between the perimeter and Bianca and the 2/1st Pioneers covering the southern sector, the garrison stood-to, expecting Rommel to attack again in force when the storm cleared, as it did during the morning. Then a large number of enemy tanks and vehicles could be seen east of 209

BATTLE OF THE SALIENT

near the minefield. At once the gunners put down a bombardment so intense that the vehicles promptly cleared out and the tanks gradually withdrew behind 209. During the rest of the day the enemy made no aggressive move. He had suffered so heavily that he could not afford to go on.

The garrison's losses had been comparatively light: out of 12 "I" tanks, 2 destroyed, 2 damaged; out of 19 cruisers, 3 destroyed, 1 damaged. The severest losses had been suffered by the infantry—especially the 2/24th. On May 2nd it was below half-strength, for 314 men (including 10 officers), who had been in the forward posts were missing, most of them prisoners. One officer and 13 men were known to have been killed and 25 men wounded. That was a sad day for the battalion, but it had the compensation of knowing that but for the stubborn resistance by the forward posts, German tanks might have done much greater damage.

The enemy's tank losses had been particularly severe, as we know from a captured document, which showed that the 5th Tank Regiment went in with 81 on May 1st, but twenty-four hours later had in action only 35. The table of losses it gave explains much:

Type	Into Action—May 1st	Still in Action—May 2nd
Lights—Mk I	9	3
—Mk II	26	12
Mediums—Mk III	36	12
Heavies—Mk IV	8	6
Commander's tanks	2	2
	81	35

Only 12 of the 46 disabled tanks were completely destroyed, but before the rest were again fit for action the time for further attack had passed. Moreover the severe losses suffered by the 5th Tank Regiment apparently made Rommel reluctant to risk any tanks of his 8th Regiment. Once again the German armour had been defeated, and this time the effectiveness of minefields plus artillery fire in stopping tanks had been clearly demonstrated. Thirty-nine of the German tanks had been destroyed or disabled by mines or shells, only seven by the British tanks. This was the first time that any major attack had been broken by these tactics. The success was local but the lesson was universal. In Poland, Belgium and France, Rommel and the German tank battalions had never struck any resistance so effective as that of Tobruk. Their failure shook the morale of the tank crews in particular. As one German officer wrote in his diary. "What we experienced in Poland and the Western Front was only a promenade compared to this."

When he learned what the 5th Tank Regiment lost on May 1st, Rommel must have realized that he could not afford to continue incurring such severe casualties, especially as he had to keep at least one battalion of tanks watching the Egyptian frontier. In two actions within a fortnight one of his crack tank regiments had been so badly knocked about that it needed substantial reinforcement and re-equipment. If he tried to batter his way through Tobruk's minefields and past Tobruk's guns, he would probably lose twice as many tanks as he had lost on May 1st. Inside its perimeter there were 220 square miles; of these he had captured only six, and he was little nearer to capturing Tobruk. The garrison had stopped him on May 1st without the use of Morshead's final reserves. The Germans had not penetrated even as far as the Blue Line except at Bianca, and Morshead still held in reserve a dozen tanks and the 18th Infantry Brigade. With the enemy attack stopped and his tanks forced to withdraw outside the perimeter, the time had come for another counter-stroke by the garrison. On the night of May 3rd Morshead sent in Brigadier G. F. Wootten's 18th Brigade in a determined attempt to regain the lost ground.

Brigadier George Frederick Wootten, one of the first graduates of Duntroon, was generally regarded by the men of his year as one of the ablest of them. He went straight from Duntroon to the 1st A.I.F. and on Gallipoli was Adjutant of the 1st Battalion. By the end of the war he was a staff officer on Haig's G.H.Q., had won the D.S.O. and been mentioned in dispatches five times. After that war, he did a brilliant course at the Camberley Staff College, but in 1923 he left the Army and studied Law. He practised as a solicitor until he went away with the 2nd A.I.F. as C.O. 2/2nd Battalion. Early in 1941 he succeeded Morshead as Commander 18th Infantry Brigade, and commanded it at Giarabub, in Tobruk and later at Milne Bay and Buna. In April 1943 he succeeded Morshead as G.O.C., 9th Division and led it to new triumphs at Lae and Finschafen. In these campaigns, he proved himself one of the most shrewd and long-headed commanders in the A.I.F. His Falstaffian appearance is misleading; in spite of his bulk, he is extremely nimble in mind. The task he now undertook called for all his ability.

BATTLE OF THE SALIENT

Phase IV. The Second Counter-attack

At a conference on May 2nd Murray, Wootten and Lloyd had urged Morshead to counter-attack with the 18th Brigade either that night or at dawn next day; but because of the duststorm and the general uncertainty as to the enemy's position and intention, Morshead decided to wait. Before employing his reserve brigade to regain any ground, he wanted to be reasonably sure that he would not need it to stop another enemy thrust. Consequently it was not until the morning of the 3rd, when Rommel still showed no signs of pressing on, that Morshead decided to make this counter-attack.

The plan was for two battalions to attack the shoulders of the Salient on the general line of the old perimeter, retake the lost posts and cut off the enemy spearhead. The 2/12th were to attack from the north against S6 and S7, and the 2/9th from the south-east against R8 and R7. After the capture of these, both battalions were to push on to Hill 209. Meantime the 2/10th, which was holding the northern flank of the Salient, was to make deep raids into enemy territory. The attack was intended to start at dark, but as the 2/12th and 2/9th moved across the dusty desert to their start-lines in the late afternoon, the garrison learned for the first time what a decided advantage the enemy had in holding 209. From there he saw them coming, and shelled and mortared them as they assembled for the attack. Because of this, the battalions were delayed and zero hour had to be put forward until 8.45 p.m., by which time darkness had set in.

Then, under cover of a concentration put down by twenty-four guns, the 2/12th advanced against S6 and S7 and right into the fire from machine-guns that were waiting for them. Flares went up from the forward German positions to mark the sector being attacked and down came severe mortar and artillery fire. This hindered the advance, and the infantry could not keep up with our barrage; when that had lifted from the S6-S7 area, machine-guns firing from there brought the attack to a standstill. The troops did not know the country, and even though they made several attempts to move forward, they could not locate the enemy positions. The leading companies lost their way, and the attack petered out.

Meantime, on the southern flank the 2/9th had been more successful. They had been heavily shelled before zero, but had attacked strongly when the British barrage began. On the right,

"A" Company (under Captain E. W. Fleming) went for R8, with Lieutenant W. H. Noyes's platoon in the lead. In the darkness Noyes missed R8, but farther on found the enemy strongly established behind a stone wall. As Noyes said afterwards:

> They had more than a dozen anti-tank and machine-guns firing straight down the road that runs along the perimeter through R8 and R6, but we kept clear of their tracers and went in with the bayonet and grenades. Eventually we drove them out, but by this time I'd lost about a third of the platoon. Then down the road from R6 came three light tanks—Italian. My sergeant,[6] three men and myself sneaked up and dealt with them by lifting the turret lids and dropping hand grenades inside. The tanks burst into flame and everything opened up on them. We moved on. Near R6 we found some more Germans and Italians in shallow diggings. We cleaned up several of these positions, but we then ran into a strong party in a half-dug anti-tank ditch. We had only half a dozen men left so I decided to go back and find the rest of the company. On the way we stumbled into R8. There was no one there.

The Germans had never occupied the post and there Noyes's men were soon joined by the bulk of Captain B. M. Lovett's company, which then made another attempt to get to R6, but lost its way and finished up at R7. This post had already been strongly attacked by the 2/9th's "D" Company, led by Captain F. E. C. Loxton. Some of his men had got as far as the anti-tank ditch surrounding the post, but had eventually been driven back by flame-throwers. Lovett's company now succeeded in driving the Germans out of R7, but almost immediately were forced to withdraw by a counter-attack supported with tanks and flame-throwers.

The enemy fire grew fiercer and in the darkness and the confusion of battle it was impossible to organize fresh attacks before daylight. Soon after 3 a.m. Morshead gave the order to withdraw, rather than risk having his troops caught in the open at dawn by dive-bombers, artillery and machine-guns. They did so without further difficulty, for the enemy was already too shaken by his heavy losses to interfere. All next day his stretcher-bearers and ambulances were carrying dead and wounded away from the battlefield. Many of his casualties were caused by the raids launched by the 2/10th against the northern flank of the Salient during the main attacks. A platoon led by Lieutenant F. W. Cook charged one machine-gun post with the bayonet and accounted for eighteen Germans. In another post Private A. T. Taylor with a tommy gun killed six Germans single-handed.

By dawn on May 4th the 2/9th and the 2/12th were back in reserve behind the Blue Line. They had suffered 134

---
[6] R. W. Hobson.

BATTLE OF THE SALIENT

casualties, but had inflicted much heavier losses on the enemy, even though they had not regained any ground except R8.

The 18th Brigade's casualties in the action were:

	Killed	Missing	Wounded
2/9th	3	3	51
2/10th	—	6	15
2/12th	5	15	57

During the night the Australians took twenty-three prisoners.

The Germans had received a particularly severe pasting from the British gunners. Although these men had been in action almost continuously for three days and three nights, they excelled themselves on this occasion. It was a considerable achievement to amass the ammunition and work out the fire programme in the short time at their disposal. The thirty-nine guns of the 51st Field Regiment, and of the 104th and 1st R.H.A. which supported the attack, fired more than 10,000 rounds in two and a half hours. One of Braddock's guns fired 375 rounds. "By the finish," he said, "you could have fried eggs on it."

It must have been equally hot at the receiving end, for the barrage, and the 2/9th's attack in particular, made the Germans realize that they could hold the Salient only by building strong defences and packing them with their best troops. This they proceeded to do. They were so much on the defensive that during May 4th, when the 2/9th took over a sector of the Salient front south of Bianca, it soon pushed the German outposts back more than half a mile in a series of impromptu local skirmishes. Schorm's diary for May 3rd reveals something of the effect the counter-attack had on the Germans. He wrote:

At 1.15 a.m. a message to the commander: "Australians have penetrated the defences between R1 and R7. Immediately counter-attack and cover with tanks." Wireless message: "Ready for action." Oh Hell! Where to? No idea. Italians argue and gesticulate wildly. I start by going as far as the gap, then turn right. No officer knows the position. Near R7 an Italian tank is burning. The Australians have gone back leaving 26 dead behind them. The Italians are absolutely in confusion. They have been under heavy artillery fire. Of 150 men occupying R7 there are more than 100 dead or wounded.

Three days later he wrote:

Our opponents are Englishmen and Australians. Not trained attacking troops, but men with nerves and toughness, tireless, taking punishment with obstinacy, wonderful in defence. Ah well, the Greeks also spent ten years before Troy.

Schorm's reaction was apparently typical and after this the Germans were forced on to the defensive for the first time in this war. Troops who had been used to trampling all opponents underfoot regarded it as humiliating to have to dig in. The Battle of the Salient was another major defeat for Rommel, even though he did gain a small amount of territory. He had set out to capture Tobruk; actually he had captured little more than Hill 209. He had complete command of the air; overwhelming tank superiority; strong artillery support and far more infantry than the garrison. He employed the Blitzkrieg tactics of combined dive-bomber and tank assault which had succeeded so well in the Nazis' European campaigns. Probably not one German who went into the May 1st attack doubted that the Fortress would fall within a few hours, as it had done when the Australians and British had attacked it only three months earlier. For the first time in this war a determined German offensive had been broken.

This battle, like the rest, was often fought again in Tobruk messes in later months, and several times I heard it argued that Rommel might have been completely defeated and driven from Hill 209 if one or other of certain courses of action had been followed—if, according to some, the 26th Brigade had organized a strong infantry counter-attack during the night of April 30th-May 1st, or at least at dawn on the 1st; or again, if all the British tanks had been employed together for one major attack on the German tanks during May 1st; or yet again, if the counter-attack by the reserve brigade had been delivered on the night of the 2nd instead of the night of the 3rd. It is easy to fight the battle again after the dust and smoke have died away. Maybe when the full facts are known it will be discovered that if one or other, or all three, of these courses had been adopted, and if there had been more boldness in the direction of the defence, the Germans might have been driven right back beyond Hill 209. Alternatively it may be shown that the risks entailed in trying to save a little might have lost the lot. Whether these criticisms are right or wrong, the fact remains that in spite of everything Rommel could do, Morshead and his men not only held the Fortress but inflicted such heavy casualties that Rommel did not seriously attack Tobruk again in 1941.

What the checking of Rommel meant to the defence of Egypt and the general conduct of the war was well summed up in

BATTLE OF THE SALIENT

two signals Morshead received from Wavell and Churchill after this battle. They read:

"Personal Gen. MORSHEAD from C.-in-C. Your magnificent defence is upsetting enemy's plans for attack on EGYPT and giving us time to build up force for counter offensive. You could NOT repeat NOT be doing better service. Well done."

"To General MORSHEAD from PRIME MINISTER ENGLAND. The whole empire is watching your steadfast and spirited defence of this important outpost of EGYPT with gratitude and admiration."

CHAPTER XII

Rommel Changes his Tune

At midnight on May 6th a destroyer slipped into Tobruk harbour and the captain went ashore. From Navy H.Q. on the waterfront he telephoned General Morshead and said that he had a Most Secret dispatch from G.H.Q., Cairo, which he could hand only to the general himself. "Would you deliver it to my 'G.1.', Colonel Lloyd?" asked Morshead. "Very well," said the captain. "Can he come down at once? I can't afford to stay too long."

An hour later back at Fortress H.Q. Morshead broke the seals on the double envelopes and drew out a copy of an enemy radio message which G.H.Q. had intercepted. It was from the German Supreme Command in the Mediterranean—to Rommel. It had been sent on May 3rd in reply to his reports on the first two days of the Salient Battle.

When he received it, Rommel—the vain and arrogant conqueror of Cyrenaica—must have raged. It was a most severe reprimand for his conduct of the campaign and for what his superiors regarded as reckless wastage of his forces. It said that he had gone too far and too fast; that casualties on the scale of the 1700 he had suffered in the past two days were excessive and could not be supported; that he was not to attack Tobruk again, nor to advance into Egypt except for purposes of reconnaissance; and that he was to hold his present positions at Tobruk and on the frontier, conserve his forces, and make no further attacks.

For Rommel it was a "rocket"; for Morshead it was a relief, determined and confident though he was that his Fortress could and would be held. Only that afternoon there had been a small skirmish in the Salient between some of the 2/1st Pioneers and the Germans. It had shown that the enemy was there in great strength. The Australians were holding only a hastily improvised line without adequate protection of wire or minefields. In the words of Lloyd, "Until we got this 'intercept', it was a mystery to us why Rommel wasn't coming on."

The revelation in this message that the Germans had suffered 1700 casualties in the first two days was Morshead's first definite information as to the casualties his own troops had inflicted. Most of these 1700 were Germans, for the Italians played a very minor part in the attack. Axis casualties for the three days must have been about 2000, for in the 18th Brigade's counter-attack on the night of May 3rd-4th the enemy had over 100 casualties in Post R7 alone, according to a captured diary. By contrast, the garrison's losses were only 797—including 59 killed, 355 wounded and 383 missing. In the three weeks since the siege began the Axis forces must have had nearly 5000 casualties, for more than 1800 had been taken prisoner. In that period, also, about a quarter of Rommel's German tanks and very nearly half his aircraft had been destroyed or badly damaged at Tobruk and on the frontier.

With the start of the Russian campaign only seven weeks away, Hitler could not spare enough men, tanks or aircraft for Rommel to continue losses at this rate—especially as the British Navy and the R.A.F. were sinking an increasingly large proportion of the supply ships running the narrows from Sicily to Tripoli, and had made Bengazi virtually useless as a port. Sound as this policy of restraint might have been for the German Supreme Command, however, it appeared to Rommel merely the result of stupidity in high places; the decision of headquarters' blockheads, who, through jealousy, timidity or lack of faith, were robbing him of the victory that was within his grasp.

To his major-generals, von Ravenstein, Summerman and Neumann-Silkow, he railed against the decision, and declared that when he got the chance he would take Tobruk no matter what happened. He would show the Supreme Command the stupidity of its caution. But meantime frustration roused his fury, and the capture of Tobruk became an obsession. Von Ravenstein and others warned him that he would only dissipate his strength trying to take it and that the real threat was from the frontier, but Rommel would not listen. The whole conduct of his campaign in the next six months was governed by his determination to build up the forces necessary to take Tobruk. For him the issue was personal. He saw himself as the potential conqueror of Egypt and the Canal, and here he was, baulked on the threshold of triumph by this impudent garrison. Yet his Supreme Command would not let him make another attempt with what strength he had, nor would it give him sufficient reinforcements to make the capture a certainty.

When he received this reprimand, Rommel was still convinced that he could take Tobruk, if only he were allowed to go on. But his generals, and especially von Ravenstein, who had commanded the May attack and knew the strength of the defences and the tenacity of the garrison, thought otherwise. He realized it was not a single problem. There were two other vital factors —the vulnerability of the long Axis supply line, and the growing strength of the British forces on the frontier. These factors were almost as important in relation to the holding of Tobruk after the first month as were the strength and spirit of the garrison itself.

Throughout 1941 North Africa was very much a subsidiary front for Hitler. By June he had more than 150 German divisions opposing Russia, but he could still spare only two for Rommel, and in the next six months the Afrika Korps received little reinforcement. It may be that Hitler—and Rommel— thought that two German and seven Italian divisions would be able to fight their way through to Suez; both of them had consistently underestimated the fighting worth of the British forces. But it is more likely that in 1941 Rommel was not expected to conquer Egypt; that his primary job was to tie up as large a British force as possible in the Western Desert and to keep the North African front open until Russia had been dealt with and the Germans were ready to strike at Suez from the north as well.

In the face of attacks by the British Navy and the R.A.F., however, the Axis Supreme Command had a hard job in even maintaining Rommel's strength at its April level. The C.-in-C., Mediterranean, Admiral Cunningham, later stated that in the six months from May to October the Navy, the Fleet Air Arm and the R.A.F. sank one out of every three ships plying between Sicily and Tripoli. Not all these were laden with cargo when they were sunk, but, quite apart from actual sinkings, the attacks disorganized and slowed up the trans-Mediterranean traffic so much that it is doubtful whether Rommel received even two-thirds of the supplies consigned to him during this period.

With the Navy's ships and Malta's planes hounding them, Axis convoys on the Tripoli run had a bad time. Between May and November there was not a week without a successful air or naval attack on enemy shipping in the Central Mediterranean. Nevertheless the Tripoli route was far less expensive in Axis ships than was the run from Italy to Bengazi. The R.A.F. made it extremely difficult for the enemy to use this port. In the 242 days that Tobruk was besieged the R.A.F. bombed Bengazi 133 times—not counting nightly nuisance raids by one or two planes. British prisoners, who had been forced to work on the wharves there and who escaped in October, reported that the attacks were so accurate that only small ships were brought into the harbour and these seldom remained there at night.

A description of this bombing was found in the captured diary of a German officer of the 5th Tank Regiment who wrote in August:

During the night the usual air attack, as vigorous as ever, too. The English are becoming so bold that when caught in our searchlights they switch on their navigation lights and go straight for their targets. . . . Despite all the terrific barrage, not a single Englishman has been brought down yet. . . . The quays have been so blasted that the handling of cargo has become very difficult.

Some Axis shipping was saved by using Tripoli instead of Bengazi, but this wasted petrol and oil, since supplies landed there had to be hauled 900 miles by road or transport plane to Tobruk. This traffic used up so much of Rommel's petrol that what he had left for offensive operations in the Western Desert was seriously restricted. One important result was that whereas the R.A.F. regularly bombed Axis ports, bases and supply lines from Naples to Bardia, and from Sicily to Crete, Rommel never had enough petrol to engage in sustained "strategic bombing" of corresponding objectives in Egypt. Throughout the eight months that Tobruk was besieged the R.A.F.—in addition to the raids on Bengazi—made 76 on Tripoli. By contrast, the enemy made only 22 attacks on Alexandria and 21 on the Suez Canal ports. This meant that the British forces in Egypt could build up supplies almost without interruption, although nearly a hundred fighter aircraft, still in the crates in which they had been shipped, were destroyed in one disastrous raid on the Canal Zone.

Our holding of Tobruk had an important effect on the balance of air power. Rommel's planes were so busy bombing it that they were used comparatively little for bombing British airfields, bases and supply lines in Egypt. If Rommel had been free to direct against Egypt the bombers that he had to keep pounding at Tobruk, the development of British strength in the desert would have been much slower. As it was, while that went on almost uninterrupted by enemy air attack, the R.A.F. struck at Axis dromes and bases between the frontier and Bengazi almost every day. (R.A.F. communiqués from April 10th to November 18th—when the British drive to relieve Tobruk began—reported more than 350 of these attacks in addition to those on Bengazi itself. In this time the enemy made more than 800 bombing raids on Tobruk, but less than 100 on British bases and dromes in Egypt.)

Captured German diaries and prisoners' reports showed that while the loss of so much cargo was serious enough, the dislocation of supply planning was even more serious. To make sure of obtaining vital cargoes, such as spare parts for aircraft and tanks, Rommel ran an air ferry with JU52s and gliders from Crete and Derna. The JU52s could carry well over a ton and tow two gliders each carrying a ton. But he could not bring in enough this way to make up for the losses at sea. The certainty of getting vital supplies through by this means lasted only until September when British long-range Beaufighters arrived in Egypt. After this the air ferry was always in danger of interception either in flight or on the airfields near Derna, for the Beaufighter had almost double the range of the R.A.F.'s single-engined fighters.

Before these naval and air attacks could materially affect the Axis supply position, the Tobruk garrison and Wavell's forces in Egypt's Western Desert had to pass through a most critical month—from mid-April to mid-May. In April the balance of striking power was definitely with Rommel, and he could have gone on at least to Matruh if it had not been for Tobruk. However, the two successful attacks on Tripoli convoys on April 14th and 21st and Tobruk's toll of German tanks and aircraft in the first three weeks of the siege left the Axis forces in Libya weaker in mid-May than they had been in mid-April, though they were still very much stronger than the combined British forces in Tobruk and Egypt. At the beginning of May the Western Desert Force Commander (Lieutenant-General Beresford Peirse) had in the frontier area the 11th Hussars (armoured cars), one very weak brigade from the veteran 7th Armoured Division with about fifty tanks, the 6th Australian Divisional Cavalry Regiment, the armoured division's Support Group, one brigade of Guards (motorized infantry) and several regiments of field, anti-tank and A.A. artillery. His only reserves were two Australian brigades (the 21st and 25th) at Matruh, an untried Indian Division at Baguish, and a Polish brigade near Alexandria.

In May, as in April, the British continued to challenge Rommel by offensive action on the frontier. As we have seen, even before the end of April they had forced him to turn from the attack on Tobruk and secure his frontier flank by retaking Sollum and Halfaya Pass.

With the enemy holding these gateways into Libya, the British forces on the frontier had too few tanks to do much to help Tobruk at the beginning of May. Nevertheless on May 2nd a mixed column outflanked the German positions near Sollum, struck north, shot up everything it encountered and cut the Bardia road fifty miles behind the forward Axis positions. This daring diversion did not cause much material damage, but it evidently gave Rommel a shock, for he moved additional tanks from Tobruk to the frontier.

This altered the balance of tank strength there very much in the enemy's favour, but it did not curtail British activity, for Gott, the forward commander, counteracted the German advantage by bold use of mobile detachments of all arms. These became known as "Jock" columns after their originator, Lieutenant-Colonel "Jock" Campbell, who then commanded the 4th R.H.A., and later won the V.C. at Sidi Resegh. Fearless and dynamic Campbell revelled in this kind of mechanized guerrilla warfare. He organized swift-moving, hard-hitting columns containing cruiser tanks, armoured cars and carriers, 25-pounders, anti-tank and ack-ack guns, and some motorized infantry. Their strength varied between 500 and 2000 men, but they relied on speed and fire-power, not on numbers. Their main tasks were to strike at enemy supply lines and harass his flank and rear.

This harassing was valuable, but bolder and stronger action was necessary to stop the enemy from increasing his pressure on Tobruk. Wavell could not be sure that Rommel would obey the orders of the German Supreme Command, and there was the further possibility that the intercepted message was a deliberate blind.

Fortunately when they were most needed, a shipment of about fifty "I" tanks and cruisers arrived from Britain. These had been destined for Greece, but that campaign was over and in the second week of May they were hurried to the desert. With this new strength Wavell ordered Beresford Peirse to attack on the frontier before Rommel's tank regiments had recovered from their mauling at Tobruk. The plan was to drive the enemy from Halfaya and Sollum and make such a strong show of force that he might be induced to withdraw west of Tobruk. Meantime its garrison was to make a strong demonstration so as to induce Rommel to keep the bulk of his forces in that area.

Unfortunately, Morshead was given very little warning. The letter advising him of the plan and of his role took five days to reach Tobruk from Mersa Matruh. He received it on the night of the 13th and the British attack was to begin at dawn on the 15th. Despite the short notice, the garrison acted at once[1] in the Salient sector. Its deception succeeded admirably. Reconnaissance aircraft on the morning of the 15th reported enemy tanks and vehicles concentrating west of the Tobruk perimeter. On May 15th-17th there was considerable fighting at Tobruk, but the Germans on the frontier remained too strong. Rommel had taken his orders seriously, and in the previous fortnight some of his best German infantry had prepared formidable defensive positions at Halfaya, Sollum and Capuzzo.

Even so, the British succeeded in capturing Halfaya and Sollum, and reached Capuzzo but could not hold it. The German tanks and anti-tank guns proved unexpectedly strong. Inland on the desert flank the British tanks were driven back, and the infantry on the coast had to withdraw from Capuzzo and Sollum. More than thirty British tanks were lost, but Halfaya was a valuable gain because Rommel could not afford to leave the British there. He had to divert considerable forces from Tobruk before he retook the pass on May 27th. Meanwhile, Morshead gained breathing space. To make sure of holding Halfaya in future, Rommel set his troops to build stronger defences there, and on the frontier and at Capuzzo. Holding this area, however, depended much less on these fixed defences than on the balance of mobile striking power[2] on the exposed desert flank.

In the earlier campaign against the Italians, the British had clear superiority in tanks, and the "I" tank had proved almost invulnerable. Some had been temporarily disabled with damaged tracks or jammed turrets, but none had ever been penetrated by anti-tank shells. Believing that German guns would be equally ineffective, Matildas had led the attack on Halfaya Pass

---

[1] See Chapter XIV.

[2] By "mobile striking power" I mean, as indicated earlier, the combined power of tanks, mobile anti-tank guns, and field guns operating together. An armoured division is not so much a force of tanks as a force of mobile guns—some mounted in tanks, some hitched behind gun tractors.

on May 15th. There two days later I saw two "I" tanks surrounded by British tank crews, gazing wide-eyed at a clean, round, 2-inch hole straight through the 3-inch armour on the front of each tank. The holes had been made by shells from the new German 50-mm. anti-tank gun. They had done little damage inside, for their force had been spent in penetrating the armour. But there were the holes, and out through those holes that day fizzled the Tobruk garrison's hope of relief by the British forces then available.

It was not until mid-June that the British were strong enough to risk another attempt to relieve Tobruk. By then more than 150 new tanks had arrived and the 7th Armoured Division, instead of one weak brigade, had two reasonably strong brigades (the 4th and 7th) with about 230 tanks. The 4th Indian Division, which had fought so well at Sidi Barrani and Keren, was back from Eritrea. The R.A.F., reinforced by new aircraft from Britain and by half a dozen splendid South African squadrons from Abyssinia, was stronger than ever.

The plan now was for infantry and "I" tanks to over-run the frontier defences by direct attack, while about a hundred cruiser tanks by-passed the enemy defences and dealt with the German armour west of Capuzzo. (The "I" tanks were from the 4th, and the cruisers from the 7th Armoured Brigade. The British and Indian infantry used were part of the 4th Indian Division.) If these moves succeeded, the relieving forces would then drive west to Tobruk and the garrison would fight its way out to meet them. At Western Desert Force H.Q. confidence reigned; those clean, round holes in the "I" tanks at Halfaya in mid-May had been forgotten. In Tobruk hopes ran even higher, for the garrison had so much more at stake. Rumour carried the numbers of British tanks to astronomical figures, and the troops had Rommel on the run and their Alexandria leave planned long before the battle opened. The 18th Brigade got ready to lead the break-out. Every man waited eagerly for news from the frontier.

At first the news was good. On June 15th the British attacked all Rommel's frontier positions. At the coastal end (Halfaya Pass), and at the desert end (Point 208, five miles west of Capuzzo) the attacks failed. But in the centre, British and Indian infantry, supported by "I" tanks, broke right through, seized Capuzzo and stopped four German counter-attacks during the afternoon. Bardia was in danger, and the battle hung in the balance at the end of the first day. Whichever side could concentrate armoured forces strong enough to control the open desert flank would gain the battle.

Rommel threw in everything he had. Anticipating the British offensive, he had already brought part of the 5th Tank Regiment from Tobruk to support his other regiment, the 8th. Now he rushed up the balance of the 5th and concentrated all its

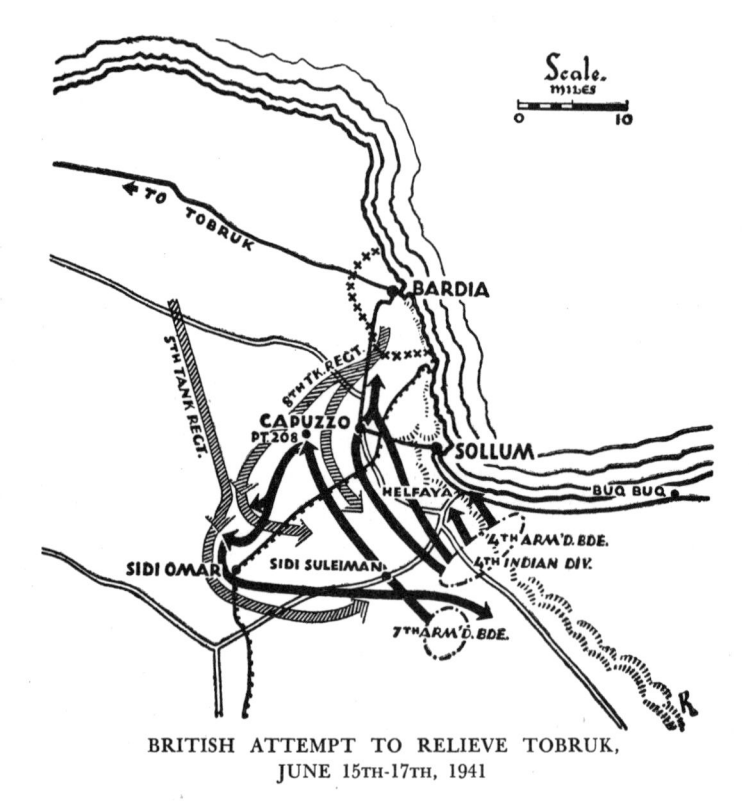

BRITISH ATTEMPT TO RELIEVE TOBRUK,
JUNE 15TH-17TH, 1941

tanks for a powerful thrust into Egypt south of the main British forces. He could afford to gamble; if he lost and had to retire, it would matter little. But Beresford Peirse could not risk all his tanks in attack. He had to keep some reserves for defence, because a deep advance by Rommel into Egypt would have serious political repercussions throughout the Middle East. He needed tank reserves also to support another diversion on the frontier, in case Rommel should attack Tobruk again.

On the second day, June 16th, thrust and counter-thrust around Capuzzo ended in stalemate. The enemy still held Halfaya, and twenty miles south-west in a series of running skirmishes his 5th Tank Regiment, with superior numbers and fire-power, forced the 7th Armoured Brigade back across the frontier. Rommel mustered every tank he could to press home his advantage. One column, with 75 tanks of the 5th Regiment, carried its outflanking movement 20 miles into Egypt south of Halfaya. Simultaneously another column fought its way through nearer the coast towards Halfaya. Threatened by these two moves, the Anglo-Indian forces, which had held Capuzzo for nearly two days, had to withdraw, leaving on the battlefield a large number of disabled, but recoverable, British tanks.

It had been a disastrous three days. Captured German documents (secret German military reports and not propaganda) allege that 143 British tanks were destroyed. This was a slight exaggeration, for the actual British losses were 123. However G.H.Q. admitted later that "two-thirds of the British armour was out of action" after the battle, and it did not claim that the Germans had lost more than 50 tanks. The battle had been decided by two factors—a new German anti-tank weapon and Rommel's bold handling of his armour. The weapon was the 88-mm. A.A. gun, used for the first time (on the frontier at least) in an anti-tank role. Rommel had only 12 of these but, if German official documents are to be believed, they knocked out 79 British tanks—one for every 20 rounds they fired.

At the two German frontier positions that held, eight of these guns destroyed 36 British tanks. The tanks, firing a 2-pounder with an effective range of 800 yards at most, were no match for the 88-mm. with its 20-pound shell that could knock out an "I" tank at a range of a mile. In these positions the 88-mm. guns were dug in flush with the ground and so well camouflaged that the British tank crews did not even know what had hit them.

On the critical first afternoon, Bardia was probably saved by one of these guns. German tanks had been driven back; mobile 88-mm. guns had been kept quiet by British shell-fire which forced their crews to take cover; the British had taken Capuzzo and there was little between them and Bardia. But lying abandoned north of Capuzzo was a solitary 88-mm. with a broken tractor. A scratch crew coupled it to a truck and got it into action. Before dark, the Germans claim, it had knocked out nine "I" tanks and blocked every British attack. By next morning the Germans had rallied enough strength to stop any further break-through. But for these guns, the frontier defences would have been overwhelmed before Rommel could have moved his tanks to save them. He handled these well. By committing all he could—even at the risk of withdrawing nearly all his German tanks from Tobruk—he gained a three to one victory. The dramatic sweep by the 5th Tank Regiment round the southern flank clinched the battle, but the way for this was prepared by the 88-mm. guns and Rommel's shrewd tactics.

He kept his tanks together in strong formations and did not use them in "penny packets". He gave them close support with artillery—especially anti-tank guns, which he placed in cleverly concealed positions to ambush British tanks. West of Capuzzo he had a dummy camp in a depression and beyond it four 88-mm. guns dug in behind the crest of a low rise. British cruisers shot up the camp without opposition, careered on over the rise and into point-blank fire, which knocked out 22 of them on the first day. North of Capuzzo on the second day, his tanks withdrew under pressure. The Germans pulled back through four well-concealed 88-mm. guns which held their fire until the British were less than 500 yards away. Eleven "I" tanks were lost.

It was probably inevitable that, in their first major clash with the much more experienced Germans, the British armoured forces should be worsted. Without the schooling of this preliminary defeat the November offensive might not have succeeded. Unfortunately, however, many of the costly mistakes of June were repeated in November. The British Command was slow to learn and slow to act on what it did learn. Senior staff officers refused to believe that the Germans were using 88-mm. guns in an anti-tank role. G.H.Q., and even Western Desert Force H.Q., which became Eighth Army H.Q., ridiculed the suggestion. Both insisted that the 50-mm. gun and the German choke-bore anti-tank rifle had caused the June losses. An Australian officer, who was captured by the Germans and escaped, told Eighth Army Intelligence in December 1941 that he had travelled on a truck carrying 88-mm. anti-tank ammunition and had been told by a gun crew that 88-mms were "very good against tanks". He was informed that the Germans were kidding him.

At last, in that same month, a British tank regiment, in taking a strongpoint at Sidi Omar, lost 48 out of its 52 "I" tanks. The 88-mm. guns, which had done most of the damage, were captured. The Cairo Military Spokesman, reflecting G.H.Q.'s continued scepticism, explained that it was only when the 88-mms were dug-in in defensive positions that they were used against tanks. It took the severe losses of June in the following year to induce Cairo to admit that Rommel used his 88-mm. as a mobile anti-tank gun.

Six months before this, correspondents in Cairo—voicing the opinion of tank crews in the field—tried to warn the British people of the alarming superiority of German tanks, anti-tank guns and general tactics. They were blocked by serried ranks of blue pencils and a red-tabbed Military Spokesman who sought to subdue them with the plea—"Gentlemen, please, let there be no criticism."

Whether Cairo admitted it or not, the appearance of the 50-mm. and 88-mm. anti-tank guns in Libya in the middle of 1941 prolonged the siege of Tobruk for nearly six months. There was no lack of courage or offensive spirit on the British side, but after the June failure it was clear that we could not attack again until we had considerably more tanks than Rommel to make up for the superior performance of his tanks and anti-tank guns. Unfortunately, it was still not realized how much superior these were.

Although the attempts to relieve Tobruk in May and June had failed, they had an important influence on Rommel's policy during the next six months. He was still determined to attack again as soon as his Supreme Command gave him sufficient forces and equipment, but the experience of May and June had evidently led him to three conclusions:

1. That he could not advance far into Egypt until he had subdued Tobruk, because of the danger that the garrison would break out and strike at his forces from the rear.

2. That taking Tobruk would not be a snap victory that could be won before the British forces from the frontier could intervene, unless he amassed much greater strength outside Tobruk and gave better protection to his frontier "flank".

3. That if the warfare of thrust and counter-thrust on the frontier went on he would never be able to assemble sufficient strength to attack Tobruk. The fighting on the frontier would have to be stabilized by building far stronger defences.

These new defences ran from Halfaya Pass south-west to Sidi Omar—twenty-five miles inland on the frontier. They were a series of four "strong-boxes", covering a deep and continuous minefield. These strong-boxes were so well defended by 88-mm.

and other anti-tank guns that any direct assault on them would be even more costly than the June attacks on Halfaya.

Behind this line—in the coastal wadis between Bardia and Tobruk—Rommel proceeded to build up dumps and workshops, and to gather artillery for an all-out attack on Tobruk. The frontier defences gave his forces some freedom from British raiding columns, and saved his tanks from the wear and tear of fluid warfare. He reasoned that if the British attempted to attack, they would have to make a wide detour round the Halfaya-Sidi Omar defences and reveal their intention so early that he could dispose his forces to meet them.

Thus, from June onward, the character of the desert war changed. On the Tobruk and Halfaya fronts, there was stalemate, as both sides concentrated on winning the supply race— the race for the initiative. Rommel had evidently gained permission from his Supreme Command to attack Tobruk when he felt he was strong enough, but with the R.A.F. and the Royal Navy pounding his supply lines and with Britain's newly formed Eighth Army in the Western Desert growing daily stronger, it was hard for him to retain his superiority in striking power.

Meantime, through the sweltering Libyan summer some of his crack Afrika Korps became disgruntled. They had been picked and trained for offensive warfare. Many of them had been fattened on the quick victories and easy loot of the European campaigns. They disliked a defensive role; still more distasteful was the task of digging holes in the unfriendly Libyan plateau, working in sandstorm and in heat that often rose to 110 degrees.

The commander of one of the German battalions holding the Tobruk Salient complained in a report written in June: "Our people know nothing about the construction of defences. We have scarcely any exercise in this phase of warfare in our peacetime training. The junior commander does not realize that positional infantry warfare is 60 per cent with the spade, 30 per cent with the field glasses, and only 10 per cent with the gun."

German diaries reveal the discontent of the rank and file and the dislocation of Rommel's supply system. "What is there for a soldier to do when there is no fighting and nothing to eat?" wrote a young tank officer in May. "This morning the bit of cheese was not even enough to go round for breakfast. The men want to attack, want to get into Tobruk. There, there's loot to be had. Replacements from Germany do not arrive. We are going to send a further indent for them in eight weeks. What rot. Oh, if only Goering knew!"

Four months later we find the same strain in the diary of a tank battalion adjutant: "There is a shortage of everything—of material, of reserve manpower. Our vehicles are on their bare rims. Poor rations have made more than 80 per cent of the regiment unfit to be sent forward. . . . Breakfast—carbolic-flavoured coffee and mouldy bacon with old Dauerbrot." The men inside beleaguered Tobruk were better off than that.

Extracts like these, published from time to time in *Tobruk Truth*, made good reading for the garrison. After the failure of the June attempt to relieve them, a wave of pessimism swept over the defenders. Hopes had been so high that the disappointment that followed was acute. But this evidence of enemy difficulties made the troops more determined than ever to hang on. Their spirit carried them through all danger, hardship and disappointment. Typical of that spirit was their reply to the leaflets that German planes scattered over Tobruk on June 24th—a week after the failure of the second attempt at relief. The leaflets read:

AUSSIES

After Crete disaster Anzac troops are now being ruthlessly sacrificed by England in Tobruch and Syria. Turkey has concluded pact of friendship with Germany. England will shortly be driven out of the Mediterranean. Offensive from Egypt to relieve you totally smashed.

YOU CANNOT ESCAPE

Our dive bombers are waiting to sink your transports. Think of your future and your people at home. Come forward. Show white flags and you will be out of danger!

SURRENDER!

Tobruk's reply was simple. A Digger took a copy of the leaflet, nailed it to the flag-pole in the main square, and underneath it wrote the garrison's answer—"Come and get it!"

CHAPTER XIII

Wouldn't It?

THE German makes a very good soldier but a very poor psychologist. In this war, as in the last, his most costly errors have sprung from an inability to appreciate the character of the men he is fighting. When the Germans pushed the Tommies and the Diggers back into Tobruk, they little realized that they were packing in dynamite and that the harder they thrust the more explosive it became.

Berlin Radio made a fatal mistake in trying to gibe and scare the Australian soldier into surrender. The longer the odds Lord Haw Haw offered against the Digger's chance of getting out, the more heavily the Digger backed himself. He and his father before him had gambled on the outcome of a drought or a strike. They had defied the bullying of man and nature and had gambled with their livelihood. It was a small step from this to gamble now with their lives. The odds were long; the fight would be hard, but they knew what was at stake.

The very scorn Lord Haw Haw heaped upon them made clear the importance of their job. It would have been better for the Axis if Goebbels had ignored the Tobruk garrison altogether. But he put them in the middle of the field, and they responded as a football team does to the hoots of its opponents' barrackers and the cheers of its own. Evidence of this was contained in a report which the British Field Censor made in October 1941. He then wrote: "The tone of the troops' mail from Tobruk is somewhat higher than that from other parts of the Western Desert, as the men realize that such a large amount of attention is focused on the Fortress."

When the siege began, Morshead was little more than a name to most of the Diggers and to all the Tommies. But Goebbels helped to make him a commanding figure, round whom the garrison could rally—not as men from Britain, Australia or India, but first and foremost as men of Tobruk.

Through the long months of stalemate after the Battle of

the Salient and the failure of the June offensive, the spirit of the Tobruk garrison was fully tested. As well as fighting the Axis divisions outside, they had to battle against dangers within —hardship, sickness and boredom.

Climatically Tobruk was healthy enough, as battle-zones go, once the Italian filth had been cleared away. The weather between March and November was not particularly bad, apart from the dust. In June and July it was often fiercely hot by day, but the heat was dry and the nights were cool. The duststorms, however, were a severe trial. They were far worse at Tobruk than in the open desert beyond. Within the perimeter thousands of wheels had churned the baked crust of the earth into a fine powder, and every wind whipped it into a choking cloud. The men breathed dust, and ate dust. Every few days the wind raised a storm that blotted out everything. But regardless of this the troops had to man their posts and guns; drive their vehicles without windscreens; unload ships or lay mines.

Next to the dust, Tobruk's greatest plagues were the flies and fleas, which the Italians left behind as a persistent fifth column. Strangely enough a few other creatures survived in this scarred wasteland—little brown mice in the open desert; big grey rats in the caves that the troops converted into dug-outs; dozens of starved Libyan dogs, many of which were adopted as unit mascots; even a few cats, jackals and gazelles, a couple of goats and one ancient sheep. This animal, known as "Larry the Lamb" was the jealously guarded mascot of a British ack-ack battery. Every night his masters placed a sentry to protect him from predatory Australians.

Fortunately one dangerous creature—the mosquito—was absent. There was no lying water and so there was no malaria. The most troublesome illness was dysentery. So long as the troops drank only chlorinated water and sanitary regulations were strictly observed, this was kept in check; but several times carelessness was followed by bad outbreaks. One week in June, 226 men went down with dysentery—three times as many as became casualties in battle. After this, stricter control reduced it, and there was remarkably little other sickness, until deficiencies in rations began to tell.

In the first three months there were no fresh, and little tinned, vegetables or fruit. Except for two interruptions by bombing, the bakeries produced reasonably good bread six days a week and this and bully-beef were always the principal rations. Bully was a great leveller. Whether you ate in the General's mess or a front line post, you got bully at least twice a day in one or other of the many disguises that ingenious cooks devised. It was varied a little by M. & V. (ready-made meat and vegetable stew, a direct descendant of the last war's "Mac-Conachie's"), tinned bacon and tinned herrings. In these months there was a fair supply of margarine, but sugar and jam were strictly rationed. As on Gallipoli, men usually had sufficient to keep them going but not enough for proper nourishment.

To make up for the lack of fresh vegetables and fruit they were given concentrates of vitamin C in the form of little white ascorbic tablets. After several months of this limited diet the troops began to break out in "desert sores", and little scratches took weeks to heal. The men worked hard and lived hard and when they eventually reached Palestine the infantry battalions found the average loss of weight was nearly two stone per man in five or six months.

By mid-July, however, the food position improved so much that the daily ration of ascorbic tablets was cut from two to one. There were reasonable supplies of tinned fruit and vegetables. A little fresh fruit and vegetables appeared in the rations about once a week, and once a month troops in reserve positions had real meat. There was more marmite, lime juice, sugar and jam. About once a fortnight from June onwards—luxury of luxuries—the canteens had a bottle of whisky or gin per officer. There was still no beer for the men, but front line troops in the Salient and those going out on patrol were given a tot of rum to keep out the cold.

In spite of desert sores, loss of weight and gradual sapping of energy, the physical condition of the troops remained reasonably good. They also stood up well to the mental and nervous strain of siege conditions. Men who have fought in both wars say that the combined air and artillery attack on Tobruk was never as fierce or as sustained as the shelling in France in the Great War. Certainly during the last four or five months few troops outside the town and harbour area were regularly bombed, and the shelling was not heavy except in the Salient and half a dozen other hot spots. In July the enemy sent over an average of 650 shells per day; by September this had increased to 1000, but on a 30-mile front this was not heavy by last war standards.

The percentage of men suffering from shock—known in this war as "bomb-happies"—was, I understand, considerably lower in Tobruk than on the Western Front in the last war. Moreover, the greater proportion of these were later returned to their units, fit for front line service. Two Australian psychiatrists (Major E. L. Cooper and Captain A. J. M. Sinclair) ran a war neurosis clinic in Tobruk for many months and achieved remarkable success in treating nervous disorders. Out of 207 patients treated between May and August, 38 per cent returned to their units without leaving Tobruk; 23 per cent became fit for front line service after treatment in Palestine; 23 per cent became fit for base duties and only 12 per cent were returned to Australia permanently unfit. It says much for the spirit of the garrison that only 3 per cent of the bomb-happy patients they examined were found to be malingerers.

While the strain on the garrison was not intense after the first month, it *was* continuous. Axis guns could shell anywhere inside the perimeter, and their bombing was so haphazard that no place could be considered safe, not even the hospitals, since they could not be placed clear of all military objectives in a fortress like Tobruk. The main hospital had to be in buildings, and consequently in the town, where the 4th A.G.H. occupied a former Italian hospital. It was near buildings the enemy had used as workshops only half a mile from the harbour, and was thus always in danger of being hit in raids on the town or shipping. Seventeen bombs landed in this hospital at various times and eye-witnesses assure me that on at least one occasion the pilots wilfully bombed it. Frequently delicate operations were carried out in the middle of an air raid, but the operating theatre was reasonably safe, for it had been so strongly protected by heavy timber and sandbags that it could withstand anything but a direct hit by a 1000-pounder.

Another hospital[1] on the beach was dive-bombed and machine-gunned several times during the first fortnight. At least one attack was deliberate, but the hospital was then not adequately marked, and was only a few hundred yards from an ack-ack position and several other legitimate targets. It was soon moved to another part of the beach two miles from the harbour—and conspicuously marked. After that, although a few strays fell close, the beach hospital was not intentionally attacked. Here the Germans certainly respected the Red Cross, for no

---

[1] This was part of the 4th A.G.H., commanded by Colonel N. L. Spiers. Surgical cases were accommodated in the town hospital; medical cases were treated at the beach section.

other such collection of tents anywhere inside the perimeter would have lasted twenty-four hours.

Similar respect was shown to the Regimental Aid Posts of front line battalions, which often had to be in places under enemy observation. Two hospital ships at Tobruk, however, were dive-bombed and one was sunk. A German pilot, shot down during one of these attacks, stated that they had orders to bomb any and every ship in the harbour.

Frequently troops were machine-gunned while swimming or sun-baking and the beaches were regularly protected by Bren guns mounted for ack-ack defence. Battalions often had greater casualties from bombing and shelling when in reserve than when in the Red Line. One day a platoon of the 2/43rd was repairing a road when a stray stick of bombs killed three and wounded five. Tobruk was like that. There was little let-up. But the very knowledge that they were hemmed in with their backs to the sea strengthened the garrison's resolve and developed a do-or-die spirit. There were a few whose nerve cracked, but generally the casual, phlegmatic, what-the-hell-anyway attitude of Diggers and Tommies carried them through.

General living conditions, however, did not ease the strain. Troops quartered in the town were reasonably comfortable. They certainly had to endure frequent bombs and occasional shells, but they became accustomed to these. Some slept secure in deep tunnels drilled out by the Italians. Others made solid shelters with sandbags, wood and slabs of concrete salvaged from wrecked buildings. Some timbered up rooms in stone houses, making them strong enough to withstand anything but a direct hit. Living in the town had advantages. The sea provided good swimming and, with the help of home-made distilleries, good drinking water. Occasionally rations could be supplemented by fish caught with the aid of hand grenades.

Those who were stationed in the intermediate zone between the coast and the perimeter lived almost permanently in an atmosphere laden with dust churned up by the traffic. Nevertheless the personnel of the various H.Q. units and the British gunners and tankmen in this area had a chance to make themselves moderately comfortable because they were seldom moved.

The Australian infantry battalions lived in much worse conditions. Every few weeks they were moved. A normal rotation was for a battalion to go from the Red Line concrete posts to the exposed positions in the Blue Line; thence to one of the inner reserve areas, and from there to the most uncomfortable Salient sector. They were probably best off in the concrete posts of the Red Line, where there was less dust and the posts were as clean and comfortable as front line positions could be. As we shall see later they were worst off in the improvised posts in the Salient.

Apart from the few who had their own salt-water distilleries, the men of Tobruk had little water with which to wash clean their dust-parched throats, and that little was brackish and chlorinated. The ration at first was half a gallon per man per day for all purposes, but after June 19th it was increased to three-quarters of a gallon. At first the water tasted like medicine, but after a while it seemed quite good unless you happened to have some sweet water with which to compare it. One night a new arrival brought some water from Alexandria. In the mess a precious jugful was passed round. We drank it neat. The troops could console themselves, however, with the thought that the enemy had water problems too. One German officer said in his diary that the water "looks like coffee and tastes like sulphur".

Whatever its drinking qualities, Tobruk water was certainly God's gift to the makers of razor blades. Even if a blade were most carefully dried, the edge rusted off after two or three shaves. The water's reluctance to lather provided a further excuse for going unshaven, especially as, until August, the troops received only one blade a fortnight. But one day Routine Orders came out with a curt comment on this unsoldierly conduct. A few days later some friendly fate guided an enemy bomb straight to the main dump of new blades, but other dumps were unharmed and the order stood.

Water was scarce enough but the beer position was well summed up by one of Tobruk's poets, who wrote:[2]

> There's militant teetotallers
> Who abhor all kinds of drink,
> There's wives who break good bottles
> And pour them down the sink;
> This place would suit them to the ground,
> We've searched in every nook,
> But booze is rare as hen's teeth in
> This place they call Tobruk.

Two or three times during the siege the garrison did receive

---

[2] This verse was written by the author of the poem that appears on page 179.

about half a pint per man, but this was barely enough to lay the dust. The men were resigned to the shortage, but few things annoyed them more than the newspaper story that beer was regularly issued to them. One of the garrison's unrecognized achievements was its destruction of the legend that the Digger cannot carry on without his beer.

As months of enemy inactivity dragged on, boredom became the garrison's greatest danger. But Morshead knew that nothing would sap the troops' morale as much as idleness. He kept them working and he kept them in contact with the enemy. The work of strengthening the defences went on from the first day to the last. Morshead was never satisfied. While the forward troops improved the Red Line, the reserve battalions built the Blue Line; and when that was finished, they started a Green Line farther in. As soon as one minefield was laid, sappers started putting down another. Up to their last night in the Salient, the troops continued digging, wiring and mining their positions.

They worked through heat and duststorm, cold and darkness, grumbling as they did so, but still capable of a laugh. In October Tobruk's tank strength was trebled by the arrival of fifty Matildas, and Australians were detailed to dig "harbours" for them as a protection against bombing. The new tank commander (Brigadier A. C. Willison) a British Regular, stopped beside one working party and listened for a moment to the Diggers cursing as they toiled. Then he said—"Tough going, boys?" "My flamin' oath," said one Australian, "but you bring us the bloody tanks and we'll dig the bastards in."

Morshead's aggressive, hard-working policy was never of greater value than after the failure of the two attempts to relieve Tobruk in May and June. The natural dejection that followed these was vigorously countered by aggressive patrolling and the garrison's self-confidence was soon restored. In his shrewd appreciation of this danger Morshead showed his quality as a leader.

During the months of boredom two things were all important to the garrison—mail and cigarettes. Throughout the bombing an Australian postal unit operated in a bank building and by August was handling up to 50 tons of mail a week. Most of this was for the Australians, as the people of Britain could still send only very small parcels and even letters came infrequently. The Australian people flooded Tobruk post office with 5000 parcels and more than 50,000 letters a week. The average weekly mail then was 700 bags inward and 350 out.

The Australian Comforts Fund, through its invaluable agents the Salvation Army and Y.M.C.A. representatives, provided the troops with writing paper, envelopes and, most valuable of all, air-mail letter cards ready-stamped. In addition the post office during one month sold £3200 worth of Australian stamps. The bulk of the mail from Tobruk was made up of souvenirs fashioned by the troops in their spare time from Stukas, Italian shell cases, hand grenades, and general wreckage. "Professional" souvenir makers did a brisk trade and I knew one shrewd corporal in an Army Field Workshops, who made several pounds a week by selling mementoes he had turned on the workshops' lathes. According to the Tobruk postal sergeant, "If there hadn't been an 11-pound limit on parcels, they'd have packed up shells, guns and all and sent them home."

Cigarettes were almost as valuable as mail in sustaining morale. As the troops were on British rations they had a free issue of 50 a week, and from June onwards they were usually able to buy another 50 each week from the canteen. In August canteen sales averaged 320 cigarettes per man. These, in addition to the free issue and those given out by the Comforts Fund, were almost enough for the average soldier. Cigarettes were the No. 1 priority cargo on all canteen ships and until July there was room for little else. But the Comforts Fund managed to find odd space on all kinds of craft—from destroyers to barges—thanks primarily to the resourcefulness and persistence of its Commissioner in Alexandria, Major Eugene ("Pat") Gorman.

The Australian Comforts Fund made no distinction between British, Indian and Australian troops and, by serving all alike, contributed much to the sense of unity in Tobruk. As one British officer wrote to Gorman: "What makes these gifts even more acceptable to a British unit is the knowledge that the A.C.F. normally caters only for Australian troops. This gesture is one of many which maintain and strengthen the spirit of comradeship amongst all troops in the Tobruk Fortress."

Shipments of both canteen and Comforts Fund cargoes increased considerably in the last few months, so much so that the Australian canteen alone had a turnover of more than £20,000 in both August and September. Unloading canteen ships was one "fatigue" for which there were plenty of volunteers, as there was always the chance of getting away with some of the cargo. A working party from one battalion, however, looted so much that the unit was denied the "privilege" of providing future unloading parties.

In addition to such occasional looting there was trouble throughout the siege with troops—mostly Australians—who "ratted" the food dumps. The number of men guilty of this was comparatively small, and they were mostly those stationed near the dumps and were not front line troops. Strong disciplinary measures were taken against any who were caught, but the practice persisted. Because of this, letters from Tobruk often gave contradictory reports about rations. But if anyone boasted of living well, he was probably one of those who shared in loot from a food dump. It is an interesting commentary on human nature that this should have happened even in a place like Tobruk, where the general spirit of comradeship was remarkably high.

An important element in maintaining morale was the supply of news. Rumour is rife in all armies and isolation from the news of the world would have had a most adverse effect on the beleaguered men, if they had not been kept informed by a daily news-sheet edited and published by Sergeant W. H. Williams.

Tobruk Truth—The Dinkum Oil came out every day in spite of enemy bombs, which once wrecked the office and several times put radio set or "printing press" out of action. Each night Williams listened to the B.B.C. news, took shorthand notes, typed the items, plus any local news or gleanings from Australian papers, on to a wax stencil and roneoed-off the copies on an antiquated cyclostyle machine. At first the news was picked up on a salvaged Italian set, and the duplicator and typewriter were also of Italian origin. When these threatened to break down, a brand new typewriter and duplicator were rushed up from Cairo, and the Comforts Fund provided a new radio. Because of the shortage of paper, the daily circulation was limited to 600, and even this was maintained at one stage only by printing the news on the back of Italian Army forms.

Tobruk Truth was the father of all the other "newspapers" in the Fortress. Many Australian and a few British units had their own roneoed news-sheets, some with picturesque names like the 2/23rd Battalion's "Mud and Blood"; the 2/24th's "Furphy Flyer"[3]; and the 2/48th's "Grubb's Gazette" (named

---

[3] A "furphy" is a rumour. Dr Bean says that the term originated in 1914 at Broadmeadows Camp, where the scavenging carts were branded with the manufacturer's name, Furphy.

after its editor, Corporal R. W. Grubb). These reproduced the main news from *Tobruk Truth*, items of local interest and readers' contributions, and they did much to build up and maintain unit spirit in conditions that often prevented even platoons in the same company from having any contact with one another. By these means rumour was kept in check, and men inside Tobruk got at least as much truth about the war as those outside it.

Very often, however, they did not know what went on within their own perimeter. For instance, a lieutenant-colonel who was rather a martinet, said to me some time after Tobruk was relieved, "My wife tells me you broadcast a concert allegedly by some Australians in Tobruk. What a hoax! There were never any concerts while I was there." I assured him that we had recorded this concert by men of the 20th Brigade in September and that British troops had held concerts almost every week throughout the latter part of the siege, but he remained unconvinced.

The 20th Brigade concert was not the only one that Australians held in Tobruk, but it was probably the best. It ran four nights to an audience of 500 Diggers on each occasion. Until a few days before, both players and audience had been in the line. They came to the concert grimy from the desert, steel helmets on their heads and rifles slung over their shoulders.

It was held in an underground ammunition chamber—one of many which the Italians had tunnelled from the rock face of a wadi near the El Adem crossroads. This man-made cave with its walls, roof and floor covered with concrete, was not acoustically sympathetic, but it was good enough. It was 20 yards wide and 50 long and held 500 men at a pinch. The stage was a rough wooden platform draped with army blankets and camouflage nets. The footlights were car headlamps shielded by cut-down kerosene tins. In the wadis and on the plateau outside British guns occasionally replied to Axis shells that landed, as they so often did, around the important road junction near by. But for two hours down in the underground "theatre" nobody heard them. The troops were a long way away: through the blue-grey haze of dust and cigarette fumes they saw a land of smoky gums and soft sunshine on rolling golden paddocks; a world of blue hills, bright lights and white breakers as they sang songs that carried them down the road to Gundagai, past a swagman and a billabong, on to Dixie, London, Lambeth, Tipperary. After six months in Tobruk they could still laugh and sing.

They sang accompanied by a piano, a saxophone, a violin, a piano-accordion and a mouth-organ—instruments with a history. The piano had once played for perfumed Italian officers as they danced in their silk-lined, velvet-collared uniforms with their painted ladies on the piazza of the "Albergo Tobruch" by the town's then-peaceful waterfront. The saxophone had often been heard in Brisbane's Tivoli and its owner, Ted Donkin, had carried it to the borders of Tripolitania and back again. To keep the dust out he used to wrap it in an army blanket and bury it in the sand. His "sax" was none the worse for all its adventures, but the same could not be said of the violin. It was of doubtful ancestry and in the absence of catgut, had been strung with army signal wire.[4] The "squeeze-box" had been suffering from asthma until an "M.O" made it fit for action by patching it with sticking plaster. These were the instruments that led the men in singing those songs that tugged so strongly at Australian hearts, when the recording of the concert was eventually broadcast by the A.B.C.

The concerts were far from mythical but there was no truth in the report that an Australian band played every day in Tobruk's main square. Where that story originated I do not know, but the London *Times* on April 25th reported: "Contrary to the German contention that Tobruk is a beleaguered city, actual conditions do not indicate such a state of affairs, says an Exchange Message from Cairo. An Australian band plays every day, and the only inconvenience is caused by bombing, against which ample accommodation is provided in underground shelters." This story was published all over the world and every war correspondent who later went to Tobruk was accused of being its author. I found that most of the phoney reports about Tobruk originated not in correspondents' dispatches, but in letters written home by troops. They wanted either to convince their friends and families that they were going through hell unperturbed or to persuade them that Tobruk was a picnic.

---

[4] The comment in the broadcast that the violin was strung with signal wire prompted several Australians to send me sets of violin strings. "If this goes on," commented A.I.F. Censor, Major George Fenton, "instead of using signal wire for violin strings, we'll be able to use violin strings for signal lines."

Some of these letters found their way into the popular weeklies and the stories they spread did considerable harm to the reputation of correspondents in general.

It was true, however, that cricket and football matches were played from time to time. The players were chiefly British gunners and tank crews, who were not under the immediate stress of holding front line posts. Almost every night near our camp ack-ack gunners played soccer. Their pitch was a bare patch of stony desert, hard on knee, elbow, and soccer ball, but that did not lessen their zest.

The Tommies occasionally played cricket and so did the Australian infantrymen. The best account of a Tobruk cricket match is in verse that will remind all Australians of "The Man from Snowy River" and "The Geebung Polo Club". And well it might, for it was written by "Banjo's" son, Private Hugh Barton Paterson.

> You've heard of Bradman, Hammond, Macartney, Woodfull, Hobbs;
> You've heard of how MacDougall topped the score,
> But now I'd like to tell how we play cricket in Tobruk
> In a way the game was never played before.
>
> The players are a mixture, they come from every rank,
> And their dress would not be quite the thing at Lords;
> But you don't need caps and flannels and expensive batting gloves
> To get the fullest sport the game affords.
>
> The wicket's rather tricky, for it's mat on desert sand,
> But for us it's really plenty good enough;
> And what with big bomb craters and holes from nine-inch shells
> The outfield could be well described as rough.
>
> The boundary's partly tank trap with the balance Dannert wire,
> And the grandstand's just a bit of sandy bank;
> Our single sightboard's furnished by a shot-down Jerry plane
> And the scorer's in a ruined "Itie" tank.
>
> One drawback is a minefield which is at the Desert end,
> And critics might find fault with this and that,
> But to us all runs are good ones, even if a man should score
> Four leg byes off the top of his tin hat.
>
> The barracking is very choice; the Hill would learn a lot
> If they could listen in to all the cries,
> As the Quartermaster-Sergeant bowls the Colonel neck and crop
> With a yorker, while some dust is in his eyes.
>
> If we drive one in the minefield we always run it out,
> For that is what our local rule defines;
> It's always good for six at least, sometimes as high as ten,
> While the fieldsman picks his way in through the mines.

> Though we never stop for shell-fire, we're not too keen on planes,
> And when the Stukas start to hover round
> You can sometimes get a wicket, if you're game enough to stay,
> By bowling as the batsmen go to ground.
>
> So when we're back in Sydney and others start to talk
> Of cricket, why we'll quell them with a look:
> You blokes have never seen a game of cricket properly played
> The way we used to play it in Tobruk.

The organization of these concerts and cricket matches was typical of the Tommies' and Diggers' determination to make the best of things. Characteristic of this was the ingenuity shown by Major H. R. Birch of the 2/23rd in arranging a dinner for the officers' mess when the battalion had finished its first five weeks in the line. In honour of the occasion and of the birthdays of the C.O. and three officers, they wanted a change from the usual fare of bully, bread and tea, and the inevitable aluminium dixies. Tobruk in May had few luxuries, but Birch went exploring. He found the canteen store almost bare, but it provided six tins of chicken-and-ham roll, one bottle of whisky and another of gin—the nucleus, at least, of a dinner.

From the Y.M.C.A.'s stock of Comforts Fund stores, Birch collected chocolate, Bonox and two small bottles of olives. From a secret reserve the quartermaster produced tins of potatoes, peas, spaghetti and peaches. But the occasion demanded more than special food. Two white tablecloths were unearthed from the linen chest of the "Albergo Tobruch"; a chipped decanter and some ersatz port were found in a former Italian officers' mess; and, as a final touch, coffee-cups and saucers and paper table-napkins were salvaged from an Italian junk heap.

A "banquet hall" was made by stretching a tarpaulin across the gap between two sides of a narrow wadi, and it was furnished with a table and seats made from sandbags and planks. The crowning elegance was a strip of dusty red carpet, borrowed for the occasion from the town hospital. The officers sat down to a five-course dinner, the first they had eaten together since the siege began; for many of them it was their last formal mess. Two days later in an attack on the enemy Salient, the 2/23rd had four officers killed and three taken prisoner.

It is not easy to generalize about Tobruk. Living conditions varied so much from sector to sector, unit to unit. It is true that most men went through the siege without seeing a football or hearing any music but the whine of bullets; without drinking anything but salty chlorinated water or tea brewed from it;

without swimming or bathing on more than four or five occasions in six months; without tasting tinned fruit or fresh vegetables more than a couple of dozen times. But it is equally true that football and cricket matches were played—by a few; that some concerts were held; that some units drank sweet water from beachside distilleries and swam almost every day. There were men who were bombed almost daily, and others who were not attacked from the air once in six months. Nothing was typical of Tobruk except bully-beef, flies, heat, dust—and boredom.

Yet all these factors combined to produce something that was typical—a spirit you found in every part of the garrison. The men might well have been dominated by an environment so unfriendly and an enemy so powerful in engines of war. But the men of Tobruk defied the enemy and rose superior to the environment. In doing this they needed more than courage, initiative and readiness to die. These carried them through the straight fight against the German, but they needed also faith in themselves, patience and sticking-power with which to combat the potential enemy within, for they had more holding-on than hard fighting from mid-May onwards.

They saw British planes in twos and threes shot out of the skies by Axis aircraft in twenties and thirties. The enemy had complete command of the air after the first few weeks, but he could never attack with impunity. They saw enemy tanks in fifties and sixties, and their own in fives and sixes, but they held on. They came under fire from heavier German artillery, mortars and machine-guns and they had few weapons with the range and calibre necessary to strike back. But they did not become discouraged and say, "We can't carry on in conditions like these; we must have this and that before we will fight." They set their teeth and fought with what they had.

Tobruk was significant not because the British and Australian troops there were basically different from Tommies or Diggers anywhere else but because Tobruk brought out the fighting best in them. The pressure from without produced a solidarity within, which left little room for complacency or individual interest. Every man, section, and unit grew to realize that the safety of the garrison in greater or lesser degree might depend on the success of his job, no matter how unimportant it might seem.

Tobruk forged such a sense of unity that what happened to one small sector seemed to have happened to the whole garrison. If the town were bombed, they were all bombed, though they may not even have seen the planes. A successful raid by ten men was a triumph for them all. This feeling underlay their determination to see the fight through together. One day in August a company commander in the 2/23rd called his best N.C.Os together. There was a good job for one of them. It meant a commission. It meant going back on the first destroyer to Alex. and on the first ship home to Australia, away from flies, grime, bully and all the discomforts and dangers of the siege.

"Any takers?" he said. Not a man volunteered.

CHAPTER XIV

Holding the Salient

FROM Hill 209 the Germans dominated a wide sweep of desert inside the perimeter, but the piece they had bitten out must have left a sour taste in their mouths. They could not afford to abandon it, because they kept a foot in the door of Tobruk by holding Hill 209. From here, when the time came to renew their attack, they might force that door wide open. But meanwhile the Salient they had established covering 209 was costly to hold. For this task Rommel was forced to use German troops that he could ill spare from the frontier area. From May to August he had only eight German battalions that could be used as infantry and it took more than a third of these to hold the Salient.

It was some days after the failure of the 18th Brigade's counter-attack on May 3rd-4th before either side established any stable line in the disputed territory. The garrison had yielded a box-shaped area a mile and a half to two miles deep and two and a half miles wide.

This was an awkward front. The desert sloped gradually upwards from the forward Australian positions to Hill 209; the rise was only about 100 feet, but it gave the enemy much better observation. The garrison had been holding $3\frac{1}{2}$ miles of the old perimeter on favourable ground, wired, mined and covered by fire from the Italian-built strongpoints. Now it had to defend a $5\frac{1}{2}$-mile front with no prepared positions, no wire and no minefields, and with the enemy sitting on top of it. In May ten companies of infantry were needed to cover the sector that in April had been held by two. (An infantry rifle company then contained 129 men, and there were four of these in a battalion.)

This placed a severe strain on Morshead's reserves. Before the May attack he had only four battalions not occupying the Red or Blue lines. Now with the 2/24th so weakened that it had to withdraw for reorganization, he was forced to use the best part of three of his four reserve battalions to hold the Salient sector. Fortunately, the 2/32nd Battalion's arrival on the night of May 4th more than counter-balanced the 2/24th's losses.

Nevertheless, Morshead's resources were sorely over-taxed and he urgently needed to shorten the Salient front so that two battalions could hold it. At this stage the Germans, apparently content with sufficient ground to screen Hill 209, had not tried to occupy all the territory yielded by the garrison on May 2nd and 3rd. In places no-man's-land was well over half a mile wide, and in the next ten days there were only occasional patrol clashes in this area. As a result of these, however, the enemy was persuaded to withdraw a little towards Hill 209 and began to establish a strong line of defensive positions.

On May 13th the 18th Brigade took over the Salient and the western sector, and was ordered to move forward until its battalions were in close contact with the Germans. Moreover, offensive action was very necessary to provide a diversion at Tobruk while British forces on the frontier launched an attack.

During the 14th and 15th the garrison did its best to convince the enemy that it was about to make a thrust towards 209. Radio messages were sent out in the hope that he would intercept them and be misled. To confirm these, trucks and light tanks were driven back and forth between the harbour area and the western sector all day on the 14th, raising foreboding dust-clouds. On the morning of the 15th the R.A.F. reported that enemy tanks were concentrating near Acroma, and that the majority of his troop-carrying vehicles in the Sollum area were withdrawing towards Tobruk.

On the morning of the 15th, as part of the deception, two platoons of the 2/12th Battalion, led by Lieutenants F. K. Haupt and K. B. Thomas and supported by three cruiser tanks, sallied forth to attack Italian positions a mile west of S15. Enemy artillery strafed the tanks as they moved out, but the Italian infantry did not stay to fight. "As they fled," said the 2/12th Battalion's operational report, "they discarded weapons, great-coats and jackets to speed their movement and our platoons were not able to keep up with them." Although it proved to be little more than a demonstration, the raid did succeed in confirming enemy fears as to the garrison's aggressive plans.

This sortie was followed twelve hours later by an advance in the northern sector of the Salient. There the 2/10th's front line, which was between 1200 and 2000 yards from that of the enemy, was moved forward after dark about 1000 yards in one sweep. This straightened the line and brought the Germans under direct machine-gun fire.

While the 2/10th was making this move the enemy attacked in force on the 2/12th's front. He was alarmed by the garrison's apparently offensive preparations and wanted to get in first with an attack which he had evidently been preparing. Good as his observation was from Hill 209, the enemy knew that he could greatly increase the garrison's difficulties by widening his salient and capturing a position known as "Figtree" on the crest of the escarpment overlooking the Derna road. From there he could dominate the flat below this escarpment and force the garrison to withdraw at least to the Blue Line in this sector, and possibly even further.

Towards midnight on the 15th-16th Posts S8, S9 and S10 came under considerable small arms fire and by 2 a.m. the whole sector was being heavily mortared and shelled. Under cover of this, Germans attacked these posts from the south, while Italians went for S15 from the west. The Italians failed completely, even though they used flame-throwers and fought strongly. A few managed to get through the wire, but by dawn the rest had been routed and fifty were soon captured by the 2/12th's patrols.

The Germans had greater success. From midnight onwards S8, S9 and S10 were covered by fire from anti-tank guns and machine-guns. Using tracer shells and bullets, the Germans cunningly guided their infantry to the Australian posts, marking each one with intersecting lines of tracer from either flank. By firing high they enabled their infantry to crawl up close to the posts before they were discovered. At S8 and S9, however, they struck stubborn opposition, which they could not subdue even with the help of tanks. At S9 they actually reached the anti-tank ditch around the post, but a counter-attack, led by Lieutenant A. L. Reid, drove them back.

Meantime another enemy party had pushed on with five tanks to S10, 500 yards behind the other two posts. While fire from the tanks kept its garrison below ground, flame-throwers sprayed the concrete trenches, until the men were virtually scorched out. Before dawn prisoners were observed being marched away from S10 and, as the signal lines to it and the other two posts had been cut, it was presumed that all three were in German hands.

Good shelling by the 51st Field Regiment fortunately prevented the tanks from doing any further damage, and before dawn on the 16th they withdrew. The 2/12th's C.O. (Lieutenant-Colonel John Field) determined to counter-attack at once, but when a platoon led by Lieutenant G. H. Rose tried to get to S10 soon after dawn it was driven back by heavy fire.

Undiscouraged, another patrol attacked about midday with strong artillery support. It had to advance across 900 yards of open desert completely covered by enemy fire, but Lieutenant E. M. Steddy audaciously led his men in, captured the post and with it a German officer and twenty-seven men. He also found

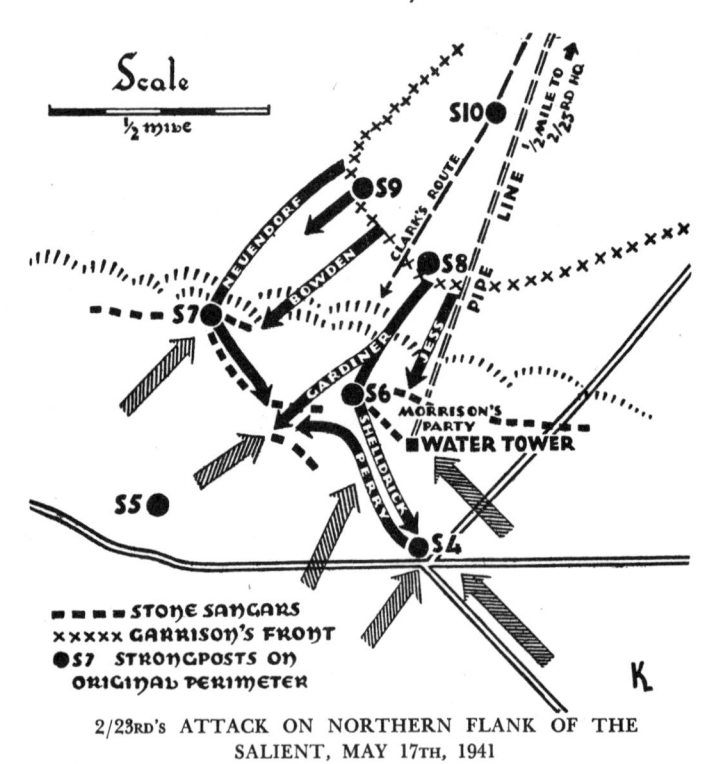

2/23RD's ATTACK ON NORTHERN FLANK OF THE SALIENT, MAY 17TH, 1941

there three Australian wounded, who had been well cared for by the enemy. Although this attack succeeded, no one could get near S8 and S9 until after dark. It was then found that these posts had beaten off half a dozen enemy assaults and had almost run out of ammunition.

Long before this news came through, preparations had been

made for the 2/23rd Battalion, supported by nine "I" tanks, to counter-attack at dawn on May 17th. It was to retake S8 and S9 and continue on to S6 and S7. These two posts were particularly valuable because they were situated on top of a sharp escarpment which commanded a clear view of S8, S9 and S10. When Morshead learned that S8 and S9 had not been lost he ordered the 2/23rd to proceed with the attack on S6 and S7 and, if possible, go on to S5 and S4.

This was no easy task, for the enemy had established himself not only in the old Italian concrete perimeter posts, but also in strongly prepared positions both east and west of them. This meant that in attacking along the line of the old perimeter the Australians would come under fire from either flank as well as from their front. It was important, however, for the garrison to regain the initiative in view of the dangerous enemy concentrations around Acroma which, it was believed, might presage another major attack.

A dawn mist hung over the desert on the 17th as two companies of the 2/23rd waited at their start-line for the barrage to begin. At 5.27 a.m. the Northumberland Fusiliers with twelve Vickers guns put down a belt of fire over S6 and S7 and the flat ground behind them. Three minutes later came a barrage from thirty-nine British guns, a few of which laid a smoke screen around Hill 209 to blind the enemy O.Ps.

When the barrage began, there was no sign of the "I" tanks that were to support the infantry, but the troops set off, expecting the tanks to overtake them. Almost immediately the enemy concentrated his full defensive fire across their path, and added a dense smoke screen. Through this and dust raised by the two barrages, the Diggers soon found they could not see twenty yards. The tanks, coming up behind them, could see nothing and lost their way. Men of the reserve platoons ran to them and hammered on the side and turrets with rocks and rifle-butts, but through the 3-inch armour of the "I" tanks, the crews could hear nothing. No one had told the infantry that on the back of each turret there was a push-button bell by which they could have attracted the crew's attention. Lost, the tanks turned back and the infantry continued on alone.

Mortars and shells fell so thick and fast among them that some men were blown off their feet by the blast, and many were wounded. Field, anti-tank and ack-ack guns provided an intense barrage, but the ack-ack guns were worst of all, for they fired shells that burst into jagged splinters fifty feet above the ground.

Moreover, the whole area was completely covered with crisscrossed fire from light and heavy machine-guns shooting on fixed lines from the front and both flanks. Nevertheless, the infantry kept on, even though about a third of them were killed or wounded before they reached the cover of the escarpment below the enemy posts.

The company on the right, under Captain Ian Malloch, made for S7, intending to attack it with a platoon from either flank. As they advanced Malloch was wounded in the arm and head, but he continued to urge his troops on. Lieutenant J. N. Bowden, also badly wounded, led the left platoon to the top of the rise, but reached it with only a handful of survivors. These captured some German sangars, not far from S7, but had not sufficient strength to attack the main concrete post. Bowden decided to wait for reinforcements, and sent three men back for help. Only one of these reached Malloch but he had no one to send, for the reserve platoon (under Lieutenant G. G. Anderson), which had been delayed while trying to put the tanks on the right course, was now held up near S9. Bowden's party was not heard of again.

Attacking from the other flank Lieutenant Trevor Neuendorf's platoon captured S7 in spite of very heavy casualties only to find that it was completely covered by enemy machine-guns in sangars behind the post. With a small party Neuendorf set out to clear this area and captured several positions, but lost nearly all his men in the process. When the Germans counter-attacked with tanks, Neuendorf and the remnant of his platoon were overwhelmed and taken prisoner. He had no anti-tank guns and no reinforcements could reach him, although some tried to do so. By 7.30 a.m. the enemy was firmly re-established in S7.

Meantime, Major W. H. Perry's company had captured S6, largely through the gallantry of Lieutenant Carl Jess. As his platoon got near the post, it was pinned down by fire from a nearby sangar. Jess led three men forward and silenced it with hand grenades, but in doing this, he was so badly wounded that when the stretcher-bearers came to him, he said, "Leave me here—I'm done. Get some other bloke who's got a chance." Jess's batman, Private H. Coxon, remained to look after him and also Sergeant Roy Jacobs, who had been wounded in both legs as he followed in behind Jess. Both Coxon and Jacobs were captured. Jess is posted "missing believed killed", but his name will be honoured forever among the 2/23rd.

HOLDING THE SALIENT

In S6 Perry's men captured nineteen Germans after a stiff fight, and Perry himself with Lieutenant G. A. Sheldrick's platoon pressed on to S4, while another platoon under Lieutenant George Gardiner was sent to clean up the sangars along the escarpment between S6 and S7.

S4 resisted strongly, but Perry's party captured it, killing most of the garrison and taking four prisoners. Perry fired a success signal, which was also a call for reinforcements, but the air was so thick with smoke and dust that the signal was not seen by the troops waiting to come to his aid.

The capture of S4 and S6 was a splendid achievement, but it was not enough. The whole area on either flank was studded with enemy machine-gun nests, and when Perry left Sheldrick in S4 and set out to escort the four prisoners back to S6, he came under fire at once from Germans still holding out between S6 and S7.

Gathering eight of his own men near S6, Perry led them against the nearest enemy position. Those left in S6 did not see him again, but in a letter written from a prisoner of war camp in Germany he described what happened.

As we rushed the sangars we ran into Gahan,[1] Gardiner and about 12 men who had attacked from a different angle but were not seen owing to the smoke. Just as we cleaned up these sangars, heavy machine-gun fire came from all angles. In a second only five of us were left standing. Immediately I ordered them into the sangars, each dragging a wounded man. Gahan and Gardiner were killed and as the light improved we saw we were almost surrounded. Yet armed only with rifles we kept up a steady fire and held them up for 2¾ hours, when they put over a thin smoke-screen.

I had just popped my head up to have another shot, when I collected on the side of the head two sandbags from the parapet, propelled by an anti-tank shell. I was knocked almost unconscious but was lucky as the shell missed me. By the time I got the sand out of my eyes, three tanks and a team of infantry were almost on top of us. My four lads had no hope and surrendered. I was assisted by a German officer who up till then was my prisoner.

Sheldrick, whom I had left at S4, hung out till the following day. His gang was completely surrounded, made several attempts to get a message back, had no water or food and had run out of ammunition.

While Perry and his men were fighting desperately to hold S6 and S4, Colonel Evans (C.O., 2/23rd) was doing his best to get help to them. But by this time the enemy was concentrating a deadly fire on the area any reinforcements had to cross. Never-

---

[1] Captain S. M. Gahan, Perry's second-in-command, the company sergeant-major, W. G. Morrison, and the survivors of Jess's platoon had been left in S6 when the others went on to S4. When Gardiner's platoon was held up, Gahan took a section from S6 to help him, leaving Morrison in the post with twenty-six men.

theless, at 7.40 a.m. Captain P. E. Spier's company set out for S6 and S7, supported by four "I" tanks. They were greeted with fire of all kinds and smoke and dust made it difficult to see more than fifty yards. This blinded the tank crews, and although they reached the escarpment near S6 they became hopelessly lost. As Spier had been ordered not to attack without the tanks, and as he saw German tanks coming up on his flank, he reluctantly turned back.

The bad visibility served one good purpose. It enabled two Bren carriers to reach S6 with ammunition and rations. The carrier-sergeant (Colin Rigg) found Perry's sergeant-major, W. G. Morrison, and 26 fit men occupying sangars around an old Italian water-tower, 200 yards south of the concrete post, from which they had been driven by severe enemy shelling. Loading five wounded men on to his carriers, Rigg went back for help.

By the time he reached Battalion H.Q. the smoke and dust had cleared and it was impossible for anyone to reach S6. About 9 a.m. when five German tanks were seen cruising round the water-tower, Morrison and his men were given up for lost, for they had no anti-tank guns. The German tanks had in fact shot up their sangars from a range of sixty yards, killing two men; but just when it had seemed that the positions would be over-run, British shells landing all around the Diggers drove the tanks off.

Nevertheless Morrison's force remained in great danger. There was no word from the platoons that had gone forward and no chance of help coming up from behind. Worst of all, the telephone line from S6 back to the Australian lines had been cut by shell-fire. Morrison called for a volunteer to make a dash across the 800 yards of open desert separating them from the nearest Australian post—S8.

"I'll go," said Corporal Fred Carleton, "I'm just the company clerk." He stripped off his equipment and ran, his six feet four making a fine target for the German machine-guns. He eluded them, but when he got near S8 the Diggers there fired on him by mistake. It was not till about midday that he eventually got through to Battalion H.Q. with the news that Morrison's garrison was still resisting but urgently needed to re-establish telephone communication with the artillery, which alone could hold off the Germans.

One of the battalion signallers, Pte. H. P. Clark, volunteered to go out and repair the line. Enemy artillery and machine-guns were still sweeping the area between S10 and S6 as Clark set off across the coverless desert dragging a field telephone with him. Half-crawling, half-sliding, he wormed his way yard by yard along the broken signal line. He repaired twelve breaks and twelve times, when he checked through, he found the line to S6 was still dead. He had now covered well over 1000 yards, but even so was more than 500 from S6. He crawled on, mended the thirteenth break and got through. Morrison, seeing him coming, had sent a man out to repair the line near S6. His job done, Clark worked his way back to S8, with snipers after him most of the way.

Over the phone, Morrison now told Evans that he still had twenty-three men alive and plenty of ammunition; that the tanks had been beaten off by artillery in the morning, but that they and German infantry were gradually closing in. Throughout the rest of the afternoon their attempts were stopped primarily by the accurate shelling which Morrison directed from a sangar beside the water-tower. No German tanks came within 400 yards of the Australian positions, but machine-gunners and snipers sneaked back into sangars which they had abandoned during the morning. Five more men were killed and five wounded, and eventually Morrison had to bring down fire almost on top of his own sangars in order to stop the advance.

Meantime, Evans was organizing another attack with the rest of the battalion, but when it was found that no tanks were available Morshead decided it would be too costly to take S7, and that S6 was useless without it. He would be content for the time being to hold the original line and Morrison would have to withdraw.

As dusk fell, German tanks were seen bearing down on the post. Morrison telephoned urgently for artillery support. It came at once, and the enemy was again checked, but it was clear that the check was only temporary. Evans told Morrison that he would have to get out before it was too late and that two carriers would be sent up for the wounded. As the carriers emerged from the half light, however, the men at the water-tower saw them head straight for an enemy anti-tank gun position, and over the phone from Morrison came this shot for shot description:

"One of the carriers has been hit point blank. It has stopped. The other has been hit. A bloke's getting out of it. He's running round to the front. They're firing at him, but he's climbed aboard and got her going. Both carriers have turned away and they're drawing back out of range."

The carriers returned to Battalion H.Q. Two of the six men who had gone out had been killed and two wounded. The others reported that S6 was being rapidly surrounded and that tanks were waiting to attack as soon as darkness protected them from British shelling.

With only a few minutes of light left, Evans ordered Morrison to make a dash for it, leaving the wounded behind; fourteen good men's lives, he said, could not be risked for the sake of the five wounded. In one minute the artillery would put down a barrage to cover them; Battalion H.Q. would send up white and green flares to guide them in. They must leave.

At six minutes past nine, Morrison shouted to his men to run. They rose from their sangars and made the best pace they could down the escarpment as the British shells thundered down behind them. The Germans saw them go and laid a screen of fire across the stretch of desert they had to cross.

Back at Evans's H.Q. the minutes dragged—9.15, 9.20, 9.25. By 9.30 they should have covered the 800 yards to S8, but there was no word of them. The enemy barrage raged on. Ten o'clock passed and 10.30. By then the German fire had died away and all hope died with it. Behind S10 in the cave which housed his H.Q., Evans said with finality—"If they were going to get through, they'd have been here by now."

But almost immediately he was contradicted by a shout from outside. Morrison and his men were safe. They had not run. They had crawled most of the distance along the shallow ditch of the old Italian pipeline. They had been pursued all the way by a machine-gun firing straight down the pipeline a foot or two above their heads. Six times they had come to points where machine-guns firing from the flanks cut across the ditch. They had watched the tracers go by and squirmed underneath them. They had not been able to get to S8 or S10 for the enemy fire on both had been too hot. They had crawled back more than a mile and a half—almost to Battalion H.Q.—before they were clear of enemy fire.

But they had brought their wounded with them.

It had been a costly day for the 2/23rd, for it had suffered 173 casualties. Of these 173 at least 25 were killed, 59 were wounded and 89 more were missing; many of the missing were taken prisoner and most of these were wounded, but nearly half are presumed to have been killed. Only two officers in the leading companies escaped unhurt; of the others four were killed, three were wounded and captured and one badly wounded. Out of the five platoons that reached the enemy posts, the half-platoon that Morrison led back was the only organized force to survive. The attack might have succeeded but for the enemy's smoke screen, which prevented the tanks finding their way to S6 and S7. Without them, all the gallantry of the infantry was in vain. The attack proved that the Germans had established a strong line running east and west along the top of the escarpment on which S6 and S7 were placed, and that the capture of these posts alone would not force them to withdraw from this general line.

The Germans realized, however, that their existing defences were not strong enough, and within a week Australians could hear pneumatic drills and concrete mixers at night as the enemy prepared pillboxes and elaborate strongpoints in the Salient. If the 2/23rd's attack did nothing else, it put the Germans definitely on the defensive. Morshead, however, could not rest content with passive resistance. Too large a proportion of his forces was still occupied holding the Salient. If an attack on the enemy's flank could not succeed, then his Salient must be reduced by concerted pressure right along the front.

Early in June, when the 20th Brigade took over this sector for the first time, Murray found that, in spite of the 2/10th's advance on the northern flank, he still needed the greater part of his three battalions to hold it, but Morshead ordered him to shorten the line so that at least one battalion could be kept in reserve.

To some extent the Germans made this task easier. Immediately after the Salient Battle, Rommel had ordered the construction of a strong defensive line behind that held by his troops on May 3rd. While his engineers were at work on this, the infantry covered them by holding a chain of outposts several hundred yards in front of these new positions. The new line, shorter and stronger, was completed by the beginning of June and thereafter the Germans did not defend these outposts as strongly as before.

Murray's battalions soon advanced their positions all along the line until they were as close as possible to these outposts. Then by intensive fire they forced the Germans to abandon their forward positions one by one, and withdraw to their basic defence chain, which ran in a rough semi-circle with a radius of about a mile and a half around Hill 209.

Even though the troops did not have to drive the Germans back at bayonet point, the brigade suffered a number of casualties[2] because the enemy had the whole front well covered with machine-guns and mortars, and protected by anti-personnel mines and booby-traps. These defences made the process of

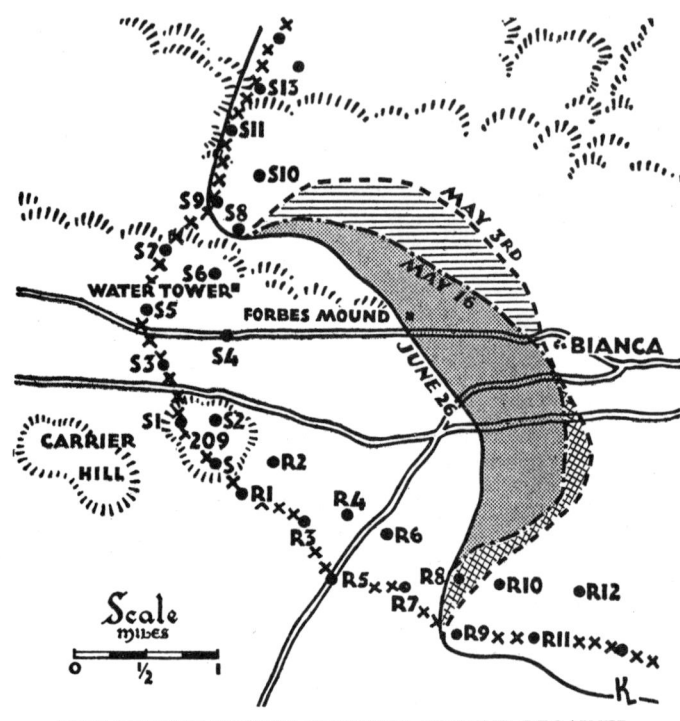

THE SALIENT SECTOR SHOWING GROUND REGAINED
BY THE GARRISON, MAY-JUNE, 1941

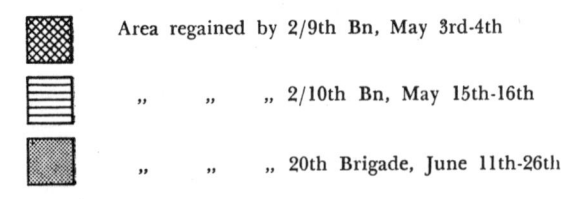

▨ Area regained by 2/9th Bn, May 3rd-4th

▤ „ „ „ 2/10th Bn, May 15th-16th

▦ „ „ „ 20th Brigade, June 11th-26th

moving the line forward slow and difficult. Before new ground could be occupied, the platoon positions had to be cleared of

---

[2] The 2/15th Battalion, for instance, in five weeks had 24 men killed and 69 wounded, even though it made no direct attacks on enemy positions.

enemy "death-traps", and then dug and wired. As all this had to be carried out after dark, each forward bound took several nights to complete.

In June the forward Australian positions were finally advanced to within 500 yards of the enemy's main line and all his outposts were driven back. By the end of the month, the brigade had gained about 1000 yards on a front of a mile and a half, thereby reducing the Salient front from more than five miles to less than four. It was now held by six infantry companies instead of the original ten. By early July, however, the forward troops were battering against the hard core of the German defences and any further westward moves could be made only at the cost of severe casualties. As they withdrew, the Germans sowed the desert so thickly with mines that Australian patrols had to move on hands and knees with the greatest caution. Even so there were many casualties. On June 29th, for instance, a patrol from the 2/15th Battalion struck a minefield only 200 yards in front of its own wire. An anti-personnel mine went off, killed an officer and drew heavy enemy machine-gun fire. As the Diggers flattened themselves out on the desert, they set off more mines which killed two men and wounded the rest.

The casualties from booby-traps and mines would have been far greater but for magnificent work by the 2/13th Field Company. It operated in this sector almost without a break and did much to make the garrison safe against further enemy attacks. The sappers' job called for courage of the highest order. As they crawled forward in the darkness they never knew what they might strike. With tense fingers they searched the desert sand for the three little prongs, which were the triggers of the powerful German "jumping-jack" mines. When these were set off a primary charge exploded, blowing a 9-pound mine, packed with shrapnel, some two feet into the air before it burst. The engineers had to be on the watch also for trip-wires, sometimes strung between camel-thorn bushes, and attached to powerful booby-traps. Having found these they had to disarm them—never quite knowing whether the Germans had not added some new device, which would explode the mine if anyone tried to delouse it.

Everything had to be handled warily. In their abandoned trenches and dug-outs the Germans had left ingenious devices. In one, the moving of an old ammunition box exploded a mine. In others, small yellow blocks, which looked like cakes of soap, had been pushed into crevices between sandbags. They contained plugs of high-explosive that went off when the blocks were disturbed. The German positions were so heavily "booby-trapped" that the troops preferred to dig new ones rather than occupy them. Months later in one ex-German dug-out I saw a large silver torch which everyone coveted but no one was game to touch. For all we knew it might have been quite harmless.

A sapper in Tobruk needed steady fingers and a quick brain. It was his wits against the enemy's and his life depended on his being able to find and disarm in pitch darkness any one of a dozen German, Italian, British or home-made mines and booby-traps. Not content with this, the engineers brought the enemy's deadly contraptions back and laid them in front of the Australian positions. Usually they improved them, fitting devices that made them "un-delousable".

The Australian sappers' informal methods were in striking contrast to the more systematic approach of the Germans who not only put down minefields in a strictly regular pattern, but made the very laying of them an elaborate parade-ground performance. A captured German manual prescribed the most formal drill. Here is an excerpt:

Laying of Un-camouflaged or Open Section Minefields
First Type: Mine-laying from column of threes: one Teller mine to one metre.

The section commander gives the *command:* "Lay mines without camouflage, from column of threes—Double." The left-hand man in each file marches ten paces. The right-hand man marches twenty paces. The centre man in each file remains stationary. All make a right turn. The section commander gives the command: "Lay first mine."

Execution: Each man lays the mine in his right hand on the ground between his feet . . .

The section commander then gives the command: "Lay second mine."

Execution: Each man takes ten paces forward and five paces to the left and lays the mine as before. Each man buries his second mine first, i.e. the mine he laid last and then his first mine.

No doubt the Germans modified this formal drill when laying minefields in the Salient, but they still put them down in a set pattern, which could be easily followed by the Diggers who merely moved along the line of the field and knew that at regular intervals they would find a mine. The Germans on the other hand had a hard job following Australian minefields. The Diggers were not fussy about accurate spacing or straight lines. If they came to a piece of rocky ground they went round where it was soft. If their pattern was a little cock-eyed, all the better for fooling the enemy. Their drill consisted of little more than —"This'll do. Put 'er in there, mate. She's right."

By the time German sappers had finished, their front in the Salient was covered by one huge minefield, but it would have been foolish for the garrison to presume that, because the Germans had mined themselves in, Tobruk was safe from further attack in this sector. Morshead still felt that the German wedge in the garrison's western flank was a serious weakness which he must remove before the enemy became strong enough to attack again. As the Germans could not be driven back by thrusting westward, he decided to try once more to pinch off their wedge by simultaneous attacks against the flanks from north and south along the line of the old perimeter. The 2/12th and 2/9th had attempted this on May 3rd before the Germans were firmly established; a fortnight later, the 2/23rd had found that the enemy had consolidated rapidly on the northern flank. Since then the Germans had been working hard for three months to make their positions impregnable. In view of this, it seemed unlikely that another attack by the garrison would have more chance of success.

Morshead, however, had broader questions to consider. The garrison's role was to do more than hold on. To keep a large number of Axis troops, and especially Germans, tied up outside Tobruk it had to be aggressive. Moreover, now that Rommel had completed his fortifications in the Salient he might well feel strong enough to man them with Italians. The Germans had to be kept there by threatening their hold on the Salient.

Morshead was confronted with a difficult decision. Reinforcements were slow in coming and reserves were so low that A.S.C. personnel had already been drafted into infantry battalions. Consequently he could not afford to employ sufficient troops to make success reasonably certain. If he struck and recovered Hill 209, the garrison's general position would be much stronger, and the regained sector could be held by one battalion instead of the two it was now taking to man the Salient positions. But he had to be sure that the nett strength of the garrison would not be reduced; that the cost of recovering the ground would not be greater than the value of the ground recovered.

Launching this attack was no easy matter, primarily because of the difficulty of obtaining accurate information about the German strength and dispositions. No air photographs were available and patrols found it hard to get close enough to examine and chart the enemy defences; harder still to get a prisoner, for the Germans sat tight behind their wire and minefields. But the Australians did know that they could not use tanks in this heavily mined area and that any infantry attack would have to be made at night.

Early in July, Brigadier A. H. L. Godfrey's[3] 24th Brigade relieved the 20th in the Salient, and before the end of the month Morshead ordered him to attack the German positions. It was decided to use the 2/43rd Battalion to attack from the south against Posts R7, R6, and R5, while the 2/28th struck at Posts S6 and S7 on the northern flank. In preparation for this, patrols intensified their search for enemy weak spots.

Several patrols from the 2/43rd penetrated deep into German territory and mapped positions, but how strongly these were held could be ascertained only from a prisoner. After several vain attempts, a patrol of seventeen, commanded by Lieutenant D. C. Siekmann, was sent out on the night of July 27th-28th to secure a prisoner at all costs. The patrol, guided by Sergeant C. H. Cawthorne, worked its way through the German minefields and forward defences without mishap. They had gone 1000 yards beyond these, when Cawthorne saw an enemy party approaching. The Australians went to ground and waited. When the Germans were ten yards away, Cawthorne dashed forward calling on them to surrender. They opened fire—wounding Cawthorne twice, but when the Australians replied, the enemy broke and ran with Cawthorne in hot pursuit. He killed one and grabbed another—an N.C.O. Two more Germans were killed. Aroused by this skirmish, the Germans in the forward positions at once sent out patrols to cut off the Australians' retreat. They might have succeeded but for Siekmann's coolness. Spotting the Germans first, he ordered his men to ground and they lay silent for fifteen minutes until the enemy gave up the search. Finally he led his patrol safely back, bringing in two wounded Diggers and the German prisoner.

In addition to this preparatory patrolling, the 2/43rd's attack was rehearsed on a specially built model of R7, but until the post was actually attacked no one realized the strength of its

---

[3] Godfrey, who had commanded the 2/6th Battalion during the 6th Division's attack on Bardia and Tobruk, had been appointed to command the 24th Brigade in February. He led it with great distinction at Tobruk and El Alamein. His death in action there was a sore loss to the A.I.F., for he was one of its finest and most popular leaders. Serving with the 5th Division in the last war he won the M.C. and in this war was awarded the D.S.O. and Bar.

defences. This was soon evident when four platoons[4] of the 2/43rd, led by Captain L. McCarter, attacked it at 3.30 a.m. on August 3rd. They went in under cover of the most severe artillery barrage the Tobruk garrison had ever laid down. More than fifty guns concentrated on enemy batteries behind Hill 209, and on the positions that the 2/43rd and 2/28th were to attack. In addition, Vickers guns of the Northumberland Fusiliers raked the tops of the enemy posts. This kept the Germans in R7 quiet while Australian sappers and infantry, led by Lieutenant R. P. Tapp, moved in to blow the wire. As soon as the garrison's barrage began, the enemy replied with heavy shell-fire right along the Salient front, but it was only when the Bangalore torpedoes exploded in the wire surrounding R7 that German machine-guns and mortars opened up in full force.

As the Bangalores went off, the infantry dashed forward. One platoon, led by Sergeant R. B. Quinn, attacked from the south, but as his leading section reached the wire, the men were silhouetted by enemy flares and machine-gun and mortar fire wiped them out. Quinn's two other sections got through the wire but ran at once into a minefield fifty yards deep and evidently extending right up to the anti-tank ditch around the post. Only eight men reached the ditch, but from its shelter they carried on a grenade duel with the Germans in machine-gun pits only a few yards away, until all except Quinn and two others had been killed or badly wounded.

Another platoon—under Lieutenant Siekmann—attacked simultaneously from the east, but did not get far through the wire. A mortar bomb landed in the middle of one section; another suffered crippling casualties on a booby-trap field outside the wire. Eventually Siekmann and three other survivors were pinned down short of the post when the Germans laid a heavy barrage right on to R7, regardless of the safety of their own men. Simultaneously machine-guns from positions behind that post turned their fire on to it. The four Australians tried to go on, but when one man was killed and another wounded, Siekmann and the third Digger crawled back dragging the wounded man with them.

Regardless of the enemy fire, Sergeant Tom Charlton led the reserve platoon in to help Quinn, but less than a dozen of his men reached the anti-tank ditch. From there, however, with

---

[4] There are three platoons—nominally with 36 men in each—to an infantry company, but these were below strength and only 129 men of the 2/43rd were engaged.

Quinn's few survivors, they fought for nearly an hour to gain the post itself. At last, when he and all his officers and most of his N.C.Os had been wounded, McCarter ordered the survivors to withdraw. Out of the 129 infantry who went in, only 23 came out unscathed. Most of the wounded were brought back before dawn, but there were still more than 30 unaccounted for. Whether they were killed, wounded or captured no one knew, but one of the 2/43rd's stretcher-bearers, Sergeant Walter Tuit, was determined to find out. About 8 a.m. he was given permission to take a truck, flying a Red Cross flag, into no-man's-land in the hope of recovering some of the casualties. As Tuit told me later:

> We didn't know what sort of reception we'd get, as almost any truck which came near the perimeter in daylight used to get shelled. But I stood on the bonnet, holding up a big Red Cross flag and hoping for the best. They didn't fire a shot. When we were 400 yards south of R7 we stopped the truck and I went forward with a stretcher-bearer named Keith Pope, and our padre, Father Gard, followed along behind us. I still had a flag, and when we were about 250 yards from the post, a German stood up with another flag like mine.
>
> He shouted what sounded like "Halten Minen". We could tell we were on the edge of a minefield because we could see the bodies of thirteen of our chaps lying there. A couple of Jerries came out with an electrical mine-detector and guided a lieutenant and a doctor out to us. I told the officer we wanted to pick up our dead and wounded. He replied in English. "Very well, but only one truck and only two men at a time. You must not come closer than this. We will send your wounded out."
>
> They brought four wounded and let the truck come up to take them away. Then they carried out the bodies of fifteen dead and helped us with those in the minefield. I told the doctor we were four short and he replied that three of our wounded had been taken away in ambulances early that morning; another, badly wounded, had chosen to stay because his brother had been taken prisoner. When the last of our dead had been brought to us, the lieutenant told me we were not to move until they were all back in the post and had taken in their flag. He went back; his men went below. He lowered his flag and I lowered mine. I saluted him, and he saluted back, but he gave me the salute of the Reichswehr, not of the Nazis. Our armistice was over.

During the day there was some characteristic German showmanship, evidently designed to impress the Diggers with the good conditions under which the Germans were living. Tuit reported that those who came near him were all cleanly and neatly dressed, freshly shaved and with their hair brilliantined. One German ostentatiously had a bath in the open, using plenty of water. Another brought Tuit several drinks—cold tea, sweet Derna water and finally a fresh lemon squash.

It was no fault of the attacking troops that they failed. The enemy defences proved to be very much stronger than expected, but in spite of this, and of the heavy casualties and early loss of most of their leaders, the troops fought their way courageously through to the posts. So few reached there that they had no chance of success.

The German account of the attack contained in the records of the 2nd Battalion of the 115th Motorized Infantry Regiment, which was holding this part of the Salient, claims that the Germans lost only four killed and six wounded in R7, but Tuit reported that six enemy ambulances—of a type which carried half a dozen men—came up to R7 during the day. This means that either the German battalion records are wrong or else the ambulances were used to bring up military stores and/or reinforcements.

Meantime on the northern flank the attack by Captain R. A. E. Conway's company of the 2/28th had drawn the enemy's full defensive fire in front of and around S6 and S7, and this took heavy toll of the infantry advancing to storm the posts. The commander of the platoon that went for S6 (Lieutenant J. M. Head) was wounded and half his men became casualties as they approached. They had to advance over a rise, and were thus easy targets in the moonlight. Barely a dozen got to the wire and, even though they fought for more than an hour, they could not bring to bear upon the post and the sangars near it sufficient fire to keep the German machine-guns quiet. The survivors had no chance of reaching S6 and before dawn they withdrew.

In the meantime two platoons had gone for S7. Wearing rubber-soled desert boots, they had worked their way through the enemy's lines west of S7 without disturbing his outposts, and had come at it from behind. The barrage under which they advanced was heavy and accurate—so much so that five direct hits were scored on S7 itself. (This and the fact that the troops slipped past the outposts undetected, is stated in the records of the 2nd Battalion, 104th Motorized Infantry Regiment, which held this part of the line.) However, the infantry suffered heavily from enemy artillery and mortars as they moved in to attack and, as soon as the wire surrounding the post was blown, they came under fierce machine-gun fire from sangars behind and on either flank of S7. The result was that only Lieutenant H. T. Coppock and two men out of the leading platoon reached the post in the first rush. Some Germans got away but four were killed and six captured.

Coppock had been ordered to fire a Very light success signal as soon as he reached the post, but when he looked for the flare cartridges, which had been carried in a bag strapped to his back, he found it had been shot away. He could give no signal, and Lieutenant S. C. McHenry's platoon and Conway's Company H.Q., which were waiting to come in, hung back. Worse still, two signalmen, who reached the post a few minutes later, having laid a line from the nearest Australian post, S9, found that shell-fire had cut the wire. Coppock immediately sent a man back to contact Conway but he did not get through, and when no help arrived Coppock, although badly wounded, set out himself to obtain assistance.

He had barely left when Conway with McHenry and the remnant of the latter's platoon reached the post and found it held by the two signalmen and several of Coppock's men, who had been wounded but had managed to crawl to the post. Conway at once fired a success signal, but by this time it was nearly light, and when reinforcements tried to reach the post heavy fire stopped them.

At dawn about sixty Germans attacked but were beaten off, and all that day Conway held on with McHenry, nine fit men, ten wounded and the six German prisoners. The enemy, apparently mindful of his experience on May 17th, did not attack again in daylight, though he did shell and mortar the post, and prevented reinforcements reaching it. It was clear that the Germans were only waiting for nightfall before counter-attacking. Hoping to get help in time, Conway sent the two signalmen (W. G. Delfs and L. L. White) as soon as it was dark to lay a phone line back to S9 and take a message to his C.O., Lieutenant-Colonel J. E. Lloyd. As the signalmen left the post in the moonlight enemy machine-guns opened fire on them, but by wriggling 300 yards on their stomachs and crawling most of the remaining distance, they got through.

At 9.15 p.m.—even before the signallers reached S9—Very light signals from S7 indicated that Conway's small garrison was being attacked. Lloyd tried to send help, but heavy enemy fire between S9 and S7 made this impossible. Before dawn on the 4th, a patrol from the 2/32nd Battalion got nearly to S7, but found the Germans were already strongly re-established there. The attempt to regain S7 and S6 had already cost the 2/28th 82 casualties out of 135 men who went into the attack. It was decided that further losses would be futile. Even if S7 could be recaptured, it could not be held unless the escarpment that ran through the two posts was taken as well. Morshead could not spare sufficient troops to undertake that task. (The German records state that their casualties in this attack on S7 and S6

HOLDING THE SALIENT

were 18 killed and 32 wounded. These are surprisingly low, but as the figures were given in an official document and not a propaganda statement they are probably correct.)

This was the last attempt the garrison made to re-take the Salient or even to reduce the German hold. The enemy was so strongly established that no direct assault on it would have a chance of success, unless such could be supported by far heavier artillery fire than Tobruk could put down. The German account of the action suggests that the August attack might have succeeded if the Tobruk artillery had concentrated on the heavy machine-guns in the German reserve line, instead of on the Axis artillery behind Hill 209. But what the Australian infantry really needed was sufficient artillery support to neutralize the fire from both field and machine-guns simultaneously. Tobruk did not have enough guns to do that.

After this failure the garrison concentrated on making its defences as impregnable as the enemy's. This was a dangerous job. The Germans had built their main line at a time when our nearest posts were 1000 yards or more away; but now the Australians had to work within 500 yards of an enemy whose machine-gunners sprang to action on the slightest provocation. Nevertheless, during its last spell in the Salient in August and September, Tovell's 26th Brigade did magnificent work laying new minefields and re-wiring the whole sector.

This task was carried out with particular energy by the 2/24th Battalion. Deeply concerned because they had been holding Hill 209 when the Germans broke through, Spowers and his men were determined that by the time they had finished work on the line no German would ever get through again. The 2/24th had a spell in each sector of the Salient during this period, and it completed the re-wiring and mining of most of its positions. It was hard and hazardous work as is shown by these comments of Captain A. W. Oakley, who was second-in-command of a company:

During this time we put a triple concertina fence round most of the 6000-yard Salient front, and dog-legged it, so that our machine-guns could fire down the legs of the wire. Then we laid blocks of mines on our side so that German delousing parties could not easily get at them. To make things harder, we covered the minefield with a maze of trip-wires and booby-traps.

The hardest part was dog-legging the wire, for we were holding the outside of a semicircle and we had to be careful that we didn't direct fire from one of our posts on to another. The only way we could fix the line of the wire was to take compass bearings on tracers or flares fired straight up into the air from the posts and from the angles in the wire. As all this had to be done at night amid a tangle of old wire, mines and booby-traps, with the enemy only 150 to 500 yards away, it was no easy task. In our company alone we had four officers and about 25 men killed or wounded by mines and booby-traps, and a number of other casualties from enemy fire in four weeks. One night on a reconnaissance two officers were killed and my O.C., Bill Sheehan, was badly wounded when a "jumping-jack" mine exploded. Sheehan was hurried back to hospital with such severe wounds in the lung that our M.O. gave him little chance. But that same night he drew a plan of all the ground he had covered and sent it out to me by "Don R". His action saved us nights of reconnaissance and no doubt a number of lives as well. By some miracle Sheehan recovered. Without his plan we should never have finished the task we'd set ourselves—the wiring of our company's front before we were relieved.

The Australians, however, did not rest content with strengthening their defences. They maintained the upper hand by severe fire from weapons most of which had been captured. The Germans fought strongly back, especially with their mortars, which were so accurate that they frequently landed bombs right into Australian machine-gun pits. Unfortunately these could not be effectively answered by British mortars, which had a comparatively short range. To be of any real value they had to be fired from the forward infantry posts, but as soon as one opened up it "drew the crabs".

Tobruk, however, had a number of captured Italian mortars, with nearly three times the range of the British weapons. By using these dug-in behind the front line, the garrison managed to keep enemy mortars fairly quiet without drawing retaliation on our forward infantry. Before this was done, however, the morale of the troops suffered considerably because they had nothing with which to hit back at the weapon that caused most casualties. German mortars were particularly active at night, but at first artillery was not used to counter them since night firing gave away the gun positions. In the later months a few guns were moved into special pits each night, and from these fired on the flashes of enemy mortars with considerable success.

To keep the Germans on the defensive the 26th Brigade severely blitzed any positions that became troublesome. In these harassing shoots one small German strongpost would be plastered with machine-gun, mortar and artillery fire for fifteen to twenty minutes. The moral effect of these sudden and heavy concentrations on a small area was greater than that of the enemy's widespread and incoordinated fire. By systematically dealing with each strongpoint in turn, the garrison forced the Germans to move position repeatedly and to keep relatively quiet.

By these tactics the Australians gained a moral advantage which had very important material results. Apart from covering

HOLDING THE SALIENT

their front by fixed-line fire, the Germans in later months seldom opened up except in retaliation. In country where movement was possible only at night and over ground swept by hostile machine-guns, the side that "called the tune", as the Australians did, had a great advantage.

In spite of the record of Gallipoli, Australians have been popularly regarded as attacking troops who lack the patience necessary for prolonged defence. This view was confounded by the Diggers who held the Tobruk Salient. The weeks they spent there were made up of days of boring, cramped, sweltering idleness; nights of watching, working and firing. The Diggers hated the job but they stuck it out. The full measure of their success was not known until certain German documents fell into our hands. These included a report by Major Ballerstedt, C.O. 2nd Battalion, 115th Motorized Infantry Regiment, which held part of the Salient. It ran:

> The Australians, who are the men our troops have had opposite them so far, are extraordinarily tough fighters. The German is more active in the attack, but the enemy stakes his life in the defence and fights to the last with extreme cunning. Our men, usually easy-going and unsuspecting, fall easily into his traps, especially as a result of their experiences in the closing stages of the European Campaign.
>
> The Australian is unquestionably superior to the German soldier: i. In the use of individual weapons, especially as snipers. ii. In the use of ground camouflage. iii. In his gift of observation, and the drawing of correct conclusions from his observation. iv. In using every means of taking us by surprise.
>
> Enemy snipers achieve astounding results. They shoot at anything they recognize. Several N.C.Os of the battalion have been shot through the head with the first bullet while making observations in the front line. Protruding sights in gun directors have been shot off, observation slits and loopholes have been fired on, and hit, as soon as they were seen to be in use (i.e. when the light background became dark). For this reason loopholes must be kept plugged with a wooden plug to be taken out when used so that they always show dark.
>
> The enemy shoots very accurately with his mortars. He generally uses these in conjunction with a sniper, or machine-gun. The greatest mistake in such cases is to leave cover and try to withdraw over open ground. It is necessary to dig several alternative positions connected by crawl trenches.

This tribute does much to explain why the Australians were able to keep the Germans on the defensive. It shows, too, why Rommel felt it necessary to build such strong fortifications in the Salient and to pack them with so many of his best troops. After the 20th Brigade shortened the line in June, the garrison held it with only two battalions. On the other hand, even though Rommel had the advantage of stronger ground and defences, he had to man the Salient with three motorized infantry battalions, and to hold two companies of special troops and one tank battalion in reserve.

From captured documents we now know that the Germans held the Salient in very considerable depth from their front line posts right back to Hill 209. The documents show that from May until mid-August the Germans had in the Salient the 2nd Battalion of the 115th Motorized Infantry Regiment on the southern flank, this Regiment's 1st Battalion in the centre, and the 104th Regiment's 2nd Battalion on the northern flank. In support they had two "Oasis Companies"—special desert troops of the Afrika Korps—one battalion of the 5th Tank Regiment, the 115th Artillery Regiment and one battalion plus two companies of anti-tank guns. The defences of the Salient were constructed by the 33rd Engineer Battalion, which began to straighten the line on May 19th and finished the job by June 1st. Almost immediately the Germans abandoned the area east of this new line, but in this territory the German engineers left 2300 anti-tank mines and 1750 anti-personnel mines and booby-traps. In mid-August, the three original infantry battalions were relieved by three new battalions of the 90th German Light Division, and so long as Australians held the Salient no Italians were put into the line opposite them.

Covering the 5300-yard front they eventually held between R7 and S7, the Germans had more than 200 machine-guns and 72 anti-tank guns. Half of these were crammed into their front line posts, giving them a machine-gun for every 50 yards and an anti-tank gun for every 150. Even with all its captured weapons the garrison never had such heavy fire-power as this, but what it had, it used to excellent advantage.

Potentially the Salient was a dagger in the side of the Tobruk garrison just as the garrison itself was a dagger in the side of the Axis forces in Cyrenaica. But from June onwards the Salient did not prove the embarrassment to Morshead that the Tobruk garrison did to Rommel. The Germans in the Salient were forced on to the defensive; the Tobruk garrison, operating against Rommel's flank, never ceased twisting the dagger. The cost to the Germans of holding the Salient might have been worth while if it had kept the rest of the garrison quiet. But Tobruk's answer to this threat was not static defence but increasing aggression on every other sector of the front.

CHAPTER XV

Salient Scenes

HOLDING the Salient was a matter of patience as much as courage, for boredom and discomfort were persistent enemies. In the pages that follow I have set down what I saw and heard while living for several days among the troops who held these positions.

ROOM WITHOUT BATH

All day we lay in a dug-out just big enough for three Diggers and me stretched out. Four feet above us was a roof of corrugated iron resting on sleepers and over that sandbags, earth and bits of camel-bush, which made the top of the dug-out just one more piece of desert to German snipers scanning the level plain from 500 yards away. The late afternoon sun beat down on the sandbags. We were clammy with sweat. The wind died away and dust stopped drifting in through the small air vent and the narrow low doorway that led to the crawl trench outside. The air was heavy with dust, cigarette smoke and the general fug we'd been breathing in and out for the past thirteen hours. We waited for darkness when we could stretch our legs and fill our lungs with fresh, cool air, and the troops could crack at the Hun who had been lying all day in his dug-out, too.

Every so often we'd hear the rumble of guns, and shells would whistle high overhead. The gunners were having their evening "hate", but the enemy's shells were landing well back. His machine-guns had been silent since dawn. Even his mortars had not been landing with their usual unheralded crump around our forward posts. It had been a quiet day—like so many since the hard battles in the Salient in May.

I woke about seven in the evening and started to scratch. I seemed to be itching all over—the itchiness of being dirty. You get that way after the flies and fleas have been at you all day. You don't know whether you've been bitten or not, and you just scratch as a matter of routine. In the far corner Mick was doing a bit of hunting. He had his shirt off. Seriously, deliberately he ran his thumb nail under the seam and a slow smile of success spread across his face. "Got you, you little ———. That makes four less anyway!"

Over by the phone Ernie, the platoon commander, was censoring letters, which had to go back to Company H.Q. with the ration party after dark. He was only a sergeant and should not have been exercising an officer's privilege of censoring letters, but his battalion (the 2/24th) was still so short of officers that this rule was not strictly observed in the case of platoon commanders whose commissions were about to come through any day.

Ernie had shaved since lunch and then "bathed" in his shaving water. He said he felt a new man. The phone beside him buzzed. "Ernie's here," he said, ". . . Say again . . . oh . . . ammo. . . . Send us up 500 Bren and 500 Breda . . . yeah . . . got plenty o' smokes . . . an' look, what's the ration with that writin' paper? . . . What? . . . Three envelopes and eight sheets a man . . . an' I got to censor the lot . . . O.K. . . . What? . . . Oh, pretty quiet down here . . . not even enough to make life interestin' . . . No, nothin' else—not unless you got some bloody beer."

Beer? Even Charlie woke up at that; a Queensland miner, he still had a miner's thirst. He didn't do very well on a waterbottle a day. "Beer," he said, "there ain't no such thing. I 'aven't 'ad four beers in the last six months, and we won't get no more now till they get us out of 'ere; an' Gawd knows when that'll be."

Mick chipped in again—"I know what I'll do when I get out. I'm going to a pub and I'm going to have a hot bath and splash the water all over the floor—I'm going to *waste* it. Then I'll drain out the mud and fill the bath again with clean water and I'll lie there and wallow. And while I'm lying there they can bring me iced beer. And when I've had enough of the bath, and I've had a feed, I'll just get into bed and they can bring me beer and more beer. I've got a six months' thirst!"

Charlie broke in—"Well, if you was given the choice of beer or a bath right now, what'd you pick?"

"I'd rather have a bath," said Ernie. "One beer now'd only take the dust off my throat. Even a bottle wouldn't do any real good. I'd rather get clean in a decent bath and get on some clean clobber instead of the lousy things that you live in here day and night till you stink."

They all agreed with Ernie, but right then a cup of tea would have done. We hadn't had one all day. We didn't have a primus and we couldn't light a fire. The enemy hadn't picked up this post and the boys didn't want to give him a trail of smoke on which to lay his machine-guns.

We'd been up all night and during the day the flies and fleas had done their best to stop us sleeping. We'd had a quiet night, but the troops were still weary. The tucker had been late getting up from the company cook-house, and the bully stew and tea were almost cold by the time they reached the forward posts. The carrying party had been held up by enemy machine-guns firing during those few hours just after dark when there was almost a gentleman's agreement not to fire at all, so that both sides could get their evening meal.

Usually from dark until midnight you could safely move around the Salient posts, but about twelve o'clock the fun started. By day you couldn't move at all. In the dead flat desert the machine-gunners and snipers on both sides could see every move. And so for thirteen hours of daylight both sides lay quiet and fought vermin and boredom. In most parts you couldn't even stand up, for the unyielding Libyan rock made the digging of deep trenches impossible in this sector. This meant that you lay in a stuffy dug-out all day and sat in a cramped shallow weapon pit all night. You might stretch your legs going back to Company H.Q. after dark to guide the ration party forward. That was exercise but it was no pleasure stroll, for you never knew when the Hun would forget the rules and start sweeping the desert with machine-guns.

You couldn't dig communication trenches leading back to Company and Battalion H.Q., as in France during the last war, and for hundreds of yards back behind the front there was no dead ground to give you cover. In fact, most of the time you were safer in the front line posts than walking about on the plain. You might also find some exercise in working on the posts at night—repairing the wire or digging deeper weapon pits and trenches; but you couldn't do much between bursts of fire. You had to keep the upper hand by giving the Germans more than burst for burst. Some nights these private machine-gun battles developed into willing combats with fire from mortars and artillery added. During the night you took your turn in the listening post a couple of hundred yards out in no-man's-land —lying in an 18-inch trench; straining your eyes and ears; slowly growing numb with cold. Then came the stand-to, and you waited for dawn with its uneasy quiet.

Once it was light, if anyone happened to be wounded or ill, he had to lie there until dark, while his mates gave him what attention they could. One afternoon in a forward post a sergeant was badly wounded. His mates couldn't move him back in daylight, so a Digger telephoned to Company H.Q. While he was speaking a mortar cut the line, but the Digger crawled out some distance under enemy fire and repaired it. From telephoned directions he dressed the wounds and kept the sergeant alive until he could be taken out on a stretcher. It wasn't altogether a sweet job in the Salient posts. Quite apart from discomfort and the nervous strain of holding the most vital part of the perimeter, there was the constant struggle with boredom.

There was little to do in the drawn-out daylight hours in a muggy, cramped dug-out. You could try to make up for lost sleep; or write a few letters—only there wasn't much to tell; or read a well-thumbed magazine or book that was lying round the dug-out—but you'd probably read them before; you could smoke cigarette after cigarette—if you had enough. The supply was better than it had been—fifty a week as an issue; perhaps another fifty from the canteen or the Comforts Fund. But you needed every cigarette you could get when time hung heavy on your hands.

Boredom and discomfort took your appetite away. You had a hot meal at night. That was usually fairly good—these days anyhow—bully-beef stew with vegetables; tea and a pudding, sometimes stewed fruit. But for other meals you couldn't cook anything. If you didn't possess a primus—and few posts did—you just had bread and marg., jam and cheese, washed down with chlorinated water for breakfast and lunch.

Usually you didn't feel hungry enough to tackle the ration of cold bully, let alone the cold tinned bacon or salt herrings. There were about twenty tins of these stacked in a corner of the dug-out.

"Do you ever tackle the bacon or the goldfish, Ernie?"

"No," he said, "don't feel like it. We've told them not to send any more but it's on the ration scale; so up it comes. We can't cook the bacon and there's no water here for washing dixies."

"Anyhow they make you too thirsty," said Charlie. "The Jerries've got the right idea. We found some of their stuff in a dug-out we took. There was cubes of chocolate, concentrated sugar, milk tablets, dried fruits, lemon drink tablets to put in your water bottle and that sorta thing."

"A few things like that'd make all the difference," said Mick. "The blokes wouldn't be too bored to eat then. What they don't understand back there is that in these dug-posts boredom's worse than the Boche."

But they made the best of it. Late in the afternoon Paddy— a kid of nineteen who had been sleeping in the other dug-out— breezed in. "Blasted fleas kept me awake all day," he said. "Still, I can't quite make up my mind what to do to-night. Dunno whether to go to the pictures or take me girl friend down to the beach."

"Why don't you pour yourself out a long cool beer and think it over?" said Mick.

Soon after dark a Digger came over from another post; his face was glum. "They got Pete last night," he said. "He was out in the listenin' post and he copped a stray burst as he was comin' in."

The dug-out was heavy with silence until Ernie said, "So they got Pete, eh? In a listenin'-post . . . Wouldn't it? We were mates when we joined up. A bloke doesn't mind so much if he gets knocked in a stunt. He more or less expects that, but to cop it out in a listenin'-post—I don't want to go that way. That makes his section pretty weak; only five blokes now instead of ten. I wish those reos[1] would come over from Aussie a bit quicker. We could do with 'em."

"Couldn't we?" said Mick. "I wouldn't mind going home for a bit. There's lots of chaps I know there, cobbers of mine— once. They aren't married and they aren't keeping families or anyone, except themselves. I'd like to go back and tell 'em what I think. One of our fellows wrote a poem about 'My Friends Who Stayed at Home'. They reckon he got killed a few days later. He was rough, but he was dinkum, like his poem. Want to hear it?"

He lit a smoky hurricane and pulled a crumpled piece of paper from his pocket. In his voice as he read, I sensed a feeling that was widespread among the men who had fought so stubbornly, cheerfully and gallantly to hold Tobruk. It was one of disappointment and resentment. They were bitter because they felt that they'd been let down by some of their own people. To some extent it was unreasoning, unquestioning resentment;

---

[1] Reinforcements.

but it was real and widespread. The men didn't stop to think that there were many vital jobs to be done in Australia if they were to be kept fighting. All they knew was that newspapers from home still contained stories of strikes and political squabbles. Not unnaturally, they blamed these for the shortage of equipment and reinforcements. They had seen many of their best mates fall in an unequal struggle and they knew how slowly others arrived from Australia to take their places. What they felt and said was bluntly expressed in the verses Mick read:[2]

> I'm pullin' off my colours, I'll throw away my web,
> I'm goin' down to Cairo to get a beer an' bed.
> I'm tired o' bein' a soldier, so 'elp me Gawd I am;
> Of dust an' salty water; of bully, marg. an' jam;
> Of fightin' Huns an' Dagoes out here all on our own,
> While sittin' back in Aussie, are my friends who stayed at home.
>
> Now when I told my mother I'd volunteered to fight,
> She said, "God bless you, Digger, an' bring you back all right."
> But they called me "chocolate soldier" an' "five bob tourist" too,
> They said, "You'll never see the front—or even get a view."
> They said, "You'll have a picnic no matter where you roam."
> But they weren't game to face it, my friends who stayed at home.
>
> They're not such bad shots either—along the rabbit track;
> For rabbits aren't so dangerous; an' rabbits don't hit back.
> They shine before the barmaid; they brag, they're full of skitin',
> But at the corner of the street is where they do their fightin'.
> A billiard cue their rifle, a bar their battle zone,
> For there there are no bullets for my friends who stayed at home.
>
> I'll bet they're walkin' down the street, their chests puffed out with pride,
> An' skitin' to their cobbers how they saved their worthless hide.
> While out here in the desert if a bloke should show his head
> He'll just as likely get it filled with some damn German's lead.
> But give me the old Lee-Enfield; I'll buckle me webbin' about.
> Though I'm only a flamin' private, I'll see this business out,
> And if I stop a bullet, I'll die without a moan,
> Though they put the kibosh on me—my friends who stayed at home.

No one said anything when Mick finished reading. He took out the makings. "And the bloke who wrote that stopped one," he said. "Wonder what's stopping those blokes back home?"

"They Gotta be Good to Get You"

All we could see ahead was a trail of dust, as we followed a truck laden with mail, rations and ammunition. It was nearly

---

[2] Although hundreds of Diggers in Tobruk firmly believed that this poem had been written by one of the garrison, I understand that it is a last war veteran. It is quoted here because so many Australians in Tobruk adopted it as the expression of their own viewpoint.

dark and for once the enemy was not shelling as we drove across the flat in front of the Blue Line minefield and made for a twisted wadi that led to the headquarters of the battalion holding the northern sector of the Salient.

The track was a trough of brown powder, which swirled up under the floor-boards of our open "pick-up"—a sturdy little Morris truck specially built for war in the desert. It had no hood or wind-shield, and the dust made me cough. "Can't take it, eh?" said the Digger at the wheel. "I'll try it out here where it's not churned up, but you'll probably get your guts bounced out as we go over the camel-thorn."

He lugged the wheel over, but it was better on the track in spite of the dust. The camel-thorn bushes gather drifting sand in their tangle of branches until they form solid hummocks about a foot high, and too irregularly spaced for a truck to straddle or dodge them. At last we reached the mouth of the wadi. There was no track, but the driver found his way round huge boulders, across deep gutters and along the rough rock-face, with the truck often tilted at an angle of 30 degrees or more.

At the head of the wadi we found Battalion H.Q. housed in a number of small, wide-mouthed caverns which nature had hollowed out of the rock. The troops had sand-bagged the entrances to the caverns and made "dug-outs". The C.O.'s quarters were heavy with the smell of Scotch. Half an hour before an enemy shell had gone through the sandbag wall of the next dug-out. It hadn't gone off, but it had broken the battalion's last bottle of whisky.

The dug-out was just big enough to hold the colonel's stretcher, a table made from packing-cases, three petrol cases nailed together to form a "chest-of-drawers", and two rickety chairs scrounged from a house in the town. The colonel spread out his maps and explained how they held the Salient by giving more than they got. Before he'd finished, I found that even a colonel's dug-out in Tobruk had its colony of fleas.

It was dark when we resumed our journey forward, but with uncanny eyesight the driver picked out the track—a line of churned dust. Riding on the step was a Digger who knew the way through the minefields. A couple of nights before a truck had blown up there and had drawn the full fury of the enemy's fire on itself and its passengers.

Here and there we came to a sentry. The colonel had warned us to remember the password because, he said, "these men don't wait to ask questions". He didn't know his own sentries. The challenge and the passing were typically Australian.

"That you Pete?"

"Yeah, mate, 'oo's that?"

"Mick 'ere. On yer go."

It was the same when we continued on foot. Not once this night—nor on any other night—did I hear a password. It would have taken a smart German, however, to trick them. One time two Diggers, lying in a listening-post in no-man's-land, saw two shadowy figures coming towards them. "Who are you?" challenged one Digger. "We are Aussie soldiers," came the answer. The Diggers replied with a tommy gun.

After half an hour's bumping along we reached a slight hollow, beyond which vehicles could not go. A chink of light from a hole in the desert beckoned us. We lifted a groundsheet and dropped down a small hole into an old water-cistern—roughly pear-shaped and about thirty feet by twenty. Through the fug of dust and cigarette smoke glowed the light of several hurricane lamps, burning evil-smelling Italian oil. It was a Company H.Q. Men were sitting round eating, smoking and talking. Their evening meal had just arrived and they were tackling it before it got cold. Dust, stirred by restless feet, went in with every mouthful. It was warm and stuffy in the cistern but at least you could have a light and a smoke.

From the roof hung sticky fly-catchers blanketed with victims. On a natural, flat rock table in the middle lay an odd assortment of dirty mess dixies, dusty-lipped tins of jam and margarine, the ends of two loaves of bread, a couple of Bren magazines and a tommy gun. You had to be careful not to trip over a half-sleeping Digger, an empty dixie or a can of water on the floor.

In one corner the company sergeant-major was trying to hear above the surge of speech a message from Battalion H.Q. In another the O.C. of the company was holding a platoon commanders' conference. By the light of a senile torch they pored over a map.

Conference over, we went on by foot for half a mile to the forward posts. As usual there were no landmarks so the guide took a signal wire in his hand and we found the first post easily.

It was S10—one of the Italian-built concrete posts. "Follow me and stick to the track," said the guide, as he led us in through the minefield and the barbed wire—much battered by shelling but draped with booby-traps like a Christmas tree.

SALIENT SCENES

There was not a sound of war, but in the weapon pits on top of the post Diggers were squatting beside each machine-gun. Inside we tripped over men sleeping fully clothed on the concrete floor of the narrow corridor-trench, which was cluttered up with empty dixies, boxes of ammunition, rifles and accumulated junk. We stumbled over cursing figures till we came to a small concrete room opening off a side trench. It was about six feet square. Its furniture was a couple of ammunition boxes and a table made from petrol cases. The Italians had meant it to be a "shell-proof" command post, but the roof was cracked and crumbling and only the steel reinforcement kept it from falling in.

Following my upward glance at the roof, a Digger said: "They've got their finger on this blasted place. They can land a bloody shell on 'ere any time they like. When there's a blitz on, we cop all the muck in the world. It's the only entertainment we get."

"Shut up, will you," said another Digger, with his ear to the phone in the corner. "The news is comin' on." The battalion sigs were picking up the B.B.C. news and "piping" it out along the signal lines to the forward posts. The Digger at the phone began taking notes.

There was silence, more or less, until he put the phone down. He read out the headlines: "Roosevelt and Churchill meet at sea—Nazis reckon they've surrounded Odessa—" and finally, "At Tobruk patrol activity only."

"Patrol activity only," echoed a Digger with heavy sarcasm. "The bloke who wrote that oughta been 'ere last night. I suppose the Aussie papers've still got bands playin' in Tobruk's main square."

It was hardly the moment to introduce a correspondent who broadcast for the B.B.C. Someone produced a dixie of tea, brewed over an Italian primus, and the platoon commander—a young sergeant—began telling me about the post.

"You won't see much here," he said. "This is in the second line, and we do little except send out patrols. In some ways it's better in a front line post, like S9. There you can hit back. We're at the receiving end most of the time here, but it's better than being in the dug-posts in the Salient itself. Like to go over to one?"

Outside it wasn't as quiet as it had been. Every few seconds a German machine-gun would spit out a burst of red tracer bullets. Fifty yards to our right streaks of light shot by like live

Morse code. "That's a fixed line from Spandau Joe—down an old Italian pipeline," said the sergeant. "The post we're going to is on the far side of that. If we make it snappy we'll get across before the next burst. The pipeline's an easy route to follow and he puts one down there every now and then."

We went on. There was no signal wire to guide us but the track was marked by a thin hessian tape strung between camel-thorn bushes. The post was very crude—three sandbagged circular machine-gun pits about four feet deep and five feet across. They were connected by shallow crawl trenches, off which opened two low dug-outs, roofed over with boards, corrugated iron and sandbags. The desert here was soft grey sand instead of the usual rock and brown earth. The corporal in charge of the post said they had a job preventing the walls of the pits and trenches from falling in. "Even sandbags don't help much," he said, "because heavy Jerry mortars landing round the post blow the sides in anyway."

It was after eleven. The troops had finished their meal and, in front of the post, some of them were putting up more barbed wire, muttering curses as they struggled with an obstreperous coil.

Suddenly from somewhere in the darkness two German machine-guns came to life. Bullets sang past the post, followed by sharp cracks like the back-lash of a stockwhip. We bent our heads below the parapet; the men working on the wire hopped back to their trenches and in a few seconds their guns were firing. There were only the corporal and six men in the post, but they had four automatic weapons and an anti-tank rifle between them. To their own tommy gun and Bren they had added a captured Fiat medium machine-gun and a light Breda. They gave the Germans a stirring reply.

After five minutes it seemed that every enemy machine-gun for a mile around was firing on us. The Australian posts on either side joined in and the whole front was ablaze. From the German lines, four or five hundred yards away, went up flare after flare. They certainly knew where this post was. One machine-gun, firing on fixed lines, sent a stream of tracers a few feet above our heads every minute or so.

"That's a big bastard—probably a Schwartzloe," said the corporal. "Fires from somewhere near the water-tower. Too far away for us. If we had a Vickers or a decent mortar we might get him. But our mortars haven't got the range. If we bring 'em up here, they draw the crabs. If we put 'em back behind somewhere, they can't reach the water-tower."

After a quarter of an hour the enemy's flares went up less often; one by one his guns stopped; but the big Schwartzloe still stuttered out occasional bursts and a few heavy mortars landed behind us. One more flare hung in the sky and spluttered out, leaving the now-silent German lines shrouded in darkness.

The Australian posts on either side of us fell silent too, but the corporal said, "Keep 'er goin', boys. Jerry started it." Turning to me he added, "If we didn't give 'em more than they give us, we couldn't even stick our heads out. We usually stir 'em up, but we're keepin' things quiet to-night. We've got some blokes comin' up with mines. They should've been here before this started, but those mortars must've landed bloody near 'em."

Our guns kept going a little longer but the Germans didn't want to renew the fight. "O.K.," said the corporal. "We'd better get on with the wiring." Grumbling a little, the troops scrambled out of the machine-gun pits. As he went, a Digger mumbled, "Gawd struth, corp., one thing you've always got plenty of round 'ere—and that's blasted barbed wire."

A few minutes later half a dozen figures loomed up out of the darkness. It was the mine-carrying party. "Did you cop much o' that, Joe?" asked the corporal.

"My oath, we did," replied Joe. "The M.Gs was all right, but them mortars damn near blew me tin 'at off. You can 'ave that game. Lyin' out there with a box o' mines beside you, an' Jerry mortars givin' you the works. Got a water-bottle?"

He took a swig, and then went on—"Brought some mail for yer. It come up too late for the ration party. I got a letter from 'ome meself to-day. A bloke's a flamin' mug—diggin' 'ere in the desert, an' back in Aussie rabbit-skins is eight-an'-six a pound."

I went back with the mine-carrying party. The front was lively again. Every few seconds a flare went up or a machine-gun burst whipped past. I was walking with Joe, and I found myself ducking involuntarily when anything happened. A couple of times we all flattened out on the sand and camel-thorn when something seemed to come rather close. But for the most part Joe walked nonchalantly on.

As we approached the Company H.Q. in the foggy cistern, I said to him, "Do you usually cop much on the way up at night, Joe?" "Well," he said, "you do an' you don't; but they gotta be good to get you."

CHAPTER XVI

The Battle for No-Man's Land

AFTER the failure of his two smash and grab attacks Rommel settled down to contain Tobruk. As the enemy rested on the defensive, Morshead and his men might well have done the same—sitting passively behind their defences. Had they done that, however, Tobruk would have played a much smaller part in the defence of Egypt in 1941; it might in fact have been lost. Morshead knew that the Battle for Tobruk—and even for Egypt —would be largely fought in the no-man's-land outside his perimeter. The more offensive his garrison was, the greater the force Rommel would need to keep watching it, and the smaller the force he would have available to attack Egypt. "From the first day I determined that no-man's-land would be *our* land," Morshead once told me.

Comfort, as well as security, made this policy necessary. He knew that if the Axis positions around other parts of the perimeter should ever be advanced as near to the garrison's line as they were in the Salient, life would become extremely difficult. After the May battle the Salient posts were the only ones within easy range of enemy mortars and machine-guns. Only in that sector did the enemy have extensive observation of the area inside the perimeter. Elsewhere the forward troops could walk around in daylight with impunity, could drive their trucks almost to the Red Line, and were reasonably free from the danger of surprise attack.

They kept this freedom and made Tobruk a constant menace to Rommel by means of patrols, which struck almost nightly at the Axis positions around Tobruk.[1] These patrols kept the enemy so far back that no-man's-land remained anything from a mile to four miles wide. Technically, Tobruk was invested,

---

[1] There were, of course, many patrols and raids besides those described in this chapter. The ones I have dealt with are chosen as typical examples and are therefore not referred to in strict chronological order. Most of these took place while I was in Tobruk, and the details were checked by personal interview at the time.

BATTLE FOR NO-MAN'S-LAND

but from May onwards the Axis forces outside were more on the defensive than the garrison inside.

The policy of patrolling no-man's-land by day and night began early. At the Easter week-end the troops learned the need for patrols at night to stop the enemy from reconnoitring the anti-tank ditch, wire and minefields; to keep track of enemy movements in no-man's-land, so as to gain warning of any preparations for attack or for the building of new enemy strongpoints. Consequently, an elaborate system of patrolling was established, particularly in the southern sector where the enemy's forward positions were well back from the perimeter. The three battalions holding this sector normally had about three hundred men on patrol each night.

These patrols were divided into several classes. First there was the inter-post, which became known in the 2/17th Battalion as the "love and kisses" patrol. This nickname arose in a strange way. The practice in the forward posts was for two men in, say, Post R_{53} to patrol to a point half-way between the posts on either side—R_{55} and R_{51}. (The first line of posts bore odd numbers; the second even numbers.) It was very difficult, however, to time the meetings and so, to avoid one patrol having to wait for the other, a simple system of checking-in was arranged. On the ground at each half-way point they kept two sticks: crossed, they represented "kisses" and lying side by side they represented the code word "love". If R_{53}'s code word was "love", that for R_{55} and R_{51} would be "kisses". Thus, if the patrol from R_{53} found the sticks were crossed, it knew that the other had been there, and laid them side by side to indicate that it had checked in since the other's last visit. In addition to the inter-post patrol there were similar parties watching the anti-tank ditch and barbed wire. Farther out there were covering patrols consisting usually of an N.C.O. and half a dozen men, sent either on special reconnaissance to observe an enemy working party or position, or else to cover a certain "beat" and give warning of enemy movement and also to shoot up anyone they encountered.

The offensive raids for which the garrison became famous were even more important than these defensive patrols. When the Germans and Italians began to dig themselves in, patrols discovered and mapped their positions, shot up working parties, and, even when the posts were finished, raided them in hardhitting night attacks.

Once the enemy became established, however, daring daylight

raids like those which Forbes, Rattray and Hutchinson had led in April became impossible. Nevertheless, the enemy still had to be closely watched by day, particularly during duststorms, for both sides had learned to use these to cover preparations for an attack. Consequently, the garrison maintained almost the same system of protective patrols during a duststorm as it did at night. These patrols were the most unpopular job in Tobruk, for the men had no protection except anti-gas goggles over their eyes and handkerchiefs over their noses and mouths.

On clear days no-man's-land was policed mainly by "silent cops"—parties of two or three men, who lay-up in small holes as far as three miles outside the perimeter. There they waited, watched, reported enemy movements by telephone, and sometimes directed the artillery or a Bren carrier patrol to a suitable target. These outposts were known by names such as "Plonk", "Bondi", "Bash", "Jack", and "Jill". In the latter months of the siege the garrison even set up a 40-foot observation pole more than a mile out in no-man's-land in the south-eastern sector.

In addition to these observation posts, the garrison frequently sent Bren carriers to patrol no-man's-land. They were ideal for this task, being low enough to sneak up to enemy positions and observe without being observed; having sufficient fire-power to cause plenty of damage in a surprise raid and enough speed to get away from enemy tanks. They were used for all kinds of tasks—investigating suspicious movement; shooting up enemy positions or working parties; covering daylight patrols; acting as mobile observation posts for the artillery; or bringing in wounded.

After the Battle of the Salient the Tobruk defenders feared that the enemy might try to drive a wedge into the eastern perimeter as he had done in the west. He had already established himself astride the Bardia road, and now began strengthening and extending this position, particularly by placing field guns in the wadis between the road and the sea. To delay these preparations and to keep a close watch on them, Brigadier Godfrey, whose 24th Brigade was then holding the eastern sector, ordered his forward battalions to carry out offensive patrols with Bren carriers.

On May 9th a carrier patrol from the 2/43rd Battalion shot up an Italian strongpost and brought back two prisoners. Next morning another of its patrols surprised an Italian working party of about 300 and strafed them severely until enemy tanks drove the raiders back. The enemy replied by sending four tanks either to attack or to make a close reconnaissance of the 2/43rd's front. These were driven off, but Godfrey decided that stronger action was needed to keep the enemy on the defensive.

Consequently, before dawn on May 13th, "D" Company of the 2/43rd Battalion, commanded by Captain M. R. Jeanes and supported by eight tanks and seven carriers, set out to attack the positions astride the Bardia Road a mile east of the perimeter. The attack was dogged by misfortune. The enemy was not caught unawares, for apparently he heard the tanks rumbling up in the still night air and was waiting for them.

To make matters worse, three "I" tanks and three carriers, which were to silence an enemy strongpoint on the right of the attacking infantry, missed their way in the dark. Instead of going for the enemy position, they bore down on Jeanes's troops as they lay-up waiting to attack, and opened fire on them. Luckily their fire was inaccurate, but it brought every enemy weapon into action. From the strongpoint, which the tanks were to have silenced, Jeanes counted no less than seventeen machine-guns firing. Disregarding the fire from our own tanks as well as the enemy, the infantry went in to attack, but were soon pinned down. Jeanes himself ran from tank to tank, trying to warn the crews of their mistake, but even though he smashed his rifle battering on their sides, he could not attract the crews' attention.

Finally, the tanks turned away to deal with the unsubdued strongpoint on the flank, but in doing so ran into heavy anti-tank fire, which disabled two and damaged the third. Undeterred by this, the three Bren carriers attacked the strongpoint and kept it quiet while the tank crews were rescued. Two carriers, however, were destroyed and their gallant commander, Lieutenant L. J. Pratt, was killed.

A final mishap stopped the infantry attack before it reached the main enemy positions. As they moved forward, three green flares went up. "Three greens" was the withdrawal signal for the tanks, and thinking that the latter must have fired this, the infantry began to retire. It seems now that the flares were sent up by the enemy, who had chosen the same signal as a call for "defensive fire". Not suspecting this, the infantry continued to move back under increasingly heavy fire. Jeanes could not rally them in time and so ordered a general withdrawal under cover of a smoke screen laid by the carriers. This was so effective that in spite of the mishaps the 2/43rd lost only two men killed and seven wounded.

The enemy did not follow up this success, however, and Australian carriers by day and infantry by night continued to make no-man's-land their own. The enemy by this time was devoting all his attention to strengthening his positions in the Salient and astride the Derna and Bardia roads. In mid-May he also set his infantry and engineers to complete a chain of strongposts in the west from the sea to the Salient and on to the El Adem road. Covering the 12-mile gap between the El Adem and Bardia roads, however, Rommel had merely mobile patrols from the Ariete Armoured Division.

Offensive Patrols

Two events on May 30th abruptly reminded Rommel that it would take more than this to keep the garrison quiet in that sector. Five miles south of the perimeter that afternoon two enemy lorries were blown up as they ploughed through the deep dust of a by-pass track which led to Bardia. They were the victims of mines laid the night before by Lieutenant H. R. Beer and six men of the 2/48th Battalion. Between dark and dawn Beer's party had tramped in thin sand-shoes more than ten miles over rough desert. They had evaded enemy patrols and outposts and laid six mines in the conveniently dusty track. Then for two hours they had lain in wait beside the road with their tommy guns ready to pour fire into any victim. Much to their disappointment no vehicle appeared before the time came for them to leave in order to be clear of enemy territory before daylight. But observers in no-man's-land next afternoon saw the results of their work.

Late that afternoon enemy tanks ran into trouble in this sector. For some days they had been policing the area north of the by-pass road, so as to curb the activities of the Tobruk carrier patrols, which had been directing artillery shoots. The garrison did not ignore the challenge. Morshead sent out a British artillery observation officer in a cruiser tank with a roving mission to shell anything he saw, and with a covering force of three cruisers and three light tanks. Ten enemy tanks that tried to interfere were driven off, and the British officer continued to direct the artillery fire until the enemy brought up eighteen tanks. In a moving fight which lasted nearly till dark one of these was destroyed and two others damaged before the British tanks withdrew under a protective barrage.

This sortie inspired the 2/17th's carrier platoon commander,

BATTLE FOR NO-MAN'S-LAND

Lieutenant L. C. Maclarn, to tackle some enemy tanks with his Bren carriers. Moving out through the wire a few mornings later he blandly told an inquisitive Digger in one post, "Just going out to get a couple of Jerry tanks, old boy." He ran into more trouble than he expected and his carriers came racing back in a cloud of dust. A number of enemy tanks had loomed up out of the heat haze at a range of 500 yards, but he had brazenly engaged them with machine-guns, even though the tanks had armament powerful enough to blow his carriers sky-high. It was sheer cheek, but without such impudence the garrison could not have established and kept the upper hand.

Apart from occasional skirmishes there was little contact with the enemy in the southern sector during May and June; both sides were busy strengthening their existing positions, and the wide gap in the enemy defensive system between the El Adem and Bardia roads remained. As we have seen, however, when the British attacked on the Egyptian frontier in June, the garrison got ready to fight its way out. Air reconnaissance must have revealed this intention to Rommel, for at once his troops began preparing defensive positions to close that gap. He evidently hoped that the completion of these would prevent a major break-out, and protect the by-pass road and the artillery batteries which he proceeded to amass in preparation for a final assault on Tobruk.

The first enemy move was to lay a minefield across the open desert about three miles south of the perimeter. At first this was not covered by fire from his infantry positions and it served mainly to provide the garrison with a much-needed supply of mines. On July 1st, for instance, under cover of the afternoon heat haze and a slight duststorm, Lieutenant-Colonel Allan Spowers, C.O. 2/24th Battalion, led a pirating party of more than fifty out to this minefield. Brazenly they drove three miles into no-man's-land in three trucks, escorted by three Bren carriers. They brought back 500 German anti-tank mines and relaid them inside their own wire. There were many other mine-pirating sorties, although none on so large a scale. But the several thousand mines these yielded were a valuable addition to the garrison's defences.

It took the Italians five months to complete the chain of defences covering this south-eastern gap. If they worked by day, they were harried by field guns and carriers; at night by infantry patrols. Consequently, their policy was to build an initial position far enough back from the perimeter to be reasonably safe from attack. From this they would send out working parties at night to dig a new position half a mile or so farther forward. When this was completed troops would occupy it and the work on the next position would begin. This leap-frogging process was slow and wasted much labour. But, unless they were first prepared to fight out the battle for no-man's-land, there was no alternative.

To hasten the completion of these defences, the Italians sometimes worked by day, but that was risky, as one of their working parties found on August 1st. Before dawn Lieutenant E. M. Pinkney and seven men of the 2/13th established themselves in shallow trenches beside a track along which the Italians had been seen moving to a position that they were preparing a mile and a half south of the perimeter. After they had lain all day in the baking sun their patience was at last rewarded. Along came three parties of Italians, half a dozen in each, and one headed straight for the Australians.

As Pinkney told me later:

When they were only twenty yards away we rose like ghosts out of the desert and told them to surrender. They replied by opening fire, but they hadn't a chance against our Brens and tommy guns. We killed four and took one prisoner. The other two parties, which were some distance away, cleared out, pursued by our bullets.

Typical of the operations by carriers was a raid led by Lieutenant R. S. Rudkin of the 2/17th early in October. Before dawn three carriers moved out more than a mile and lay-up in a slight depression about half a mile from an Italian strongpoint. As soon as it was light they sneaked forward into open ground and turned their Bren guns on to the Italians, who were shaking out their blankets and making their beds before going to rest after a night's vigil. These daylight attacks evidently made the Italians jittery, but it was never possible to get in close enough by day to be certain of inflicting severe casualties. However, darkness gave the Australian and Indian patrols the chance to hit hard at close range. To protect their working parties the Italians usually put out covering patrols with machine-guns on either flank of the position they were digging, but even these did not save them from frequent attack.

One moonlight night in October, for instance, Sergeant N. J. Smith and three men of the 2/17th, armed with two tommy guns and two rifles, were patrolling in the El Adem sector when they saw fifty Italians near a minefield, digging energetically, and two covering parties, each about ten strong, moving out to the flanks. The Diggers decided to walk boldly towards them in the moonlight. The bluff succeeded; less than a hundred yards from the Italians the four men lay down and turned their tommy guns and rifles on to the massed working party. When the Australians found their ammunition running out, they dashed to safety followed by wild bursts of fire.

The enemy was not saved from such punishing night raids even when he had completed his strongposts. These were not easy to attack for they were well prepared for all-round defence. Each post was protected by mines, booby-traps and barbed wire, and defended by machine-guns, anti-tank and usually field artillery as well. Each was manned by anything from fifty to a hundred men established sometimes in stone sangars, sometimes in trenches, dug-outs and weapon pits, often drilled and blasted out of the rocky desert.

Attacks on these positions succeeded only because of thorough reconnaissance, good planning and great courage. In the flat, featureless desert, it was very difficult to find the way, even in moonlight. While an officer or N.C.O. kept direction by compass and the stars, another member of the patrol measured the distance travelled by counting paces. An error of only fifty yards in a 4000 yard trek might take the patrol past its objective. In the darkness it was also extremely difficult to keep control of a large raiding party. On rare occasions fifty men were sent out, but the usual number was anything from ten to twenty.

Before these raids there were generally at least two reconnaissances by an officer or N.C.O. and two or three men. They crawled to within fifty yards of the post, and studied the lay-out of the defences and the routine of the garrison. Often they lay doggo watching and listening for an hour or two. They noted the minefields, booby-traps and wire; the location and character of the weapons; the position of sentries and outposts; and the routes the enemy used for bringing in supplies. It was important also to note the habits of the garrison—when they fed; what patrols they sent out; what was their reaction to an alarm. Sometimes in order to test this, a patrol made a demonstration some distance out, while two or three men lay up beside the post to watch.

Reconnaissance patrols were dangerous and nerve-racking. Sometimes they ended badly. One night in August Lieutenant R. C. Garnsey and another man of the 2/17th were surprised behind the enemy lines. They made a dash for it. Garnsey got away but the last he heard from his companion was "I'm O.K., but I won't be back."

Sometimes they ended humorously. Another night Lieutenant H. G. Byron-Moore and a small patrol of the 2/23rd had nearly reached their objective when they heard a noise behind them. Down they went; looked round, saw nothing; listened, heard nothing. They went on. A few seconds later—that noise again. This time they traced it—to a donkey. With much shooing and throwing of stones they tried to drive it away, but everywhere the party went that donkey had to go. At last in desperation the Diggers turned for home, but it still trailed them right back to our minefield. As it trotted over the mines, the men threw themselves to the ground—just in time. When the smoke and dust of the explosion cleared away, the donkey was still there kicking up its heels, impatient at the delay.

From information gathered by patrols the Intelligence section produced sketches of the defences and a map with notes of what had been discovered as to the strength and habits of enemy posts near by. After the colonel and the officer chosen to lead the raid had worked out the plan of attack from this information, the raiding party were told the scheme in detail, and shown either on a map or a sand-table model exactly what each man had to do. Sometimes a model of the post to be raided was constructed inside the perimeter, and the attack rehearsed, first by day and then by night. This thoroughness was well rewarded.

On the eve of the raid the patrol was usually given a good hot meal and a tot of rum before it set out. In the last few months of the defence, the troops were well equipped for patrolling. They had special boots—with thick, soft rubber soles; special patrol suits—one-piece, khaki overalls with reinforced elbows and knees to save them when crawling over stony and thorny ground. But before this they made the best of what they had. To deaden their footsteps, the Australians often wore thick socks over their boots; occasionally they attacked in stockinged feet. The Indians made themselves silent sandals out of strips of old motor-tyre.

Each man carried two or three grenades, and a patrol of a dozen normally had one man with a Bren, to be fired from the hip, as many as six with tommy guns, and the remainder with rifles and fixed bayonets. Almost invariably the raiders attacked without artillery support, relying on surprise; but often they withdrew under a protective barrage. Mortars and Bren carriers were usually sent out to positions half a mile or a mile from the enemy post so that they too could give covering fire as the attackers withdrew. The Bren carriers were also used for bringing in wounded. To guide any who were lost or cut off, single tracer bullets were fired every few minutes from the post to which the patrol was to return. One company in the 2/15th often guided its men home with music from the saxophone which Ted Donkin played in front line posts with all the persuasiveness he later revealed in Tobruk concerts. And never did the strains of "Waltzing Matilda" and "Roll Out the Barrel" reach such receptive ears.

Finding the objective was the hardest part of the patrol leader's job. Often the men were saved much foot-slogging by being taken a mile or so outside the wire in trucks to some well-marked spot, from which an accurate compass bearing could be taken. But from there the leader had to rely on his pace-counter and his compass. It was not easy for the pace-counter to maintain steps of regular length while walking over rough ground, studded with camel-thorn, and it was seldom possible to follow one compass bearing direct to the objective. Usually, in order to achieve surprise, the enemy post had to be attacked from the flank or rear and that demanded a dog-leg approach, with considerable margin for error.

Sometimes, however, the enemy unwittingly guided our patrols to a post—in one case "by the strong smell of cigar smoke", and in another by the strains of a gramophone which was providing an Italian labour squad with music while it worked. Often the Italians revealed their positions—and their nervousness—by excited chatter.

Once a patrol had reached the enemy position there was still the problem of getting into it. Even courage did not make up for bad reconnaissance as a patrol of the 2/10th found to its cost on the night of July 20th-21st. The battalion had been ordered to raid an enemy position, known as "Fig Tree," about a mile and a half south-west of the perimeter. There was only one preliminary reconnaissance and the four Australians who made it found the Italian garrison asleep. They could not resist the temptation to strike then and there. Crawling up to the enemy sangars they tossed hand grenades inside and followed in with bayonet and tommy gun. Enemy casualties were optimistically reported as twenty killed and ten wounded. The patrol stated that there was *no* barbed wire around the post and that it could easily be raided again.

On the strength of this a platoon, commanded by Lieutenant

M. R. Ellenby, was sent out the following night to attack the post after a preliminary strafing by artillery and Vickers guns. Under cover of this, Ellenby and his men approached the post; seventy-five yards from it he called on them to charge, but the enemy was on the alert. They were met by heavy machine-gun fire from the post they were attacking and also from those on either flank. After thirty yards they ran into trip-wires; stumbling on another twenty, they were stopped short by a concertina wire fence. Only Ellenby and one of his tommy-gunners, Private George Booker, found a way through. While the rest of the men were freeing themselves from the wire, Ellenby and Booker dashed for the Italian machine-gun pits. Ellenby had nine hand grenades and had thrown seven of them before he fell—wounded in the arm and head.

Booker crawled over to him and was told—"Blow three blasts on my whistle—that's the withdrawal signal. Don't worry about me; get the others out." Booker blew the signal, and then, collecting another man, Mick Fallon, helped Ellenby back through the wire. As they got clear of it, Ellenby was hit a third time—in the leg.

Fallon, a wheat lumper in Port Lincoln before the war, said he would carry Ellenby in, while Booker went back for a stretcher. By this time the enemy was plastering no-man's-land with shells, mortar bombs and machine-gun fire. "Whenever we heard a shell or a mortar coming," Ellenby told me later, "Mick would put me on the ground and crouch down to shield me. It took him two and a half hours to carry me a mile and a half to the stretcher party. But if it hadn't been for him, I would have been out there still."

Instead of misfiring as it did, however, this raid might have been a great success if the previous night's patrol had done its reconnaissance thoroughly and found the barbed wire, rather than easy victims.

By contrast a raid by an officer and ten men of the 2/15th Battalion on the night of August 30th-31st gained a brilliant success—at a cost of two men killed and one missing—primarily because of the thorough reconnaissance, on which their C.O., Lieutenant-Colonel R. W. Ogle, always insisted. The objective was an Italian strongpoint east of the El Adem road, and the raiders were led by Captain F. L. Bode, a giant of a man, who had been a noted amateur boxer in Queensland. The hero of the attack was Sergeant R. A. Patrick, a slip of a lad, who barely looked his twenty-one years and who before the war had been a clerk in a country store. He made the two reconnaissances, which were the basis of the raid's success, and was personally responsible for at least five of the fifteen Italians believed to have been killed.

The following day I sat in Ogle's dug-out while the raiders were being interrogated. Patrick told his story just as if he were describing a football match:

About 3000 yards out we came to the enemy minefield a little to the west of the post we were going for. We crawled through that and then moved round till we were behind the post. Still crawling, we got over the low trip-wire behind it and were within forty yards of the post, when the Ities sent up a flare and opened with a Breda. We went down flat.

The firing stopped and Captain Bode said "Come on boys, up and at 'em." We charged. Another flare went up behind us and the Ities must have seen us silhouetted against its light. They swung four machine-guns straight on to us and a volley of hand grenades burst in our path. For a few seconds the dust and flash blinded us, but we went on. In the confusion I ran past the machine-gun pit that I was going for, and a hand grenade—one of the useless Itie money-box type—hit my tin hat. The explosion knocked me down but it didn't hurt me. As I lay there, the fight was going on all around, and I could hear Ities shouting and screaming and our tommy guns firing and grenades bursting.

I rolled over and pitched two grenades into the nearest trench and made a dash for the end machine-gun post. I jumped into the pit on top of three Italians, and bayoneted two before my bayonet snapped. I got the third with my revolver as he made for a dug-out where there were at least two other men. I let them have most of my magazine. Another Italian jumped into the pit and I shot him too. He didn't have any papers so I took his shoulder-badges, jumped up and went for my life.

I cleared the concertina wire in front of the post, but caught my foot in a trip-wire. Luckily it brought me down, for just then a machine-gun burst got the chap next to me. I wriggled over to him, but he was so badly hit I couldn't do anything to help. I took his last two grenades; crawled out through the booby-traps and then threw one grenade at a machine-gun that was still firing. As this burst, I made a dash for it, and a hundred yards out reached a shell-hole. I waited till it was all quiet again, and then came back.

This patrol did everything but take prisoners, although it nearly captured two. Bode was wounded early in the attack, but kept his tommy gun going until he ran out of ammunition. He then caught two Italians in a trench, grabbed each by the scruff of the neck and was about to drag them out when a grenade burst in front of him. The blast spattered his face and chest with pieces of metal, so he "banged their heads together and threw 'em back". Nearly blinded by the explosion, Bode came in singing, "My eyes are dim I cannot see."

Sometimes attacks on enemy positions came about by accident. One night in July two officers (Lieutenants P. S. Hayman and J. T. Finlay) and fifteen men of the 2/24th Battalion went out

to shoot up Italians who were laying a minefield three and a
half miles south-east of the perimeter. In searching for them,
the Diggers stumbled right into the undefended rear of a half-
finished Italian strongpoint. They did not realize where they
were until Italians rising from trenches at their feet began
shouting "Australianos". The "Australianos" replied with grenades, tommy guns and bayonets, but enemy positions on either
flank immediately turned all their fire on to this post. Finlay
and Hayman were wounded but, when one of their men was
hit, they went back to rescue him. Both were wounded again
and they had to leave him behind lest they should prejudice
their chance of getting the rest of the patrol back through the
minefield. This was a ticklish job, but an engineer, Lance-
Sergeant H. J. Spreadborough of the 2/4th Field Company,
guided everyone safely through. "He almost put each man's foot
down for him—step by step," said one of the men when they
got back.

The raid which evidently most impressed the enemy was that
made by the 2/12th Battalion on the night of July 11th-12th.
Led by Lieutenant A. L. Reid and Sergeant N. H. Russell, two
parties, each of nineteen, raided a heavily defended enemy
position astride the El Adem road. They attacked under cover
of strong artillery and Vickers gun fire; dealt severely with one
Italian strongpost and put a covering force to flight; and then
withdrew leaving more than 50 enemy dead or wounded and
bringing back five prisoners. Three men of the 2/12th did not
return and one officer and nine other ranks were wounded.

On the Axis radio this successful, but not unusual, raid
became an "attempt to break out with tanks". Rome was so
pleased with this line of talk that on July 15th it broadcast a
long and entirely fictitious account which began: "During the
past few days the British forces in Tobruk have repeatedly tried
to attack the German and Italian troops and to break through
their lines."

It went on to tell how the Tobruk garrison had made three
vain attempts on the 11th and 12th to break out, and added:

The enemy have been forced to realize the impossibility of changing their
unhappy condition as besieged men. The progressive and systematic work of
the Axis land and air forces, the destruction of warehouses and the blocking
of supplies to the stronghold render the British situation at Tobruk more
unsupportable, difficult and precarious with each passing day.

Rome's outcry was evidence of the raid's success and Morshead
sent congratulations and the following message to Lieutenant-

Colonel John Field, the 2/12th's C.O.: "I am glad you are seizing every opportunity to inflict casualties on our unneighbourly enemy and to harass him. It is good for him and also for us. And remember what the Good Book says, 'It is more blessed to give than to receive.' "

The following week, on the night of July 17th-18th, "B" Company of the 2/28th Battalion on the Derna road sector showed that the garrison's patrols could penetrate deep into the enemy defences if they wished. Led by Major M. A. Buntine, two platoons moved out at midnight to attack an enemy position known as "White Knoll", a mile west of the defences. The raiders found White Knoll itself unoccupied but, as they pushed on, they ran into heavy fire from defences farther west. Undaunted, they advanced with mortar and artillery support and broke through three lines of Italian positions. After fighting their way half a mile into enemy territory, the attacking platoons withdrew only when their ammunition began to run short. Buntine's sole casualty was one man slightly wounded, but nineteen Italians were killed for certain and twice as many wounded. Eight of them were killed by Corporal W. L. France; single-handed he accounted for two enemy machine-gun posts.

Another Australian patrol, which got behind the enemy's forward defences in the Bardia road sector, had at least one prisoner to show for its efforts, although he was obtained in a rather unorthodox fashion. One moonlight night Captain R. Rattray, Lieutenant N. E. McMaster and 14 men of the 2/23rd Battalion were discovered by the enemy when they were half-way between the forward and the supporting positions which the Italians had constructed astride the Bardia road. The enemy at once sent out two strong fighting patrols of Germans and Italians to box Rattray's party in. As one patrol came towards them, the Diggers held the fire of their ten tommy guns until it was only fifty yards away. The enemy patrol was stopped in its tracks and Rattray's men began to crawl slowly backwards.

When the Australian fire ceased the Germans rallied the Italians and moved forward again. This time they were halted so sharply that they made no further attempt to come on. The Diggers continued to crawl backwards. Rattray told me afterwards:

As we went we saw the shadowy figure of a soldier moving out from the forward enemy position to the patrol, which we had pinned down. Every few yards he would stop and give a low whistle. When he whistled the third time, McMaster whistled back. The figure turned towards us and as he got nearer we could hear him calling, "Herr Leutnant! Herr Leutnant!" McMaster called back "Si, si, Comradio!" and the Itie walked right into our arms. We had been sent out to get a prisoner and so now we could go back. But we still had to crawl 600 yards before we were clear of the second patrol which was waiting to cut off our retreat. Next day we all had badly lacerated knees, hands and elbows, but we had the unusual distinction of having whistled a prisoner in.

Individually these raids were not of great military importance, but their combined result was to give the Tobruk garrison a remarkable freedom of movement, in addition to forcing the enemy on to the defensive. He was compelled to waste time, men and material making strong fortifications, and even when these were completed it took at least one German and three or four Italian divisions to man them and keep in check the one and a half divisions inside the perimeter. (Italian infantry divisions are only about half the normal strength of Australian infantry divisions—7000 men as against 14,000. However, the Australian brigades in Tobruk were so much below strength that the total garrison between May and September was less than 23,000. The investing force in September numbered well over 40,000. It consisted of the 21st German Armoured Division, plus some infantry battalions of the German 90th Light Division; the 27th Brescia, 17th Pavia and 25th Bologna Infantry Divisions, plus part at least of the 132nd Ariete Armoured Division.)

If it had not been for these raids, Rommel could have left merely a light covering force holding Tobruk. As it was, he had three times as many troops outside it as he had on the Egyptian frontier watching the rising strength of the Eighth Army. As well as tying-up enemy forces, these patrols inflicted not inconsiderable casualties.

More significant than casualties, however, was the damage done to the enemy's morale. The Italians became so nervous that the smallest alarm brought down defensive fire right along their front. One night when a raid was made on the Derna road sector, we recorded a running commentary on the action from Post S19. We could not see much but there was plenty of sound and fury for the Italians let fly with everything they had and wasted nearly a thousand shells, providing us with a lively broadcast.

Italian morale was not improved by the V for Victory campaign which the 20th Brigade organized in the southern sector in July and August. Murray had leaflets stencilled with "V Per Vittorio" and ordered that these be attached "by the use of clips, string, nails, pins, etc., to enemy bodies, posts, wire, sandbags, sangars, etc., by patrols". The result was to make the Italians even more nervous than before, as day after day they found these Victory leaflets stuck in their own defences by patrols which usually they had not heard.

Axis Counter-measures

The measure of the Tobruk patrol successes was indicated by the steps that both the Germans and Italians took to protect themselves. Early in the siege the enemy gave up counter-patrolling and stayed behind his defences. In July on the Bardia road sector Italian officers—in an attempt to force their men to patrol—ordered them to build cairns of stones at the end of each leg of their route. At first the 2/48th Battalion, which was then manning this sector, thought the cairns must be artillery ranging marks, or some new form of booby-trap. The first cairn was taken to pieces with much care. A sergeant tied a piece of cord round the top stone, withdrew a discreet fifty yards, lay flat, tensed his nerves for the expected explosion and pulled the cord. The stone flopped harmlessly to the ground. Stone by stone he took the cairn apart, his annoyance mounting all the time.

When a prisoner finally revealed why these were built, the Diggers decided not to disturb the Italians at work, but to go out after them and dismantle the cairns before daylight. Following this there must have been some rather tense scenes in the Italian trenches when bewildered N.C.Os tried to point out to their officers the cairns they had built the night before.

The best the Germans could do was to induce the Italians to attack the garrison's outposts at dusk. They tried this several times in July on the sector between the sea and the Derna road, which was held by the 18th Indian Cavalry Regiment. On July 19th about 200 Italians advancing to "attack", took to their heels when they ran into 24 Indians. A few days later they made another move. This time they approached the Indian posts shouting and talking excitedly, but when the Indians opened fire at a range of over half a mile, they hastily withdrew under artillery protection. Apparently they had advanced with so much noise either to cover their nervousness or else to give early warning of their approach in the hope that the Indians would open fire at long range and allow them to withdraw in safety without too much loss of face.

As a substitute for patrols the enemy established listening-posts a few hundred yards in front of his main positions. We have evidence of how ineffectively two of these were manned. On June 20th a small party from the 2/1st Pioneers sent in the following report: "Moving out we came on a hole in the ground in which there were two Italians. One was asleep, the other drowsy. We wakened them with the bayonet and had no further trouble."

An Italian diary revealed the reactions of another outpost when its occupants heard suspicious noises on the night of July 12th. The author seems to have had a lively sense of humour, for his diary entries read:

Great alarm to-night at our O.P.
1. Suspicious noises are heard.
2. Patrol leaves O.P. in a rush; takes refuge in main post.
3. Capt. L. arms himself to the teeth with rifle, pistol, hand grenades, etc. and throws away the telephone.
4. Lieut. A. makes a heroic forward reconnaissance of about 300 yards.
5. Lieut. S. gets a good smack on the head with a rifle.
6. My batman takes refuge in the tent with a rifle in each hand.
7. It is established that there are no British in the area. The suspicious noises came from our own transport.
8. The O.P. is manned again. The telephone is recovered and a shot or two is then fired.

When the outposts failed to give protection, the Italians installed searchlights, with which they swept no-man's-land. These provided a fine target for Australian machine-guns. Lieutenant L. C. Maclarn of the 2/17th dealt with them even more effectively one night by getting in behind the Italian lines and cutting a large section out of the electric cable that fed the lights.

The next enemy move was to attack the "silent cops" which the garrison maintained several miles outside the perimeter in the south-east. He first tried to make them untenable by shelling; several times the men in the outposts had to withdraw but they always returned next day.

When shelling failed, Italian infantry were sent to attack the farthest outpost, known as "Jim", and situated at an old well about three miles south-east of the perimeter. Late on the afternoon of August 9th this post's garrison (Captain Ray Leakey, M.C., a British tank officer, Privates L. Bennett and C. Hayes of the 2/23rd Battalion) saw twenty-seven Italians approaching. Leakey called for artillery fire, but before the guns opened up the Italians attacked, closing in from three sides. Leakey and his two men held their fire until the enemy were less than a hundred yards away. Then they opened up with a Bren and a tommy gun. The Italians did not come on. Eighteen were killed outright and most of the remaining nine were wounded. Just before sunset the enemy brought up a larger force and Leakey and his men had to withdraw. That night the Italians came out and buried their dead, but did not stay. Next morning the 2/23rd manned the outpost again.

Apparently discouraged by this failure, the enemy made no further move against the silent cops during the next four weeks. Then on the night of September 13th-14th, while the 24th Brigade were making two raids on Italian positions near by, a force of German tanks and infantry attacked the outpost "Jack" three miles east of the perimeter.

The first Australian raid on this night was made by Captain J. A. Johnstone and twenty-three men of the 2/28th Battalion. They went for an Italian position, known as "White Cairn", three miles south-east of the perimeter. The enemy had not finished wiring and booby-trapping the post, and the patrol had little trouble in getting in and taking him by surprise. Out of the Italian garrison of about twenty-five, they killed ten, wounded another ten and brought back four prisoners. Two of the raiders were wounded.

This attack was simple compared with one made later that night by three officers and fifty-eight men of the 2/32nd Battalion on a very heavily defended Italian strongpost south-west of White Cairn. It was held by more than a hundred men armed with a dozen machine-guns and mortars, at least two 75-mm. field pieces and two 47-mm. anti-tank guns. Captain R. Joshua, who planned and commanded the attack, had led two previous patrols against this post. One night they lost their way; another night the attack misfired. But he and his men would not be beaten. They laid out a model of the enemy position inside the perimeter and rehearsed the attack by day and night, until Joshua was satisfied that they would not fail again.

Warned by the previous attempt, however, the enemy were on the alert and when the attackers were still seventy-five yards from the post they came under fire so heavy that they could not tell whether their engineers had blown the wire or not. When they reached the wire, Joshua found it still intact. He sent his men to ground while engineers blew the gaps, but by this time every weapon in the strongpost had been turned against them and fire from supporting positions came down on the Australians as they fought their way through to the guns they had come to destroy. They blew up one field gun with gun cotton and one anti-tank gun with grenades; at least twenty Italians were killed and two were brought back.

Joshua's patrol was outnumbered two to one, but when the enemy this same night attacked the seven Western Australians of the 2/28th Battalion who were manning the outpost "Jack", he sent half a dozen tanks and more than a hundred men against them. From this outpost at half past one in the morning came a telephone call: "Send help at once . . . for God's sake hurry. They're within twenty yards of us." Behind the speaker's voice there was the sound of firing as the seven Diggers fought to hold the enemy back. Then there was silence. Bren carriers went out at once, but they found that the Germans were too strongly established.

The enemy held "Jack", but he waited another month before striking again at any other outposts. Then he began a general forward move to clear the south-eastern and eastern sectors of no-man's-land, and for this purpose brought up tanks to do the work his infantry would not tackle. This was his final admission of inability to deal with the Australian patrols.

THE BATTLE FOR "PLONK"

On the night of October 9th-10th German tanks over-ran the outpost "Bondi", manned by nine Tommies of the 2nd Queen's, two and a half miles south of the perimeter's south-eastern corner. From "Bondi" about twenty German tanks headed north-west towards another outpost, "Plonk", situated at Bir El Azazi, a mile south of the perimeter and two miles east of the El Adem road. The Tobruk garrison was ready for them. For the first time Morshead had some tanks to spare and a commander (Brigadier A. C. Willison) who was prepared to use them boldly. During the previous month gallant British auxiliary lighters had run the gauntlet from Mersa Matruh to Tobruk carrying the fifty-two "I" tanks of the 4th Royal Tank Regiment, commanded by Lieutenant-Colonel W. C. L. O'Carroll.

As the German tanks headed towards "Plonk", fifteen of O'Carroll's Matildas were already moving in its direction. On the previous night enemy troops had been seen working under cover of tanks on a new minefield south-east of "Plonk". Consequently, on this night Morshead had ordered O'Carroll to cover the 2/17th's standing patrol at "Plonk", and attack any German tanks that appeared in the area.

BATTLE FOR NO-MAN'S-LAND

As the British tanks moved out to "Plonk" about 9.30 p.m., Captain I. F. McMaster, of the 2/17th, who was guiding them, saw two figures coming towards him. They were Tommies from "Bondi", bringing the first news of its capture. Until then the tanks had been going slowly so that they should not be heard. Now they raced for "Plonk" at full speed. There they found that the 2/17th's patrol was still intact, though it had been very heavily shelled. There had been no sign of the enemy, but a few minutes later the rumble of tanks, coming from the direction of "Bondi", gave warning of German intentions.

The British disappeared into the night heading south-east to meet them. One tank returned almost immediately with engine trouble. This was fortunate, because four enemy tanks soon approached from the south-west. By this time the lone Matilda was sitting hull-down in the middle of the four low mounds at "Plonk". Its commander held his fire and the Germans did not see it until they were a hundred yards away. As they slowly closed in on "Plonk", McMaster decided it was time to withdraw his small infantry patrol, which had no adequate anti-tank weapons. It was barely clear when the German tanks opened fire. By this time they had approached within fifty yards, but the "I" tank held its ground and fired back. Sparks flew from the tanks as shells ricochetted from their heavily armoured sides. One enemy tank was hit point blank by an armour-piercing shell, but managed to pull out of the fight. The others followed it, little knowing that with one of their last shells they had jammed the turret of the "I" tank and made it defenceless.

Meantime, east of "Plonk" the other fourteen "I" tanks were roaring across the desert in search of the main German force. Crew commanders, heads high above their turrets, strained their eyes to distinguish in the blackness the shapes that might be enemy tanks. The rival forces were only 150 yards apart when our tanks first saw theirs and immediately opened fire. The commander of one British tank later described the running dog-fight that followed:

We opened fire at a range of about 100 yards and the German tanks scattered. We spread out and chased them, each of us picking one to tackle. All we could see was a series of black blobs, blurred by smoke and dust. By contrast, the sudden flashes of guns and the flares of tracer shells were almost blinding. Their tanks had more speed and they used it—200 yards away they were out of sight. Judging from the sparks that flew we scored some hits, but most of their fire was wild and they didn't stay to fight it out.

The Germans made no further move against "Plonk" that

night and Morshead decided to garrison it with a platoon of infantry and two anti-tank guns and to protect it with wire and mines. The plan was opposed by Murray and by the C.O. of the 2/17th, Lieutenant-Colonel Crawford, who both felt that "Plonk" could not be defended by so small a garrison and that Tobruk could not afford to place in such an exposed position a force strong enough to hold out against enemy tanks. Morshead, however, was always reluctant to see the enemy occupy any ground the garrison had once held and knew the importance of at least delaying the closing-in process that Rommel had evidently begun.

An hour before dark it became clear that the enemy, too, had designs on "Plonk". The 2/17th's advance party found no enemy near there but the battalion's front was heavily shelled. At dark Captain Frank Windeyer tried to take out the main party with trucks carrying anti-tank guns, mines and wire, but they ran into very heavy artillery fire. One of the anti-tank trucks was knocked out and the other was disabled; Windeyer was mortally wounded and several others were hit. The party withdrew, followed all the way by a barrage of increasing fury.

Under cover of this the enemy moved in to occupy "Plonk", closely observed by Lieutenant G. T. Reid, one of the ablest and most experienced patrol leaders in Tobruk, who had taken two men out through the shelling to within 300 yards of "Plonk". From there he counted eleven tanks, five trucks and about forty men near the mounds.

These provided a perfect artillery target, but the Tobruk guns had so few alternative positions that they preferred not to reveal their location by firing at night. Consequently, they did not shell "Plonk" until dawn, but then their fire was so accurate that the enemy garrison was thrown into confusion. Vehicles, hastily loaded with troops, tools and stores, were driven away at top speed. After an hour's bombardment the outpost was again deserted.

The final round of the battle for "Plonk" was fought on the night of October 11th-12th. By then Morshead had abandoned the idea of occupying it and had ordered the establishment of a new outpost nearer the perimeter. To cover this and harass the Germans, Reid and forty men prepared to raid "Plonk" under cover of artillery and "I" tanks. In their first attempt to get there, the tanks were late in starting and lost the advantage of the artillery concentration. At midnight eight Matildas tried again, but the enemy, warned of their approach, shelled them heavily as they moved out.

When they got near "Plonk", they found eight or nine enemy tanks already there, covering infantry who were digging in. This time the Germans held their ground and the eight Matildas cruised past them in line ahead formation, firing broadsides at a range of about a hundred yards. As soon as they were abreast of the enemy they turned sharply and closed in.

The German tanks fought back stubbornly, supported by artillery which shelled German and British tanks indiscriminately. In spite of this, as the Matildas moved in with their machine-guns and 2-pounders blazing, the enemy infantry retreated, closely followed by their tanks. When the British reached "Plonk", half a dozen fresh German tanks advanced from the west, but their attack was eventually beaten off. It was an hour and a half before the area was finally cleared, but the enemy shelling continued and made it impossible for Reid's party to go in. The tanks having cleared "Plonk", however, the infantry were not needed and before dawn the British tanks moved back to cover the new outpost, "Cooma", nearer the perimeter. Soon after first light the enemy was again observed digging in at "Plonk" under cover of tanks. British guns shelled it, but by this time the Axis infantry was well enough dug-in to stay there regardless of the bombardment. "Plonk" passed into the hands of the enemy.

The threat from the south during the battle for "Plonk" did not keep the garrison on the defensive elsewhere. In the Derna road sector, the 2/43rd Battalion, which was about to leave Tobruk, gave the Italians a parting shock. On two consecutive nights several small patrols struck deep into enemy territory, ambushed Italian working parties from ranges of 10 and 20 yards, and inflicted at least 75 casualties. One patrol, led by Captain W. E. L. Catchlove, killed 15 out of a party of 16 Italians and captured the survivor. Having roused the enemy's fears and suspicions by these attacks, the 2/43rd lay low the following night, but on the next they had their final laugh.

They had already discovered what Very lights the enemy sent up as a signal for general defensive fire. Consequently, on this night the 2/43rd gave the enemy front a short, sharp strafe and when the Italians were thoroughly roused, a lone Digger, some distance out in no-man's-land, put up the enemy's own defensive fire signal. Along the whole sector every Italian weapon opened up. For the next hour and a half shells, mortars and machine-gun bullets were flying everywhere in no-man's-land. The Italians wasted more than 700 shells, and the men of the 2/43rd—remembering the unfortunate mistake caused by the conflicting signals when they made their first attack in May—sat back in their concrete posts and grinned.

During the next five weeks the outposts that the Australians had maintained in the south and south-east all passed into the hands of the enemy.

This was probably inevitable, but the process was undoubtedly hastened by the withdrawal of the 9th Division. The units of the 70th British Division, which relieved it, were below strength, and could not maintain such an intensive system of patrols. Moreover they did not know the country and it was naturally some weeks before they were familiar with it. During this change-over period, the enemy, feeling less pressure from the garrison's patrols, and knowing that the troops were new, moved his positions forward under cover of tanks, until virtually all the perimeter was within range of hostile machine-guns. The result was that by mid-November the Tobruk garrison was in a weaker position than it had been at any time since May. It had less freedom and Rommel was much better able to launch a surprise assault. It was clear that as soon as he had consolidated his control of no-man's-land and gathered sufficient strength, he would attack Tobruk in force. For the garrison the vital question was—would he be ready to strike before the Eighth Army could launch its long-awaited offensive from the frontier? But the Australians could feel satisfied that by keeping command of no-man's-land during so many months they had delayed Rommel's preparations and given the Eighth Army time to recover from its severe losses in the June engagement and to build up fresh strength. They had also given it most valuable information about enemy dispositions and movements. The Tobruk garrison could peek into Rommel's back-yard. Traffic on the by-pass road was closely watched from the perimeter and day to day fluctuations in traffic provided a useful index of future activity on the frontier. Patrols quickly detected any big movement of troops to or from Tobruk. Reports compiled by Morshead's extremely able G.III (Intelligence), Captain L. K. Shave, told Eighth Army H.Q. much that it could not have learnt from any other source. Although the Diggers did not realize it, the scraps of information they picked up outside Tobruk were of great value to the British troops who were holding the frontier.

On the last night that the 2/17th Battalion were in the line

BATTLE FOR NO-MAN'S-LAND

I was at a forward post when their final Tobruk patrol went out. They took with them a rough wooden cross with a Digger's name and number painted on it. Tied to it was a note in stumbling French, asking the Italians to place the cross over the grave of an Australian who had been killed in the battle for "Plonk". The patrol left the cross in the enemy minefield where it was sure to be seen. In this gesture I felt they were paying their last tribute to all their mates who had fallen in the Battle for No-man's-land.

CHAPTER XVII

"We Never Say 'No' "

SOME of the British gunners in Tobruk sang very well, as I discovered when I sat with them round their gun-pit in the long evenings. Their favourite song was about gunners, and its chorus ran:

> Merry, oh merry, oh merry, are we,
> We are the boys of the artillery.
> Sing high, sing low, wherever we go
> Artillery gunners we never say "No".

The last line was certainly the motto of every Tobruk gunner. British artillery was the rock on which the two main German assaults in April and May finally broke. In the months of virtual stalemate which followed, it had an equally important role, and life in the garrison would have been much more hazardous if the enemy had been able to shell without fear of prompt reprisal. While Australian patrols held the enemy infantry well back from the perimeter in all sectors, except the Salient, the British and Australian artillery kept the Axis guns subdued. The Tobruk artillery was commanded by Brigadier L. E. Thompson, a British regular soldier. Under him were some of the finest artillery regiments in an Army renowned for its gunners: the 1st, 104th and 107th Regiments of the R.H.A., and the 51st Army Field Regiment. The only Australian field gunners were those of the 2/12th Field Regiment—and the Bush Artillery.

The enemy's artillery had several important advantages. The first was in observation. Because of the flatness of the desert, the duststorms and the heat haze, which restricted visibility from about eleven until four o'clock almost every day, it was extremely difficult to gain good observation from ground-level. When the enemy took Hill 209, he captured the garrison's best observation post, and gained a sweeping view of the area inside the perimeter as far east as the El Adem road. From 209 he overlooked the important gun-positions in the Pilastrino area, and made it dangerous for any but isolated vehicles to move in the area south and west of Pilastrino during daylight.

In addition, he had the advantage of unrestricted aerial observation, which was doubly important because the Tobruk gunners had no planes to spot for them, and few aerial photographs. Enemy reconnaissance planes came over at will to photograph, pick targets and direct shoots, but the ack-ack gunners kept them above 20,000 feet. After one JU88 had been shot down at 23,000 feet, the Germans used ME110s and Henschels, which had a higher ceiling. Their effectiveness as "spotting planes", however, was largely frustrated by "jamming" their radio sets. The Tobruk counter-battery staff discovered that the Germans used four frequencies—two for speech and two for Morse. Australian signalmen had a grand time tapping out the V for Victory call-sign on the Morse frequencies and interjecting with a few uncensored items on the speech wavelengths.

Enemy aerial observation was also hampered by effective camouflage. It is extremely difficult to conceal guns in the desert, but they can be camouflaged so that the enemy is unable to tell which positions are dummies and which are real. By holding their fire when reconnaissance planes came over and by frequently changing position, Tobruk gunners kept the enemy guessing. One troop of the 1st R.H.A. for a while had wooden guns covered by net screens half a mile from its real guns which were camouflaged to look like trucks.

Mere camouflage was not enough, for there were not many alternative battery positions. The artillery relied for protection primarily on the 25-pounder's capacity to shell Axis field guns from positions which these could not reach. The enemy, however, could move his guns to new positions almost every day. The Tobruk gunners adopted all kinds of subterfuge to hide their guns. Sometimes they fired through a dust-screen raised by trucks driven up and down in front of their gun-pits. At other times they fired artillery of varying calibre simultaneously from different positions. This stopped the enemy from identifying what guns were in action and which positions were being used.

To mislead him further the garrison destroyed landmarks, which he used for ranging—the fort at Pilastrino, buildings at the El Adem road junction, roadside telegraph poles and the funnels of ships in the harbour. To draw his fire on to worthless targets they made a number of dummy tanks out of metal piping, wood and hessian. One morning in July the Germans woke up to find a dozen new "tanks" near the Derna road. They shelled these spasmodically for a couple of days before realizing their mistake. Beside the Bardia road in the eastern sector there was a small white house which the enemy frequently shelled. To encourage him the 2/43rd Battalion sent men every morning and evening for some weeks to light a fire inside it. As the smoke rose, down came enemy shells.

Tobruk gunners took considerable risks in their efforts to gain observation. They often directed fire from outposts several miles beyond the perimeter; from tanks and carriers on patrol in no-man's-land; from tall pole O.Ps inside, and even outside, the wire. Many of these had been put up by the Italians and the enemy, knowing their exact positions, regularly shelled them with shrapnel. To trick the Axis gunners some poles were permanently "manned" by dummies, so that they could never tell whether these were really occupied. The 2/23rd Battalion raised a pole O.P. even in the Salient. It took the enemy 20 shells to knock it down. They put up a second. It went down after 32 rounds. A third stood; after 98 misses the enemy gave up the contest and the Diggers were soon able to occupy it with safety. To some extent these ruses countered the enemy's advantage in observation, but nothing compensated for the lack of spotting planes.

The enemy was also better supplied with ammunition—at least for his Italian guns. At both Bardia and Derna there were vast dumps that we had not had time to destroy. The garrison, on the other hand, was forced to husband its limited resources. Tobruk had ammunition for three or four months when the siege began, but in the first six weeks the artillery fired fifty tons on many days and on some as much as a hundred. This was considerably more than had been anticipated. To make matters worse, enemy bombers in June blew up one of Tobruk's largest ammunition dumps and for some weeks the guns were limited to ten rounds per gun per day. They exceeded this only when the garrison made a raid.

When the ammunition situation was at its worst Captain E. Baillieu and thirty men of the 2/24th Battalion brought in 110 rounds of 25-pounder ammunition, which the 6th Division had left outside the perimeter. This was no easy task. The shells in boxes of four had to be carried from a dump close to enemy positions two miles back to a waiting truck. As every shell cost £5 to manufacture and transport to Tobruk, Baillieu's men reckoned that on that night at least they had earned their pay. In later months the position improved, but ammunition was still rationed because the garrison had to build up reserves for the coming British offensive.

The Axis artillery was kept reasonably quiet only because of excellent work by the garrison's gunners and the British counter-battery staff, under Lieutenant-Colonel B. E. Klein.[1] In the absence of our aircraft, the counter-battery staff had to rely on flash-spotting and sound-ranging in fixing enemy battery positions. This was carried out by the 4th Durham Survey Regiment, but these methods did not work well by day, when the enemy did most of his shelling. At night he used various tricks to upset the counter-battery calculations. He fired mortars and guns simultaneously, hoping their flashes would be confused. The flash-spotters might have been misled, but the sound-rangers soon revealed the deception.

He also tried moving his guns frequently and firing them from many positions. Gradually, however, the garrison learned where most of these were and, as soon as an enemy battery opened up, Klein's staff knew it would probably be in one of several well-plotted sites. As a quick rough-and-ready check, they used the "flash-to-bang" method. In this, observers would clock the time from the moment they saw the flash until they heard the "bang" of the gun. After allowing for wind and temperature they could quickly calculate the approximate range. Knowing this, they could then pick out which of several known positions the guns were using.

This method worked particularly well in dealing with the big guns, which shelled the harbour from the Bardia road sector from mid-June onwards. The first of these was christened "Bardia Bill"; and when a second gun began shelling from this area, the title was applied to both. These guns were apparently 155-mm. siege or naval guns. Firing from the Wadi Belgassem, they could just reach the town eight and a half miles away. At first it was difficult to silence them because they changed position almost every night. Eventually the counter-battery staff "fixed" eleven positions so accurately that "Bardia Bill" seldom got off more than half a dozen rounds before its location was pin-pointed and shells were falling round it.

The guns that dealt with "Bardia Bill" were four 60-pounders, manned by the 2/12th Field Regiment, four 25-pounders of the 104th R.H.A., and two 149-mm. coast defence guns on the headland east of the town. Whenever there was shipping in the harbour, the crews of all these guns stood ready for action, and

---

[1] "Counter-battery" is the term used to describe action to silence enemy guns. Klein, who was Counter-Battery Officer on 1st Australian Corps H.Q., was lent to Brigadier Thompson in that capacity for two months.

their reply was so prompt and accurate that the shelling of
the harbour did remarkably little damage. One day in September,
there were seven small vessels in port and, anticipating a
Stuka raid, Bill Macfarlane[2] and I had set up our recording
gear on the waterfront. No Stukas came but "Bardia Bill"
searched the harbour in the late afternoon with twenty-six shells.
Not one landed within a hundred yards of a tanker, which was
the main target, and only three exploded.

Towards the end of July Rommel brought up more heavy
artillery. On the escarpment near El Adem, he had a 210-mm.
gun, which the counter-battery artillery could not effectively
shell. He also established behind Hill 209 a couple of big guns,
which became jointly known as "Salient Sue". "Sue" could
barely reach the harbour but one of Tobruk's main pumping
stations in the Wadi Auda was just about her length. The soft
earth of the wadi bed was cratered all around the stone building
that housed the plant, before she eventually hit it twice. Fortunately
the pump was below ground and was not even scratched.

The counter-battery work was so accurate that eventually
Klein's staff had pin-pointed more than a hundred alternative
battery positions, as well as those of twenty long-range mortars
and forty pole O.Ps. The value of this achievement was tested in
the attack on the Salient early in August. Then twenty-four guns
were devoted to silencing enemy artillery and for the most part
they were successful, as captured documents show; but Rommel
had too many guns for the garrison to deal with them all.

Later that month, a daring attempt was made by the 2/13th
Battalion to silence some troublesome artillery by direct attack.
The enemy had several batteries on high ground west of the
El Adem road and about half a mile behind his forward infantry
positions. The guns were located, and the raid made possible,
mainly through bold reconnaissance by Lieutenant J. B. Martin.
He began by finding and plotting the enemy minefield two
miles south of the perimeter. When he had located gaps between
the enemy's forward posts, he led deep patrols in behind them
on the next three nights. On the third night he went with eleven
men 1000 yards inside the minefield until they reached a road
used by enemy supply trucks. They moved westward for half
a mile looking for the guns. After waiting and searching for

---

[2] All the recordings made by the A.B.C. Field Unit in Tobruk were cut
by its engineer, Bill Macfarlane, who operated the recording equipment
in front line posts and gun-positions, in dug-outs and open desert, in
darkness and duststorm.

over an hour, they saw the guns fire 300 yards west of them.
Martin took a bearing on their flashes, while another patrol took
a bearing on them from a different direction. Simultaneously
the guns were flash-spotted from inside the perimeter.

Following this discovery, on the night of August 17th-18th
three officers and fifty men set out to blow up the guns. In
spite of its size, the patrol moved through the minefield and up
to the gun-positions without being detected, only to find that
the guns had gone. For nearly two hours the assault parties
prowled behind the enemy lines looking for the guns or for
any worthwhile target on which to use their explosives. All they
could do was to disrupt enemy communications by cutting
telephone lines. When the time came to withdraw, one of the
officers, Lieutenant E. R. Bucknell,[3] found his party was two
men short. Sending the rest home, he went back and eventually
discovered them searching for their boots. Because of the
shortage of sand-shoes some men had removed their boots so
that they would not be heard, but these two had mislaid theirs
in the dark. One man's feet were badly cut, so Bucknell gave
him his own boots and walked back in his stockings.

This raid failed, but several others brought back booty, which
was invaluable to the Bush Artillery. When the Australian
battalions first used captured guns, few of them had sights or
instruments. In many cases the range could be varied only by
putting another chock under the wheels, or taking one away.
Consequently when raiding parties brought in vital parts from
guns that they could not tow home, the Bush Artillerymen were
delighted. The unlimited ammunition left in Tobruk by the
Italians made these guns most valuable—they could continue
firing when rationing restricted others. Moreover, the Italian
149-mm. guns out-ranged the 25-pounders and helped to make
up for the garrison's shortage of medium artillery.

The regular gunners of the R.H.A. regarded with some amuse-
ment the initial efforts of the Australian infantry who had
turned gunners. But before long the Bush Artillery was directed
from the regular observation posts and the gunners were
honoured by requests from the R.H.A. to fire on targets that it
could not reach. From an infantryman's plaything the Bush
Artillery became an important part of Tobruk's artillery
defences. Some of these guns were manned by spare crews from
the anti-tank companies; others by odd personnel of the

---

[3] The other officers were Captain O. M. Walsoe and Lieutenant J. B. Martin.

battalions—batmen, cooks, clerks and drivers. They soon found it was no soft job. Several guns were blown up when shells exploded in the barrel; and after this many pieces of Bush Artillery were fired with the aid of a length of rope by remote control from the comparative safety of a sangar. These guns, being more active than the regular ones, had the added disadvantage of "drawing the crabs"; so much so that the normal routine was "a dozen rounds and dash for cover".

Because of this, units stationed near any Bush Artillery regarded its support with some misgiving. One gun was particularly unpopular with neighbouring troops. Located in a wadi beside the Pilastrino road, its crew charged passers-by "two piastres a pop" for the doubtful privilege of firing the gun. The crew's position was financially strategic, but they were not on the best of terms with a reserve battalion that had its H.Q. in the same wadi. Whenever business was brisk for the gunners, enemy reprisals made life uncomfortable for their neighbours. The battalion had its Signals and Intelligence offices in a dug-out thirty yards from the gun. Every time it fired sandbags deposited a little more of their contents on the maps, documents and telephone exchange. The blast even threatened to bring down the whole structure. Finally, the colonel appealed to Brigadier Thompson and the gun was removed, much to the indignation of the crew who swore they would sue for "loss of business".

An additional danger to all guns was the enemy's bombing. Next to the harbour and the ack-ack positions, field guns were the favourite dive-bomber targets. But thanks to the excellent defence by British and Australian light ack-ack batteries not one was knocked out in the first six months. The 8th Australian Light A.A. Battery, commanded by Major P. W. Stokes, bore the brunt of these air attacks, for it covered the guns in the important Pilastrino sector. Using 18 captured 20-mm. Bredas, this battery had to defend more than 50 field pieces, and several of the main supply dumps. It was difficult in Tobruk to allot particular "kills" to particular batteries, but these gunners are probably entitled to claim 15 "certainties", 19 "probables" and 46 planes damaged in six months.

They fought their guns so well that even though they were directly attacked by Stukas several times not a man was ever hit while engaging the enemy. Most of their casualties came from shell-fire, for they were in one of the favourite enemy target areas. The men stood to their guns right through air raids, but there was a quick scatter for dug-outs and gun-pits whenever any shelling began. One day as the shells came down, two Diggers raced for a gun-pit. As they dived in, the leading man said—"We beat the bastards that time." "What do you mean—beat 'em?" said his cobber. "One bit's run a dead heat with me flamin' tail."

The enemy shelling was seldom as accurate as this and it caused remarkably few casualties. How many casualties the garrison's shells inflicted not even the gunners knew, but G.H.Q. in its airy fastness in Cairo evidently considered that it should be given a detailed tally. During October Brigadier Thompson received a delightful memorandum from G.H.Q asking him to forward a return in triplicate showing how many (*a*) Germans and (*b*) Italians had been (*a*) killed and (*b*) wounded by shellfire in the previous three months. The request drew an appropriate reply from the colonel of one R.H.A. regiment but I doubt if it reached G.H.Q. He wrote:

As any honest sportsman knows, the matter of the infliction of casualties is, in most cases, unless one can pick up one's bird, purely a matter of conjecture. As I wish to be thought honest, I am resorting to pure mathematics and to history. In the Great War the ratio given was one ton of ammunition for one casualty. Of the total rounds then fired under 5% were observed. In Tobruk, I estimate that 25% of the rounds fired were observed. Consequently we may claim five casualties per ton.

As for certain casualties—on one occasion in the Salient after a shoot an officer reported having seen a priest descend from a vehicle, so it is reasonable to assume that he can claim at least one German. Some months ago a wounded Italian was seized upon and medically examined as to the cause of his trouble. So short of ammunition were the infantry at the time, that the machine-gunners began searching for their bullet. However, the doctor awarded the honours to the R.H.A.

Such are the difficulties under which I labour in providing a convincing answer to your inquiries, but now for figures:

Known Enemy Casualties
  Germans 1
  Italians (after being claimed by the infantry) 1

Estimated Enemy Casualties
  Rounds fired by Regiment 38,001
  Less two rounds for above casualties   2
                                      ─────
                             Say, 38,000 = 424 tons
  For observed rounds (25% of above tonnage)—
    (estimated one casualty per 20 rds for 9500 rds)
    casualties 475
  For unobserved rounds for remaining 318 tons—
    (estimated one casualty per 2 tons or 180 rds, allowing
    for wide open spaces) casualties 159
                                                  ─────
              Total enemy casualties (Perhaps)   636
                                                  ─────

Although the garrison could not give G.H.Q. a more precise estimate of casualties, the Axis gunners always had much the worse of the artillery duels. They were never completely silenced, but they became increasingly reluctant to stir up trouble. Enemy infantry and transport took care not to appear in daylight within range of the garrison's guns. Even Rommel's by-pass road was not far enough out. The 60-pounders and two captured 88-mm. ack-ack guns consistently shelled both it and the El Adem drome, and they certainly hindered the flow of Rommel's supplies to the frontier.

For the most part the work of the British gunners was unobtrusive, but it was none the less vital to the defence. As we have seen, in every crisis they had a decisive influence, and contributed substantially to the tactics of defence against tanks. In the Easter Battle they demonstrated the great value of the 25-pounder as an anti-tank gun in a direct fight. In the Battle of the Salient, they showed the effectiveness of heavy shelling combined with minefields in breaking up tank attacks. After this, as we saw in the fighting on May 17th, the German tanks were reluctant to face their fire.

No one knew better than the Australian infantry how much the garrison owed to the British artillery. They saw German tanks turn back and Axis infantry break and run when the British shells landed amongst them. They saw troublesome enemy guns and mortars promptly strafed as soon as they opened fire on forward posts. They knew that again and again fighting patrols had returned safely from raids largely because of the blanket of fire the British gunners put down behind them.

In view of all this it was unfortunate that the Australian Press tended to speak of Tobruk as though it were solely an A.I.F. achievement. A rather more directly informed journal, the news-sheet of the 2/48th Battalion one day in May printed a tribute that voiced the opinion of every Australian in the garrison. It published messages that Morshead had received from the British and Australian Prime Ministers and from Wavell after the second big German attack had been stopped. Then it added:

While these messages are appreciated . . . we must not forget that the greater part of the praise for what has been done here so far is due to the British artillery regiments. They have done a magnificent job. While we are not a Prime Minister nor a C.-in-C., we would like to express our most sincere and heartfelt thanks for what the British gunners have done for this garrison.

CHAPTER XVIII

Smashing the Stuka Parade

IN the wardroom of H.M.S. *Decoy* one morning early in August 1941, I picked up a copy of the *A.I.F. News*. Splurged across the front page was an article about Tobruk by the Australian war correspondent, Reg. Glennie. The first sentence ran, "Dust, Dive-bombers, Derelict Ships and Death". Maybe the officers of *Decoy* left this around deliberately to cheer their passengers as the destroyer churned through the Mediterranean to Tobruk.

For four months these game little destroyers of the R.N. and the R.A.N. had been running this gauntlet. Not all had come through unscathed. Already H.M.A.S *Waterhen* and H.M.S. *Defender* had been sunk, and Nazi bombers were to send other warships to the bottom in the next four months before the land route was opened again.

Meantime the destroyers and a few game little merchant ships, caiques and lighters maintained Tobruk's life-line, in spite of bomb, shell and submarine. But already the Luftwaffe had made things so hot that the destroyers could only come in when there was little or no moon. In the early months the Germans had not tried dive-bombing at night and the destroyers could afford to brave their high-level attacks. But in July the Germans found that they could pick up the destroyers in the moonlight because of the white foam in their wake, and in the darkness the ships' gunners could not see the diving planes until it was too late.

We were on the first run of the month and there would be the waning moon to guide the bombers to us as we got near Tobruk, but the crew hoped it would not be bright enough. Their main worry was the last half-hour before dark, when the escorting fighters had left. In this period the Stukas tried to stop the destroyer-ferry so consistently that the run from Sidi Barrani onwards was known as "Bomb Alley".

Dive-bombers seemed as yet a long way off as we lay in the sun on the deck. The day seemed brighter, the Med. bluer and the ship's wash whiter than ever before. We had left Alexandria at 8.30 a.m., slipping out of a harbour packed with merchantmen and warships, which Axis bombers had never been able to hit. On this trip there were three destroyers, *Decoy*, *Havock* and *Kingston*, each laden with fifty tons of freight and nearly a hundred troops.

Cargo and passengers took up almost every inch of the skimpy deck space. The troops were sprawled out on the cargo and almost in the scuppers, drinking in the sun. Most of them were going up for the first time; some were old-timers, returning for more after being invalided out sick or wounded, and telling newcomers terrible tales of a Tobruk that lay somewhere between purgatory and hell. But there was evidence that it was not so very bad, for amongst us were four Diggers, hitch-hiking back of their own accord. After a few weeks in hospital in Palestine they had scorned convalescent leave, "hitched" their way 400 miles to Alexandria, and "jumped" the destroyer. Strictly they were A.W.L., but they were not going to loiter in a Palestine camp while their cobbers were fighting at Tobruk.

Most of the cargo was cigarettes, mail and ammunition. On the three destroyers there were four million cigarettes—mostly South African brands, which are faintly Turkish—enough to give every man in the garrison the weekly ration of fifty for the next three weeks. As important as these were the dozens of bags of mail—more than three tons of it on our destroyer alone. And then boxes and boxes of ammunition—long, dark-green iron cases with 3.7-inch A.A. shells in them; shorter, squatter green cases of 25-pounder; green-lettered, rope-handled boxes of .303 rifle and machine-gun ammunition; some made in South Africa, some in the U.S.A. Another American contribution was hundreds of cases of dried fruits marked "American Red Cross in Greece". Too late for the Greeks, they had been switched to Tobruk. The rest of the cargo was utilitarian bully-beef, canned cabbage, tinned carrots, dried fruits, a new barrel for a Bofors A.A. gun, a track for a tank, a motor-car engine, and a pile of stretchers for wounded.

Sitting incongruously beside one stack of ammunition was a British officer's brand new kit. He had been in the Base Ordnance Depot in Cairo for five years and this was his first time in the field. He had fitted himself out well with a bright green canvas valise and stretcher, a blue-painted, brass-hinged wardrobe trunk, a smart new suitcase, and a khaki kitbag. With him was a Scotch terrier!

I tossed him the paper with the glaring lead—"Dust, Dive-bombers——"

"Not much of a place for a dog," I said. "Do you take him everywhere?"

"Yes," he replied. "I brought him out from England five years ago and war or no war I take him with me. He doesn't mind the desert, but I don't know how he'll like the dive-bombing."

This dog was not the strangest thing imported to Tobruk. Other British officers arrived during the siege bringing tennis racquets and golf clubs. One canteen ship came in with a large shipment of nurses' underwear that had been ordered some months before the German counter-attack, when A.I.F. nurses were at Barce. Another time some bright wit in Alexandria shipped to Tobruk twenty-four dozen gin bottles, but he sent them up empty, so that the troops could fill them with "Molotov cocktail". Empty!

About 3.30 p.m. we pass the white sandhills of Mersa Matruh. Two hours later we are level with Sidi Barrani, keeping well out to sea away from bombers based on Bardia. A.A. gunners move to action stations. Then a warning—shouted through a megaphone—"Plus six unidentified twenty miles south." Guns swing that way—even the 4.7s rise to the high-angle ack-ack position

Eight specks loom out of the blue, but they are distinctly Hurricanes, coming to cover us as we run through Bomb Alley. The leading plane fires a Very light recognition signal and over they come, 5000 feet up, sweeping back and forth above the three destroyers with the afternoon sun glinting on silver wings and fuselage as they bank and turn.

The destroyers quicken their speed—thirty-two knots now—and spray breaks over the after-deck. On we go, destroyer throbbing under our feet; fighters droning overhead. We are safe while they are with us. An hour later another warning—one flight heads southward to intercept; the other keeps circling above. But soon we see the four Hurricanes returning with eight specks trailing behind them—more Hurricanes—to relieve the others and carry on till half an hour before dark. They must leave then, otherwise they might crack up on landing.

"Looks as though we'll be all right to-night," says a sub-lieutenant standing beside me. "We haven't been in for nearly a week, so Jerry won't be expecting us and he hasn't had a 'recce' out. Last month he had a crack at us most nights at dusk after the fighters had gone."

Finally they wheel away and we continue alone, hoping for the best, but just before dark one lone reconnaissance plane sweeps in from the west, circles once well out of range and goes back to his base with the target for to-night.

The next four hours drag slowly through as the setting moon silhouettes us on a silver sea, turning our wake into a phosphorescent trail. On the deck we wait—salt spray spattering faces and knees as the destroyer plunges into the night. Waiting—waiting—waiting—ears straining for the drone of bombers.

Then above the roar of engines, wind and sea, from the rear gun-platform an officer shouts through a megaphone: "Stand by. Action stations." We wait again. Then, "Stand by. Enemy aircraft."

Suddenly we're snatching at the nearest rail or bulkhead as the destroyer heels over in a wild zigzag and seems to leap forward. On the slippery deck the cargo slides crashing into the scuppers and spray drenches everything.

Above the turmoil that voice again, "Stand by. Blitz barrage." Behind us a great white swath of wash is even more tell-tale than before, but they'll have seen us now and the only way to trick them is to zigzag. I look across at *Havock*—a great stream of black smoke is pouring from her funnels. Then we hear the bomber's drone and *Havock's* guns stab the darkness with red flashes. She rolls over in a 90-degree turn and a hundred yards or so ahead of her a great white water-spout tells us that the Stuka has missed its mark.

Out of the darkness ahead we see two pin-points of light, the harbour lights of Tobruk, shielded from the air but visible to us. We slacken speed. There is no wash now, and a welcome cloud cloaks the moon and other bombers cannot see us.

But they are over Tobruk and are going for the harbour. We can hear the muffled crack of the ack-ack guns and see the flashes of bursting shells high in the sky; only the "heavies" are firing, so apparently the bombers are well up.

We slip in between the lights, past the black ghosts of wrecks, under the lee of the white sepulchre of a town. The ack-ack is still speeding the raider home, but another is coming in—lower. The Bofors are firing too, so it must be well under 10,000 feet. But we have no time to think of the fireworks display above us. As *Decoy* stops moving two barges and two launches come alongside. Troops clamber over the side, pitching their kitbags ahead of them. Unloading parties swarm aboard and slide ammunition down wooden chutes into one barge, while the rest

SMASHING THE STUKA PARADE

of the cargo is dumped anyhow into the other. As soon as the troops are off, the crew start bringing wounded aboard in stretchers.

They are getting a warm farewell. One stick of bombs screams down on the south shore of the harbour; the next is closer—in the water 500 yards away. The old hands continue working, unworried, but some of the new ones, like us, pause momentarily, shrinking down behind the destroyer's after-screen. From the man with the megaphone comes a sharp rebuke—"What are you stopping for? Those bloody bombs are nothing to do with you."

We take no notice of the next two sticks which fall in the town and at last everything is unloaded. The engine throb quickens and the destroyer is lost in the blackness just thirty-two minutes after the barges came alongside. Fifty tons of cargo and nearly a hundred men taken off; fifteen to twenty stretcher-cases embarked, and all in half an hour.

The guns were going again as we left the jetty and went bumping out of the town in a 3-tonner. For the next hour, they were coming over in ones and twos every ten minutes or so. As the drone of one died away, we could hear the next coming in, the greeting of the guns, the rumble of bursting bombs and then the ack-ack's spasmodic farewell fire. We thought it was a fairly warm welcome but for Tobruk it was just an ordinary night.

Month after month the Navy had been bringing its ships into these dangerous waters and, by doing so, had made possible the holding of Tobruk. When the siege began the garrison had food and ammunition for three, and possibly four, months, but it had to hold for eight. In April and May enemy air attacks on shipping both inside and outside the harbour were so severe that the maintenance of supplies was a most hazardous task. During the first month when ships tried to approach Tobruk in daylight, more than 50 per cent of the cargo vessels were turned back by Stukas and several were sunk. Valiant destroyers managed to slip through at night but Cunningham could not spare enough ships at this time—especially after the losses off Greece and later off Crete—to maintain the supply of anything but absolute essentials. In fact Tobruk's food reserves would have been seriously depleted if naval and merchant vessels had not evacuated more than 12,000 surplus personnel during the first month.

Even with the garrison reduced to 23,000 the maintenance of

adequate supplies was most difficult. Tobruk had no proper unloading facilities, for British bombs had destroyed the main wharf and the other was soon badly damaged by the Luftwaffe and blocked by a wreck. This left only one small oiling jetty which was little more than a pipeline on piles, and so most cargo had to be unloaded into barges or on to half-sunken wrecks. This task was doubly difficult because enemy bombing soon made daylight unloading impracticable.

As it was similarly difficult for shipping to make the run along the Cyrenaican coast to Tobruk in daylight, the garrison during May and June was forced to rely for supplies and reinforcements almost entirely on destroyers which could come in, unload and get out again under cover of darkness. Even if the destroyers escaped bombing this was a perilous run. Their crews never knew what fresh wreck might be lying in the harbour, or whether mines had drifted into or been laid in the narrow channel, or again whether the enemy had put up dummy harbour lights to mislead them. Added to these was the possibility that an enemy submarine would be lying in wait along the route the destroyers had to take in entering the harbour. H.M.A.S. *Stuart* attacked submarines near Tobruk on two occasions at the end of June.

Undeterred by these hazards, destroyers maintained their ferry service almost nightly, for the Navy knew that without the supplies these brought in, the garrison would eventually have to starve or surrender. None appreciated this more than the troops themselves. Their thanks found expression in the grace I heard a Tobruk padre say one day—"For what we are about to eat, thank God and the British Fleet." The padre could well have included the anti-aircraft gunners, because without the protection they provided, even the British Navy could hardly have used the Tobruk harbour.

The A.A. gunners' victory was not quickly or easily won. Rommel used every possible technique to silence them and close the harbour. His airmen tried dive-bombing, high-level bombing, low-level minelaying, mixed bombing—combined dive and high-level, or high-level and minelaying. He went for the ships inside the harbour and outside; by day and night. When bombing proved ineffective, he tried shelling.

To counter these attacks the garrison had only seventy guns in action on April 10th, and by the end of the month only eighty-eight—more than half of which had been captured from the Italians. A third of these were "heavies" and of the remaining light ack-ack guns, half had to be kept outside the harbour area to cover the field artillery.

The guns available were:

Heavy Guns	Light Guns
24 3.7-inch (British)	17 Bofors—40-mm.—(British)
4 102-mm. (Italian)	43 Breda (all 20-mm. Italian except one twin 37-mm.)

These guns were mostly manned by men from Scotland and England. Out of seven batteries, only one was Australian—the 8th Battery of the 3rd Light A.A. Regiment. Few of the gunners had been in action before and fewer still had faced a dive-bomber attack until they came to Tobruk. Some compensation for their lack of experience was provided by the inspiration and soldierly genius of their commander, Brigadier J. N. Slater, a British regular gunner of magnificent spirit, energy and originality. No anti-aircraft commander had been faced with the problem which he had to tackle—that of defeating the dive-bomber with ack-ack guns alone, and, in particular, of protecting these from direct dive-bomber attack. The tactics Slater and his gunners used had to be developed and tried out while the battle was on.

The measure of their success is shown in this: on the first fifty-four days of the siege, the harbour and town area was raided in daylight by 807 dive-bombers; in the last fifty-four days that I was there, there was one daylight dive-bombing attack on this area by one Stuka.

The first fifty-four days in Tobruk were certainly the worst. This initial phase, which lasted from April 10th to June 2nd, was one of intensive dive-bombing, directed first at the ships in the harbour and then at the ack-ack guns. By June 2nd the ack-ack gunners had engaged more than 1550 aircraft and all but 106 of these had come over in daylight.

In the last three weeks of April, there was at least one Stuka raid every day and in spite of the anti-aircraft barrage the harbour became virtually unusable in daylight. When no ships were there, the Stukas bombed jetties on the north shore, general port installations and the town—frequently going for the ack-ack guns simultaneously. To defeat this attack, the guns around the harbour at first put up an umbrella barrage at about 3000 feet.

This was not enough. The German pilots dived through the

barrage, or round and under it. They came down as low as 600 feet before dropping their bombs. They were game and, though a few paid, most got away with it. Their main worry at this time was the Hurricanes of No. 73 Squadron, but these were seldom warned early enough to intercept any bomber before it dropped its load.

The harbour area could be protected only by more effective ack-ack fire. This was provided by "thickening the barrage" with more guns, as they became available, and by spreading their fire over the area between 3000 and 6000 feet, instead of concentrating it at one level. Thus Stuka pilots had to face a belt of fire for 3000 feet of their dive. To counter their trick of coming down along the edge of the barrage and then diving under it, this was made to swing backwards and forwards across the harbour, so that a pilot never knew where its edge would be. He might start his dive clear of the barrage and suddenly find that it had swung right into his line of flight. Similarly gunners used to vary the height of the barrage. Some days its ceiling was 5000 feet; on others 7000, and pilots were frequently tricked. These two improvements made the barrage much more effective and any Stukas that did brave their way through it came under direct fire of two or more of the twelve Bofors placed around the harbour. After the end of April these "killed the bird" more often than not, if a Stuka came really low.

Stung by the force and accuracy of this fire, the Germans turned their dive-bombers against the ack-ack guns themselves. In a fierce attack on April 27th, they went for the four heavy gun-positions, each of which had four 3.7-inch guns. The attack began with a number of medium bombers and fighters (JU88s and ME109s) coming in very high to draw the fire from the heavy guns. While the 3.7s were blazing away at 20,000 feet, fifty JU87s stole in well below them in four formations, each of which went for one heavy-gun position.

From two of these positions, the JU87s were spotted and engaged on their run in. As the guns swung on to them, each formation split into four groups of three or four and down they came—attacking each of these two gun-positions from four points of the compass. With the concentration of fire broken up, each gun had to deal with three or four Stukas diving directly for it.

It took nerve to stand up to the attack but every gun kept firing as the bombs came down. From the moment the first bombs exploded, the crews were smothered with dust and smoke, but they fired on without faltering even though they could see nothing. In spite of this, the Stukas went through with their dives, but not one bomb landed on either position. Even the near-misses—fifty and a hundred yards away—did no damage, for the guns were well dug-in and had strong parapets. Not one man on these eight guns was killed or wounded.

On the other two heavy-gun positions it was a different story. The JU87s that attacked one site were spotted as they came in, but the gunners did not engage them very effectively. On the other site the gunners were still busy dealing with the high-level attack when the first of the Stukas' bombs burst in the middle of the circle of four gun-pits, which were only about fifteen yards apart. The Stukas had all dived straight out of the sun and the gunners, disconcerted by this and the surprise, took cover as soon as the first bombs landed. The pilots had an open go. Practically every bomb was placed right on the positions. To make matters worse, the guns were not well dug-in and their parapets were not substantial. Five men were killed and forty-one wounded. Two guns on each site were put out of action for two days, and other ack-ack equipment was damaged.

The comparison between the fate of these and the other two gun-positions taught a grim but encouraging lesson. If the guns fought the dive-bombers all the way down their crews were reasonably safe. If they did not, both guns and crews would be lucky to escape.

Slater immediately instructed every battery that in the face of dive-bombing no one who had a weapon to fire was to go to ground. Every gun must keep in action and all those who were not manning an ack-ack gun must engage the diving planes with rifles or light automatics. Every gun was to be dug in as deep as possible and protected by a parapet capable of withstanding a 1000-pounder, landing ten yards away.

These measures helped the gunners to look after themselves fairly well and with each attack they gained more confidence and skill. Guns were damaged from time to time, but, from April to the end of October at least, not one was completely knocked out, and none was put out of action for more than a day or two. On only three other occasions did the dive-bombers silence a position during an attack and by the end of May the gunners had the upper hand.

The anti-aircraft guns, however, had to do more than defend themselves. Rommel had so many planes that he could afford to launch one attack strong enough to keep all the heavy guns occupied while he sent another against the harbour. Naturally if all the heavy guns were to be engaged in beating off direct attacks on their own positions, they could not keep up the harbour barrage. This danger was averted primarily by deception. A number of dummy gun-sites were established near the main heavy ack-ack positions. These were remarkably well constructed—so well that you could drive within a hundred yards of a dummy site without realizing that it was not genuine. They had dummy guns, dummy men, trucks, and ammunition dumps. Moreover, the dummies were fitted with special mechanism that produced "gun-flashes" and dust-clouds when the nearby guns were fired. By having real guns in a position one day and dummy guns there the next, the deception was completed.

The result was that the Stukas, diving at dust-clouds from which flashes came, attacked dummy sites as often as real ones. As the danger of direct attack on the guns was thus virtually halved, the gunners could concentrate on their primary task of maintaining the harbour barrage. To make sure of this, Slater ordered that no gun-site was to use more than one gun for its own defence except in very unusual circumstances, but it took considerable courage on the gunners' part to keep three of their four guns firing the barrage when they knew that Stukas were diving straight for them. To give better protection from low-diving attacks, however, one light ack-ack gun was placed near each position.

This system worked magnificently. The barrage was maintained, the guns were defended, and the Germans wasted a lot of their bombs on the dummy sites. On one occasion thirty-five JU87s and eight JU88s attacked the harbour and seven heavy-gun sites. Three of the sites attacked were dummies and each of the other four defended itself with only one of its two guns. (As part of the deception policy, some sites at times had two real guns, and two dummies.) The harbour barrage suffered very little and the enemy had three planes shot down and six hard hit.

Frustrated in his attempts to silence the guns and close the harbour in the first month, Rommel turned his bombers against Tobruk's water resources, in the hope of "thirsting" the garrison out. Tobruk's main supply came from two distilleries on the south side of the harbour, which purified sea-water, and from

SMASHING THE STUKA PARADE

two pumping stations in the Wadi Auda (two miles west of the town), which raised sub-artesian water that was more than a little brackish. These were all operated by the 2/4th Field Park Company, even though its only trained engineer was a staff-sergeant, E. D. Wakeham. An additional supply was provided by a pumping station in the Wadi es Sehel, which formed part of the western boundary of the defences. This plant, housed in an underground room with blue-painted walls and a red-tiled floor, was actually in no-man's-land. Nevertheless, troops regularly went out there for a shower. This was never bombed—apparently because the enemy hoped to capture it intact and not, as the Diggers believed, because the enemy himself pumped water from this source. The other plants, however, were subjected to heavy and repeated attacks during May and early June. Luckily none was hit.

Finally the enemy was induced to abandon his attacks by further clever deception. After one attack on the distilleries a camouflage section poured dirty oil over the buildings to make it appear that they had been hit. They finished the job in half an hour and the reconnaissance plane that came over later evidently saw black shadows that looked like gaping holes in the roofs of the buildings. They were not directly attacked again.

The attacks on the water supply were part of Rommel's attempt to bomb Tobruk into submission after his tank attacks failed. He was able to keep all shipping—except very small caiques and other minor craft—out of the harbour in daylight during the rest of May, but the ack-ack guns still defied him. All through that month the battle between dive-bombers and gunners went on, and frequently the German Radio claimed that the Tobruk ack-ack had been silenced.

In the Berlin *Nationblatt* on May 12th a German war correspondent, named Billhardt, gave a glowing and optimistic account of the air attacks on the harbour. He wrote:

Over Tobruk the sky is seldom silent. The sound of our motors continually terrifies the Tommies, chases them to their guns and forces them to hang the sky with steel curtains and black anti-aircraft clouds, until dive attacks by our Stukas with bombs and machine-gun fire destroy them or force them to take cover. The anti-aircraft artillery of Tobruk enjoyed our highest respect—once. Then the Stukas dropped their bombs, and since then the anti-aircraft shelling from Tobruk has become very much weaker. After each attack the younger pilots are twice as eager next day to fly still more madly into the middle of the anti-aircraft barrage—to get on to their objectives still more exactly. To batter Tobruk till it is ready for storming will be a nice piece of work.

Herr Billhardt's pilots had ample chance to prove these words good when Rommel made an all-out attempt to silence the ack-ack guns in the week ending June 2nd, but they found that the Tobruk defences were stronger than ever. There were now twenty-eight heavy guns in action compared with sixteen in April and the harbour was ringed with twelve Bofors guns instead of six. The gunners even manned the 3-inch dual-purpose gun on the deck of the gunboat H.M.S. *Ladybird*, which lay half-sunken in the harbour. She was the victim of a dive-bomber raid, but a tattered White Ensign still flew proudly from her mast.

That week's blitz began on May 26th with an attack by six JU87s on a new heavy-gun position on North Point—the headland north of the harbour. The crews of these four guns had never been in action before, but they braved the Stukas, blew one to bits with a direct hit, and watched a nearby Bofors bring down another.

On the 29th the dive-bombers switched their main attack to the harbour, but the gunners scored their biggest victory to date. Out of thirty dive-bombers, four crashed, another probably crashed, and four more limped home, unlikely to fly again. But their bombs sank two lighters and one small ship.

Undeterred by their losses, the Stukas came back on June 1st for another defeat. Twenty-four out of forty JU87s went for the heavy guns while the rest attacked the harbour. Twelve dived on the North Point guns, but in the face of their fire, few came below 3000 feet, and one that did was destroyed in mid-air. Not one bomb fell within 150 yards of the guns and some pilots sheered off and dropped their bombs in the sea. Altogether four were shot down for certain, and at least six more were badly damaged.

The final round was fought next day, when the Germans sent in sixty Stukas—thirty of them against the impudent North Point guns. To see whether the planes really went through with the attack, they sent three Henschels to observe the results of the bombing from a safe height above the barrage. But, Henschels or no Henschels, the pilots would not face the anti-aircraft fire.

In the first two raids of this week they had come down one after the other in steep dives at an angle of about 70 degrees. On June 1st they had dived steeply but had been forced to release their bombs above the barrage—too high for accuracy. On June 2nd they changed their tactics and tried shallow diving from

SMASHING THE STUKA PARADE

different directions, but this made no difference to the gunners. Once again the North Point guns blew a plane out of the sky and the bombs fell even farther from the mark than before. The Germans did not press home their attack, but this raid was just as costly as that of the previous day. Four JU87s were shot down, four were probably destroyed and four more damaged.

June 2nd saw the end of the first phase of the battle between the gunners and dive-bombers and the scoreboard then showed:

AXIS LOSSES			TOBRUK LOSSES	
Aircraft			*Ships*	
By A.A.	—Certainly destroyed ..	57	Sunk	5
	Probably destroyed ..	44	*Guns*	
	Damaged	96	Destroyed	Nil
By R.A.F.	—Certainly destroyed ..	30	Damaged (but in action within 48 hours)	16
	Probably destroyed ..	4		
Air Crew			*A.A. Personnel*	
Killed	At least	150[1]	Killed	10
			Wounded	72

The enemy's most serious losses had been in dive-bombers and their crews, since 80 per cent of the planes shot down were single-engined JU87s. For a few weeks the Germans used twin-engined JU88s for dive-bombing as well, but these were sitting shots for the gunners. On April 20th, when eleven of them dive-bombed the town, the R.A.F. shot down four, the ack-ack got three and probably destroyed two more.

Unfortunately for Rommel, his most courageous pilots—those who dived lowest—were the ones generally brought down, and almost invariably they crashed to death. Thus by June 2nd he had lost the pick of his German dive-bomber crews, and thereafter had to make increasing use of Italians, who were neither as skilful nor as courageous. With the Russian campaign soon absorbing nearly all the aircraft and pilots Hitler could spare, Rommel could no longer incur losses as severe as those his airmen had suffered at the end of May.

For all these losses Rommel had little to show. His aircraft had sunk in Tobruk harbour only two small naval vessels, two troop-transports and one small cargo ship. In addition a larger

---

[1] See Chapter XIX. The Tobruk A.A. Command's estimate of the number of planes shot down was very conservative, and the actual enemy plane losses were probably 50 per cent greater than those claimed. Hence this estimate of personnel killed.

number of vessels was sunk outside the harbour approaching or leaving Tobruk. Some of these sinkings would have been avoided if G.H.Q., Cairo, had given earlier heed to Tobruk's request that no ships, other than very minor craft, should be sent in during daylight.

In defying the dive-bombers, the Tobruk anti-aircraft gunners did more than keep the harbour open and destroy enemy aircraft. They gained a moral triumph and set an example for Allied gunners and enemy pilots everywhere. For the first time in this war, ack-ack gunners showed that Stukas could be beaten by men who stood to their guns.

CHAPTER XIX

Keeping the Harbour Open

ALTHOUGH the German dive-bombers were defeated as decisively as their tanks in April and May, the air assault against the Fortress had to go on. If Rommel could not capture Tobruk, at least he had to stop the garrison becoming strong enough to break out and harass his flank and lines of communication. If he could not silence the ack-ack defences and close the harbour, he must restrict its use as much as possible.

As Stuka raids had become too expensive, Rommel was forced to rely on high-level bombing to impose his air blockade. The percentage of attacks delivered by dive-bombers dropped from 68 per cent in the first phase to 18 per cent in the second, which lasted from June 3rd to August 3rd. During this period his losses were cut down by more than 80 per cent, only eleven planes being shot down for certain, compared with eighty-seven in the previous eight weeks. The effectiveness of the bombing, however, was reduced almost as much. In the absence of the dive-bombers in June, the small ships' traffic increased. In attempts to stop this, the Stukas came back in force on July 1st and 4th, but their pilots—many of them now Italians—were reluctant to dive below 6000 feet.

In the first attack only one plane was shot down, but all the forty-six Stukas dropped their bombs above the barrage and not one ship was hit. Thirty dive-bombers were sent back three days later accompanied by "Gestapo" Henschels and apparently ordered to go in below the barrage. They did so, but the Bofors shot down five and the "heavies" got another. Two more were probably destroyed and six hit. Again they missed the ships. This was their costliest defeat and except for two other fleeting appearances, the Stukas left the skies to the high-level bombers from then until August.

Axis daylight attacks were mostly delivered by single planes or small formations of three or four, which sneaked in at anything from 18,000 to 25,000 feet. The ack-ack fire kept them high and more often than not threw them off their targets. The result was that normal high-level bombing had merely a nuisance value and, if the enemy hit any worthwhile target, it was largely by good luck. Being frequently thwarted by the barrage if they made a regular run in, some German pilots tried various tricks and certain planes became so well known by their tactics that the ack-ack gunners gave them pet-names. At one stage for about a month there were three JU88s that specialized in bombing the supply dumps every morning just about the time the ration trucks were drawing stocks. They were nick-named "Pip", "Squeak" and "Wilfrid" after three saucy British comic-strip characters. One by one the barrage got them.

They lasted about three weeks, but two other JU88s, "Mickey" and "Minnie", lived twice as long. They had a special trick. One would come roaring out of the sun in a shallow dive while the other approached from a different direction with its engine throttled back. Finally one of them had three feet shot off the end of its wing and the combination was broken up. The JU88 which did more damage than any dozen dive-bombers, was one known as "Jimmy". He specialized in hit-and-run attacks, and would glide in out of the sun with his engine just ticking over, drop his bombs and roar away before the guns had time to get on to him. On August 12th "Jimmy" landed a stick of bombs on an ammunition dump near 9th Division H.Q. For several hours huge clouds of smoke hung over the area and thunderous explosions could be heard in the farthest perimeter posts. "Jimmy", evidently delighted with his success, came back for more; but the dump was composed largely of useless Italian ammunition, which the Ordnance branch was about to dump in the sea. "Jimmy" saved it the trouble.

However, these nuisance raids did cause more casualties than dive-bombing, primarily because the first warning was usually the bursting bombs. One morning "Jimmy" caught some ack-ack gunners lining up for their cigarette issue. One stick of bombs killed eleven and wounded nearly twice as many. What appeared to be haphazard nuisance bombing was not always so. At one time bombs were being consistently dropped on a patch of open desert where there was no visible target. This was regarded merely as bad bombing until one day Stukas dived deliberately on the area. Investigation revealed a large buried petrol dump which the Italians had forgotten to explode before Tobruk fell.

The high-level bombing became less effective as the anti-

KEEPING THE HARBOUR OPEN

aircraft defences improved, and small ships and lighters were eventually able to unload in the harbour in daylight. The additional supplies these brought were extremely important, because more varied rations were urgently needed, and reserves of petrol, ammunition and food had to be built up to support the eventual British offensive.

During July there were two most important supply developments. The Navy tried sending in two auxiliary lighters—each carrying 120 tons—every forty-eight hours. At first these arrived one night, unloaded the next and left the following night, but by the middle of the month the ack-ack defences had so subdued the Stukas that Morshead authorized daylight unloading. In the absence of dive-bombers twenty-two lighters, eight small cargo vessels and four schooners landed their cargoes safely during July. These, plus thirty-four trips by destroyers and two by a cruiser, resulted in the delivery of 5076 tons of stores during the month—an increase of more than 50 per cent on the figures for June.

The troops benefited directly from this improvement. The inward mail for July rose to more than two thousand bags. One ship brought in sufficient meat for seven or eight issues per man. The ration of fresh vegetables and oranges improved so much that the daily dosage of ascorbic tablets could be reduced from two to one. The razor blade allowance was increased from one a fortnight to one a week and, most significant of all, there was one issue of nearly a pint of beer per man.

In spite of this general improvement, however, a serious petrol situation was only just averted. This was easily the most hazardous cargo shipped to Tobruk, since the tankers which brought it were slow and vulnerable. Because of this, rigid economy was enforced but by mid-June the garrison was using 6000 gallons (about 27 tons) a day, and there was barely a month's reserve in hand, and less if heavy fighting were to develop.

In response to Morshead's urgent request, Middle East dispatched the tanker *Pass of Balmaha* with 750 tons of petrol for Tobruk on June 22nd. As escort, she had two sloops, H.M.S. *Auckland* and H.M.A.S. *Parramatta*. Nearing Tobruk late on the afternoon of June 24th, this vital convoy was attacked by forty-eight Stukas in three formations. The story of what followed is well told in *Parramatta's* own account:

As they worked round in order to dive from the direction of the sun, both *Auckland* and *Parramatta* opened with the heaviest barrage their guns could give. The pandemonium was terrific. Added to the bark of gunfire and the continuous staccato of machine-guns, was the angry hornet noise of dive-bombers swooping down from every direction; then the hiss of falling bombs, followed, in some cases, by the roar of an explosion. The enemy machines concentrated two-thirds of their attack on *Auckland* and the remainder on *Parramatta* and *Pass of Balmaha*. *Auckland* was suddenly obscured by thick brown smoke. She had been hit; the whole of the stern section above water had been blown to pieces. With the foremost guns still firing, she managed to continue at about 10 knots with the wheel jammed hard a-port, yet, for some unaccountable reason turning rapidly to starboard. To the amazement, therefore, of *Parramatta*, the next thing she saw was *Auckland* emerge from the smoke and head straight at her. Just in time *Parramatta* managed to put her wheel over to avoid collision, but *Auckland* presented a pathetic sight, with no stern visible, heeling heavily to port, her available guns still firing at the diving aircraft.

Almost immediately she was hit again by three bombs simultaneously, but she continued firing until the enemy had dropped all their bombs and flown away. When the enemy drew off, she lay stopped, flames and smoke pouring from her decks and the ship listing more heavily to port. As her end was obviously near, orders were given to abandon ship, and boats and rafts were already in the water. *Parramatta* closed and stopped to windward of the sinking vessel, where she dropped whalers, skiffs, lifebelts and floats. Suddenly there was a terrific explosion in *Auckland*, which lifted her slowly and steadily about six feet into the air. Her back broke, and she settled down with an increased list to port, and at 1829 hours rolled over and sank. Another attack was obviously developing, and it was impossible for *Parramatta* to stop and pick up survivors at the time. As she was gathering way the attack came in a deliberate low-level bombing by six Savoias 79. *Parramatta* and *Pass of Balmaha* successfully evaded damage, whereupon the aircraft machine-gunned *Auckland* survivors in the water, but happily did little harm.

As the sun began to sink towards the horizon—and how anxiously every one watched it!—the sky became alive with aircraft. At first it was hoped that British fighters were among them and attacking the bomber formations, but it was soon discovered that all in sight were hostile. At 1955 the attack developed, and from that moment the air seemed so full of shrieking and diving planes that it was impossible to count them. There was always one formation overhead falling about like leaves and diving in succession, another formation moving forward into position, and a third splitting up and approaching at an angle of 45 degrees. For the best part of an hour and a half attacks continued, until at length, as the sun touched the horizon at 2025, the enemy drew off. Shortly after, to the great relief of every one on *Parramatta*, we sighted the destroyers *Waterhen* and *Vendetta*. We had begun to feel lonely, and the arrival of these destroyers was much appreciated. The work of picking up survivors was quickly carried out, and with 162 on board, *Parramatta* proceeded towards Alexandria, while *Waterhen* took *Pass of Balmaha* in tow and delivered her safely at Tobruk. Thus, another 750 tons of petrol reached its destination.

Thanks to the consideration of the Italians in leaving their bulk pumping and storage facilities intact, this cargo and a further 150 tons of petrol were safely off-loaded at Tobruk before the end of June. It was fortunate that they were, for on July 9th the bulk petrol pumping plant was put out of action for a month by a direct hit. The enemy had struck a fortnight too late, for by this time Tobruk had seventy days' supply. Not satisfied with this, however, Morshead had cased petrol shipped in to maintain stocks while the plant was being repaired and one night a small party of Diggers unloaded 50,000 gallons of cased petrol between dark and dawn. Further economy reduced the daily consumption to 4500 gallons, and the petrol crisis was weathered.

The voyage of *Pass of Balmaha* was probably the most important individual run ever made to Tobruk, but the main means of general supply was always the destroyer-ferry. This was maintained almost entirely by British and Australian ships of the Tenth Flotilla. At one time or another the "Spud Run", as the Navy called it, was made by all the Australian destroyers in the Mediterranean—*Vendetta, Stuart, Waterhen, Vampire, Voyager, Napier, Nestor* and *Nizam*. *Vendetta* eventually established a record with twenty-eight trips; *Stuart* made twenty-two and *Waterhen* had made nearly as many when she was sunk as a result of German bombing on June 29th. A near-miss holed the engine-room; H.M.S. *Defender* took her in tow but could not save her, though all the crew was rescued.

Waterhen's finest exploit on the Tobruk run was probably her attempt to save the hospital ship *Vita*, which was deliberately dive-bombed on April 14th. *Waterhen* tried to tow her, and when that proved impossible, rescued 437 patients, six doctors, six nurses and forty-one sick-berth attendants and took them to Alexandria.

The enemy was well aware of the importance of the destroyer-ferry and did his utmost to stop it by bombing the harbour at night when the ships were in, but the barrage was so effective that no destroyer was ever hit. Night attacks on the harbour could have succeeded only if the dive-bombers had knocked out the guns in daylight. When they failed in this, the dive-bombers tried to intercept the destroyers off Sollum in the late afternoon. From June onwards, as we have seen, R.A.F. fighters escorted the destroyers, and after nine Stukas had been shot down in one action, the enemy was less persistent with these attacks.

Finally he did gain a limited success. His dive-bombing of the destroyers at sea by night became so accurate that it was too dangerous for them to come in when the moon showed the ships' wake. Because of this there were only thirty-four destroyer trips in July, but by sending three or four destroyers in each night during the "no moon" period, the number was increased to fifty-eight in August and sufficient supplies and reinforcements continued to reach Tobruk. Even then dive-bombers made the ferry run risky and on several occasions I saw troops coming off a destroyer drenched with spray thrown up by a near-miss.

Apart from such attacks on ships outside the harbour, the enemy air force during June and most of July relied on the night bombing of Tobruk to stop the destroyer-ferry. Most of these raids were made by single bombers from about 13,000 feet. By putting up a barrage in the oncoming bomber's path— as revealed by radio location equipment—the ack-ack guns forced as many as half of them to drop their bombs wide of any real target.

It was not until late in July that any serious threat developed from these night attacks. Then heavier night bombing, together with minelaying attacks and increased shelling by big guns, set new problems. The minelaying was particularly serious and on July 30th the destroyers could not be unloaded and some auxiliary lighters had to turn back. These developments and the renewal of dive-bombing introduced the third phase in the battle to keep the harbour open. It began on August 3rd with the reappearance of the Stukas, and during the next four weeks they made twelve attacks.

By this time the Navy had added a new weapon to the harbour barrage in the form of three 20-barrel rocket-projectors. Each of these barrels fired a rocket, which burst open some distance above the harbour barrage and released two small white parachutes trailing a considerable length of piano wire with a small bomb on the end. The result was a parachute counterpart of a balloon barrage.

When enemy pilots first met these rockets over Tobruk on August 10th they took violent avoiding action, but the leaders had already begun their dives before the rockets burst. Most of the eighteen pilots let their bombs go early in obvious panic. One plane crashed; one made for home with a parachute tangled in its rudder like a dog with a tin on its tail; two others were hit by bombs and the ack-ack damaged two more.

In spite of this, the Stukas continued their attacks throughout August, but their tactics were very different from those of the early days. Then they had dived to 600 feet before releasing their bombs. Now they very seldom came below 3000 and most of them pulled out at 6000. Moreover, instead of diving steeply, the majority made only shallow glides, let their bombs go and then turned for home. Their caution was understandable, for in five out of seven raids in late August the leading plane was shot down.

The final round in the battle between dive-bomber and ack-ack was fought on September 1st—the second anniversary of the Nazi attack on Poland. To mark the occasion Rommel launched against Tobruk more than 140 planes, 45 of them Stukas.

From an escarpment about two miles south-west of the harbour, I watched this raid. It began just before noon on a hot, glaring day. When the ack-ack gave the first warning, the black shell-bursts guided our eyes to a formation of a dozen fighters and twin-engined bombers lazing along so high that we could hardly pick out their silver wings. As the ack-ack got on to them the planes swung away to avoid the barrage. Apparently they had intended to pattern-bomb the harbour, but their bombs thudded into the desert about half-way between the town and where we stood. A yellow dust-cloud went up hundreds of feet, and was soon streaked with black smoke and red flame from a blazing fuel dump.

Before this had cleared away, the guns were going again. Behind the high-level bombers the Stukas were coming in. Two formations, each of about fifteen, were manoeuvring to begin their dives when the harbour barrage began. The air was soon spotted with puffs of smoke from bursting shells and criss-crossed with tracer fire from the Bofors; then above the barrage little white blobs unfolded like flowers in the sun. The rocket guns had hung their deadly parachutes above the bursting shells.

As these unfurled, the Stukas began diving—each formation going for a heavy-gun site. Boldly they roared into their dives, but as they got near barrage and parachutes we could see them falter and their steep dives turned into shallow swoops. But some that pulled out early aimed their bombs accurately nevertheless. As these fell, one gun-position was enveloped in dust and smoke, but even while the last of the bombs were hurtling down we could see through the haze the short vivid flashes that told us that the gunners were still fighting back, although (as we found later) one man had been killed and six wounded.

None of the Stukas tried to dive-bomb the harbour. Apparently the plan was for them to silence the guns, or at least to draw their fire, so that high-level bombers coming in behind them could pattern-bomb undisturbed. This plan miscarried. No more than half the heavy guns were needed to deal with the Stukas; the rest concentrated on breaking up the high-level formations—with such success that only one of these did any damage. It put some sixty bombs in a neat pattern all around one gun-position, but the pits were so well built that not a man was hurt and no equipment was damaged even though some bombs fell within ten yards of the pits.

In the midst of this, to the west fifteen more dive-bombers were attacking the field guns near Pilastrino. From all over the flat behind us came the staccato chatter of captured 20-mm. Bredas. Here the Stukas could afford to dive lower than they dared over the harbour, but the rumble of the last bursting bombs had barely died away before the artillery, determined to show the Germans that dive-bombers could not silence them, had every gun firing.

Meantime about fifty other planes made half-hearted attacks on the forward troops, well clear of the area defended by the ack-ack guns. Maybe these planes had been intended to attack the harbour and had been discouraged by the barrage; or possibly the attack on the perimeter was part of an over-all blitz. Some of the aircraft, however, finished by bombing and machine-gunning their own troops, much to the satisfaction of the Diggers in the forward posts.

This was an appropriate ending to Rommel's last great air assault on Tobruk while the 9th Division was there. He lost very few planes (the A.A. claimed only one shot down and three probables), for most of the pilots made only half-hearted attacks. All Rommel's 140 aircraft did less damage than had been caused in a surprise sortie a few weeks earlier by "Mickey" and "Minnie". The garrison's only casualties were the seven ack-ack gunners already mentioned.

From September 1st onwards day bombing was of small importance. The failure of the mass raid on September 1st closed the third phase of the Battle for the Harbour. Rommel's airmen had been beaten in daylight, and during the next two months 75 per cent of the bombing was carried out at night.

The re-appearance of the dive-bombers in force in the last fortnight in August had coincided with the withdrawal of the first Australians. Warned of this by his spies in Alexandria, Rommel no doubt hoped that intensive dive-bombing of ack-ack guns and harbour just before dark might dislocate embarkation facilities and weaken the defences. But dive-bombing achieved neither, and night bombers in August found the barrage heavier than ever, for there were now ninety-three ack-ack

KEEPING THE HARBOUR OPEN

guns in action. Because of this, night raids were even less successful than daylight attacks. Not once did they stop the destroyers coming in, or disorganize their unloading, or damage them while they were there. Night bombers, however, were the only weapon Rommel had left, and his increasing reliance on them was a tacit tribute to the Tobruk anti-aircraft defences. Over the six months' period the increase was rather remarkable, as this table shows:

	April (*10-30*)	May	June	July	Aug.	Sept.	Oct. (*1-9*)
Number of night bombers engaged by A.A.	32	74	132	126	205	187	152
Percentage of all bombing carried on at night	6	14	39	38	40	76[1]	75

The most serious night attacks were those made by minelaying bombers from late July onwards. In September mines were dropped almost every night during the weeks when the destroyers were running. The planes glided in from the west at about 3000 feet, following the course of the long narrow channel, dropped their mines on parachutes and made off out to sea clear of the ack-ack. High-level bombers usually came in simultaneously to cover their approach and to draw the ack-ack fire. But radio-location sets picked up the low-flying minelayers, and the moment they approached the harbour hell was let loose. One night when we were making recordings from a gun-pit beside the harbour, there were seven minelaying attacks; in five of these the bombers sheered off when they struck the ack-ack and their mines fell some distance inland. The barrage lasted barely a minute; there was a short, sharp burst of fury as though someone had flashed a jet of fire quickly on and as quickly off.

Rommel tried one other means of closing the harbour—shelling. This would have been most serious but for the excellent work of the counter-battery staff and the British and Australian gunners. We have seen already how they dealt with "Bardia Bill" and the other "harbour guns", but these could never be completely silenced and they frequently landed shells in the harbour at night before our gunners could chase the crews into their dug-outs.

Because the ack-ack dealt with "Mickey" and "Minnie" and their fellow bombers, and the artillery kept "Bardia Bill" fairly

---

[1] Excluding the mass daylight raid of September 1st, after which the Axis bombing policy changed.

quiet, the harbour was kept open month after month and the enemy paid heavily for his attempts to close it. Nevertheless, in the last part of October Rommel was to make one more serious bid to stop the destroyer-ferry at a time when the prize at stake was bigger than ever.

Before then, however, Brigadier Slater's H.Q. produced a balance sheet covering the six months from the first German attack on April 10th to October 9th. This showed that during these months more than 3000 aircraft had been engaged by the guns over the harbour area in some 750 raids. Of these aircraft 83 planes were certainly shot down, 77 were probably destroyed and 186 more were damaged. In addition 30 at least were shot down by No. 73 Squadron R.A.F. in the first fortnight of the siege, and another half-dozen at least were brought down by small arms fire outside the main anti-aircraft defence area.

No doubt the figure of eighty-three certainties is a conservative one. The Tobruk A.A. Command never claimed any plane as a certainty unless it was seen to crash either on land or in the water and unless this was confirmed by an independent report. Slater was able to check the results of three typical raids with one captured German airman. This showed:

	Tobruk Claim	German Admission
Raid 1	1 shot down 3 hard hit	1 shot down 5 damaged
Raid 2	2 shot down[2] 2 hard hit	2 shot down "all 21 surviving Stukas hit; several badly damaged"
Raid 3	5 hit	5 shot down

Since absolute accuracy was impossible, however, it was better to err on the side of under-estimation, and to apply the R.A.F.'s strict tests of "certainty" and "confirmation". This was all the more desirable, because troops in Tobruk would have been quick to spot exaggerations. Nothing strikes at the soldier's faith in his cause and his leaders more than exaggerated claims or misrepresentation in communiqués or correspondents' despatches. He wants the truth told about the batlle he is fighting, even though it may not be so good for somebody's reputation (including his own) and will not make such a good story in the home town newspapers.

---

[2] On this occasion the Australian 8th Light Battery claimed hits on more than a dozen planes, including two shot down. The A.A. Command granted it only the two certainties.

KEEPING THE HARBOUR OPEN

Now, however, we are better able to assess the Tobruk ack-ack gunners' real achievement, for we have fresh evidence from prisoners and captured documents. On the basis of this, it is fair to assume that the enemy lost about half the seventy-seven "probables" that Tobruk claimed. If this is so, Rommel's air attacks on the garrison in these six months must have cost him 150 planes shot down by ack-ack fire or the R.A.F., and twice as many damaged.

As suggested earlier, the loss of aircraft was less serious than the loss of personnel, for the pick of Rommel's pilots were killed over Tobruk. Again and again the leading dive-bomber was shot down and it was often one of the yellow-nosed Stukas of Marshal Goering's own squadron. In the end, to make sure that the Italians actually carried out their dive-bombing tasks, sheep-dog Messerschmitts chased them into action. Evidently some Italian pilots resented this so strongly that one day in September fifteen of them force-landed their JU87s in British territory in the Western Desert. They alleged that they had run out of petrol, but they were so close to their own bases that any petrol shortage could hardly have been accidental.

At the end of six months Rommel had little to show for all his expenditure of aircraft, bombs and personnèl. In more than 750 raids enemy bombers sank only seven ships and a few auxiliary lighters in the harbour, and five of these ships were sunk in the first six weeks before the ack-ack defences reached their full strength.

The men who appreciated the gunners' work most were the crews of the little ships that supplemented the destroyer-ferry. Trawlers, schooners, luggers and lighters made the perilous run from Mersa Matruh to Tobruk month after month with scant means of self-protection. These usually took a wide sweep to the north soon after leaving Matruh, so as to avoid enemy air patrols. By doing this and arriving at Tobruk just before dawn, unloading during the day and leaving again at dark, they generally managed to get in and out unscathed.

Their most dangerous time was the daylight unloading. To minimize the risks of this they lay up alongside one or another of the many wrecks in the harbour, shielded by huge camouflage nets, which made it hard for enemy reconnaissance planes to spot them. The most useful wrecks were two bombed ships, *Marco Polo* and *Liguria*, which the Italians had beached on the south shore. Their hulks, towering above the little craft, made them difficult to see and gave some protection from raiders' bombs and "Bardia Bill's" shells, while working parties unloaded the cargoes into small lighters and on to the charred decks of the wrecks themselves.

The most famous of all the small ship commanders was an Australian of the R.N.R., Lieutenant Alfred Palmer, known to everyone as "Pedlar". Before the war he had been a merchant seaman, but had finished up in Shanghai, where he commanded a company of Chinese Lancers in the Shanghai Volunteer Reserve. Soon after the outbreak of the war he joined the Royal Navy and began running small supply ships along the Mediterranean coast. From May till October he skippered a 400-ton schooner—the *Maria Giovanna*, which had been captured from the Italians off the Libyan coast—and ran a "regular weekly service" from Matruh to Tobruk. He was frequently attacked from the air but his strange assortment of scrounged anti-aircraft guns had three enemy planes to its credit.

"Pedlar" used to find his way into Tobruk harbour more by instinct than by instruments. The entrance was not easy to find and most ships at night used the Tobruk anti-aircraft fire to guide them in. One dark night when the ack-ack put up no guiding beacon, "Pedlar" complained, "How do they expect me to get in here, when there's no moon and no bloody air raid?"

Finally the Italians trapped him by a ruse. They found there were two shielded lights marking the entrance to the harbour, and set two similar lights about fifteen miles further east along the coast. One night with no air raid to guide her, *Maria Giovanna* and her gallant skipper were lured on to the rocks. The same night the enemy almost got the destroyers as well, but with better instruments they were warned in time. "Pedlar" Palmer is now a prisoner in Italy and his schooner is a wreck, but the men of Tobruk will never forget him. He brought the little things that made all the difference. For his gallantry he was awarded a Distinguished Service Cross, and no Tobruk decoration was more fully earned.

Of the "little ships", the auxiliary lighters, which ferried tanks and guns, were militarily the most important. Their greatest service was in bringing in more than fifty "I" tanks and many new guns in the two months before the relief. When the garrison eventually broke out these gave it a striking power that the enemy did not expect it would have.

The men who suffered most from the bombing were the gunners, who had to stand-to every time a "Red Warning"

KEEPING THE HARBOUR OPEN

indicated enemy aircraft in the vicinity of the Fortress. As there were more than 1600 warnings in the first 200 days of the siege, they were on the job most of the time. Their only real rest came when a duststorm or the absence of the moon made the visibility too bad for bombing. But some days the gunners stood-to more than twenty-five times and were in action a dozen. And yet they defended themselves so strongly that in the first 750 raids only 40 ack-ack gunners were killed and 129 wounded.

Macfarlane and I spent a fortnight in September living at a Bofors gun-pit beside the harbour, waiting to make recordings of a dive-bomber raid, which never came. But we did learn how one typical gun-crew lived. They were all Scotsmen except their sergeant and a lone fellow from Yorkshire, who had been living with the Scotties so long that his own rich brogue had become polluted. He even said "bonnie" instead of "champion".

They had made themselves quite comfortable. A shanty built of odd scraps of wood, tin and canvas was their mess. They had a cookhouse made with timber from a bombed building, a stove from an Italian house, and tables topped with tiles from the floor of an Italian bathroom. Their gun, bedded in concrete and stone, was protected by a solid wall of 40-gallon oil drums filled with rocks and sand. Gaps between these were packed with sandbags and Italian cement. On top of the drums was a parapet of bags filled with inedible Italian flour. Mixed with sea-water it became almost as hard as cement. This pit was so substantial that it withstood the blast of a 2000-pound bomb that landed less than twenty-five yards away and yet hurt no one. One 1000-pounder actually scored a direct hit on the parapet—but did not explode. Inside it the bomb-disposal squad found this note: "Keep it up, Tommy. This is the best we can do for you now." It bore the trade-mark of a factory in Occupied Europe.

Some of the gunners slept on the wooden floor of the pit but others had old Italian bedsteads set up outside under the camouflage net that was stretched from the top of the parapet to the ground. They had very little uninterrupted rest, however, except on their days off, when they took their bed-rolls into an old tunnel near by and slept soundly.

Like most other Tobruk gunners, they had had no previous action experience, but soon took the Stukas' measure. Their big day was May 7th. Then, according to Bill Reilly, the sergeant in charge of this gun: "The Jerries came over about midday and dive-bombed the harbour. We had our gun down cleaning it and we couldn't engage them. But they came back in the afternoon and we got our revenge. We shot down two and hit two more. The Brigadier sent us a letter of congratulation, the C.O. produced a bottle of whisky and two bottles of beer and the Q.M. gave us a buckshee issue of rum. We weren't in such good form when the Stukas came back next day."

In spite of the bombing and lack of sleep, these gunners lived fairly well. They supplemented their normal rations by "salvage". The crews of the small supply ships knew how much they owed to the ack-ack gunners, and somehow or other accidents happened during the unloading. A case of milk or tinned peaches would fall overboard—and by good luck there would be some gunners near by to rescue it from the water.

One of the most colourful and successful ack-ack gunners was a lone amateur, the Chief Movement Control Officer, red-faced, grey-haired, Irish; C. J. O'Shaughnessy was the name. He entered Tobruk a few days after it was captured, a lieutenant with a Military Medal from the last war. By the end of the siege he was a major and had won the George Medal and the Military Cross.

O'Shaughnessy claimed to be Tobruk's oldest inhabitant. He had certainly identified himself with the port, which he ran with gusto and ability. His office was a little white house on the waterfront in the most-bombed, most-shelled part of the town. In a sand-bagged pit outside it, he had twin Lewis guns with which he engaged every aircraft that came anywhere near. Nothing ever drove him from those guns. He claimed to have brought down half a dozen planes, but few of his fellow gunners gave him credit for them—until the Honours List came out. He had an unenviable job; bombs or no bombs, shells or no shells, he was on the waterfront or harbour day and night organizing and speeding up unloading; getting the ships away; or rescuing cargo from vessels that had been bombed. One day an ammunition ship was hit and set alight; thanks to O'Shaughnessy's courage and quick action the fire was put out and ship and ammunition were saved.

He was good at saving. As one of the first officers to establish himself in Tobruk, O'Shaughnessy acquired a useful stock of that excellent Italian mineral water, Recoaro, and some doubtful Italian brandy. Right until the end he always had "just a little left".

The first time I had a drink with him, he dived into a safe and emerged with a bottle of Recoaro and a bottle of brandy.

KEEPING THE HARBOUR OPEN

"These," he said confidentially, "are the last of their kind in Tobruk. All the Recoaro has gone to the hospital; all the brandy—gallons of it—had to be poured into the sea by the General's own order. Your Australian boys couldn't stand it. I couldn't stand it myself. So I managed to save just a couple of bottles. This is the last of them."

A few months later I had my farewell drink with him. The same ritual—the last bottle of Recoaro—the last bottle of brandy—for a special occasion. Were we not leaving on the destroyer that night?

We raised our glasses and drank to those men who had kept the harbour open—to O'Shaughnessy and his men; to the ack-ack; to "Pedlar" and the little ships; and above all to the Navy. Even O'Shaughnessy's inexhaustible "last" bottle hadn't enough in it to do justice to them all—for without them there could have been no Tobruk.

CHAPTER XX

So Long Tobruk

THREE officers in freshly ironed shirts and shorts and pith helmets got out at the control post and headed up the road towards 9th Div. H.Q. The traffic cop turned to the driver of their car and said:

" 'Struth, who're the blokes with the flash lids on?"

"Dontcha know?" said the driver. "They're Poles. We're all goin' ter be relieved. The boss was talkin' about it yes'dy. Won't be long now."

"Garn," said the M.P., "we ain't never goin' ter be relieved, we're 'ere for the duration. Jest another push more likely."

The traffic cop looked up the road at the receding Poles. "You'll be sorry," he said as he waved the next car through.

The M.P. outside Div. H.Q. was a man who always knew more than most. Did he not usher the General's car in and out, and talk with those who drove the Divisional staff around, and those who brought in visitors from the various units? He knew all the furphies from the H.Q. tunnels and the perimeter posts.

For the rest of this August day he was very busy dispensing the best story for months. The news that the Poles were coming was bush-telegraphed to the farthest outpost not later than that evening's rations. Round the perimeter there ran a buzz of speculation. After months of boredom and disappointment this was something.

Since the failure of the June offensive, the troops had become more or less resigned to waiting and the thought that they might be relieved by any means other than the land route had never entered their heads. Life was tedious and often difficult, but their soldierly pride made them want to see the siege through to the final break-out. They were convinced that Rommel could never take Tobruk from them, but they wanted to show that they could beat the Germans in attack as well as in defence. They also had old scores to settle.

When the Poles arrived in mid-August, the troops swung from

resignation to optimism and back again overnight according to the prevailing rumours. No one was sure whether they had come as reinforcements or relief. Then the 18th Brigade began to move out and hopes ran high. The local bookies laid ten to one against September 30th and five to one against October 31st for the relief of the 9th Division. But when the last of the 18th Brigade had gone and the withdrawal stopped hopes fell again. The 18th had been relieved, the troops thought, merely because they belonged to the 7th Division.

The M.P. outside Div. H.Q. covered his disappointment with a little philosophic pride. "They've pulled the 18th out," he said to me one day, "but us 9th Divvy blokes is goin' ter be left 'ere till the end. They couldn't 'old Tobruk without us. We'll stay till we goes out by road—an' that's dinkum."

He soon forgot this prediction when a group of British staff officers arrived in mid-September—the advance party of the 70th Division, which was to take over from the Australians. There could be no mistake this time. The "books" began to take bets about particular days, and the men added up the balances in their paybooks. There were no thoughts now of waiting to go out by road.

This relief came about only after strong and persistent urging by the G.O.C., A.I.F. (General Sir Thomas Blamey), who supported his plea to Middle East G.H.Q. with two strong arguments.

In the last war the A.I.F. divisions in France had not fought together as an Australian Corps until the end of 1917. When they were then brought together under a single command they gained fresh strength from this unity and were even more successful than before. When the 2nd A.I.F. went to the Middle East the Menzies Government requested that the divisions of the Australian Corps should be kept together.

This request was to have been granted when Blamey took the 1st Australian Corps to Greece in April 1941. The 6th Division and Corps H.Q. went first, the 7th Division was to follow almost immediately, and the 9th was to be sent over as soon as it had completed its training and equipping in Cyrenaica. Operational developments disrupted this plan, and by the time Blamey's forces returned from Greece, nearly all the 9th Division and one brigade of the 7th were shut up in Tobruk.

Keen to have his Corps together as a single fighting force, Blamey—now Deputy C.-in-C., Middle East—at once asked Wavell to relieve the A.I.F. in Tobruk. He reiterated this request with greater force after the failure of the attempt to raise the siege in June. By the end of July the rest of the A.I.F. was concentrated in Syria and Palestine, and the Australian Corps, with Lavarack now administering command, was the main strength of the newly-formed Ninth Army, which was made responsible for holding the northern flank of Suez in case the Germans should attack through Turkey or Cyprus. For this task Lavarack's Corps needed its full strength.

The failure of the June attack in the desert gave Blamey a second argument. There was then little chance of the British forces on the Egyptian frontier gathering sufficient strength to attack again much before December. In June the garrison was to have fought its way out to meet the relieving forces. After that, however, the question arose whether it would be fit to carry out this role in the next offensive if the men were left in Tobruk for another four or five months.

By July the hard conditions were beginning to tell. The infantry and ack-ack gunners were particularly war-weary, and lack of vitamins and of fresh food generally had increased the sickness rate. Australian infantry battalions, which would have to bear the brunt in any break-out, were much below strength and sufficient reinforcements for the A.I.F. were not immediately available, for the 6th Division's severe losses in Greece and Crete had barely been made good. (On May 25th the Australian units in Tobruk were about 30 per cent below strength, for they were 128 officers and 3891 other ranks short—the equivalent of more than a complete infantry brigade. The position improved after this but few infantry battalions ever had 75 per cent of their full numbers, and several of them had to be reinforced with A.S.C. personnel.) The Australian Government supported Blamey's request and made a direct application to the British War Cabinet. In London and Cairo the weight of the two Australian arguments was appreciated, but it was feared, with good reason, that relief on such a scale would be costly and extremely difficult. It involved taking in more than 15,000 British and Polish troops and bringing out as many Australians through a port which had few facilities and was regularly bombed and shelled. But Morshead, who made two special trips to Cairo to see Blamey about this, was convinced that his staff could handle its share of the responsibility.

When the Royal Navy undertook to provide the warships to transport the troops, G.H.Q. finally agreed to withdraw, in August, one Australian Brigade group consisting of the 18th Infantry

Brigade, the 16th Anti-tank Company, 2/4th Field Company, 2/4th Field Ambulance and the 51st British Field Regiment, plus the 18th Indian Cavalry. The 18th Brigade was chosen because it belonged to the 7th Division and *not*—as some of its members later proclaimed—because it had borne the brunt of the fighting at Tobruk. This group was to be replaced by the Polish Carpathian Brigade group, which for over a year had been itching for a chance to fight the Germans. G.H.Q. agreed that, if the move were successful, the remaining Australians would be withdrawn.

Few people in Cairo, however, thought that the dangers and difficulties could be overcome. So large a move could hardly be hidden from Axis spies in Alexandria. The ships could not afford to stay in the harbour much more than half an hour. In that time they would be fine targets for enemy bombs and shells. Even if no ships or troops were hit, enemy interference might delay the unloading and loading so long that the warships would not be clear of Bomb Alley off Sollum before dawn.

During the change-overs in August and September, however, Axis bombers were not very troublesome and, by bringing in eight mobile 3.7s from the outer areas each evening, the harbour barrage was made strong enough to divert most of the Axis pilots from the danger zone. In August, as we have seen, the enemy tried to clear the way for his night raiders by severe dive-bombing of the ack-ack gun-positions shortly before dark. These attacks failed and the protective barrage over the harbour was even heavier than before. "Bardia Bill" was kept quiet by counter-battery fire.

The arrival of the Poles in the third week of August caused a stir among the rather bored troops. The Poles were marked out at once by their pith helmets; their dull grey shorts and shirts; their silver insignia of rank and their very formal behaviour. They are invariably sticklers for courtesy. Privates salute corporals; lieutenants salute lieutenants. And their saluting is quite a performance—even in the field. Two officers meet—salute, shake hands, salute again. They carried this politeness into the front line. A British artillery officer told me that one day he and a Polish officer were manning an O.P. in the Salient only a few hundred yards from the enemy. The Pole put his guns right on to a target; the Englishman congratulated him. The Pole stood up, saluted and sat down only just in time to escape a sniper's bullet. After that he was less demonstrative.

They had no politeness where Germans were concerned, but they were not at all interested in the Italians. This same British officer summed up the Poles' attitude by saying: "If they see an Italian working party of fifty, they ignore it; but one German shaking out his blanket brings 'three rounds gun-fire'."

More than half the men in the Carpathian Brigade had fought against the Germans in 1939. The rest were civilians, who had left their homes and families so that they could take up the fight in the Middle East. But they reached there only after considerable dangers and hardships. Those who had been soldiers had to escape from internment camps in Hungary and Rumania or from German prisons. Some even fought their way out of Poland. Many had walked or hitch-hiked half-way across Europe in escaping.

They had originally been organized into a fighting force in Syria, but when France collapsed the Poles, defying Vichy's orders, marched into Palestine taking all their French weapons, equipment and transport with them. Then for more than a year they trained, and prepared defences, in Palestine and Egypt, but it was not till August 1941 that they got their chance at Tobruk. They made the most of it.

The Poles relieved the 18th Brigade group in August and the 24th Brigade group[1] was replaced in September by the 16th British Brigade group. Both moves went so smoothly that G.H.Q. decided to withdraw the two remaining Australian brigades on nine nights in the last half of October when the moon was changing. It was expected that Rommel would do his best to interfere; for the sake of prestige, if for no other reason, he could not allow them all to "escape".

He was baffled only by good timing and co-operation between Navy, R.A.F. and Tobruk garrison. In the late afternoon as the warships came within the range of the dive-bombers, a swarm of R.A.F. fighters gave them cover until it was nearly dark. When the warships were an hour or so out from Tobruk, British bombers and long-range fighters took off from airfields in Egypt and headed westward for enemy bases. The R.A.F. knew that Axis airmen did not operate when there was no moon, unless they used flare-lit runways. During the critical hours when the

---

[1] The 2/43rd Battalion remained, but the 2/1st Pioneers, the 2/12th Field Regiment, the 3rd Anti-tank Regiment, the 24th Anti-tank Company, the 2/7th and 2/13th Field Companies, the 2/3rd Field Ambulance and the 8th Light A.A. Battery were withdrawn at the same time. Some British units were also relieved. The 16th Brigade was part of the 70th British Division, commanded by Major-General R. M. Scobie.

enemy's bombers might have been taking off for Tobruk, the R.A.F. dropped a few bombs over his airfields and then cruised around above them, confident that he would not dare to light his flares so long as he could hear the drone of the British aircraft overhead.

As the warships approached Tobruk the 60-pounders and 25-pounders opened fire on "Bardia Bill" and the other "harbour guns". With smoke and star-shells they provided a beacon that guided warships and bombers to the enemy gun-positions. An escorting destroyer broke away from the convoy and standing off-shore shelled the big guns while British bombers dropped parachute flares above the positions and added their bombs to the Navy's shells. These three-way attacks were not made every night. Sometimes only bombers were used with the 60-pounders; sometimes only warships; sometimes both. But the result was always the same.

When the ships slipped into harbour, "Bardia Bill" was silent and the enemy bombers absent. There was only one jetty for the three destroyers and the mine-laying cruiser, which came in each night, but that did not worry the Navy. Two destroyers slid alongside half-sunken hulks that had been turned into "wharves". The cruiser was unloaded and loaded in mid-harbour from barges. After half an hour, having disembarked a thousand men, dumped anything from 100 to 200 tons of stores, and taken a thousand men aboard, the warships steamed out again into the night.

These combined attacks kept the enemy quiet while the ships were in the harbour; but on the last nights of the move, when the moon did not set for several hours after dark, "Bardia Bill" and enemy bombers attacked the waterfront in the early evening, evidently hoping to catch the waiting troops in the open. Stukas even dive-bombed by moonlight and by the light of parachute flares, but they were no more effective than the high-level bombers. This reappearance of the Stukas under cover of darkness was the final confession of their own defeat.

On the third last night of the relief, there was some excitement before the destroyers arrived. In the afternoon the departing troops, who had been in the front line until the night before, packed their kitbags, haversacks and packs till they bulged, leaving out clothes to make room for precious souvenirs fashioned out of shell-cases, grenades and fragments of wrecked planes.

About five o'clock they had their last dust-laden meal of

Tobruk stew, irrigated with chlorine-tainted tea. At dark they piled into trucks and made their final journey to the harbour. On their way they passed several heavy ack-ack guns going in to strengthen the night's barrage. As the Australian trucks crawled by, a Digger called to the gun-crews, "Good on yer Tommy; give it to 'em to-night!" The Tommies waved an envious farewell.

The guns were certainly needed. As we followed one party down to the harbour after dark, bombers were coming over, as they had been every ten minutes or so for the past hour. At the roadside on the outskirts of the town the large red air-raid flag was hanging limp, as if tired out from flying for more than 1600 "red warnings". (Tobruk's only other air-raid warning devices were the blowing of a muffled siren with a note like a bugle at Admiralty House, the Naval H.Q., and the showing of a red flag by day and of a shielded red light by night from the top of that building. Early in the siege, the Italian siren in the town had been used, but its blood-curdling note, wailing almost continuously in those days, was more nerve-racking than the bombing itself.)

The guns were going now, but the trucks, laden with silent Diggers, kept on; there was to be no stopping for anything to-night. We lumbered on slowly in the moonlight. At a bend in the road a shadowy figure waved us round a fresh bomb-crater which engineers were already repairing. We crept along to the waterfront, where another gesticulating figure stopped us. It was one of the "bomb disposal boys" with a warning: "There's a dud 500-pounder right in the middle of the road here—a Stuka dropped it half an hour ago—keep well over and for Gawd's sake keep moving. The last lot of trucks was banked up here for ten minutes and I was sure they'd cop another."

We edged past the small round grave the bomb had dug for itself, and parked the truck at the end of the jetty where there was a broad shelf between the sea and the cliff. Here guides and M.Ps were busy hustling the troops out of trucks and back to shelter either against the cliff or in one of the deep tunnels the Italians had burrowed in its face. Inside these there was a heavy fug but they were bomb-proof and provided the troops with a chance to smoke and sing as they waited impatiently for the ships to arrive.

We walked along the waterfront; it was quiet now as the drone of the trucks going back for the next load died away.

Then suddenly to the east we saw two bright flashes a short distance inland. Almost at the same moment a voice from a lookout post called—"Two from 'Bardia Bill'." There was a scurry as everybody dived for cover. We seemed to wait twenty minutes, not twenty seconds, before we heard the high-pitched whine of the oncoming shells. With a final screaming swish they plunged into the water, fortunately clear of two lighters packed with troops about to be ferried out to the wrecks that were used as landing-stages.

Quiet again—and we walked along to the Movement Control Office where clerks were busy checking the final arrangements. In the house behind the office we found a ghostly O'Shaughnessy, powdered a dirty white from head to foot with dust and plaster. A bomb had shattered an empty building across the street, but had done no other damage beyond shaking a couple of square yards of plaster off O'Shaughnessy's roof and on to Tobruk's Movement Control Chief himself. He was now sweeping out his bedroom.

"Good evenin' boys," he said. "You're just in time to help me wash the dust out of me throat." He produced the inevitable brandy and Recoaro. We were just drinking to his good fortune when the ack-ack started again. O'Shaughnessy drained his glass, dashed out the door and down the steps to his precious Lewis guns. The planes were so high that the Bofors were not bothering about them. O'Shaughnessy, ever optimistic, loosed a couple of bursts from his machine-guns, but it was the heavies that turned the raiders away. We did not even hear their bombs crash. O'Shaughnessy left his post in disgust. "They stay so high," he said, "they don't a give a fellow a chance"—and back he went to his sweeping.

We were in the middle of the town when the last raiders came over just before the moon went down. The battered buildings loomed grotesquely in the half-light. We might have been in the heart of a ghost town until two bombers drew near again. In an instant Tobruk was alive and fighting. From the ruins came the harsh crack of several machine-guns and, with the full barrage going, the sound of the guns seemed to be amplified many times in the town's empty shell. Then above the noise of ack-ack, the steady drone of engines suddenly rose to a roar as two planes dived towards the harbour. They pulled out and the roar died away, but the whine of on-coming bombs increased as the roar faded.

The bombs fell so wide that we could not tell where they had hit, but the walls of the nearest buildings shuddered. The fury of the ack-ack was soon spent and two columns of smoke and dust spiralling up from the bare hill behind the town were the only evidence that the Stukas had been over again. On top of Admiralty House the red warning light went out and across the harbour the long steady note of the "all clear" bugle sounded like a distant foghorn. The moon set and that was the last of the bombers, but the next two hours of waiting dragged by like a wet week-end.

At last the destroyers slid out of the darkness, their guns pointing skyward, their gun-crews alert beside them—in case. At fifty gun-pits round the harbour guns and gunners were equally ready. As one destroyer tied up alongside the wreck at the end of Tobruk's main wharf, British Tommies began streaming down the narrow gangway, across the wreck and on to the jetty. There was no clank of iron heels on the steel plates because they all wore rubber-soled desert boots. They needed them. The gangway was narrow and they were more heavily laden than an Arab mule. Nevertheless 300 padded off in ten minutes.

At the same time, on the destroyer and the wreck men of an Indian Labour Company were lumping huge boxes of ammunition from one ship to the other. Although the orders to the Diggers read "no noise", the Indians made a great clatter, shouting all the time and crashing the metal ammunition cases down on the steel deck. At last everything was clear and 300 Diggers had ten minutes in which to scramble aboard. They were on in five.

The destroyer began to throb. Slowly she slid out into the stream. Until this moment the Diggers had been quiet, but as they broke contact with Tobruk first one whistle then another and another shrilled out from the destroyer and from the shore came others in reply. Then a hush, until across the water echoed their own farewell—a long coo-ee.

Night after night the moves went smoothly through. It was excellent staff work and clearly showed the efficiency of Morshead's H.Q., and particularly of the officer most responsible, Major N. G. Dodds. There was no hitch until the very last night —October 25th-26th. Before then there had been no serious attacks on the harbour or the warships en route to Tobruk during the October moves. But on the evening of the 25th the enemy attacked the waterfront strongly and bombs fell perilously close to the waiting troops.[2] Finally the bombers went but the ships did not come in.

Late that afternoon they had been spotted by a reconnaissance plane. Shortly after dark enemy bombers began coming over in the moonlight. The ships successfully fought off and evaded the early attacks, but at last a direct hit sent the minelaying cruiser H.M.S. *Latona* to the bottom. One of the destroyers was damaged by a near-miss, and by the time the others had picked up *Latona's* survivors it was too late for them to go on to Tobruk.

It was almost dawn before the news reached the Diggers waiting on the Tobruk waterfront. Their disappointment deepened when they found that they could not leave before the second week in November, when the waning moon would allow the destroyers to come in again. Then, with the Eighth Army's offensive about to begin, G.H.Q. asked the A.I.F. to leave the 2/13th in Tobruk so as to give General Scobie another battalion. The 2/13th blamed their unlucky number, little realizing then that they would soon be proud to have been left behind.

In spite of the disaster on the last night the relief of the Australians was a final insult to Rommel. For six months the German Radio had been boasting that the Australians in Tobruk were caught like rats in a trap with no hope of escape; it had sneered at them as "self-supporting prisoners". It had boasted that the Stukas had made the British Navy powerless to come to their aid.

Now the same powerless Navy, which had kept the garrison supplied throughout the siege, had carried more than 15,000 men in and as many out again. The Australians whom Rommel had threatened to drive into the sea in April had thrown back all his attacks, defied and harried his forces for over six months and finally had been withdrawn to rest, refit and come back for their revenge at El Alamein in 1942.

---

[2] This contingent comprised part of 20th Brigade H.Q., the 2/13th Battalion, two companies of the 2/15th Battalion, and a few of the Divisional Staff.

CHAPTER XXI

What a Relief

BY the beginning of November 1941 Rommel was nearly ready to attack Tobruk again. For the previous six months he had concentrated on amassing strength to overwhelm the Fortress once and for all, so that he could be free to drive on towards Suez. His failures in April and May had shown that for any future assault on Tobruk he would need far more German infantry and artillery than had then been available. Now, in addition to the infantry in his two German armoured divisions, Rommel had at least three battalions of the 90th Light Division, and four other German battalions plus a regiment of special assault troops known as the "ZBV Group". To support these he had more than 200 pieces of field and medium artillery outside Tobruk and his tank strength was greater than ever.

Each German Panzer Division had at least 130 tanks and 75 per cent of these were Mark IIIs with 50-mm. guns or Mark IVs with 75-mms. When he brought the Afrika Korps to Cyrenaica, Rommel had roughly 145 tanks in each of his two divisions, but nearly half of these were light tanks. Since then the number of mediums and heavies had been increased by 20 per cent and the tanks themselves greatly improved. The Mark III now mounted a 50-mm. not a 37-mm. gun, and the new Mark IV was more heavily armour-plated. The Ariete Division, now using M13 Mediums throughout, had been well-trained and partly officered by Germans. It could no longer be taken lightly.

Rommel had paid a heavy price for these reinforcements. During the three months ending October 31st 86 Axis vessels were sunk and 61 damaged between Southern Europe and Libya by naval or air attack. In the first week of November British warships and submarines had their greatest success—sinking 19 Italian ships. By increasing use of the Crete-Derna air ferry, Rommel had partly made up for these losses, and the R.A.F. estimated that in October transport planes towing gliders were lifting from Crete as much as 400 tons a day. This was about 20 per cent of the daily needs of the Axis forces in Eastern

Cyrenaica, but interception by Beaufighters and bombing of airfields around Derna destroyed much of this freight. Rommel's main problem was that since July the R.A.F. had definitely had the best of the air battles over the frontier. For an attack on Tobruk, however, this was not so vital a matter, for the R.A.F. could not operate from the Fortress nor could it effectively intervene over Tobruk with fighters based in Egypt.

With the Afrika Korps strengthened Rommel was confident that he could take Tobruk and the Axis Mediterranean Command had evidently withdrawn its earlier objection to offensive action in Libya now that the Russian campaign was going so much in Germany's favour. Rommel needed to capture Tobruk before the Eighth Army was ready to attack. Held by the British, it weakened his defensive position because his forces could be caught between two jaws. It also debarred him from attacking elsewhere.

By early November the bulk of his forces were concentrated around Tobruk preparing to storm it before the end of the month. He had an Italian infantry division astride each of the three main roads that lead to Bardia, El Adem, and Derna, and had another in reserve at Gazala. He had a German infantry regiment and some Italians in the Salient; but he was planning his main thrust from the south-east, where he had assembled the ZBV Group and part of the 21st Armoured Division to the north of Ed Duda, a low knoll eight miles from the perimeter. In October, as we have seen, the enemy had driven back the garrison's outposts in the south-eastern sector, had closed the gap between the Italian positions astride the Bardia and the El Adem roads, and had brought all the perimeter posts under direct machine-gun and mortar fire. To cover his preparations and to guard against any attempt by the garrison to break out towards Ed Duda, the enemy had prepared between the perimeter and that knoll a series of strongposts which the garrison had named "Tiger", "Butch", "Lion" and "Wolf".

The rest of Rommel's forces were disposed so as to frustrate any British attempt to come to Tobruk's rescue. On the frontier strong defences ran from Halfaya to Sidi Omar—twenty miles inland. They were manned by the Savona Division, some German gunners and three battalions of German infantry. It was unlikely that the British would try to fight their way through this line with all its minefields and anti-tank guns.

South of Sidi Omar the open desert flank was unprotected, but Rommel had his 15th Armoured Division in the Bardia-

Gambut area, and the Ariete Armoured Division at El Gobi, fifty miles west of Sidi Omar and forty south of Tobruk. Both were strategically placed to attack the flanks of any British force that swept around the end of the frontier line and made for Tobruk. The Ariete Division was also protecting the Axis forces at Tobruk in case of attack from the Giarabub Oasis, 160 miles to the south. There, with considerable fuss, the British had been preparing what they wanted Rommel to believe was their major offensive base. Reuter's correspondent late in October was "permitted" to write a full description of the extensive preparations at Giarabub and to speculate on the possibilities of attack from there. Actually, the Giarabub force consisted of only 5000 British and Indian troops and fifty dummy tanks made of wood.

Rommel was so obsessed with the idea of taking Tobruk, of justifying himself with his own Supreme Command, and of getting his revenge on the garrison, that he had evidently lost sight of the threat from the frontier. His success in June had made him scornful of British tank commanders; he knew that their tanks and guns were inferior to those of the Germans and he evidently believed that the British could be smashed as certainly as before.

He did not appreciate what extensive preparations they had been making since June. The new C.-in-C., Middle East, General Sir Claude Auchinleck, had converted the Western Desert Force into the Eighth Army and appointed as its commander Lieutenant-General Sir Alan Cunningham, brother of the C.-in-C., Mediterranean Fleet. Sir Alan had led the British and South Africans in Abyssinia with great distinction, but he was an infantry commander with little experience of armoured warfare and none of the Western Desert.

He vigorously tackled his first major problem—that of organizing supply services for a force large enough to attack with reasonable hope of success. This was not easy, for he eventually gathered 115,000 British, Dominion, and Indian troops in the Western Desert and it was estimated that they would require 2500 tons of ammunition, food, water and petrol per day during an offensive. To provide for this, the coast railway was extended eighty-five miles west of Matruh, and the pipeline that brought water from Alexandria was laid a further twelve miles beyond the railhead. Huge supply depots were established near the frontier and as much as thirty-five miles inside Cyrenaica well south of Sidi Omar.

WHAT A RELIEF

Having overcome these supply difficulties, Cunningham mustered 700 tanks in the Western Desert and Tobruk compared with Rommel's 415. To support an attack his colleague, Air Vice-Marshal Arthur Coningham, the R.A.F.'s desert commander, had thirty-six squadrons with more than 600 front-line fighters, fighter-bombers, and bombers. In Libya Rommel had slightly more aircraft than this, but only one-third of them were flown by Germans, though reinforcements could rapidly be brought from Europe.

The primary object of all these preparations was "the destruction of the enemy armour"—to quote the Cairo Military Spokesman. The relief of Tobruk would natually follow and, using it as a base, the Eighth Army was then to drive westward through Cyrenaica and on to Tripoli. The Axis was to be cleaned out of North Africa. (This intention was, of course, never declared publicly, but Air Vice-Marshal Coningham told correspondents on November 23rd that he had bet a "fiver" that we would be in Tripoli by January 15th.) This was by no means an impossible task, provided the enemy tanks could be destroyed quickly and comparatively cheaply. The Eighth Army, however, had not intended to attack before the end of November, for the railway would not be completed until the 14th, and the necessary supplies could not be accumulated in less than a fortnight after that. But when Cunningham's Intelligence sources warned him early in November that Rommel intended to attack Tobruk about the 22nd these plans were changed. He decided the Eighth Army must strike first.

The force at his disposal then comprised:

13th Corps: 4th Indian Division; 2nd New Zealand Division; 1st Army Tank Brigade (with 153 "I" tanks and Valentines).
30th Corps: 7th Armoured Division (455 cruiser and light tanks); 1st South African Division; 22nd Guards Brigade.
Tobruk Garrison: 70th British Division; Polish Carpathian Brigade; 32nd Army Tank Brigade (93 "I" Tanks and Cruisers).
Army Troops: 2nd South African Division; 29th Indian Brigade Group (at Giarabub).

Cunningham's plan was this:[1] the 30th Corps with the 7th

---
[1] The story of this battle is not told in the same detail as other operations described in this book. The relief of Tobruk followed nineteen days of confused and hard fighting over a broad battlefield. Consequently I have dealt only with such events as directly affected Tobruk and its relief, and even these are sketched only in broad outline. Because of this, little has been said, for instance, of the splendid work of the R.A.F.

Armoured Division as its spearhead was to outflank the frontier defences and strike north towards Gambut, deal with the German armour and then move west to relieve Tobruk. On the third morning its garrison was to start fighting out to Ed Duda, and Eighth Army H.Q. was confident that by the fifth day Tobruk would be open to landward supply columns.

To protect the flanks of the armoured division during its deep thrust, the 1st South African Division was to watch the Italians at El Gobi; the 4th Indian Division was to make a demonstration against the frontier line; while the 2nd New Zealand Division skirted Sidi Omar and advanced north to Capuzzo and Bardia, thus isolating the frontier sector. To provide a further diversion, the Indians at Giarabub were to advance westward across the waist of Cyrenaica, towards Agedabia on the main Tripoli-Bengazi road, and strafe Axis supply columns moving along it.

The R.A.F. planned to subject enemy airfields as far back as Tripoli to an all-out blitz with the object of grounding the Axis air forces and gaining such superiority that Coningham's squadrons would be free to concentrate on direct support for the ground troops. By the evening of November 17th the attacking divisions were at their battle stations ready to move at dawn, after intensive bombing of Axis dromes. But that night thunder and lightning split the Libyan skies and the heaviest downpour in memory flooded the desert. Not one British aircraft left the ground and next morning the R.A.F. could not immediately swing its full strength into action. But the enemy suffered far more seriously. His airfields were in the coastal belt, where the rain was heaviest and the soil like glue; for two days almost every Axis aircraft was grounded.

Because of this and the failure of German airmen to detect the Eighth Army's approach march the day before, Rommel was taken completely by surprise. It was late in the afternoon of the 18th before his H.Q. knew that the British had attacked. "It has come in a way we did not expect," wrote a German officer on Afrika Korps H.Q., "and there's hell let loose. On the evening of the 18th while I was still continuing my afternoon sleep, there came a telephone call summoning me to pack my kit immediately. Position: the enemy is attacking with very strong forces in the southern sector." Actually, by this time the leading column was near El Gobi—fifty miles west of the frontier.

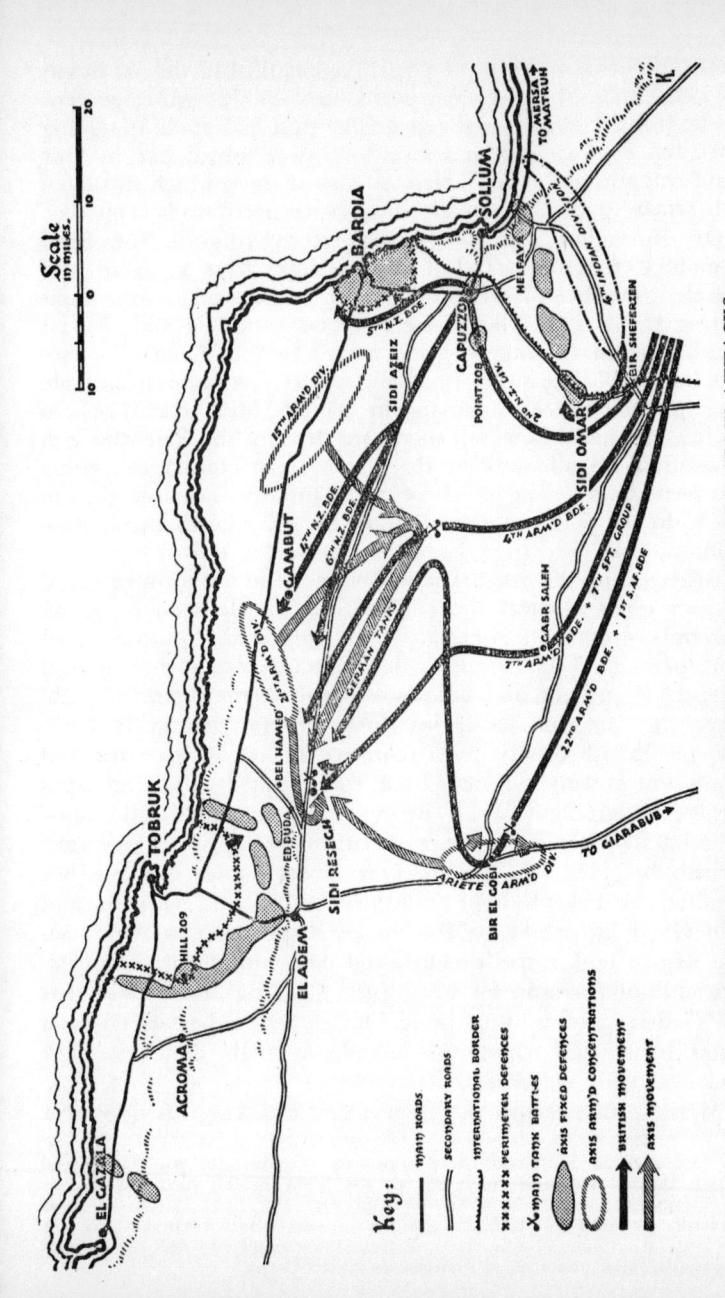

THE RELIEF OF TOBRUK—PHASE I. THE EIGHTH ARMY ATTACKS, NOVEMBER 18TH-22ND, 1941

At dawn that morning the 7th Armoured[2] and the 1st South African Divisions had sallied into Cyrenaica through huge gaps in the frontier barbed-wire fence. The rain had made the going slow, but by dark the attacking force was spread out in four main columns along the Trigh El Abd—a track which ran from Sidi Omar to El Gobi—ready to advance northwards next day.

On November 19th the most westerly column (the 22nd Armoured Brigade) attacked Italian tanks near El Gobi and disabled forty-five of them, but lost twenty-five of its own tanks during the action. The Ariete Division withdrew and the 1st South African Infantry Brigade moved into El Gobi to secure the left flank. Meantime the most easterly column had made the right flank safe by moving in behind Sidi Omar. The two middle columns now advanced north. On the left the 7th Armoured Brigade headed for Gambut, but found the going too heavy and swung north-westward towards Sidi Rezegh. On the right the 4th Armoured Brigade moved towards the Bardia-Gambut road.

Disregarding the 7th Brigade, Rommel sent an advance guard of sixty tanks to check the 4th and the first clash came late on November 19th. The Germans were considerably outnumbered but their tanks had a marked advantage over the American "lights" in armour and fire-power. At dusk the Germans withdrew after an even battle in which they lost twenty-six tanks and the British twenty. Next morning the 4th Brigade attacked again, but overnight Rommel had concentrated about 180 tanks —the main strength of his two German Armoured Divisions— to meet it. He saw a chance of cutting off the two westward British brigades, which were now seventy miles inside Libya heading for Tobruk. If he could drive south between them and Sidi Omar, he might be able to sever their supply line, keep the British tank forces divided, and deal with them piecemeal. An additional reason for hitting the 4th Brigade first was that its "General Stuarts" were no real match for the heavier German tanks. If he could cripple this brigade, he might then turn back and deal with the others.

Massing his strength in this way and attacking his opponent

---

[2] This division contained three armoured brigades—the 7th (129 mixed cruiser tanks); the 22nd (with 160 of the latest British mediums—known as "Crusaders"); the 4th (with 166 American M.3 light tanks, "General Stuarts"). In addition there was the 7th Support Group. Actually this was too large an armoured force for a divisional command and the 4th Brigade was mostly used under direct command of 30th Corps.

WHAT A RELIEF

in detail was typical of Rommel's technique. Throughout November 20th the tank battle raged thirty miles west of Capuzzo. This time the 4th Brigade was not only out-gunned, it was also out-numbered; but it fought so strongly that, although driven back, it put thirty-six German tanks out of action and lost only forty. Battered, but by no means disgraced, the British withdrew at dusk, leaving the enemy in possession of the battle-field and able to salvage many of his tanks.

While this battle was in progress, the 7th Armoured Brigade had captured Sidi Rezegh aerodrome and the 7th Support Group had established itself on the escarpment north of it and only ten miles south-east of the Tobruk perimeter. All day on the 20th the garrison had waited anxiously for the order from 30th Corps to begin its drive on Ed Duda. According to the original plan, it was to have broken out on the morning of the 20th. When no warning arrived on the 19th, hopes fell, but now the code-word came and all through the night the men in Tobruk were busily preparing to attack at dawn on November 21st.

If they could reach Ed Duda while the Eighth Army held Sidi Rezegh it would be an easy matter to join forces across the 2-mile gap between the ridges. But at dawn on the 21st, as the garrison began its attack, the 7th Armoured Brigade found the full force of Rommel's armour bearing down upon Sidi Rezegh. The British tank brigades were still split. The day before, when Rommel had struck at the 4th, the 22nd had rushed across from El Gobi to help it, but had arrived too late. Now that these two brigades had linked up, Rommel stole off in the night to tackle the 7th on its own. When they discovered the Germans had gone, the 4th and 22nd set out in pursuit, but battle had been joined around the Sidi Rezegh drome long before they reached it.

The 7th Brigade and the Support Group stopped the two German divisions at first but suffered heavy casualties. The Germans had more and better tanks and guns and it would have been wiser for the British to have yielded ground and kept their armour intact until the other brigades joined them. In the circumstances their attempt to hold ground was suicidal. Most of that day the 7th Brigade clung to Sidi Rezegh, hoping the others would arrive. But the 4th had been checked by an enemy column and the 22nd did not get there until late in the afternoon. By then the 7th had lost three-quarters of its tanks but was still in possession of the drome and escarpment. It was reinforced by the 5th South African Infantry Brigade, but its hold was still precarious. The Germans had gained armoured superiority and were clearly preparing for another big assault next morning. The 4th Brigade had not yet appeared.

The crucial question was this—could the British hold Sidi Rezegh until the Tobruk garrison reached Ed Duda? Its attack that morning had been led by the 2nd Battalion of the Black Watch and "I" tanks of the 4th R.T.R. Piped into battle, the Highlanders had taken one enemy strongpoint—"Tiger"—in a brilliant bayonet charge, in which nearly half their men became casualties. The tanks had also suffered heavily from minefields and anti-tank guns. Another strongpoint, "Butch", was taken that afternoon and the toll of prisoners reached 1100—half of them German. At the end of the day, however, the leading Tobruk troops were barely a third of the way to Ed Duda and there was still much hard fighting ahead of them. The German defences were stronger and deeper than had been expected, and they were manned by the crack troops whom Rommel had assembled for the assault on Tobruk. The gap between the garrison and the relieving forces was only seven miles, but it was clear that Ed Duda could not be reached the following day as had been planned.

Meantime the concentration of German armour around Sidi Rezegh had left the area immediately behind the Halfaya-Sidi Omar line clear of German tanks, and the Eighth Army could now complete the envelopment of the frontier defences. The 2nd New Zealand Division, supported by "I" tanks, did this by thrusting northwards behind the line on November 21st. By next morning it had captured Capuzzo, cut the water pipeline, which supplied Halfaya, and placed a brigade to picket Bardia. There was now little chance of the Axis forces on the frontier joining in the main battle around Sidi Rezegh.

This was renewed with increasing vigour on the morning of November 22nd. The Germans made a feint from the east at dawn and then slammed in their main assault with a hundred tanks from the west. For a while the 7th and 22nd Brigades held them off, but their losses were so heavy that, even with the arrival of the 4th Brigade, the British were still outnumbered. In the afternoon the Germans attacked with tanks and lorried infantry, supported by an intense artillery barrage. The 7th Support Group was driven from the Sidi Rezegh escarpment and the British tanks had to withdraw from the airfield. By nightfall the Germans were in full possession of the area. More

WHAT A RELIEF

important, in three days they had wiped out the numerical advantage with which the 7th Armoured Division had started.

In a determined effort to restore the situation, Cunningham ordered the New Zealand commander (Major-General B. C. Freyberg) to leave one brigade masking Bardia and Capuzzo, and to move westward with the bulk of his division and strike at the rear of the German armour between Gambut and Sidi Rezegh. If it could attack west, while the Tobruk garrison moved south and the 7th Armoured Division and the South Africans drove north, the Germans might yet be forced from Sidi Rezegh. That was the plan on November 23rd. The southward thrust from Tobruk was slow, but the New Zealanders came up from the east like a storm. By midday their 4th Infantry Brigade had taken Gambut and their 6th had linked up with the 5th South African Brigade, which was holding a position south-east of Sidi Rezegh, covering the 7th Armoured Division while it reorganized.

Early that afternoon, however, before the Eighth Army could consolidate along this line, German tanks and infantry attacked from the north. While the South Africans were fully occupied in holding off these, another seventy German tanks swept in from the south-west, scattering the Brigade's supply vehicles and capturing its H.Q. The tanks drove on with guns blazing, right through the exposed infantry positions and back again. So long as ammunition lasted the South Africans kept up the fight, but before dark the survivors of this gallant brigade had become a column of prisoners. Its total casualties including captured and missing were nearly 4000.

The 22nd Armoured Brigade had done its best to save them, but had been distracted by a well-timed Italian tank attack from the west. By nightfall the men of the Tobruk garrison must have regarded the campaign as already lost. They were still only half way out to Ed Duda and the armoured hand that had been stretched out to meet them had now been forced back. The gap between the 7th Armoured Division and Tobruk had widened in twenty-four hours from seven miles to about thirty-five. The nearest New Zealanders were still astride the Trigh Capuzzo, twenty miles from the Tobruk perimeter, but the balance of armoured strength, on which the garrison pinned its hopes, had now passed to the Germans.

Rommel had succeeded thus far by remarkably bold and able handling of his tanks. He summed up the secret of his own success when he said to a captured British tank brigadier after the battle: "What difference does it make if you have two tanks to my one, when you spread them out and let me smash them in detail? You presented me with three brigades in succession." He had kept all his tanks together. Cunningham had deliberately divided his, and even when he knew that Rommel was attacking the 4th Brigade alone, he still did not send the others to its aid. Until more than a third of the 7th Armoured Division's tanks had been destroyed, Rommel never had to engage its three brigades together.

Added to the advantage Cunningham gave him, Rommel's use of field and anti-tank guns in close support of his tanks made them more formidable. He repeated the trick, which he had used so well in the June battle, of withdrawing his tanks through a screen of 88-mm. and 50-mm. guns and luring British armour into their deadly fire. Greatest advantage of all was the superior quality of his tanks and guns. The 50-mm. on the Mark IIIs fired a $4\frac{1}{2}$-pound shell and was effective at 1400 yards; the 2-pounder on the British tanks was of little use beyond 800. Thus, while the British were too far away to open fire, the Germans could engage them from the steady platform of a stationary tank. If the Germans were forced to withdraw, they could get away comfortably under cover of their 88-mm. guns, which were effective at 2000 yards and more. The British tried to use the 25-pounder in the same role. It was excellent in defence, but was of less value in attack because it had not the mobility or range of the 88-mm. The result was that after five days the German armour had gone very near to destroying the force that had set out to destroy it.

This was a heavy set-back to the Army that had gone into battle with such high hopes and with these words of Mr Churchill ringing in their ears: "For the first time British and Empire troops will meet the Germans with ample equipment in modern weapons of all kinds." Many correspondents in the desert felt at the time that this had yet to be proved, but Eighth Army H.Q. and G.H.Q. Cairo, had been confident of complete victory. Their optimism persisted even after the experience of the first five days.

The basic reason for this was that no accurate system of checking enemy tank losses had been worked out. In the confusion of battles fought amid clouds of dust, tank crews could not easily tell how many tanks they had hit, and often the same victim must have been claimed by several crews. Further, there was a tendency to count disabled tanks as destroyed, even though the Germans were left in possession of the battlefield after most encounters and had an excellent recovery system—something the Eighth Army lacked.

When the campaign began to go badly and it was clear that the early claims of German losses had been exaggerated, the Army tried to blame the optimistic over-statements on to war correspondents and the Prime Minister's son, Major Randolph Churchill, who was then head of the Information and Propaganda section at G.H.Q. Acting as liaison between Eighth Army H.Q. and correspondents in the desert, however, he did little more than pass on what that H.Q. told him. Admittedly his enthusiasm modified the natural scepticism of the correspondents, but faulty information was still the main reason for the over-optimism, and when correspondents tried to warn the British people of the real position they were stopped by G.H.Q.

In many cases the exaggerated dispatches of the first week came not so much from the desert as from Cairo, where the newspaper "string-men"—known as the "2nd Eleven"—had to rely on the communiqués and the embellishments of the "Military Spokesman". He was probably the greatest optimist of all, and he was not Randolph Churchill, as was suggested in the House of Commons. Following this Cairo lead, London editors, bent on feeding victory-hungry readers, added another layer of optimism and after the first few days their headlines shouted complete victory. When the truth seeped through and searching questions were asked in the House about the Cairo Military Spokesman, the officer in question left his deputy to carry on. The deputy immediately warned correspondents that what he said might be used but not quoted as coming from any Military Spokesman.

This drew from an American correspondent, Sam Brewer, the drawled inquiry: "Well, colonel, that maybe O.K. for you, but our papers won't take it on our say-so. We've got to quote some source. What would you rather be—a 'Military Spokesman' or an 'authoritative circle'?"

Although not as severe as Cairo had claimed, Rommel's tank losses had been heavy, and his reserves were not as great as those of the Eighth Army. At this stage he probably did not have many more than a hundred German and seventy-five Italian tanks fit for action, though a number of others were being repaired. The 7th Armoured Division had less than a hundred tanks, but fifty more were on their way from the railhead and another fifty en route from Alexandria. In addition there were still about sixty infantry tanks in Tobruk and with 13th Corps. In June these had proved too slow for effective use in an open tank battle, but they still had to be reckoned with.

Evidently realizing this, Rommel decided to make a bold throw. On the morning of November 24th he sent General von Ravenstein[3] on a diversionary raid with thirty to forty tanks, plus a battalion of lorried infantry and several batteries of field and anti-tank artillery. Rommel ordered this column to move south from Sidi Rezegh to the Trigh El Abd and then east to the frontier near Sidi Omar, where the British had over-run part of the defended locality two days earlier, and on into Egypt to link up with the Halfaya garrison.

Shooting up everything in sight, the column outflanked the 7th Armoured Division, scattered its transport and over-ran its supply dumps; put 30th Corps H.Q. to flight and generally herded across the frontier all the administrative and supply vehicles on which the forward troops depended. On the way it was severely bombed and strafed by the R.A.F., which hindered but could not stop its advance. On the afternoon of the 24th thousands of British vehicles were streaming eastwards across the frontier as hard as they could go. A "flap" was on and once a flap starts in the desert it is difficult to stop, but fortunately the boundary fence provided a place at which to rally the disorganized troops. Even so the German use of many captured British and South African trucks made reorganization difficult. No one could tell friend from foe, as Damien Parer and I found that afternoon, when we drove our truck straight towards a column, which we did not realize was German until an anti-tank gun opened fire on us. We got away in time, in spite of Parer's immediate reaction which was to stall the truck, switch off the engine and step furiously on the starter. Suddenly the truck roared into action again and shot off across the desert spurred on by several shells which were no match for Parer's speed.

All that night Eighth Army H.Q. was ready for a sudden move, and R.A.F. fighters were withdrawn from some of the advanced dromes. Next morning, however, the German raiders were again heavily attacked from the air and were finally halted

---

[3] von Ravenstein commanded the 21st Armoured Division, and was later captured by the New Zealanders near Sidi Rezegh.

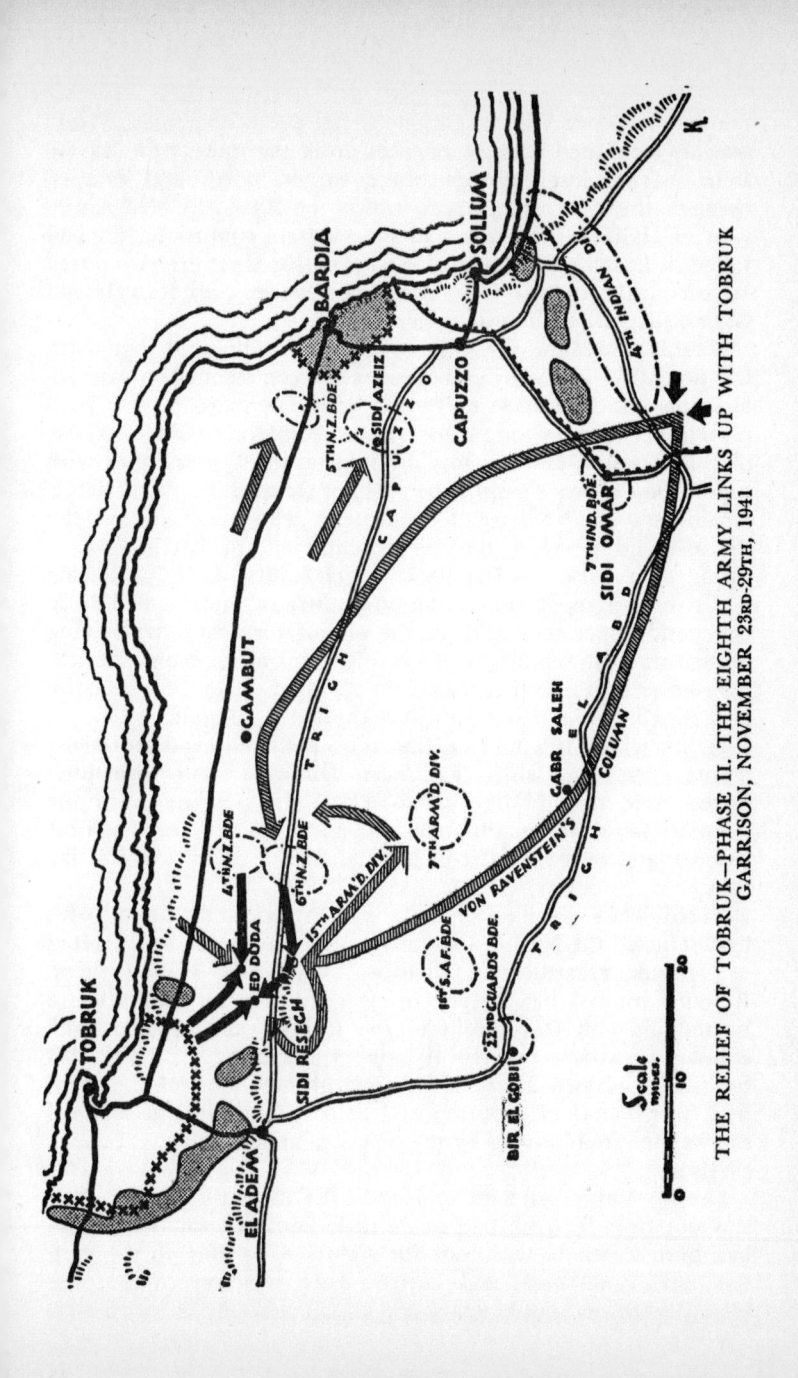

THE RELIEF OF TOBRUK—PHASE II. THE EIGHTH ARMY LINKS UP WITH TOBRUK GARRISON, NOVEMBER 23RD-29TH, 1941

ten miles east of the frontier by a few tanks and guns. When another armoured column attacked from the south, von Ravenstein, having lost eighteen tanks, turned north and escaped through the frontier defences, which the Axis still held southwest of Halfaya. The raid had spread great confusion, but had failed in its main objective which was to force the 7th Armoured Division to withdraw from the area between Sidi Rezegh and Gabr Saleh, where it was re-organizing.

By this time, however, Cunningham was convinced that there was no chance of relieving Tobruk. He recommended to Auchinleck that the Eighth Army should withdraw to its former positions in Egypt, re-group and refit. Auchinleck would not hear of this. He flew at once to Cunningham's H.Q., bringing with him a new Army Commander, Major-General N. M. Ritchie. Auchinleck had to have a commander who believed that the battle could be won, but his appointment of Ritchie was a complete surprise. As Deputy Chief of Staff at G.H.Q., Ritchie had gained a reputation as an administrator, but he had little command experience and, at the age of forty-four, was young by British Army standards for so important a command. He was still, however, to be little more than a chief of staff, for Auchinleck stayed in the desert to direct the battle himself.

He knew that it would be disastrous, politically and militarily, if the campaign, which had been launched with such high hopes, were now to be abandoned. If the pressure from the frontier were not maintained, Rommel might turn against Tobruk and overwhelm it before the Eighth Army could strike back.

Auchinleck's order to all ranks was "Attack and Pursue", and he instructed the New Zealanders to press on at once to the relief of Tobruk, regardless of what was happening behind them. Rommel himself had helped to clear the way for this advance by sending von Ravenstein to the frontier and another tank column to attack the 7th Armoured Division. By doing this he had withdrawn from the Sidi Rezegh area most of the tanks with which he had captured and held it. He had thus opened the way for fresh attacks by the New Zealanders and the Tobruk garrison.

During November 23rd and 24th, the infantry fighting their way out from Tobruk had made little headway, for their tanks had been forced to withdraw for maintenance. But on the 25th the tanks came back, and Fortress H.Q. was warned that the New Zealanders would make an all-out attempt to reach Sidi

Rezegh the following day. The garrison must get to Ed Duda by then. Early on the 26th, British infantry captured "Wolf", the last stronghold covering their objective, but there was no sign of the relieving forces. Throughout that morning the garrison's observers eagerly scanned the crest of the El Adem escarpment with their field glasses, but they looked in vain. About one o'clock several small specks appeared upon the skyline. They were tanks. Ours or theirs? German reinforcements for Ed Duda or British relieving forces? From one of the tanks three red flares went up; a pause; and then three more. That was the Eighth Army's signal—relief was at last in sight.

With fresh verve the British swept on to Ed Duda and by four o'clock men of the Essex Regiment and the Northumberland Fusiliers had driven the last German from the ridge. Tobruk had done its part, but there was still a 2-mile gap to Sidi Rezegh and the New Zealanders were not yet there. Soon after dark, however, they fought their way through to both Sidi Rezegh and Bel Hamed, an important rise two miles east of Ed Duda. By one o'clock next morning the 19th New Zealand Battalion, with a squadron of British "I" tanks, reached Ed Duda itself. At last Tobruk and the Eighth Army were linked, but it was too early to say that the garrison was relieved—in fact the general feeling was well expressed in the famous comment by the G.O.C., 13th Corps, when his H.Q. followed the New Zealanders inside the perimeter: "Tobruk may be relieved, but it's not nearly as relieved as I am." Already Rommel was mustering his armoured forces around Gambut for another major blow.

The 7th Armoured Division was also refitting near Gabr Saleh, and in the meantime the battle became fluid. There was no organized fighting and small mobile columns from both sides roamed at large in the area between Tobruk and the frontier. The British have a special aptitude for fighting of this kind and "Jock" columns and small tank formations destroyed a number of German tanks in impromptu skirmishes. The battle was so fluid that while British supply columns were moving north to Tobruk, Axis convoys were moving east across this route in an attempt to reach the beleaguered forces on the frontier and at Bardia. It was more like naval than land warfare. Convoys were slipping through and "destroyers" were worrying them, while the main "battle-fleets" prepared for another action. Nominally, the Germans around Gambut were cut off from their troops on the frontier and from those at El Adem, but the Eighth Army's line of communication with the head of the corridor the garrison had made through the defences screening Tobruk was little more secure than a convoy route across the Atlantic.

By November 29th Rommel felt strong enough to make a thorough-going attack on the Sidi Rezegh-Bel Hamed-Ed Duda triangle, which was the head of the Tobruk corridor. Sending in the 15th Armoured Division from the west and the 21st, plus some Italians, to attack from the east, he planned to chop off the head of the corridor with two concerted blows. The Eighth Army intercepted a radio message giving these orders. At once fifty British tanks moved north to intervene while "Jock" columns were sent to harass the rear and flanks of both the German armoured forces.

Early in the afternoon the attack was launched. The New Zealanders on Bel Hamed and Sidi Rezegh held their ground, but the 1st Battalion of the Essex Regiment, which was holding the western slope of Ed Duda, was driven back by German infantry supported by more than fifty tanks. At dark the enemy was strongly established on the western end of the Ed Duda ridge, and, if the rest of it were to be lost, the corridor wall would collapse and the garrison would have to withdraw inside the perimeter. Already the Tobruk commander, General Scobie, had eight of his fourteen infantry battalions holding the corridor and those inside were dangerously spread out. But Eighth Army H.Q. had sent this most urgent warning—"At all costs the corridor must be held."

The task of regaining the lost ground on Ed Duda was given to the only Australians still in Tobruk—the 2/13th Battalion. They had moved out to a reserve position on the northern slope of the rise the night before, and all through November 29th had been heavily shelled. Late that afternoon the artillery fire increased as the Germans attacked and before dark the Essex had been driven back and the Australians knew that they would have the crucial task of counter-attacking that night. They welcomed the chance, realizing that on their success or failure the relief of Tobruk might depend. They knew that Scobie had told their C.O. (Lieutenant-Colonel Burrows), "Whatever happens we must hold Ed Duda."

In bright moonlight shortly after ten o'clock Burrows led his two attacking companies up the northern slopes of Ed Duda towards their start-line. As they went a stray shell landed in the middle of one platoon. Seven men were killed and ten

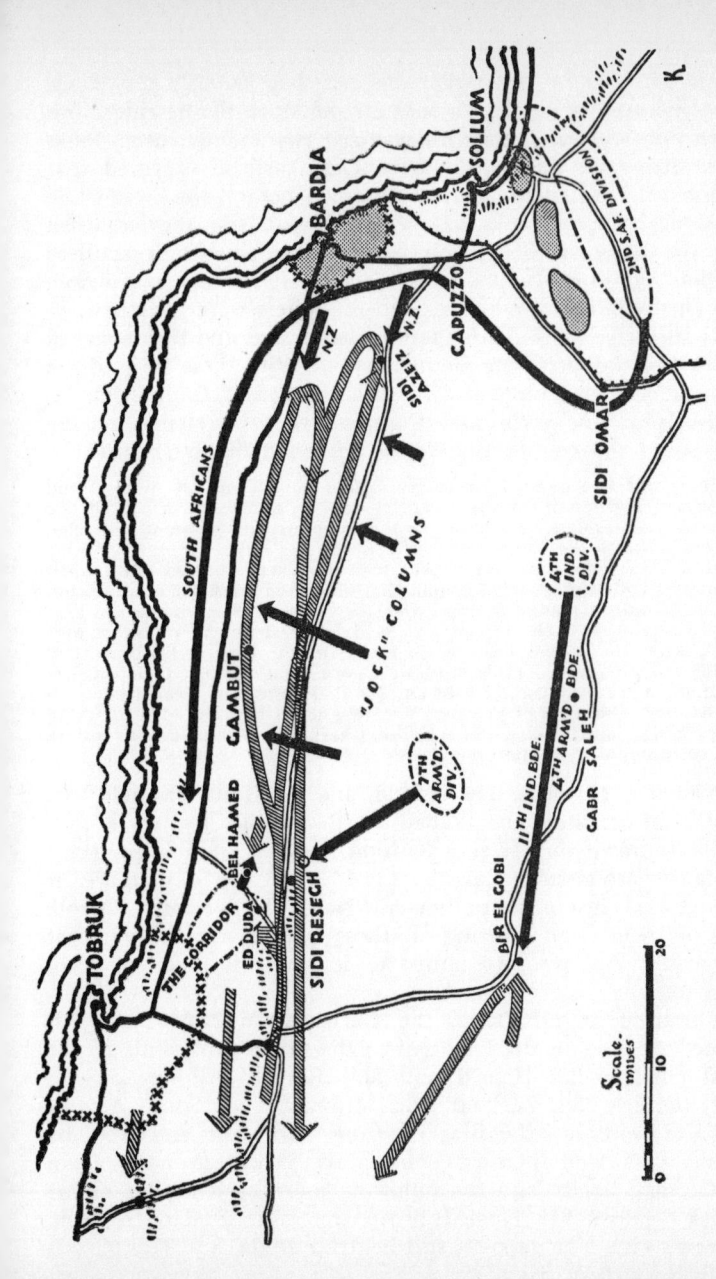

THE RELIEF OF TOBRUK—PHASE III. ENEMY CUTS EIGHTH ARMY'S LINK WITH TOBRUK BUT FAILS TO RELIEVE BARDIA, NOVEMBER 30th–DECEMBER 10th, 1941

wounded, but the other platoons marched steadily on. Their start-line was the crest of a fold on the slope of the ridge; but when they reached it Burrows saw that twenty-four enemy tanks were sitting on the positions the Germans had captured that afternoon. He told his men to lie down behind the crest while he went back for tanks. He returned with six; they attacked but the Germans held their ground. He called for artillery support and down came a heavy barrage. It was not long before two enemy tanks were blazing and the others were in retreat.

By this time more British tanks had arrived and they engaged the last of the retreating German tanks. With these clear of the position, Burrows unleashed his two companies, Captain O. M. Walsoe's on the right and Captain H. T. Graham's on the left, about 160 men in all. Walsoe described this afterwards:

Suddenly we were away. I remember calling out "Come on Aussies" and seeing the long line of steadily advancing men on either side of me. Up the slope we went and as we neared the top we heard the jabber of a foreign tongue in which we could soon distinguish *"Englander kommen"*. I fired a green Very light and with a wild roar our chaps charged down upon them. The sight and sound of us must have been too much for the Germans. A few desultory bursts of fire and then they cracked. Some broke and ran; some, cowering in their weapon pits, held up their hands. We swept over them, across the by-pass road, which ran along the back of Ed Duda, and on for several hundred yards until we'd gone right through their infantry positions. A few odd pockets held on, but they were soon cleared out with the bayonet. Our tally of prisoners was 167—more than our total attacking force. It was hard to stop the men from keeping up the pursuit, but we had to consolidate on the ground we'd recovered.

What the 2/13th gained it held, and Ed Duda was held too, in spite of persistent enemy shelling. Two nights later the 2/13th was withdrawn to a reserve position in which it suffered heavy casualties from enemy artillery fire. After two days there, it moved back inside the perimeter. "Never did we think," wrote one of them later, "during all those months in Tobruk, that we would ever want to return to it, but this night we were glad to."

Thwarted at Ed Duda, the Germans on November 30th turned their main strength against the other two points of the vital triangle—Bel Hamed and Sidi Rezegh. All day on the 30th the 6th New Zealand Brigade and the 1st South African Brigade were heavily attacked from both east and west by enemy tanks and infantry. Before dark Sidi Rezegh was again in German hands, and the following morning a similar pincer attack against Bel Hamed drove the New Zealanders from there as well. The garrison still held Ed Duda, but Tobruk was again isolated.

WHAT A RELIEF

The Germans were now in command of the Trigh Capuzzo from El Adem eastwards through Sidi Rezegh almost as far as Fort Capuzzo itself. On the first four days of December, enemy columns took advantage of this freedom and moved eastwards in an attempt to relieve Bardia and Capuzzo, which were still being covered by the 5th New Zealand Brigade. But every day his southern flank was harassed by "Jock" columns, which shot up transport and raided the area around Gambut where Rommel was holding his remaining forces. The R.A.F. and these columns, striking hard and swiftly, took heavy toll of the enemy's transport and stubborn resistance by the New Zealanders outside Capuzzo finally checked him.

While the Germans were thrusting east along the Trigh Capuzzo, the Eighth Army was counter-thrusting west along the Trigh El Abd towards El Gobi, threatening Rommel's desert flank. This threat became serious when Indian infantry and British tanks recaptured El Gobi on December 4th, and drove the remnants of the Ariete Division north-west towards Gazala. This British success, combined with the recapture of Bel Hamed by the New Zealanders, and the final failure of three attacks on the 4th Battalion of the Border Regiment at Ed Duda, evidently made Rommel realize that he could no longer maintain his position between Tobruk and Bardia. On the morning of December 5th the R.A.F. reported that enemy transport was streaming west past Tobruk, and was being bombed all the way.

Already British tanks and "Jock" columns were driving north-west in the hope of cutting off the Axis retreat. To counter this move and give him time to reorganize on the general line Tobruk-El Adem-El Gobi, Rommel on December 6th sent eighty tanks south to El Gobi. On the 7th they were driven back in disorder and the Tobruk-El Gobi line was turned. There was nothing for Rommel but further retreat.

On December 7th the Germans were still holding positions in the Tobruk Salient and along the western face of the perimeter, but there were only odd pockets and stragglers to the east and south-east. That day South Africans advancing along the road from Bardia and the 11th Hussars moving up through Sidi Rezegh re-established contact with the Tobruk garrison. In their wake came a huge supply column of hundreds of vehicles. Relief at long last was a fact, even though the Germans were still clinging to their positions in the Salient and checking a westward advance while the main Axis forces re-grouped around

Gazala. On the night of December 9th-10th the Polish Brigade regained part of the Salient and by next morning the Germans and Italians had abandoned their positions around Hill 209 and were headed westward in full flight. Tobruk, which had been held as a Fortress for 242 days—fifty-five days longer than Mafeking—was finally free.

Epilogue

ON December 10th 1941, when the last of Rommel's forces broke away from Tobruk, it was eight months to the day since they had first made contact with the perimeter. During that time those thin defences had turned the tide of war in the Middle East. By going on to Tobruk in the previous January, Wavell had been able to clinch the advantages won at Sidi Barrani and Bardia, and to complete Mussolini's humiliation. More than this, the capture of Tobruk greatly strengthened the defences of Egypt, as was shown by the way Rommel disposed his forces in Cyrenaica. From June onwards, as we have seen, two divisions watched the frontier; two were held in reserve west and south of Tobruk; and five more were needed to hem in the garrison's one and a half divisions. This was the measure of its triumph.

It is, however, too much to claim that Tobruk stopped Rommel capturing Alexandria and the Suez Canal in 1941. Rommel hardly had sufficient forces for such a task. I doubt whether he had been sent to Libya for that purpose. His job was rather to secure this sector of the German right flank while Russia was attacked, to tie up British forces and to protect the air bases from which the Axis could challenge British naval power in the Central Mediterranean. There is now little reason for thinking, as many did at the time, that the German campaigns in Libya and the Balkans early in 1941 were part of a major drive on the Middle East. They were, I believe, merely preliminary moves in the attack on Russia.

By the end of 1940 Hitler, having lost the Battle for Britain, must have realized that he could not invade the British Isles, unless he could bring much greater strength to bear; and he could not do this until the threat to his eastern frontier had been removed. In spite of the Nazi-Soviet Non-Aggression pact, Hitler then had more than 140 divisions and several thousand aircraft on the Russian border. The decision to attack Russia must have been made no later than January 1941, and in preparation for this offensive Hitler needed to safeguard his southern flank and, if possible, to strengthen it. In Albania the Italians were suffering defeat after defeat and, so long as the Greeks fought on, the Allies had in Europe a foothold which they might try to extend. Hence the campaign against Yugoslavia and Greece was an essential preliminary to the attack on Russia.

Hitler's grand strategy required not only the conquest of the Balkans but also the encirclement of Turkey. This intention was clearly shown by the size and character of the force he sent to Greece and Crete—an armoured division, six infantry divisions, and two of air-borne troops. The latter were primarily intended for the attack on Cyprus *not* Crete, which he expected to take without much opposition. After that he had apparently planned to make an air-borne invasion of Cyprus from the Dodecanese and, with the help of Vichy, to go on from Cyprus to Syria and to Iraq where revolt was organized. This development was blocked by the severe losses of the Luftwaffe and the Nazi airborne divisions in the battle for Crete. Had this plan succeeded, Hitler would not only have made this flank secure, but he might also have forced Turkey to provide him with a back door to the Caucasus and a front door to Asia.

Even though the Germans were halted at Crete, Turkey might not have been saved if Tobruk had fallen in May 1941. The defence of the Middle East through 1940-1 was almost as much a political as a military problem. For many years Axis propagandists had been campaigning against Britain in Egypt, Palestine, and the Moslem lands generally. This campaign had been helped by the prestige which the Germans had won through their European victories in the first eighteen months of the war. Germany—in Moslem eyes—was irresistible, and Britain's military reputation could hardly have been lower. In view of this, an advance by Rommel to Mersa Matruh—or worse still to El Alamein—in May 1941 would have had disastrous political consequences, not only in Egypt, where the Axis had friends and agents in the highest places, but throughout the Middle East. Britain's forces were probably capable of holding Rommel at El Alamein in that year, but they would almost certainly have been seriously embarrassed by civil uprisings extending from Egypt to Iran.

If Rommel had reached El Alamein at the time of our expulsion from Greece and Crete, it is difficult to see how

EPILOGUE

Turkey could have withstood German pressure, especially as the Axis then had such air superiority that the British Fleet might well have been forced to leave the Eastern Mediterranean. With it would have gone the main bulwark of Britain's prestige. Even as it was, the Turks were dragooned into signing a "Treaty of Friendship" and a new trade agreement with Germany on the eve of the Nazi attack on Russia. A year later, when Rommel reached El Alamein, the political consequences were not so serious. The belief that Germany's power was irresistible had been disproved at Tobruk, and Hitler's crack troops had been defeated and driven back in both Russia and Libya. But in April and May of 1941, between Hitler and a great politico-military triumph in the Middle East there stood little but Tobruk.

Because he was denied this triumph, Hitler's attempt to envelop Turkey failed. He then tried to frighten the Turks into surrender, but Stalin evidently warned him that any move against them would bring Russia in on their side. Hitler turned to attack the Soviet without further ado. Had Crete not proved so costly and Tobruk so stubborn, Russia would almost certainly have found herself invaded a month earlier than she was and attacked, moreover, on her southern flank as well as her western front.

Tobruk had an important effect on the course of the war for further reasons. Here the Germans suffered their first defeat on land. The Tobruk garrison showed that they could be beaten and how to beat them. It demonstrated that the Blitzkrieg, break-through tactics could be defeated by resolute infantry, who held their ground; by minefields and artillery fire; by defence in depth and by individual courage. It showed that the dreaded dive-bomber could be beaten off by ack-ack gunners who fought strongly back. Until this siege the dive-bomber had so dominated the gunner that the approved tactics were that gun crews went to ground when directly attacked.

Tobruk put an end to that and also to the theory, so current after the campaigns in Western Europe and the Balkans, that ground troops could not hold their positions against an enemy who had complete command of the air. Admittedly the conditions in Tobruk were very different from those which had enabled the Nazis to use their aircraft so successfully in Greece and Crete, but that did not lessen the effect of Tobruk's example on the rest of Wavell's forces. After these further retreats and evacuations, there was a danger that the Luftwaffe might gain a decided moral ascendancy over the British troops—especially those who had as yet no action experience against the Germans and had not fully recovered from the pessimism that followed Dunkirk. The success of the Tobruk garrison in dealing with both tanks and dive-bombers and fighting back month after month *with no air support at all* was most timely and heartening —not only for the Middle East forces, but for the Allies on every front.

Long before the war, the Germans began undermining the resistance of their enemies and prospective victims by sedulously spreading the doctrines of the inevitable success of the side strong enough to take the offensive; the certain supremacy of the force with superior engines of war; and the clear advantage of the young, sturdy Totalitarian nations over the effete democracies. Their successes in 1940 were *prima facie* proof of their case and Allied troops developed an inferiority complex, which was heightened by Germany's continued superiority in armament. Gallant though Dunkirk had been, nothing had happened on land to disprove the German doctrines—until Tobruk. But the Tommies and Diggers then showed that resolute men could defy superior mechanized power, so long as they refused to be intimidated. Before we could begin to defeat Hitler, this psychological supremacy of the machine over man had to be broken. Tobruk did that, and did more. It gave Britain time to recover from the disasters of Greece and Crete, and to re-organize the defence of Egypt; time for American aid to become effective and fresh supplies and reinforcements to arrive from Britain. It set an example of courage in the face of superior strength; of firm spirit in spite of hardship; of cheerful defiance and offensive defence.

Tobruk not only leg-roped Rommel, it also made possible his defeat in the November offensive. If the British had not been holding Tobruk—if they had not been able to strike at Rommel from two flanks simultaneously—the November attack would have failed as certainly as had that in June. By November 23rd, when the Germans had regained Sidi Rezegh and put out of action half the British tanks, the Eighth Army had lost that armoured superiority on which its success primarily depended. If Rommel had then been free to concentrate all his strength to drive the remaining British tanks back across the frontier, he would have won the day. Only fear of the British garrison in Tobruk stopped him from doing that. No wonder Rommel and the Germans came to hate the very name "Tobruk"—so

EPILOGUE

much so that after they later captured the Fortress in June 1942, Hitler renamed it "Rommel".

It is not unfair to say that as the November offensive developed the outcome was as much the relief of the Eighth Army as the relief of Tobruk. In this final triumph the A.I.F. had been represented only by the 2/13th but that battalion's recapture of the lost ground at Ed Duda on November 29th was the turning-point in one of the major crises of the campaign. The 2/13th had gained there at least a token revenge for all the Australians who had fought to hold Tobruk.

There was much in common between these men and the original Anzacs. Although the one was a successful defence and the other an offensive which failed, the same spirit was engendered in Tobruk and on Gallipoli. In both, the constant threat of an enemy who hemmed them in with their backs to the sea bound men together in unbreakable comradeship. Because of this, Tobruk and the spirit it typified became woven into the pattern of the Australian heritage, just as surely as Gallipoli was twenty-six years before.

Like Gallipoli, Tobruk has been made almost part of Australian soil by those who fought and died there. Most of the members of the A.I.F.[1], who were killed in the defence of Tobruk, lie buried in its War Cemetery. A few days before he left Tobruk General Morshead unveiled a memorial and there was a short ceremony at the cemetery in honour of those who lay there. In a broadcast at the time I described the ceremony in these words:

"At the setting of the sun we are met to honour those whose sun has set, but whose names shall live. Here beside the road that runs from Bardia to Tobruk the smooth brown sand of the desert is broken by 800 white crosses and the mounds of 800 graves—the graves of those who have died fighting for their country at Tobruk. In the west the sun has just set, but the sky is still streaked with light and a restless wind sweeps a fine dust-cloud across the cemetery. From the escarpment to the south comes the occasional thunder of guns; along the road from time to time trucks, armoured cars and tanks roar past on their way to or from the front; half a mile away troops are shaking out their blankets. The ordinary life of war goes on while we are

---

[1] In the withdrawal from Bengazi, the defence and relief of Tobruk, at least 776 officers and men of the A.I.F. were killed or died of wounds. Some of these have no known grave. Most of the 65 Australians posted missing are now presumed to have been killed also. The full list of A.I.F. casualties in this and other Middle East Campaigns is given in Appendix I.

gathered to do homage to those who have found peace only in death.

"Silhouetted against the evening sky is their memorial—a plain grey concrete obelisk—bearing the inscription:

> THIS IS HALLOWED GROUND FOR HERE LIE
> THOSE WHO DIED FOR THEIR COUNTRY
>
> *At the going down of the sun and in
> the morning we will remember them.*

"Over this inscription is draped a Union Jack and around the memorial are now gathered those who have come to honour fallen comrades. Each unit in the Tobruk Fortress has a representative here. There are officers and men of the British, Australian, Polish and Indian forces; officers and men of the Army, Navy and Air Force, for members of all three services are buried here. Now they stand in solemn silence awaiting the arrival of the Fortress Commander who will unveil the memorial. After that there will be a short service of dedication conducted by an Australian and a British chaplain.

"This will be a simple ceremony. Here within the sound and range of enemy guns anything elaborate would be out of place. Here soldiers, sailors and airmen are gathered to honour fellow soldiers, sailors and airmen. They have come straight from their tasks of war. Some from front-line posts; some from gun-positions; some from headquarters' dug-outs; some from dock-side or aerodrome. Some have come in their everyday dress—their shorts, shirts and steel helmets; some are in warmer battle dress; a few are wearing uniforms for which they've had no use these last six front-line months. There is to be no display, no pomp and ceremony, no glittering uniforms, no regimental bands, no speeches. Just two chaplains in khaki, one bugler and a hundred men gathered round a plain memorial draped with a Union Jack.

"Some of the graves are not yet completed. Some are only mounds of earth ringed with rough rock. Most of them have been bordered with a concrete wall and covered with white tiles on which there is a cross or a rising sun in dark stone. More than 500 of the men buried here are Australians. Some gave their lives when we first took Tobruk, but most have died in the defence of the Fortress. As well as the Australians, there are several hundred troops from the British Isles, Indians and Poles and a few Jewish volunteers from Palestine. There are two

Greek sailors, a New Zealander and a South African and several members of the Libyan force which joined the Army of the Nile after Cyrenaica was first conquered. The Mohammedans are buried in a sector by themselves, and so are the Germans and Italians. But it does not matter whether they are friend or foe; Christian, Hebrew or Mohammedan; European or Asiatic. They are men who gave their lives for their country and as such we honour them.

"But as nearly all those who are buried here died in the heroic defence of Tobruk, it is fitting that we should think specially of them. Their example of defiance and self-sacrifice is an inspiration to those who are left to fight on. Tobruk stands unconquered to-day because of the courage of men like these. The drifting sands may sweep across this cemetery and cover these crosses and this memorial as they have covered the monuments which the Phoenicians, Greeks and Romans raised along this barren coast. But the sands neither of the desert nor of time will obscure the splendid achievement of the men of Tobruk. Their real monument is their name and their most honoured resting place is in the grateful hearts of their fellow men."

APPENDIX I
TOBRUK GARRISON

a. **Formations and Units**

The principal units in the garrison from April till mid-August 1941 were:

Australian

H.Q. 9th Australian Division and Divisional Troops.

Infantry

18th Brigade: 2/9th, 2/10th, 2/12th Battalions.
20th Brigade: 2/13th, 2/15th, 2/17th Battalions.
24th Brigade: 2/28th, 2/32nd, 2/43rd Battalions.
26th Brigade: 2/23rd, 2/24th, 2/48th Battalions.

Artillery

2/12th Field Regiment; 3rd Anti-tank Regiment (less one battery); 16th, 20th, 24th, 26th Anti-tank Companies; 8th Light A.A. Battery.

Engineers and Pioneers

2/1st Pioneer Battalion; 2/3rd, 2/4th, 2/7th, 2/13th Field Companies; 2/4th Field Park Company.

Medical Units

4th General Hospital; 2/2nd Casualty Clearing Station (until July 20th); 2/3rd, 2/4th, 2/8th, 2/11th Field Ambulances.

Miscellaneous Ordnance, A.S.C. and Postal Units.

British

Artillery

Field: H.Q. R.A.; 1st, 104th and 107th Regiments R.H.A.; 51st Army Field Regiment; 4th Durham Survey Regiment.
Anti-tank: 3rd R.H.A. (less one battery).
Anti-aircraft: 4th A.A. Brigade H.Q.; 51st Heavy A.A. Regiment H.Q.; (152nd, 153rd, 235th Heavy A.A. Batteries); 14th Light A.A. Regiment H.Q.; (39th, 40th, 57th and part of 1st Light A.A. Batteries); 306th Searchlight Battery
Coast: 206th and 530th C.A. Batteries.

Machine-Gunners

1st Royal Northumberland Fusiliers.

Armoured Forces

3rd Armoured Brigade, now including 1st R.T.R. (23 cruiser tanks); one squadron, 7th R.T.R. (4 and later 12 "I" tanks); Composite Regiment, mostly from 3rd Hussars (light tanks) and King's Dragoon Guards (armoured cars).

Engineers
551st Army Troops Company.

Miscellaneous
One Company of Special Service Troops (Commandos).
A.S.C., Ordnance and Port Authority Personnel.

Indian

18th Indian Cavalry Regiment (dismounted).

Others

During the early months of the siege there were in Tobruk some Palestinian and Cypriot troops who worked on the waterfront, and a Libyan Labour Battalion that had been raised during the first desert campaign.

So far as I know the only fighting units that saw the siege right through from April to December were:

British: 1st Royal Northumberland Fusiliers; 1st, 104th, 107th Regiments R.H.A.; 1st R.T.R.; 39th and 40th Light A.A. Batteries.

Australian: 2/13th Battalion.

---

b. Strength

The numerical strength of the garrison at various times is shown by the following table:

April 12th	35,307
April 21st	33,109
May 2nd	22,800 (approx.)
June 30th	22,305
July 30th	22,026
August 31st	22,996
September 30th	25,029

The relative strengths of the British, Australian, Indian and later Polish troops is shown by this table:

	A.I.F	British	Poles
April 21st	14,817	18,292 (inc. about 550 Indians)*	
June 30th	14,326	7,979 (inc. 500 Indians)	
August 31st (after 1st flight of A.I.F. had left)	12,400	5,775 (inc. 300 Indians)	4,821
September 30th (after departure of 2nd flight)	7,716	12,441	4,872

---

* The Indian troops are included with the British because most of their officers were British.

APPENDIX I

c. Casualties

The casualties suffered by the A.I.F. during the siege of Tobruk, in the other Middle East campaigns and in New Guinea up to January 1943 are shown in the following table:

Middle East

	Killed in action or died of wounds	Wounded in action	Missing	Prisoners	Total
First Libyan Campaign (Dec. 1940 to Feb. 1941)	264	932	9	24	1229
Tobruk Siege (Including the withdrawal from Bengazi, March to October, 1941)	726	2057	61	951	3795
Second Libyan Campaign (Relief of Tobruk—November-December, 1941)	50	55	4	3	112
Greece-Crete	518	494	174	5033	6219
Syria	411	1144	2	Nil	1557
Palestine	1	6	Nil	Nil	7
El Alamein	1177	3629	193	795	5794
Total	3147	8317	443	6806	18,713

New Guinea

	Killed in action or died of wounds	Wounded in action	Missing	Prisoners	Total
(To end of Buna Campaign)	2110	3833	269		6212

APPENDIX II

HONOURS AND AWARDS

For gallantry and outstanding service during the capture, siege and relief of Tobruk more than 240 officers and men of the A.I.F. were decorated, and their names are set out in this appendix. So far as I know this list is complete, but some names may have been inadvertently omitted, others may have been wrongly included. For instance, some members of the 9th Division who were decorated during 1942 may have received their awards as much for their good work at Tobruk as at El Alamein, but I have not included them in this list.

It has been rather difficult to work out a satisfactory basis for the inclusion of the names of men who were decorated after the first Libyan campaign, for in many cases the decorations were awarded for the recipient's work in the campaign as a whole. Where this was the case the name appears in this list, but I have not included the names of those whose decoration was awarded for a particular act at, say, Bardia or Derna, even though their general good service at the capture of Tobruk may have indirectly contributed to the decision in the awarding of decorations. The ranks given are those held by the recipients at the time the awards were made. Every care has been taken to see that this list is accurate, but I hope that those whose names unfortunately may have been omitted will appreciate the difficulties involved.

Victoria Cross (V.C.)
Cpl. J. H. Edmondson.

Companion of the Most Honourable Order of the Bath (C.B.)
Brigadier A. S. Allen, C.B.E., D.S.O., V.D.

Knight Commander of the Most Excellent Order of the British Empire (K.B.E.)
Major-General I. G. Mackay, C.M.G., D.S.O., V.D.
Major-General L. J. Morshead, C.M.G., C.B.E., D.S.O., E.D.

Commander of the Most Excellent Order of the British Empire (C.B.E.)
Col. F. H. Berryman, D.S.O.
T/Col. T. P. Cook, O.B.E., E.D.
Col. H. C. Disher.
Brig. E. F. Herring, D.S.O., M.C., E.D.
Col. C. E. M. Lloyd.
Brig. H. C. H. Robertson, D.S.O.
Brig. S. G. Savige, D.S.O., M.C., E.D.
Col. N. L. Spiers, V.D.

APPENDIX II

Officer of the Most Excellent Order of the British Empire (O.B.E.)

Maj. H. T. Allan
Lieut.-Col. A. Brown, D.S.O., M.C.
Lieut.-Col. W. E. Cremor, E.D.
Lieut.-Col. T. P. Cook, E.D.
Maj. G. A. Davis
Lieut.-Col. B. S. Hanson
Lieut.-Col. C. W. B. Littlejohn

Lieut.-Col. N. B. Loveridge
Maj. F. W. MacLean
Maj. G. H. O'Brien
T/Lieut.-Col. N. H. W. Saxby
Lieut.-Col. D. N. Veron
Lieut.-Col. J. A. Watson
Maj. W. W. Wearne
Lieut.-Col. E. W. Woodward

Member of the Most Excellent Order of the British Empire (M.B.E.)

Lieut. E. C. V. Adams
Lieut. D. D. Balfour-Ogilvie
Capt. J. A. Bishop
Capt. G. D. T. Cooper
Lieut. H. A. Davidson-Craig
Lieut. H. G. Davies
Capt. A. H. Dixon

Capt. R. Drummond
Capt. M. Feitel
Capt. A. Fryberg
T/Capt. P. G. I. Northey
Lieut. A. H. Pearson
Lieut. G. P. Wild
Capt. T. H. Winchester

Distinguished Service Order (D.S.O.)

Maj. J. N. Abbott
Maj. R. K. Anderson
Lieut.-Col. L. E. S. Barker
Maj. G. H. Brock
Lieut.-Col. F. A. Burrows, M.M., E.D
Maj. I. R. Campbell
Lieut.-Col. F. O. Chilton.
Lieut.-Col. J. W. Crawford, E.D.
Lieut.-Col. I. N. Dougherty
Lieut.-Col. K. W. Eather
Lieut.-Col. V. T. England
Lieut.-Col. B. Evans
Capt. W. Forbes
Lieut.-Col. H. G. Furnell

Maj. A. S. Gehrmann
Lieut.-Col. A. H. L. Godfrey, M.C., E.D.
Maj. J. F. Herbertson
Capt. J. A. Hutchinson
Lieut.-Col. J. E. Lloyd, M.C.
Lieut.-Col. L. C. Lucas, M.C., V.D.
Maj. D. Macarthur Onslow
T/Col. J. Mann
Lieut.-Col. J. E. G. Martin, O.B.E.
Maj. A. G. Torr
Lieut.-Col. T. G. Walker
Lieut.-Col. W. J. V. Windeyer

Bar to Distinguished Service Order

Brig. A. H. L. Godfrey, D.S.O., M.C., E.D.
Brig. J. J. Murray, D.S.O., M.C., V.D.

Brig. R. W. Tovell, D.S.O., E.D.
Brig. G. F. Wootten, D.S.O.

Military Cross (M.C.)

Lieut. J. L. Allen
Capt. J. W. Balfe
Lieut. G. Beckingsale
Lieut. H. R. Beer
Capt. F. L. Bode
Lieut. E. R. Bucknell
Lieut. J. R. Burrell
Lieut. W. S. Cantelo
Capt. W. E. L. Catchlove
Capt. W. W. Cobb
Lieut. F. W. Cook
Lieut. S. C. Diffey

Lieut. H. L. E. Dunkley
Lieut. M. R. Ellenby
Lieut. J. T. Finlay
Lieut. E. H. Gerard
Lieut. P. R. Gilmour
Capt. D. L. B. Goslett
Capt. S. J. M. Goulston
Capt. E. A. Handley
Lieut. P. S. Hayman
Capt. J. G. Hendry
Lieut. E. C. Hennessy
Capt. J. H. Hodge

Military Cross (M.C.)—Continued

Capt. R. Joshua
Capt. L. McCarter
Lieut. J. E. Macdonald
Lieut. G. F. McDonnell
Capt. R. W. F. McDonald
Lieut. F. A. Mackell
T/Capt. L. C. Maclarn
Capt. R. E. McPherson
Capt. G. I. Malloch
Lieut. T. Mills
Capt. D. O. Muller
Lieut. A. C. Murchison
Lieut. H. W. Nicholls
Capt. C. H. B. Norman
Lieut. W. H. Noyes

Lieut. J. W. Overall
Lieut. J. L. Perry
Capt. R. Rattray
Lieut. A. L. Reid
Lieut. J. S. Rosel
Capt. J. J. Ryan
Lieut. D. C. Siekmann
Capt. A. L. F. Taylor
Lieut. H. L. Thompson
T/Capt. N. A. Vickery
Capt. O. M. Walsoe
Lieut. E. R. Wilmoth
Lieut. J. H. Wilton
Lieut. R. A. Yates

Medal for Distinguished Conduct in the Field (D.C.M.)

Sgt J. W. Barnard
Sgt L. W. C. Batty
Sgt E. F. Boland
Sgt J. W. Christisen
Sigmn K. R. Clift
A/Sgt R. W. Hobson
L/Sgt J. G. Hunt
WO II B. H. Macdougal
Sgt V. D. McQuillan
Pte O. Z. Neall
Pte L. R. Passmore

L/Sgt E. R. Peel
Cpl A. A. Picket
A/Sgt N. H. Russell
Sgt J. E. Searle
Cpl G. O. Smithers
WO II W. H. Stenning
L/Cpl A. J. Taylor
Sgt H. L. Watts
Cpl J. K. Weston
Sgt K. W. Young

Military Medal (M.M.)

Sgt W. M. Allison
Cpl C. A. Amos
Pte P. M. Anderson
Cpl L. G. Armstrong
Cpl F. C. Aston
Gnr R. J. Baldwin
Pte L. Bennett
Pte N. Blundell
L/Cpl F. O. Booth
Sigmn W. A. Bruce
Pte W. C. Button
Sgt C. H. Cawthorne
L/Sgt R. J. Chambers
Sgt T. Charlton
Pte H. P. Clark
Gnr E. J. Courtney
Sgt A. Crawford
Cpl. W. B. Curren
Spr M. L. Daly
Pte R. G. Daniells
WO II J. H. Deane
Cpl C. R. Dodd
Spr J. Dodd
Cpl A. E. Dunbar
Pte E. O. J. Dunning
Pte H. Ferres

Cpl W. L. France
Cpl D. L. Fraser
L/Cpl H. D. Genner
L/Sgt C. Gilbert
Cpl L. Gracie
Cpl J. C. Gray
Cpl L. R. Goode
Pte C. G. Hackett
Sigmn A. C. Hammond
WO II A. J. Harrison
A/Cpl C. B. Hayes
Sgt P. R. Hook
Pte J. Hunt
L/Cpl D. W. Hutchinson
Sgt. W. C. Jarman
Sgt. E. J. Johnston
L/Sgt T. L. Johnson
Sgt G. H. Jones
Pte J. McG. Kelly
Cpl M. J. Kennedy
Sgt A. H. Knight
Pte C. Lamond
Sgt E. B. Lodge
Sgt L. M. Long
A/Sgt G. Lucas
A/Cpl F. R. Lynch

APPENDIX II

Military Medal (M.M.)—Continued

Sgt R. P. McG. Lee
Pte R. A. McBain
Sgt G. W. D. McCarthy
Tpr C. L. McCarthy
Sgt R. McL. McElroy
Pte D. M. McGinty
Spr T. J. McGreevy
Pte G. S. McGrow
Sgt A. A. McIlrick
Sgt B. L. McKay
Sigmn R. D. McKeague
L/Sgt J. M. McWilliam
Spr W. Madams
L/Sgt J. W. Maynes
A/Sgt J. V. P. Mooney
Pte F. Munnich
Sgt V. E. Nash
L/Cpl H. B. Nutt
Pte H. O'Brien
Pte M. J. O'Connell
Pte B. P. O'Donnell
Spr G. Parsonage

Sgt R. A. Patrick
Pte L. T. Perkins
WO II R. B. Quinn
Pte D. E. Rayner
Sgt E. J. Richards
Sgt C. G. Rigg
A/Sgt L. Rodda
L/Sgt F. G. Rodda
A/Sgt H. T. Sayers
Sgt R. W. Shepheard
Pte K. Smith
Pte J. L. Spavin
L/Cpl C. T. Stanford
Sgt L. L. Stone
L/Sgt G. A. Stuckey
Sgt E. B. Thurman
Pte E. T. Unwin
Pte. J. Vardy
A/Cpl G. G. Williams
Pte F. Wright
Sgt A. J. Wyatt

George Medal

Cpl W. L. Bowman

Spr J. W. G. Gleaves

Medal of the Order of the British Empire for Meritorious Service (B.E.M.)

Sgt R. W. Anderson
Sgt L. Austin

Bdr R. Auton
Pte R. Muirhead

Polish Decorations

Krzyz Waleczynch

Lieut.-Col. F. A. Burrows, M.M., E.D.

Virtuti Militari

Major-General L. J. Morshead, C.M.G., C.B.E., D.S.O., E.D.

APPENDIX III

THE MAIN EVENTS OF 1941

The following table sets out the main events of 1941, showing in italics those which are dealt with in this book:

JANUARY:

- 3rd. 6th Australian Division and British forces attack Bardia.
- 5th. Italian resistance at Bardia ends.
- 10th. First battle in the Mediterranean between the Royal Navy and the Luftwaffe—H.M. Aircraft-Carrier *Illustrious* damaged.
- 21st. *6th Australian Division and British forces attack Tobruk.*
- 22nd. *Italian resistance at Tobruk ends.*

FEBRUARY:

- 7th. Australians occupy Bengazi: British round up the last of Graziani's forces in Cyrenaica.
- 9th. Mr Churchill appeals to the United States, "Give us the tools and we will finish the job."
- 25th. First clash between British and German mechanized patrols in Libya, west of El Agheila.

MARCH:

- 1st. Bulgaria joins Axis and German troops enter the country.
- 11th. President Roosevelt signs the "Lend-Lease" Bill.
- 24th. Germans capture El Agheila.
- 25th. Yugoslavia joins Axis.
- 27th. Bloodless revolution in Yugoslavia: pro-Axis Government overthrown. Fall of Keren, chief Italian fortress in Eritrea.
- 28th-29th. Italian fleet routed at Battle of Matapan, off Crete.
- 31st. *Axis forces drive British from Mersa Brega and Rommel begins counter-offensive into Cyrenaica.*

APRIL:

- 4th. *British evacuate Bengazi.*
- 6th. Germans invade Yugoslavia and Greece.
  British and Australian forces begin general withdrawal in Cyrenaica.
- 8th. Fiercest German raid on Coventry.
- 10th. *Last British and Australian units withdraw inside Tobruk perimeter. Siege begins.*
- 13th. Germans capture Bardia and reach Egyptian frontier at Sollum.
- 14th. *First serious German attack on Tobruk repulsed.*
- 24th. Evacuation of Anglo-Anzac forces from Greece begins.
- 27th. Germans enter Athens.
- 30th. *Rommel launches second serious attack on Tobruk.*

APPENDIX III

MAY

- 1st-3rd. *Attack on Tobruk continues, but peters out.*
- 10th. R.A.F. night-fighters shoot down 33 German planes over London.
- 12th. Rudolph Hess lands in Scotland.
- 15th-16th. *First British attempt to relieve Tobruk by attack from Egypt fails.*
- 16th-17th. *German attempt to widen breach in Tobruk perimeter repulsed.*
- 20th. Duke of Aosta, Viceroy of Abyssinia surrenders. Germans begin air-borne attack on Crete.
- 30th. Evacuation of Anglo-Anzac forces from Crete begins.
- 31st. British troops complete pacification of Iraq. Rebels seek armistice.

JUNE:

- 8th. British, Australian, Free French and Indian troops invade Syria.
- 15th-17th. *Second British attempt to relieve Tobruk by attack from Egypt fails.*
- 18th. Turkey signs treaty of friendship with Germany.
- 22nd. Germany invades U.S.S.R.

JULY:

- 1st. General Auchinleck (C.-in-C., India) exchanges posts with General Wavell (C.-in-C., Middle East).
- 7th. U.S. Forces occupy Iceland and Greenland.
- 12th. Syrian campaign ends: Armistice signed at Acre.

AUGUST:

- 3rd. *Tobruk garrison attempts to retake German Salient, but fails.*
- 12th. Mr Churchill and President Roosevelt approve draft of Atlantic Charter. (This Charter was never signed.)
- 13th. Germans occupy Smolensk, threaten Kiev and Odessa.
- 25th. British and Soviet troops invade Iran.
- 28th. British and Soviet troops complete occupation of Iran.

SEPTEMBER:

- 1st. *Rommel launches heaviest air attack on Tobruk with 140 planes.*
- 11th. President Roosevelt announces that U.S. fleet ordered to destroy Axis forces operating in "American defensive waters".
- 15th-16th. Two Axis columns penetrate 35 miles into Egypt but are turned back.

OCTOBER:

- 7th. President Roosevelt announces plan for revision of Neutrality Act to permit American merchantmen to carry "Lend-Lease" goods to Britain.
- 16th. Germans take Odessa.
- 29th. Germans take Kharkov and threaten Moscow and Rostov.

NOVEMBER:

- 5th. German advance checked at Moscow's outer defences.
- 18th. *British begin counter-offensive in Libya for relief of Tobruk.*
- 22nd. Germans capture Rostov but are driven out five days later.
- 27th. Germans only 20 miles from Moscow.

DECEMBER:

- 7th. Japanese attack on Pearl Harbour.
  Siege of Tobruk is raised.
- 8th. Britain and U.S.A. declare war on Japan.
- 10th. *Rommel's forces in full retreat break off contact with Tobruk.*
- 25th. British re-capture Bengazi.

INDEX

INDEX*

Abbot, *Maj.* J. N., 20, 21
A.B.C. Field Unit, 246*n*
Acroma, A.I.F. withdrawal to, 79, 80; enemy concentrations at, 82, 117, 124, 128, 142, 144, 187
Aerial photographs, of Tobruk (Jan.), 12, 15; of German defences not available (June), 197, (Aug.) 243
Afrika Korps, 206, 294; composition of (March), 65; training of, in Germany, 66; difficulty of reinforcing, 156; reaction of, to desert warfare, 116-17; strengthening of (Nov.), 290, 291
Agedabia (Map p. 75), 68, 70, 284
A.I.F. *See* Australian Imperial Force
A.I.F. News, 251
Airente (Map p. 33), 32, 40, 86
Air-raid warnings in Tobruk, 286
Alcohol, scarcity of, in Tobruk, 170, 173-4, 267, 279
Allen, *Brig.* Arthur, commands 16th Brigade, 14; sketch of, 14; in planning the attack on Tobruk, 14, 15; during the attack, 20, 27
Ammunition, lack of A.P., and use of H.E. by 25-pounders, 101*n*; amount used in Allied counter-attack (May 2), 151; average German expenditure of, in shelling Tobruk, 170; dump, garrison's, destroyed by enemy (June), 244; garrison's expenditure of, restricted, 244; enemy's superior supplies of, 244-5; Italian, in Tobruk, for captured guns, 247; delivered by destroyer-ferry to Tobruk, 252; dump, Italian, destroyed by enemy (Aug. 12), 266. *See also* Artillery, Anti-tank guns
Anderson, *Lieut.* G. G., 188
Anderson, *Maj.* R. K. (quoted), 50
Anti-aircraft batteries—*British and Australian*, during siege, 87, 120, 126, 257; task of, and results in six months, 248-9; protecting the harbour from enemy bombers, 254-5;
number of guns in action (April), 256-7; their victory over German bombers, 256-64; barrage put up by, 257-8; tactics adopted by, in face of direct attack, 258-9, 260; casualties of, 259, 263, 271, 272, 277; dummy gun-sites established near, 260; losses inflicted on enemy by, 260, 262, 263; enemy blitz on (May 26-June 2), 262-3; force enemy to resort to high-level bombing (June 3-Aug. 3), 265-6; effectiveness of their barrage over harbour, 269, 270; in the attack of Sept. 1, 271-2; number of guns in action (Aug.), 272-3; estimate of enemy aircraft engaged and shot down by (Apr. 10-Oct. 9), 274-5; life of the gun-crews of, 276-8; strengthening of harbour barrage to cover troop movements (Aug.-Sept.), 283. *German*, 88-mm. A.A. guns used in anti-tank role, 103*n*, 163-5. *Italian*, in defence of Tobruk, 8; guns of, used against Australian infantry, 37-8, 39. *See also* Artillery
Anti-tank defence, ineffectiveness of Italian minefields as, 11, 21; garrison's system of minefields, 86; dug-in tanks for, 86; garrison's strengthened by last-minute arrival of guns from Mechili, 91; garrison uses Italian field guns for, 91; tactics and value of 25-pounders as, 101-2; garrison employs heavy shelling plus minefields as (May 1-2), 147-8, 250
Anti-tank ditch, 6, 15, 20, 27, 94
Anti-tank guns, Allied shortage of, 80; number and distribution of Allied, 86, 87; German 50-mm. and 88-mm., 161, 163-5; superiority of German to British, 299-300
Army of the Nile, after Sidi Barrani victory, 1, 2; advance to El Agheila, 63. *See* Cyrenaica Force
Artillery—*British and Australian*, in first assault on Tobruk, 12-13, 19-

* Names which appear only in the list of honours and awards, Appendix II, are not indexed.

INDEX

Artillery—*continued*
20, 25-6, 28-9, 38, 39, 40, 42; shortage of in 6th Australian Division, 35-6; excellence of, a decisive factor in Tobruk victory, 49; in holding the Er Regima escarpment, 71-2, 73; available to defend Tobruk, 85, 86, 87, 91, 93; in the Easter battle, 93-5, 96, 100, 101, 102, 103; in the Battle of the Salient (antitank), 130-1, 131-2, 133, 137, 142, 145-7; before the counter-attack of May 2, 149, 151; before the counter-attack of May 17, 187; barrage before the attack of Aug. 3, 199, 201, 203; inadequate fire-power of (Aug. 3 attack), 203, 204; importance of its role, 242, 250; use of camouflage by, 243-4; devices of, for spotting enemy guns, 244, 245; counter-battery work of, 245-6, 273, 283, 285; types of, used against "Bardia Bill", 245-6; use of captured Italian by Bush Artillery, 247-8; danger to, of enemy bombing, 248; difficulty of assessing enemy casualties from, 249; what the garrison owed to the British gunners, 250; in the battle for "Plonk", 238; covering the withdrawal of A.I.F. from Tobruk, 285. *German*, in the assault on Er Regima, 72, 73; in the first assault on Tobruk, 97, 103; in the Battle of the Salient, 128-9, 133, 137, 140, 142, 146, 149, 150; superiority of their 50-mm. and 80-mm. anti-tank guns, 161, 163-5, 300; average daily shelling of Tobruk, 170; in the A.I.F. counter-attack of May 17, 187, 192; in the A.I.F. attack of Aug. 3, 199, 201; strength of, in the Salient (May-Aug.), 206; in the battle for "Plonk", 238, 239; advantages of, in observation, 242-3; attempts of, to mislead British counter-battery staff, 245, 246; heavy types of, 245-6; shelling of garrison's field guns by, 248-9; bested in artillery duels, 250; use of heavy guns against harbour, 273, 283, 285, 287; strength of outside Tobruk (Nov.), 290. *Italian*, in defence of Tobruk, 7-8, 34, 35, 37-8, 39, 41, 42, 47, 49, 57; captured at Tobruk, 48, 57; during A.I.F. patrol activity, 239-40. *See also* Anti-aircraft batteries, Anti-tank guns

Aston, *Cpl* F. C., 130

Auchinleck, *Gen.* Sir Claude, C.-in-C. Middle East, 14, 292, 304
Auckland, H.M.S., 267-8
Australian Air Force. *See* R.A.A.F.
Australian Comforts Fund, services of, in Tobruk, 175
Australian Imperial Force, constitution of, in Tobruk, 88-9, 91; harmony of, with British in Tobruk, 89-90, 175, 181; short of equipment at Tobruk, 90, 91, 93; general tactics of, in holding Tobruk, 107-8, 111; units of, below strength in Tobruk, 232, 282; withdrawal of first units of (Aug.), 272; replaced by British and Polish troops in Tobruk, 280-9; reasons for withdrawal of, from Tobruk, 281-2; effect of Tobruk conditions on, 282; formations and units of, at Tobruk, 319; strength of forces in Tobruk, 320; casualties of, at Tobruk, in Middle East and in New Guinea up to Jan. 1943, 321. *See also* Diggers and under individual formations and units.

CORPS, *1st Australian*, 68, 281, 282
DIVISIONS—*6th Division*, in the assault on Tobruk, 3, 8, 12, 26, 49, 55, 89, 244; weakness of, in artillery, 36; its commander, 52; relieved in Libya, 68; in Greece, 281, 282. *7th Division*, 68, 80, 81, 88, 281, 283; its commander in the Syrian campaign, 14. *9th Division*, relieves 6th Division in Libya (Mar. 8), 68; its role before the siege, 69, 71, 74, 76, 78, 79, 82, 83 (*see also* Cyrenaica Force); its training and equipment incomplete, 84, 112-13; composition of, 88; during the siege, *see under* units below; withdrawal of, from Tobruk, 240, 280-9; originally intended for Greece, 281

BRIGADES—*16th Brigade*, 9, 27, 36; its role in taking Tobruk, 10, 14, 15, 26, 37, 44, 46; its commander, 14. *17th Brigade*, 9, 12, 66; part played by, in the assault on Tobruk, 10, 44, 47-8; its commander, 47. *18th Brigade*, transferred from 9th to 7th Division, 68; sent to Tobruk before siege, 80; left in reserve at start, 88; previously commanded by Morshead, 112; its commander, 148; counter-attacks on the Salient (May 3), 148-51, 155, 183; casualties, 151, 155; prepared to lead break-

INDEX

Australian Imperial Force—*continued*
out from Tobruk (June), 161; takes over Salient sector (May 13), 184; its patrols in El Adem sector (July), 227-8, 230-1; leaves Tobruk (Aug.), 280, 282-3, 284. *19th Brigade*, 9; in the assault on Tobruk, 10, 12, 25, 26, 28, 31, 44, 51; its commander, 14. *20th Brigade*, transferred from 7th to 9th Division, 68; during the withdrawal to Tobruk, 68, 69, 71, 74, 80, 88; its commander, 68-9; astride the El Adem road, 93; part in Easter Battle, 93-106; its concert in Tobruk, 177-8; ground regained by, in the Salient (June 11-26), 193-5, 205; casualties, 194; its V for Victory campaign, 232; leaves Tobruk, 289*n*. *21st Brigade*, 158. *24th Brigade*, 68, 69, 80, 88; its commander, 198*n*; holding the Salient sector (July-Aug.), 198; attacks in Salient (Aug.), 198-203; holding the eastern sector (May), 220; raids by, on Italian positions (Sept. 13-14), 235; leaves Tobruk (Sept.), 284. *25th Brigade*, 65, 158. *26th Brigade*, 88; transferred from 7th to 9th Division, 68; before the siege, 69, 74, 78, 80; its commander, 78; holding the western sector, 116; and the battle of the Salient, 128-31, 134-7, 139-45, 152; strengthens Salient defences (Aug.-Sept.), 203; keeps Germans on defensive, 204
BATTALIONS—*2/1 Battalion*, 9; its advance to Bardia road, 22, 24, 25, 27; moves to the El Adem road and beyond, 30, 42. *2/2 Battalion*, its role in the capture of Tobruk, 22; over-runs enemy gun positions, 24, 25-6; advances towards El Adem road and beyond, 30, 42. *2/3 Battalion*, 9, 15, 41; begins the assault on Tobruk, 16, 18, 19-21, 22, 24, 25, 27, 30; captures further posts on the El Adem road, 41-3. *2/4 Battalion*, 9; in the Tobruk assault, 28, 30, 36; its advance to Solaro, 32, 37, 38-9; prepares to enter Tobruk, 44. *2/5 Battalion*, 9, 48. *2/6 Battalion*, 9; in the Tobruk assault, 25, 27, 28, 30, 48; at Fort Cheteita, 47. *2/7 Battalion*, 9; enters the Tobruk perimeter, 25, 26, 30, 48; collects prisoners, 47. *2/8 Battalion*, 9, 46; captures the El Adem crossroads, 28-30; in the drive to Pilastrino, 32, 35-8, 41, 42. *2/9 Battalion*, counter-attacks against posts R7 and R8 (May 3-4), 149-50, 197; casualties, 150-1; ground regained by, in Salient (May 3-4), 191. *2/10 Battalion*, in the Battle of the Salient, 142, 146; raids by, on northern flank (May 3-4), 149, 150; casualties, 151; advances in northern sector (May 12), 184-5, 194; raids "Fig Tree" (July 20-1), 227-8. *2/11 Battalion*, 9; its role in the Tobruk assault, 28, 30, 32, 40-1; platoon of, saves water distilleries, 41. *2/12 Battalion*, attacks Salient posts S6 and S7 (May 3), 149, 150, 197; casualties, 150-1; offensive patrols by, in Salient sector (May 15-16), 184-6; raid by (July 11-12), 230-1. *2/13 Battalion*, 82, 93; holding the Er Regima escarpment (Apr. 4), 71-4, 79; at Martuba (Apr. 6-7), 77, 78; in the Easter Battle, 93, 94, 95; patrol disrupts German diversion (May 1), 132; raids Italian working parties (Aug. 1), 224; raids enemy gun positions (Aug. 17-18), 246-7; stays in Tobruk, 289; part played by, in the relief of Tobruk (Nov.), 306-8. *2/15 Battalion*, 129, 289*n*; H.Q. captured by enemy (Apr. 6), 78; during the Easter Battle, 93, 106; casualties in Salient sector (June), 194*n*; 195; guides its patrols home with saxophone, 227; raiding operations by (Aug. 30-1), 228-9. *2/17 Battalion*, 74, 234; in the Easter Battle, 93-5, 97-100, 103-4, 106; its "love and kisses" patrols, 219; raids on Italian positions by (Oct.), 224; typical patrols of (Oct.), 224-5; its patrol at the outpost "Plonk", 236-7; its attempt to garrison "Plonk", 238; final Tobruk patrol of, 240-1. *2/23 Battalion*, holding the western sector, 116; raids Italian positions, 120, 121-4, 231-2; in the Salient Battle, 128-9, 140-1; its news-sheet, 176; its officers' mess dinner at Tobruk, 180; attacks on northern flank of Salient (May 17), 186-94, 197; casualties, 192; patrol incident with donkey, 226; defends outpost "Jim", 234-5; erects pole O.P. in Salient, 244; *2/24 Battalion*, 208; in the western sector (Apr.), 116, 117; in the Battle of the Salient, 128-9, 130-1, 137, 140, 142, 144, 145; casu-

INDEX

Australian Imperial Force—*continued*
alties, 147; its news-sheet, 176, withdraws for reorganization, 183, 184; strengthening the defences on the Salient (Aug.-Sept.), 203-4; casualties, 204; in a mine-pirating sortie, 223; raiding operations by (July), 229-30; bringing ammunition from outside the perimeter, 244. *2/28 Battalion*, before the Easter Battle 92; attacks German positions in the Salient (Aug. 3), 198, 199, 201-3; casualties, 202; raids "White Knoll" (July 17-18), 231; raids "White Cairn" (Sept. 13-14), 235; mans the outpost "Jack", 236. *2/32 Battalion*, arrives in Tobruk (May 4), 88, 184; part in attack on Salient (Aug. 3), 202; raids Italian strongpost (Sept. 13-14), 235. *2/43 Battalion*, 172, 244, 284*n*; attacks German positions in the Salient (Aug. 3), 198-201; casualties, 200; raids by (May 9-13), 220-1; final patrols by, 239-40. *2/48 Battalion*, 118, 123; before the siege, 77, 82; patrols by, on western sector (Apr. 15-16), 116, 117-18; casualties, 118; in the raid on Carrier Hill (Apr. 22), 120-1; casualties, 123*n*, 145*n*; minelaying by patrol of (May 30), 222; mans Bardia road sector, 233; its news-sheet, 176, 250
6TH DIVISIONAL CAVALRY REGIMENT, 9, 158; part played by carriers of, in the Tobruk assault, 26, 28, 50; in Western Desert (May), 158
ARTILLERY—*2/1 Field Regiment*, 9. *2/2 Field Regiment*, 9. *2/3 Field Regiment*, 9, 38, 49. *2/12 Field Regiment*, 242, 245, 284*n*. *3rd Anti-tank Regiment*, 76, 77, 91, 102, 284*n*. *16th Anti-tank Company*, 9, 283. *17th Anti-tank Company*, 9. *24th Anti-tank Company*, 129, 130, 284*n*. *26th Anti-tank Company*, 129, 131. *8th Light A.A. Battery*, 78, 248, 257, 284*n*. See also Bush Artillery.
ENGINEERS AND PIONEERS—*2/1 Pioneer Battalion*, used as infantry, 85*n*; in the Battle of the Salient, 140, 146; skirmish with enemy in the Salient, 154; on patrol, 234; leaves Tobruk, 284*n*. *2/1 Field Company*, 9; preparing for the assault on Tobruk, 11, 16; clears way for infantry and tanks, 18, 21. *2/2 Field Company*, 9. *2/4 Field Company*, 230, 283. *2/7 Field Company*, 284*n*. *2/8 Field Company*, 9. *2/13 Field Company*, its splendid work in the Salient, 195, 284*n*. *2/4 Field Park Company*, 261
MEDICAL UNITS—*4th General Hospital*, 171; *2/3 Field Ambulance*, 284*n*. *2/4 Field Ambulance*, 283; *2/8 Field Ambulance*, 78
ARMY SERVICE CORPS, personnel of, drafted to infantry battalions in Tobruk, 88-9, 197, 282
Australian Navy, bombards Axis forces, 115; running the gauntlet to Tobruk, 251, 256, 267-9

Babini, *Gen.*, 8
Baillieu, *Capt.* E., 244
Balfe, *Maj.* J. W., in the first German attack on Tobruk, 93, 95, 96, 97, 99, 100; quoted, 94, 94-5, 96-7, 106
Ballerstedt, *Maj.* (German officer), 205
Bamford, *Lieut.* H. O., 15
Bangalore torpedoes, 11, 16, 20, 199
Barberis, *Gen.* Umberto, 36
Barce (Map p. 75), 71, 73, 253; Australian withdrawal to, 74
Bardia (Maps pp. 75, 295), 3, 4, 253, 311, 315; A.I.F. capture of, 1, 2, 12, 25; Italian prisoners and weapons taken at, 48; occupied by Axis troops, 97; raided by British commandos, 115; almost retaken by British (June), 163; enemy positions astride road to, 220, 222, 231, 233, 243, 245, 291; in the Eighth Army's November offensive, 294, 298, 299, 304, 308, 309
"Bardia Bill", 245-6, 273, 283, 285, 287
Barnard, *Sgt* J. W., 122-3
Barnes, *Squadron-Leader* Peter Wykeham, 125
Battalions, Australian. See under Australian Imperial Force
Batten, *Sgt-Maj.* Reg., quoted, 101
Batty, *Sgt* L. W. C., 121
Bean, *Dr* C. E. W., 52, 176*n*; quoted, 109-10
Beaufighters, long-range, arrive in Egypt, 158
Beckingsale, *Lieut.* G., 11
Beda Fomm, 7*n*, 70; Italian prisoners and equipment taken at, 48
Beer, *Lieut.* H. R., 222
Bel Hamed (Maps pp. 295, 307), 305, 306, 308, 309
Bengazi (Map p. 75), harbour made untenable by Luftwaffe, 63, 67-8;

INDEX

Bengazi—*continued*
20th Brigade's withdrawal to, 69; Australian attempt to hold enemy at, 70; bombed by R.A.F., 155, 157; withdrawal from, 315n
Benina aerodrome, 68, 70, 72
Bennett, *Pte* L., 234
Bergonzoli, *Gen.*, 7
Berryman, *Col.* F. H., 51, 52; sketch of, 52-3
Bettsworth, *Sgt*, quoted, 133-4
Benzie, *Maj.* A. E., 104; quoted, 104
Bianca (Map p. 143), 142, 145, 146, 148
Billhardt (German war correspondent), 261, 262
Birch, *Maj.* H. R., 180
Bird, *Capt.* A. C., 139
Bir El Azazi, 236
Birks, Col. H. L., 138
Blamey, *Gen.* Sir Thomas, G.O.C. A.I.F., 35; urges evacuation of A.I.F. from Tobruk, 281-2
Blue Line, the, 86, 87, 88, 92, 101, 102, 111, 119, 141, 142, 145, 150, 172, 174, 183, 185
Bode, *Capt.* F. L., 228, 229
Bofors guns, 254, 257, 258, 262, 265
"Bomb Alley", 251, 253, 283
"Bondi" (outpost), 236, 237
Booby-traps, Italian, 11, 18; German, 195-6
Booker, *Pte* George, 228
Bowden, *Lieut.* J. N., 141, 188
Boyes anti-tank rifle, 29n
Braddock, *Capt.*, 146, 151
Breda guns, 257
Bren carriers, in the attack on Tobruk, 9, 26, 29, 31; tactics employed by, 50-1; use of, in offensive patrols, 220-1, 223, 224, 226-7
Brewer, Sam (war correspondent), 301
Brigades. See *under* Australian Imperial Force, British Army
British Air Force. See R.A.F.
British Army, in the first Libyan campaign and the withdrawal to Tobruk. See Army of the Nile, Cyrenaica Force; artillery units of, in Tobruk, 84, 88, 89, 91; harmony between A.I.F. and, in Tobruk, 89-90; diversionary attacks by, on the frontier (Apr.-May), 115, 127, 159; strength of frontier forces, 158-9; offensive action by, on the frontier, 159-60; in the attempt to relieve Tobruk (June), 161-4; Command slow to learn by costly mistakes, 164-5; the part played by its artillery at Tobruk, 250; formations and units at Tobruk, 319-20. See *also* Eighth Army, Western Desert Force
CORPS—*13th Corps*, 2, 3, 48-9, 53, 293, 302, 305. *30th Corps*, 293, 296n, 297, 302
DIVISIONS—*2nd Armoured Division*, in the withdrawal from Cyrenaica, 64, 70, 76, 80. *7th Armoured Division*, 3, 49; in the first Libyan offensive, 8, 47, 63; at Beda Fomm, 48n; in the frontier area, 80, 158; reinforced (June), 161; in the November offensive, 293-4, 296, 299, 301, 302, 304, 305; composition of, 296n; losses and reinforcements, 301-2. *70th Infantry Division*, 109; relieves 9th Australian Division in Tobruk, 240, 281, 284n, 293
SUPPORT GROUPS—*2nd Support Group*, 70, 71. *7th Support Group*, 80, 84, 93, 158, 296n, 297, 298
BRIGADES—*16th Infantry Brigade*, arrives in Tobruk (Sept.), 284. *3rd Armoured Brigade*, at El Agheila, 68, 69; withdraws with heavy losses, 70-1, 74, 76. *4th Armoured Brigade*, 161, 296n; in the November offensive, 296, 297, 298. *7th Armoured Brigade*, 161, 163, 296n; in the November offensive, 296, 297, 298. *22nd Armoured Brigade*, in the November offensive, 296, 296n, 297, 298, 299. *1st Army Tank Brigade*, 293. *32nd Army Tank Brigade*, 293. *22nd Guards Brigade*, 80, 84, 115, 293
INFANTRY UNITS—*Black Watch* (2nd Bn), 298. *Border Regiment* (4th Bn), 309. *Cheshire Regiment* (1st Bn), 9. *Essex Regiment* (1st Bn), at Ed Duda, 305, 306. *Queen's Regiment* (2nd Bn), 236. *Royal Northumberland Fusiliers* (1st Bn), 9, 26, 30, 42, 89, 129, 146, 187, 199; at Ed Duda, 305
ARMOURED UNITS—*3rd Hussars* (Light Tanks), 70. *11th Hussars* (Armoured Cars), 158; in the relief of Tobruk, 309. *1st R.T.R.*, in the first German assault on Tobruk, 94, 104; in the Battle of the Salient, 136. *4th R.T.R.*, in the battle for "Plonk" (Oct. 10-12), 236-9; in the November offensive, 298. *5th R.T.R.*, at El Agheila, 70. *6th*

INDEX

British Army—*continued*
R.T.R., at El Agheila, 70. *7th R.T.R.*, 9, 42, 120
ARTILLERY UNITS—*1st R.H.A.*, 9, 242, 243; in the Easter Battle, 94, 96, 101; in the Battle of the Salient, 151. *3rd R.H.A.* (Anti-tank), 9; in the capture of Tobruk, 26, 37; in the Battle of the Salient, 129, 133. *4th R.H.A.*, 9; "Jock" columns of, 159. *104th R.H.A.*, 9, 38, 39, 242, 245. *107th R.H.A.*, 242. *7th Medium Regiment*, 9. *64th Medium Regiment*, 9. *4th Durham Survey Regiment*, 245. See also Appendix I
British Navy, in the assault on Tobruk, 8, 9, 16, 19; destroys Axis convoys, 67, 155, 156-7, 290; taking troops and supplies to Greece, 67; bombards Axis forces, 115; running the gauntlet to Tobruk, 251, 255-6; its role in keeping up Tobruk supplies, 267-9; anti-aircraft rocket-projectors introduced by, 270; part played by, in the relief of the A.I.F. in Tobruk, 282, 284-5, 288-9
Brocksopp, *Lieut.* A. E., 118
Brown, *Col.* Arnold, 85n
Bryant, *Lieut.* D., quoted, 119
Bucknell, *Lieut.* E. R., 247
Buntine, *Maj.* M. A., 231
Burgess, *Sgt* Jim, 29
Burrows, *Lieut.-Col.* F. A., commanding 2/13 Bn., at Er Regima, 71; at Ed Duda, 306, 308
"Bush Artillery", 91, 92-3, 242, 247-8
"Butch" (German strongpoint), 291; falls to British, 298
Byron-Moore, *Lieut.* H. G., 226

Cairo Military Spokesman, 293, 301
Camouflage of British gun-positions and tanks, 243-4
Campbell, *Capt.* Don, 29, 36
Campbell, *Maj.* Ian, 14, 15-16
Campbell, *Lieut.-Col.* Jock, 159
Cann, *Lieut.* S. B., 11, 18
Canteen ships, unloading of, 175-6
Capuzzo (Maps pp. 158, 295), British attacks on, 115, 160; British seize, then withdraw from, 161, 163-4; in the November offensive, 294, 297, 298, 299, 308, 309
Carleton, *Cpl* Fred, 190
Carpathian Brigade, 283, 284, 293
Carrier Hill, 119, 120
Carriers. See Bren carriers
Casualties, few Australian, in attack on Tobruk, 46; Italian, in first Libyan campaign, 48; Axis and Allied, in the Salient Battle, 154, 155; Axis, in the first three weeks of the siege, 155; A.I.F., in Tobruk, the Middle East and New Guinea, up to Jan. 1943, 321. See also under Formations and Units
Catchlove, *Capt.* W. E. L., 239
Cavalry tactics (6th Australian Division) in the Tobruk assault, 50-1
Cawthorne, *Sgt* C. H., 198
Challen, *Capt.* Hugh, 29, 35
Charlton, *Sgt* Tom, 199
Cheteita, Fort (Map p. 33), 47
Chilton, *Lieut.-Col.* F. O., 25, 26
Christie, *Lieut.* J. S., 141
Churchill, *Maj.* Randolph, 301
Churchill, *Rt Hon.* Winston, his signal to Wavell in Dec. 1940, 1, 2; congratulates Morshead on defence of Tobruk, 153; quoted, 300
Cigarettes, supply of, in Tobruk, 175, 210, 252
Clark, *Pte* H. P., 190-1
Comforts Fund, services of, in Tobruk, 175
Company, composition of infantry rifle (A.I.F.), 183
Concerts in Tobruk, 177-8
Coningham, *Air Vice-Marshal* Arthur, 293, 294
Conkey, *Capt.* H. S., 39
Conway, *Capt.* R. A. E., 201, 202
Cook, *Col.* T. P., 80
Cook, *Lieut.* F. W., 150
"Cooma" (outpost), 239
Coombes, *Capt.* C. J. A., 29, 35
Cooper, *Maj.* E. L., 171
Coppock, *Lieut.* H. T., 201-2
Correspondents, war, attitude of Army to, 34
Counter-battery staff, 13, 245n, 246, 273, 283
Coxon, *Pte* H., 188
Crawford, *Lieut.-Col.* J. W., 99, 103, 238; quoted, 104
Crete, significance of campaign in, 312
Crete-Derna air ferry (Axis), 290
Cricket in Tobruk, 179-80
Crummey, *Lance-Cpl* W., 122
Crusader tanks, 296n
Cunningham, *Admiral Sir* Andrew, 1, 67, 80, 156, 255
Cunningham, *Lieut.-Gen. Sir* Alan, commands Eighth Army, 292, 304; his supply problem, 292; forces at his disposal, 293; his plan of attack, 293-4; his tank tactics, 300

INDEX 337

"Cyrcom" (Cyrenaica Command H.Q.), 69, 96; failure to appreciate enemy strength and intentions (Mar.-Apr.), 66, 68, 70-1; ignorance of battle situation (Apr. 5), 74; Lavarack takes command of, 81; transferred to Maaten Baguish, 108

Cyrenaica Force, impossibility of its holding Cyrenaica, 63-5 (Mar.-Apr.); its inferiority in armour, 64-5, 68, 69; begins withdrawal (Mar. 15), 69; defending the Er Regima escarpment, 69-70, 71-3; driven from El Agheila, 70; withdraws to Mechili and Derna, 71; withdraws to Barce, 74; withdraws from Mechili, 76-7; withdraws from Martuba, 78; withdraws to Gazala and Acroma, 79; its retreat covered by R.A.F. and R.A.A.F., 79-80; withdrawal to Tobruk and decision to stand, 80-3. *See also* Tobruk, A.I.F.

Daniells, *Pte* R. G., 117, 121
Davey, *Lieut.* W. A., 11
Dawson, *Lieut.* B., 11
Decorations, A.I.F., 322-5
Decoy, H.M.S., 251, 252, 254
Defender, H.M.S., 251, 269
Delfs, Pte W. G., 202
Della Mura, *Gen.*, 7, 31, 32
Derna (Map p. 75), 3, 8, 53, 54; Allied withdrawal through, 71, 77, 78; Germans advance through, 74, 82, 92; road sector, 231, 233, 239, 243, 291; ammunition dumps at, 244
Desert warfare, factors governing, 64
Destroyer-ferry from Alexandria to Tobruk, 251-6, 267, 269-70
Diggers, behaviour of, in taking Tobruk, 54-5; their attitude to the war, 61; unity of, with Tommies at Tobruk, 89-90, 175, 181; their spirit in Tobruk, 168, 174, 181-2; German impressions of, 205
Dill, *Gen. Sir* John, 69, 80
Divisions. *See under* nationality
Dodds, *Maj.* N. G., 288
Donkin, *Pte* Ted, 178, 227
Dougherty, *Lieut.-Col.* I. N., 38, 39; quoted, 39-40
Duststorms, delay British assault on Tobruk (Jan.), 3; delay German attack on Tobruk (Apr.), 80, 84, 92; in the Salient Battle, 131, 142, 145, 146; effect of, on troops in Tobruk, 169; used to cover preparations for attack, 220
Dysentery in Tobruk, 169

Easter Battle, the, 91-108
Eastern sector (Tobruk), enemy threat to, 220, 236
Eather, *Lieut.-Col.* K. W., 22
Ed Duda (Map p. 295), during the relief of Tobruk (Nov.), 291, 294, 297, 298, 305, 306, 308, 309, 315
Eden, *Hon.* Anthony, 80
Edmondson, *Cpl* Jack, first V.C. in 2nd A.I.F., 98-9
Eighth Army, 289, 291; growing strength of, 166, 232; Western Desert Force becomes, 292; organization and supplies of, 292-3; composition of, 293; planned movements of, 293-4; in the November offensive and the relief of Tobruk, 294-309
El Adem (Maps pp. 75, 99), 6, 9, 10, 80, 84, 242, 243; crossroads, 19th Brigade's thrust to, 10, 15, 31; prisoners' cage near, 35; Allied reserves at, 86; German drive towards (Apr. 15), 100, 101; enemy positions astride road to, 222, 223, 230, 246, 291; the escarpment near, 246, 305; in the November offensive, 306, 308, 309
El Agheila (Map p. 75), 63, 64, 66, 68, 69, 70; British driven from (Mar. 24), 70
El Alamein, 64, 289, 312; A.I.F. casualties at, 321
Eland, *Pte* S., 73
El Gobi (Map p. 295), 292, 294, 296, 297, 309; recaptured by British, 309
Ellenby, *Lieut.* M. R., 227-8
England, *Lieut.-Col.* V. T., 20, 42
Er Regima (Map p. 75), 69, 70, 71; Australians holding escarpment at, 71-3; withdrawal from, 73-4
Evans, *Lieut.-Col.* Bernard, 189, 191-2

Fallon, *Pte* Mick, 228
Fascism, and the Italian attitude to war, 60-1
Fearnside, *Cpl* G. H., 82
Fenton, *Maj.* George, 178*n*
Field, *Lieut.-Col.* John, 186, 231
"Fig Tree", hill inside perimeter, 185; enemy strongpost at Bir El Carmusa, 227
Finlay, *Lieut.* J. T., 229, 230
Flame-throwers, use of, by Germans, 139*n*

INDEX

"Flash-to-bang" method in calculating enemy artillery's range, 245
"Flash-spotting", in fixing enemy gun positions, 13, 245
Fleet Air Arm, at Taranto, 1; bombs Tripoli (Apr.), 67; sinks Axis ships between Sicily and Tripoli, 156-7
Fleming, *Capt.* E. W., 150
Fleming, *Lieut.* Allan, 36; quoted, 36, 37, 38
Food in Tobruk, 169-70, 180, 210-11; delivered by destroyer-ferry, 252, 267
Football in Tobruk, 179
Forbes, *Capt.* W., 120-1, 145
Forbes Mound (Map p. 143), 145
France, *Cpl* W. L., 231
Francis, *Cpl* A. A., 139
French marines (Free), 47
Freyberg, *Maj.-Gen.* B. C., commands 2nd N.Z. Division, 299
Furnell, *Col.* H. G., 113*n*
"Furphy Flyer", 176

Gabr Saleh (Map p. 295), 304, 305
Gahan, *Capt.* S. M., 189*n*
Gambier-Parry, *Maj.-Gen.* M. D., commands 2nd Armoured Division at El Agheila, 70, 71; his view of Rommel's intentions, 71; at Mechili, 76; taken prisoner, 77, 82
Gambling banned in Tobruk, 112
Gambut (Map p. 295), aerodrome at, 3; in the November offensive, 292, 294, 296, 299, 305, 309
Gard, *Father*, 200
Gardiner, *Lieut.* G., 189
Gardner, *Capt.* Philip, 42
Garnsey, *Lieut.* R. C., 225
Gazala (Map 295), withdrawal of 9th Division to, 74, 79; in the November offensive, 291, 308, 309
Gebel Akdar, 71
Gebhardt, *Capt.* Peter, quoted, 131
Geikie, *Lieut.* W. B. A., 99
General Stuart tanks, 296, 296*n*
German Air Force. *See* Luftwaffe
German Army (Afrika Korps), inevitability of success in Cyrenaica drive, 63-5; its advantage in armour, 64-5, 90; constitution of its forces (March), 65; training of, in Germany, 66; brought to Libya, 67; drives British from El Agheila, 70; takes Er Regima, 72-4; takes Mechili, 76-7; British and Australian prisoners taken by, 77-8; closes in on Tobruk, 78-80; members of, taken prisoner in Tobruk, 88, 107, 151, 186; in the first attack on Tobruk, 93-108; takes, loses and retakes Sollum and Halfaya, 115, 127; preparing for the second assault on Tobruk, 115-16, 124-5, 127; reaction of, to desert warfare, 116-17, 166; attitude of to Australian and British troops (May 3-4), 151-2; difficulty of reinforcing and supplying, 156, 166; drops leaflets in Tobruk, 167; its stronger position in the Salient, 183-4; strengthening the Salient defences (May), 193; its casualties in the A.I.F. attack of Aug. 3, 201; strength of, in the Salient sector, 206; strength of, outside Tobruk (Sept.), 232, (Nov.), 290-2; reinforcements to (Aug.-Oct.), 290; number of tanks in Panzer Divisions of, 290; defences of, around Tobruk, 291-2; in the Nov.-Dec. battle with the Eighth Army, 294-309; prisoners from, taken by the Eighth Army, 298. *See also* Afrika Korps

DIVISIONS—*15th Armoured Division*, 65, 116, 120, 291; in the British November offensive, 296, 306. *21st Armoured Division*, 65, 232, 291; in the British November offensive, 296, 204. *5th Light Motorized Division*, 65, 97. *90th Light Division*, 206, 232, 290
ZBV GROUP, 290, 291
INFANTRY—*115th Motorized Infantry Regiment*, 201, 205, 206. *104th Motorized Infantry Regiment*, 201, 206. *2nd Machine-gun Battalion*, 129. *8th Machine-gun Battalion*, 99, 102-3, 107, 116
ARTILLERY AND ENGINEERS—*115th Artillery Regiment*, 206. *33rd Panzer Pioneers (33rd Engineer Battalion)*, 129, 133, 134, 206
TANKS—*5th Tank Regiment*, 115, 130*n*, 157, 206; in the first assault on Tobruk, 97, 100, 101; in the Battle of the Salient, 140, 147, 148; on the frontier, 162, 163, 164. *8th Tank Regiment*, 115-16, 147, 162

G.H.Q., Cairo, Rommel's intentions not appreciated at (Mar.), 66-8; and the decision to defend Tobruk, 80-1; Cyrcom's message to, before Easter Battle, 96; intercepts signal to Rommel, 154; admits heavy British tank losses on frontier, 163; sceptical of German use of 88-mm. guns in anti-tank role, 164-5; fails

INDEX

G.H.Q., Cairo—*continued*
  to heed Tobruk's request not to send in ships by day, 264; its exaggerated estimate of German losses in the November battle, 301
Giarabub, 9, 294; British feign attack from oasis at, 292, 294
Gilmour, *Lieut.* P. R., 11
Glennie, Reg. (war correspondent), 45, 251
Gliders used to transport Axis supplies, 158, 290
Godfrey, *Brig.* A. H. L., quoted, 62; commands 24th Brigade, 198; takes command of Salient sector before August attack, 198; sketch of, 198*n*; organizes offensive patrols in eastern sector (May), 220, 221
Goering, *Marshal*, 275
Gorman, *Maj.* Eugene, 175
Gott, *Brig.* W. E. H., 80; commands 7th Support Group at El Adem, 80, 84; in the withdrawal to the frontier, 93, 97; delays German drive in Egypt, 115; his use of mobile detachments in the attempt to relieve pressure on Tobruk, 159
Graham, *Capt.* H. T., 308
Graziani, *Marshal* Rodolfo, 3, 53
Great Sand Sea, 64
Greece, men and equipment sent to, 63; effect of expedition to, on Libyan campaign, 63-4; expulsion of British and Australian troops from, 127; object of German campaign in, 312; A.I.F. casualties in, 321
Green, *Lieut.* Arnold, 57
Green Line (Tobruk defences), 174
Grubb, *Cpl* R. W., 177
"Grubb's Gazette", 176-7
Gunners. *See* Artillery

Halfaya Pass (Maps pp. 159, 295), taken by Germans (Apr. 13), 115; retaken by British (Apr. 15), 115; recaptured by Axis (Apr. 26), 127, 159; retaken by British (May 15-17), 160; retaken by Germans and held (May 27), 160, 163; German defences from, to Sidi Omar, 165-6, 291, 298, 302
Hand-grenades, British, 30*n*; use of, in dealing with tank crews, 35; in the Salient Battle, 150
Handley, *Capt.* E. A., 72-3
Harbour, Battle for the (at Tobruk), first phase (to June 3), 265; second phase (June 3-Aug. 3), 265-70; third phase (Aug. 3-Sept. 1), 270-2. *See also* Tobruk, Anti-aircraft batteries
Harding, *Brig.* G., 81
Hassett, *Capt.* F. G., 15
Haupt, *Lieut.* F. K., 184
Havock, H.M.S., 252, 254
Hayes, *Pte* C., 234
Hayman, *Lieut.* P. S., 229, 230
Hayman, *Maj.* Gordon, 40
Head, *Lieut.* J. M., 201
Hennessy, *Lieut.* E. C., 30, 44
Herring, *Brig.* E. F., in planning the assault on Tobruk, 12, 13-14, 16; sketch of, 13; as an artillery commander, 49, 50; succeeds to command of 6th Division, 49; his subsequent career, 49
Hetherington, John (war correspondent), 45
Hewitt, *Cpl* G. V., 132
Hill 209 (Maps pp. 135, 143), 118, 119, 120, 127, 129, 132, 133, 193, 197, 246; captured by the enemy (May 1), 140, 141, 152; A.I.F. attempt to retake, 141, 142, 145, 149; advantages to enemy of holding, 183, 193, 242; retaken by Allied forces (Dec. 10), 310
Hitler, Adolf, regards North Africa as subsidiary front, 155, 156, 263; his strategy in 1940-1, 311-12
Hobson, *Sgt* R. W., 150*n*
Hodge, *Capt.* J. H., 25
Honours and awards, A.I.F., 322-5
Hospitals in Tobruk, Axis bombing of, 171-2
Hutchinson, *Lieut.* J. A., 122-3; quoted, 122

"I" tanks, description of, 3*n*; role of, in assault on Tobruk, 9, 50; in action, 21-4, 37, 42; reinforcements arrive at Tobruk, 115, 174, 236; used in "penny packets" (May 1), 138; vulnerable to German 50-mm. and 88-mm. guns, 161, 163-4; their role in the battle for "Plonk", 236-9
Indian Army, its forces in Tobruk, 88; in the frontier area (May), 159; Labour Company of, 288
FORMATIONS AND UNITS—*4th Indian Division*, 49, 161, 293, 294; *3rd Indian Motor Brigade*, 76. *29th Indian Brigade Group*, 293. *18th Indian Cavalry Regiment* (dismounted), at Mechili, 76; in Tobruk, 85*n*, 88, 106, 233; withdrawn from Tobruk, 283

340 INDEX

Infantry, part played by, in capture of Tobruk, 51; shortage of, in Tobruk, 84; relative strength of Australian and Italian divisions, 232. *See under names of armies*

Intelligence, warns of large German forces in Tripoli and Tunisia (Mar.), 66; uses information gathered by Tobruk patrols, 226

Isaksson, *Lieut*. O. H., 117

Italian Air Force, after the capture of Bardia, 8; personnel of, used in bombing Tobruk, 263, 264, 275

Italian Army, strength of, in Cyrenaica, after the fall of Bardia and Sidi Barrani, 3, 7-8; resistance of, in the Allied assault on Tobruk, 22-4, 26, 28-9, 30, 31, 32, 34, 35-8, 39, 40, 41-2; prisoners from, at Tobruk, 27, 30, 34-5, 39-40, 41, 42, 43-4, 47, 48, at Bardia, 48, at Beda Fomm, 48, at Sidi Barrani, 48; destruction of ammunition etc. by, in Tobruk, 40, 41, 43, 45, 46-7, 57; surrender of, at Tobruk, 44-5, 46-7; reasons for quick collapse of, 46; losses of, at Tobruk, 48; its stores of food and wine in Tobruk, 58; way of life in desert warfare, 59-60; attitude to war, compared with British and Australian, 60-1; in Rommel's army, 65; left by Rommel to maintain pressure on Tobruk, 116-24; prisoners taken during the siege, 117, 118, 121, 123-4, 185; in the battle of the Salient, 140, 141, 151, 155; routed on the Salient sector (May 15-16), 184, 185; working on defences in southeastern sector, 223-4; its positions raided by Australian patrols, 224-5, 227, 229-32, 235; strength of infantry divisions of, 232; forces outside Tobruk, 232; reluctant patrol activities of, 233-5; nervousness of, 227, 232, 233, 234; its part in Nov.-Dec. operations, 291, 292, 296, 299, 309

FORMATIONS AND UNITS—*Tenth Army*, 1. *132nd Ariete Armoured Division*, 65; outside Tobruk, 97, 140, 222, 232; at El Gobi, 292, 296, 309. *27th Brescia Division*, 232. *25th Bologna Division*, 232. *17th Pavia Division*, 232. *55th Savona Division*, 291. *60th Infantry Division*, 8. *61st Division*, 7. *62nd Trento Regiment*, 118

Italian Navy, at Taranto, 1; in the Allied assault on Tobruk, 8, 41; its personnel at Tobruk, 45, 47, 48

Jacobs, *Sgt* Roy, 188
"Jack" (outpost), 235, 236
James, *Lieut*. R. W., 122
Jeanes, *Capt*. M. R., 221
Jeffrey, *Squadron-Leader* Peter, 79
Jenkins, *Lieut*. Claude, 117
Jess, *Lieut*. Carl, 188, 189n
"Jim" (outpost), 234
"Jimmy" (JU88), 266
"Jock" columns, 159, 305, 306, 309
Johnston, *Sgt* E. J., 11
Johnstone, *Capt*. J. A., 235
Joshua, *Capt*. R., 235-6
"Jumping-jack" mines, 195

Kelly, *Sgt* R. L. F., 77
Keren, 161
Key, *Maj*. A. S., 36
Khamsin, the, 84
Kimber, *Lieut*. D. G., quoted, 121, 123
Kingston, H.M.S., 252
Klein, *Lieut.-Col*. B. E., 245, 246
Knights, *Capt*. R. W., 15

Ladybird, H.M.S., 262
Latona, H.M.S., 289
Lavarack, *Maj.-Gen*. J. D., commands 7th Australian Division, 80; arrives with Wavell in Tobruk, 80; given command in Cyrenaica, 81; organizes stand at Tobruk, 82; gives Morshead command of Tobruk perimeter, 84; his decision to hold the old Italian perimeter, 85; directing the defence of Tobruk (Apr. 11-12), 95; his Order of the Day after the Easter Battle, 108; leaves Tobruk, 108; Wavell sends congratulations to, 108; commands 1st Australian Corps in Syria, 108, 282
Leaflets, German, to the Tobruk garrison, 96, 167; British, to Italians outside Tobruk, 118
Leakey, *Capt*. Ray, 234, 235
Legg, *Sgt* F. H., quoted, 82
Libyan Labour Battalion, 320
Lighters, auxiliary, unloading of, 267, 275-6; ferrying of tanks and guns to Tobruk by, 276
Liguria, s.s., 41, 275
"Lion" (strongpost), 291
Lloyd, *Col*. C. E. M., 69, 81, 149, 154; "G.1" to Morshead, 113; sketch of, 113-14

INDEX

Lloyd, *Lieut.-Col.* J. E., 202
Long, Gavin (war correspondent), 45
Long, *Sgt* L. M., 42
Longmore, *Air Chief Marshal Sir* Arthur, 80
Looting of canteen cargoes and food dumps in Tobruk, 175-6
Louch, *Lieut.-Col.* T. S., 28
Loughrey, *Maj.* J., 144
Lovett, *Capt.* B. M., 150
Loxton, *Capt.* F. E. C., 150
Luftwaffe, bombs Bengazi harbour, 63, 67-8; strength of, in Libya (Mar.), 65, 67, 68; checked by R.A.A.F. during Allied withdrawal from Cyrenaica (Apr.), 79; during the Easter Battle, 96, 106; attacks Tobruk harbour, 119-20, 126, 254-5, 256, 257-8, 260, 262-3, 265, 269, 270; rules the air over Tobruk, 125-6, 142; losses of, over Tobruk, 126, 155, 260, 262, 263, 265, 274, 275; in the Battle of the Salient, 128, 133, 139, 146; petrol shortage prevents more extensive bombing by, 157-8; and the Axis air ferry from Crete and Derna, 158; reconnaissance by, 243, 254; moonlight attacks by, 251, 269-70; attacks ships bringing supplies to Tobruk, 251, 254-6, 263-4, 267-8, 269-70; its unsuccessful attempts to silence the garrison's anti-aircraft guns, 256-64, 270-2; abandons daylight dive-bombing of harbour and town, 257; number of its aircraft engaged over Tobruk, 257, 273, 274; results of attacks by, 263-4, 275; attempts to impose air blockade on Tobruk, 265-78; decrease in dive-bombing attacks by (June 3-Aug. 3), 265; daylight attacks by, 265-6; high-level bombing by (June-Aug.), 265-7, 270-2; tricks adopted by pilots of, to elude A.A., 266; dive-bombing tactics of, 266; tactics of, in August and September, 270-1; renewal of dive-bombing by (Aug. 3), 270-2; minelaying by, 270, 273; bombing attacks of, mostly at night (Sept.), 272-3; number of raids by, 274, 277; during the withdrawal of the A.I.F., 285, 286, 287-8, 289; strength of in November, 293

Maaten Baguish, 108
Macarthur-Onslow, *Maj.* Denzil, 9, 10, 45; his cavalry tactics in the assault on Tobruk, 50-1

McBain, *Pte* R. A., 20
McCarter, *Capt.* L., 199, 200
McCarthy, *Capt.* J., 39
McDonald, *Maj.* H. H., 29, 35
Macdonald, *Lieut.* J. E., 21
McDonald, *Capt.* R. W. F., 21
McDougal, *Warrant-Officer* Bruce, 42
McElroy, *Sgt* R. M., 103
Macfarlane, W. T., 246, 277
McGinty, *Pte* D. M., 24
McHenry, *Lieut.* S. C., 202
Mackay, *Maj.-Gen.* Iven G., commands 6th Australian Division, 8; his part in planning the attack on Tobruk, 8, 9, 10, 11, 14, 15, 17, 44, 48, 51, 53, 116; becomes C.-in-C. Home Forces in Australia, 49; sketch of, 52; his staff officers, 52-3
Mackell, *Lieut.* Austin, 97-9, 100; quoted, 98
Maclarn, *Lieut.* L. C., 223, 234
McLeish, *Cpl* Bob, quoted, 134
McMaster, *Capt.* I. F., 237
McMaster, *Lieut.* N. E., 231, 232
McMillan, Dick (war correspondent), 35
Mail in Tobruk, distributed during battle at 16th Brigade H.Q., 28; brought by destroyers, 252; handling of, 174-5
Malloch, *Capt.* Ian, 140, 188
Manella, *Gen.* Petasso, 7, 40
Mann, *Col.* J., 113*n*
Marco Polo, s.s., 41, 275
Maria Giovanna, 276
Marlan, *Lieut.-Col.* R. F., 78
Martin, *Lieut.* J. B., 246, 247*n*
Martuba, 77, 78
Matildas. *See* "I" tanks
Mechili (Map p. 75), 8, 69, 70, 80; taken by Germans, 74, 76-7; Germans continue thrust from, 82
Mersa Brega, 70
Mersa Matruh, 5, 80, 81, 158, 253, 312; coastal railway extended from, 292
"Mickey", (JU 88), 266
Mills bomb, 29*n*
Mills, *Sgt* G. 44
Mills, *Lieut.* Tom, 41, 51
Minefields, Italian, around Tobruk, 11, 20; laid by garrison around Tobruk, 85, 86, 119, 196-7, 222; inadequacy of, 91-2, 119; delousing of, by enemy (Apr. 30), 129; sowed by Germans on the Salient front, 195-7; delousing of German, by Australians, 195-6; German method

INDEX

Minefields—*continued*
  of laying, 196; laid by enemy south of the perimeter, 223; pirated by A.I.F. patrols, 223
Mines laid in Tobruk harbour by enemy aircraft, 270, 273
"Minnie" (JU88), 266
Mitchell, *Lieut.-Col.* J. W., 29, 36, 37
Morphett, *Lieut.* H. C., quoted, 144
Morrison, *Sgt-Maj.* W. G., 189, 190, 191-2
Morshead, *Maj.-Gen. Sir* Leslie James, at the capture of Tobruk, 45; commanding the newly-formed 9th Division, 68; his men incompletely trained and equipped, 68; advises withdrawal from El Agheila, 69; anticipates German drive to Mechili, 70; advises withdrawal to Gazala, 74; his conference with Wavell and the decision to hold Tobruk, 81; given command of Tobruk perimeter, 84, 85; organizing the defences of Tobruk, 85; his determination to hold Tobruk, 87; Wavell's Easter message to, 97; directing the defence in the first German attack on Tobruk, 104; sketch of, 109-12; his character, 110-13; quoted, 111, 123, 230-1; given complete command of Tobruk Fortress, 113; his staff officers, 113-14; orders laying of minefield inside the perimeter, 119; in the Battle of the Salient (May), 130*n*, 132, 141-2, 145, 148, 149, 150; his tank tactics, 133, 136, 138-9, 148; receives congratulations from Wavell and Churchill, 153, 250; and the intercepted German message reprimanding Rommel, 154-5; ordered to attack on May 15, 160; his methods of keeping up morale, 174; his difficulties in holding the Salient sector, 183-4; orders shortening of Salient front (May), 184; (June), 193; his orders regarding 2/23 Bn attack (May 17), 187, 192; the objects of his strategy, 197, 218; plans attack to remove German wedge on western flank, 197-8; planning offensive patrols, 222; directing the battle for "Plonk", 236, 238; organizing the withdrawal of the A.I.F. from Tobruk, 282, 288; unveiling the memorial at Tobruk, 315
Mortars, mounted on carriers, 26; range of British, Italian and German, 204; garrison's tactics in dealing with German, 204
Msus (Map p. 75), 70-1, 76
"Mud and Blood", 176
Munro, *Lieut.-Col.* E. E., 76, 77
Murray, *Brig.* John, commands 20th Brigade, 68, 93, 193; sketch of, 68-9; his advice to Morshead, 149, 238; his V for Victory campaign, 232-3
Mussolini, 1, 2, 48, 311; his glamorizing of war, 60; his exaggeration of Allied forces to justify defeat, 60
"My Friends Who Stayed at Home", 211-12

Napier, H.M.A.S., 269
Nash, *Sgt* V. E., 11
Nationblatt (Berlin), 261
Neame, *Lieut.-Gen. Sir* Philip, commands all British forces in Cyrenaica, 66; his failure to appreciate German strength, 66, 69, 70; orders holding of Barce escarpment (Apr. 6), 74; taken prisoner, 77-8, 80
Nervous disorders in Tobruk, 170-1
Nestor, H.M.A.S., 269
Neuendorf, *Lieut.* Trevor, 188
Neumann-Silkow, *Maj.-Gen.*, 155
New Guinea, A.I.F. casualties in, 321
News-sheets in Tobruk, 176-7
New Zealand Army, role of, in the relief of Tobruk (Nov.), 294, 298, 299, 304-6, 308-9
  FORMATIONS AND UNITS—*2nd Division*, 293, 294, 298, 299. *4th Brigade*, 299. *5th Brigade*, 308. *6th Brigade*, 299, 308. *19th Battalion*, 305
Ninth Army, 282
Nizam, H.M.A.S., 269
Noble, *Sgt-Maj.* E. A., 142, 144; quoted, 142-4
No-man's-land, in the Salient sector, 184; recovering casualties in (Aug. 3), 200; Tobruk garrison's control of, 218-19, 232; patrols in, 219-33; Axis activities in, 233-40; enemy gains greater control of, 240-1
Norman, *Capt.* C. H. B., 130*n*
North Point, 262, 263
Noton, *Lieut.-Col.* A. L., 113*n*
Noyes, *Lieut.* W. H., 150; quoted, 150

Oakley, *Capt.* A. W., quoted, 203-4
O'Brien, *Maj.* George, 13
Observation posts, in no-man's-land, 220; poles used as, 244
O'Carroll, *Lieut.-Col.* W. C. L., 236

INDEX

O'Connor, *Lieut.-Gen.* Richard, commands 13th Corps, 2, 53; before the Tobruk assault, 2-3, 8; the constitution of his 13th Corps, 48-9; and the Allied withdrawal in Cyrenaica, 71, 74; taken prisoner, 77-8, 80

Ogle, *Lieut.-Col.* R. W., 228, 229

O'Shaughnessy, *Maj.* C. J., 278-9, 287

Outposts, A.I.F., pass to enemy in south and south-east sectors, 240. *See also* Posts

Palestine, troops from, 320; A.I.F. casualties in, 321

Palmer, *Lieut.* Alfred, 276

Panzer Divisions, 290. *See also* German Army

Parer, Damien (war photographer), 27, 302

Parramatta, H.M.A.S., 267-8

Pass of Balmaha, s.s., 267-8, 269

Paterson, *Pte* H. B., quoted, 173, 179-80

Patrick, *Sgt* R. A., 228-9; quoted, 229

Patrols, object and effect of A.I.F., 218-19, 232; types of, 219; reconnaissance, 219, 220, 225-6; offensive, 222-33; use of Bren carriers in, 220-1, 223, 224, 226-7; equipment and preparation for, 226

Peirse, *Lieut.-Gen.* N. M. Beresford, commands Western Desert Force, 108, 158; strength of his forces in May, 158-9; commands attack on frontier (May), 159-60; in the second British attempt to relieve Tobruk (June), 162

Perry, *Maj.* W. H., 188-9, 190; quoted, 189

Petrol, shortage of, in Tobruk, 267; supplies of, supplemented, 267-9

Pilastrino (Map p. 33), 28, 31, 86, 242, 248; the fort at, 28, 31; A.I.F. drive to, 32, 35, 37, 42; garrison destroys fort at, 243

Pinkney, *Lieut.* E. M., 224

"Pirie Street", 142, 144

Pitman, *Lieut.* C. G., 99

Platoons, composition of A.I.F., 199

"Plonk" (outpost), the tank battle for, 236-9

Pohnhardt, *Col.*, 116

Polish forces, in North Africa, 80, 159; replace 18th Brigade in Tobruk, 280-1, 283-4, 293; in Palestine, 284; regain part of Salient (Dec. 9-10), 309, 310; strength of, in Tobruk, 320

Pope, *Pte* Keith, 200

Posts, defensive around Tobruk, 6-7; captured by A.I.F. in the Tobruk assault, 11, 18, 19, 20, 21, 22, 24, 25, 26, 27, 42; southern, unsuccessfully attacked by enemy in Easter Battle, 97, 99, 100, 103, 106; naming of, north and south of Hill 209, 128; enemy infiltration behind western (Apr. 30), 129; captured and held by enemy in the Battle of the Salient, 130, 133-4, 136, 137, 139, 140, 141, 142, 149, 150, 151; counter-attacked by 2/48 Bn (May 1-2), 141-5; counter-attacked by 18th Brigade (May 3-4), 149-51; effect on garrison of those lost in western sector, 183-4; further German attacks on western (May 15-16), 185-6; counter-attacked by 2/23 Bn (May 17), 186-94; 24th Brigade's counter-attack on (Aug.), 198-203; held by enemy in the Salient, defences of, 206

Pratt, *Lieut.* L. J., 221

Prisoners, Australian, taken in the Salient Battle, 130; Axis, in Tobruk, 88, 155; German, taken by garrison, 106, 107, 151, 186; Italian, taken in the Allied assault on Tobruk, 27, 30, 34-5, 39-40, 41, 42, 43-4, 47, 48; taken at Bardia, Beda Fomm and Sidi Barrani, 48; captured during Axis attacks on Tobruk, 117, 118, 121, 123-4

Pulver, *Col.* B. W., 113*n*

Qattara Depression, 64

Quinn, *Sgt* R. B., 199, 200

R.A.A.F., No. 3 Squadron, covering the Allied withdrawal in Cyrenaica, 68, 70, 79

R.A.F., role of, in the Allied assault on Tobruk, 5, 8, 9, 16, 19, 31, 32, 34, 41, 49, 57; loses air superiority, 62, 63, 65, 68; on reconnaissance from Tobruk, 66, 93, 97, 126, 127; bombs Tripoli (Apr.), 67; in the Easter Battle, 96, 106; on reconnaissance and strafing enemy (Apr.), 124; its remaining fighters withdrawn from Tobruk (Apr. 26), 125; losses and weakness of (Apr.-May), 125-6; German planes brought down by, 126; sinks Axis ships between Sicily and Tripoli, 155, 156-7; raids Bengazi, 155, 157; bombs Axis ports and supply lines,

INDEX

R.A.F.—*continued*
157-8, 290-1; reinforced (June), 161; protecting the destroyer-ferry to Tobruk, 253; success against JU88s over Tobruk (Apr. 20), 263; tally of enemy aircraft destroyed by, at Tobruk, 263; covering the replacement of Australian by British and Polish troops in Tobruk, 284, 285; strength of its desert force (Nov.), 293; plans attacks to cover advance of Eighth Army (Nov.), 294; in the Eighth Army's offensive, 302, 309. *No. 73 Squadron*, 96, 125, 258; covering the Allied withdrawal in Cyrenaica, 79; number of enemy planes shot down by, 262, 274

R.A.N. *See* Australian Navy

R.N. *See* British Navy

Ras El Medauuar, 118

Rattray, *Capt.* Rupert, 121, 231; quoted, 122, 231-2

Reconnaissance, patrols, 219, 220, 225-6; importance of, in patrol work, 225, 226, 227-8; German advantage in aerial, 243

Red Line, the, 85, 86, 87, 88, 172, 173, 174, 183, 218

Regiments. *See under* A.I.F., British Army

Reid, *Lieut.* A. L., 185, 230

Reid, *Lieut.* G. T., 238, 239

Reilly, *Sgt* Bill, quoted, 277-8

R.H.A., 88, 89, 95, 100, 249. *See under* British Army

R.T.R. *See under* British Army

Rigg, *Sgt* Colin, 190

Ritchie, *Maj.-Gen.* N. M., 304

Robertson, *Brig.* H. C. H., commands 19th Brigade, 14; sketch of, 14-15; his plan for the attack on Tobruk, 15, 28; holds press conference at El Adem crossroads, 31; his plan to capture Tobruk garrison H.Q., 32-4; and the Australian entry into Tobruk, 44-5; receives surrender of Admiral, 45

Rocket-projectors, 270

Rolfe, *Capt.* C. B. N., 39

Rommel, *Lieut.-Gen.* Erwin, 8*n*; forces opposing him in Cyrenaica, 64; his career, 65-6; his forces in Tripoli (Mar.), 65; training the Afrika Korps in Germany, 66; his drive into Cyrenaica begins (Mar.), 67; armoured superiority of his forces, 70, 97; possible objectives of his desert drive, 71, 74, 92; before the attack on Tobruk, 92; gathers forces for a major assault on Tobruk (Apr. 13), 97; diverts forces from Tobruk to frontier to meet British attack, 115-16; preparing for an all-out attack on Tobruk, 116, 120, 124, 127; his forces outside Tobruk (Apr. 26), 127; in the Battle of the Salient, 132, 132-3, 147-8, 149, 152; his tank tactics, 132-3, 164; seriously checked by failure to take Tobruk on May 1-3, 152; his superiority in arms and aircraft (May), 152; reprimanded by German Supreme Command for Salient Battle losses (May 1-2), 154-5; his determination to take Tobruk, 155-6; receives few reinforcements, 156; his supply difficulties and petrol shortage, 157-8; strength of his forces (Apr.-May), 158; meeting British thrusts from the frontier (May-June), 159, 161-2; his frontier defences, 160, 165-6; his policy after June, 165; uses German troops in Salient area, 183; strengthens defences on the Salient front (May), 193, 197, 205-6; his advantage on the Salient, 205-6; strength of his forces holding the Salient, 206; garrison's offensive tactics tie up his forces at Tobruk, 218, 222, 232, 240; strengthens defences between El Adem and Bardia roads, 222, 223; strength of his forces holding Tobruk and on the frontier, 232; his growing control of no-man's-land, 240; his superiority in artillery, 246; his attempts to silence Tobruk's anti-aircraft guns, 256, 259, 262; bombs Tobruk harbour and water-supply, 260, 261; his losses in the air over Tobruk, 263, 275; his attempts to impose an air blockade on Tobruk, 265, 272, 273, 274, 275; and the replacement of Australian by Polish and British troops in Tobruk, 284, 289; his preparation for storming Tobruk, 290, 291, 292; strength of his forces in November, 290-2; his intention to attack Tobruk about Nov. 22, 293; surprised by Eighth Army's attack, 294; his tank tactics in the November battle with the Eighth Army, 296, 297, 298, 299, 300, 302, 304, 305, 309; his tank losses in the November battle, 301; forced to retreat, 309

INDEX

Rose, *Lieut.* G. H., 186
Rosel, *Lieut.* J. S., 140
Rowan, *Capt.* J. G., 47
Royal Navy. *See* British Navy
Rudkin, *Lieut.* R. S., 224
Rule, *Sgt* E. D., 92; quoted, 92-3
Russell, *Sgt* N. H., 230
Russia, German forces opposing (June), 156

Salient, the Battle of the, 128-53; first German thrust, 128-32; German tactics in reducing perimeter posts, 133-4; enemy tanks checked, 136-9; British tank casualties and tactics, 138; German advance checked on northern flank, 140-1; Allied counter-attack puts enemy on defensive, 141-7; Allied losses, 147; German tank losses, 147-8; second Allied counter-attack, 149-51; 18th Brigade's casualties, 151; the results of the battle, 152-3, 154-5; casualties (Allied and German), 155
Salient Sector, length of front to be held in, 183; strength required to hold, 183-4, 193; enemy's advantage in holding, 183-4, 205-6; offensive patrols by A.I.F. in (May 15-16), 184-6; counter-attack by A.I.F. on northern flank of, 186-94; ground regained by garrison in (May-June), 193-5; Germans build shorter defence line behind May 3 positions in, 194; attempt by 24th Brigade to remove German wedge in (Aug. 3), 198-203; strength of enemy defences in, 200-1, 203, 206; strengthening of Allied defences in (Aug.-Sept.), 203-4; Germans kept on defensive in the, 204-6; German forces holding, 206, 291; life of Diggers in the, 207-17
"Salient Sue", 246
Sandstorms. *See* Duststorms
Sangars, 34*n*
San Giorgio, 34, 41, 44
Savige, *Capt.* J. R., 47
Savige, *Brig.* S. G., 47-8, 66
Schorm, *Lieut.*, his diary quoted, 101, 105, 107, 124, 131, 141, 151, 152
Scobie, *Maj.-Gen.* R. M., succeeds Morshead in command at Tobruk, 109, 284*n*, 289, 306
Shave, *Capt.* L. K., 78, 240
Sheehan, *Capt.* W., 204
Sheldrick, *Lieut.* G. A., 189

Shipping, attacks on Axis, 156-7, 290; British, attacked by Luftwaffe, 251-2, 254-6, 257, 261, 263-4, 265, 267-9, 275
Siekmann, *Lieut.* D. C., 198, 199
Sidi Barrani (Map p. 75), 63, 161, 251, 253; British victory at, 1, 2, 311; Italian prisoners and equipment taken at, 48
Sidi Omar (Maps pp. 159, 295), 164, 294, 296, 302; German defences from Halfaya Pass to, 165-6, 291, 298
Sidi Resegh (Map p. 295), 159, 296, 297, 298, 299, 302, 305, 306, 308, 314
"Silent cops" in no-man's-land, 220; enemy attacks on, 234-5
Simmonds, *Sgt* Roy, 73
Sinclair, *Capt.* A. J. M., 171
Slater, *Brig.* J. N., commands A.A. defences in Tobruk, 257, 259, 260
Smith, *Sgt* N. J., 224
Solaro (Map p. 33), 32, 37, 38, 39
Sollum (Map p. 75), 2, 3, 283; threatened by Axis, 97; captured by Germans and retaken by British (Apr. 13-15), 115; recaptured by Axis (Apr. 26), 127, 159; retaken and lost again by British (May), 160
South African air squadrons, reinforce R.A.F., 161
South African Forces—*1st Division*, 293, 294, 296. *2nd Division*, 293. *1st Brigade*, 296, 308. *5th Brigade*, 297, 299
Spavin, *Pte* J. L., 121
Spender, *Rt* Hon. Percy, 36
Spiers, *Col.* N. L., 171*n*
Spiers, *Capt.* P. E., 190
Spowers, *Lieut.-Col.* Allan, 128, 129, 140, 203, 223; quoted, 129
Spreadborough, *Lance-Sgt.* H. J., 230
Steddy, *Lieut.* E. M., 186
Stockley, *Sgt* —, quoted, 138
Stokes, *Maj.* P. W., 248
Stone, *Sgt.* L. L., 21, 42
"Strong-boxes" in German frontier defences, 165-6
Strongposts, German, from the sea to the Salient and on to the El Adem road, 222; in south-eastern sector, 291. *See also* Posts
Stuart, H.M.A.S., 115, 256, 269
Summerman, *Maj.-Gen.*, of Afrika Korps, 155
Supplies, Allied problems regarding, before assault on Tobruk, 3-4; Axis difficulties in building up, 156-7,

Supplies—*continued*
166-7, 290-1; building up of British, in Egypt, 157-8; for Tobruk, destroyer-ferry maintains, 251-6, 267; for the Eighth Army, 292-3
Support Group, constitution of, 80*n*; 2nd, 70-1; 7th, 80, 93, 97, 158, 297-8
Syria, A.I.F. casualties in, 321

Tactics, Australian, in dealing with strongposts (Jan.), 22-5, 30; Australian cavalry, in the Tobruk assault, 50-1; factors governing, in desert warfare, 64; German tank, 100, 133-4, 164; Australian infantry, in meeting German tank attacks, 100, 103, 107-8; British and Australian tank (May 1-2), 138-9; German, in the Salient Battle, 130, 133-4; garrison's, in Salient Battle, 152; offensive rather than defensive, of Tobruk garrison, 111; 218-20; use of "Jock" columns, 159; Australian, in holding the Salient, 204-5; Axis, against Australian patrols, 233-4
Tanks—*British and Australian*, in the Tobruk assault, 9, 22-5, 42, 50-1; compared with German, 64-5; in the withdrawal from Cyrenaica, 70, 80; dug-in, for anti-tank defence, 86, 92; weakness of, in Tobruk, 86-7, 133; in the first Tobruk battle (Apr.), 104-5; engagement with German tanks (May 1), 136-8; losses of (May 1-3), 138, 147; tactics of, 138-9; weakness of, on the frontier, 159; reinforcements of, on the frontier (May and June), 159, 161; losses of, on the frontier (May), 160; vulnerability of "I", to German 50-mm. and 88-mm. guns, 161, 163-5; strength of, in June, 161; plan to overrun frontier, 161-2; failure of June thrust by, and heavy losses sustained, 163-5; in A.I.F. patrols (May), 21, 222; in the battle for "Plonk" (Oct. 9-10), 236-9; dummies of, 243, 292; strength of, in November, 293; inferiority to German tanks in November battle, 296, 300. *See also* "I" tanks. *German*, Mark III and Mark IV, 65; in the assault on Er Regima, 72, 73; strength of, in Cyrenaica, 80; in the Tobruk Easter Battle, 93-5, 100-3, 104-7; engaged over open sights by British gunners, 101-2; strength of in Libya (Apr.), 115-16; the first thrust by, in the Battle of the Salient, 130-2; strength of, outside Tobruk (May), 132-3; tactics of, in reducing perimeter posts, 133-4; in the battle of May 1 with the R.T.R., 136-9; their south-eastern drive checked, 140; mistaken for British, 144; effectiveness of minefields and artillery in stopping, 147; losses of in the Battle of the Salient (May 1-2), 147-8; destroyed in the first three weeks of the siege, 155; diverted from Tobruk to the frontier (May-June), 159, 160, 162; success of Rommel's tactics with, 163-4; on the Salient (May 15-17), 185, 190, 191; tackled by Bren carriers on patrol, 222-3; use of, to clear no-man's-land, 236; in the battle for "Plonk", 236-9; in Panzer Divisions, 290; strength of, in November, 293; their superiority in the November battle, 296, 300; losses in November, 301; in the attacks of Nov. 24 and 29, 302-4, 305-8. *Italian*, strength of, opposing British forces before Tobruk assault, 3, 8; in the assault, 36-7; captured at Tobruk, 48, 92; light, as pill-boxes, 48; with Rommel's forces, 65, 97; in action at Tobruk, 94; in Salient Battle, 140; in November offensive, 290, 296, 299, 308
Tapp, *Lieut*. R. P., 199
Taranto, 1
Taylor, *Pte* A. T., 150
Thomas, *Lieut*. K. B., 184
Thompson, *Brig*. L. E., 242, 245*n*, 248, 249
Thurman, *Sgt* E., quoted, 137
"Tiger" (German strongpost), 291; falls to British, 298
Times, London, 178
Tmimi (Map p. 75), German thrust to, 74-6, 77, 78
Tobruk (Maps pp. 75), 2, 3; topography of, 5-6; town of, 5, 54, 56-9; harbour of, 5, 57; Italian defences of, 5-8, 10-11, 28-9; rainfall of, 6; strongpoints of, 6-7; planning the assault on, 9-17; Fortress H.Q., 15, 32, 39, 112; first phase of Allied assault on (Map p. 23), 18-31; water supply of, 41, 57-8, 172, 173, 260-1; final assault on, 32-44; capture of, 45; mopping up after the fall of, 46-53; Italian equipment and stores captured in, 48, 57, 58; factors in

INDEX

Tobruk—*continued*
victory at, 49-53; peacetime life of Italians in, 56; normal population of, 56; withdrawal of Cyrenaica force to, 79-80; decision to make stand at, 81; decision regarding defence of the perimeter at, 84, 85; Australian and British defences of, 84-8, 119-20, 124-5, 203-4; coastal defences of, 87; constitution of Allied forces in, 88-9, 91, 319-20; the repelling of the first German assault on, 91-116; cut off by enemy, 93; prisoners taken by garrison in, 106, 107, 117, 118, 121, 123-4, 151, 186; early patrol activities from, 116-24; harbour bombed by Luftwaffe, 119-20, 126, 254-5, 265-79; anti-aircraft defence of, 126 (*See also* Anti-aircraft batteries); German capture of perimeter posts at (May 1-3), 130, 133-4, 136-7, 139-40, 141; British and Australian casualties in (May 1-3), 147; German concentration on, eases pressure on Egypt, 157-8; first attempt to relieve, by Western Desert Force (May 15-17), 159-61; demonstration by garrison to synchronize with British frontier thrust (May 15), 160; second attempt to relieve (June), 161-4; influence of new German anti-tank guns in prolonging siege of, 165; German attitude to garrison of, 168; spirit of garrison in, 168, 174, 181-2; general living conditions at, during the siege, 169-82; health of troops in, 169, 170-1; climate of, 169; food supplies in, 169-70, 176, 180; effect of bombing and shelling of, 170, 171-2, 181; news-sheets in, 176-7; concerts and sports in, 177-80; scenes from the Salient at, 207-17; strength of garrison (May-Sept.), 232; garrison at, its control of no-man's-land restricted, 240-1; heavy guns shell harbour at, 245-6; difficulties of maintaining supplies to, 251, 255-6; surplus personnel at, evacuated, 255-6; replacement of A.I.F. by British and Polish troops in, 280-9; German forces concentrate round (Nov.), 290-2; Rommel's determination to take, 290, 291, 292; the relief of (Nov.-Dec.), 290-309; composition of garrison at (Nov.), 293; Eighth Army plan to relieve, 293-4; part played by garrison in relief of, 297, 298, 299, 304-5, 306-8; A.I.F. casualties at, 321; honours and awards to men serving at, 322-5. *See also* Posts, Salient
"Tobruk Tom", 57
Tobruk Truth, 167, 176-7
Tocra (Map p. 75), 69, 70
Tommies and Diggers, unity of, in Tobruk, 89-90, 175, 181
Torr, *Maj.* Alec, 11
Tovell, *Brig.* R. W., 78, 78*n*, 116, 120, 140, 203
Trigh El Abd, 296, 302, 309
Tripoli, German forces in, 65, 66, 67; shelling and bombing of Axis shipping at, 67, 157; Axis supplies landed at, in preference to Bengazi, 157; as objective in November drive, 293
Tuit, *Sgt* Walter, 200, 201; quoted, 200
Turnbull, *Flying-Officer* Peter, 79
Two-up banned in Tobruk, 112

Vampire, H.M.A.S., 269
Vasey, Col. G. A., 51, 52; sketch of, 52-3
Vendetta, H.M.A.S., 268, 269
Veron, *Lieut.-Col.* D. N., 113*n*
V for Victory campaign, 232-3
Vichy France, helps Axis in North Africa, 67
Vietina, *Admiral* Massimiliano, 45
Vita, 269
von Ravenstein, *Maj.-Gen.*, 155, 156, 302, 304
Voyager, H.M.A.S., 269

Wadi Auda, 246, 261
Wadi Belgassem, 245
Wadi es Sehel, 261
Wakeham, *Staff-Sgt* C. D., 261
Walsoe, *Capt.* O. M., 247*n*, 308; quoted, 308
War correspondents, Army's attitude to, 34
Ward, Edward (war correspondent), 35, 43, 45, 55-6
Wardle, *Lieut.* A., 117
Water, distilleries, destruction of, foiled, 40; sources of supply of, 57-8; ration in Tobruk, 124, 173; supplies in Tobruk, 172; enemy attempt to destroy, 260-1
Waterhen, H.M.A.S., 251, 268, 269
Watson, *Lieut.-Col.* J. A., 113*n*
Wavell, *Gen. Sir* Archibald, Churchill's message to, after Sidi Barrani victory, 1; and the impossibility of

Wavell, *Gen.* Sir Archibald—*continued*
holding Cyrenaica in 1941, 63, 64-6; strength of his forces in the Middle East, 64; his miscalculation of Rommel's intentions, 66; meets Morshead at Beda Fomm, 69; sends O'Connor to advise Cyrcom, 71; arrival at Tobruk (Apr. 8), 80; his instructions regarding the holding of Tobruk, 81; appoints Lavarack to Cyrenaica command, 81; the difficulties of his task and his character, 81-2; leaves Tobruk for Cairo and Greece, 81-2; suggests shorter Tobruk defence line, 84; his Easter Sunday message to Morshead, 97; his message to Lavarack after the Easter Battle, 108; and the diverting of German forces from Tobruk to the frontier, 115; congratulates Morshead on the defence of Tobruk, 153, 250; the critical period for his Western Desert forces (Apr.-May), 158; orders attack on frontier (June), 159-60; urged to evacuate A.I.F. from Tobruk, 281

Western Desert Force, H.Q., 108; strength of (May), 158-9; cuts Bardia road behind Axis positions, 159; use of "Jock" columns by, 159; its first attempt to relieve Tobruk (May), 159-61; its second attempt (June), 161-4; converted to Eighth Army, 292

White, *Col.* A. P. O., 113*n*
White, *Pte* L. L., 202
"White Cairn", 235
"White Knoll", 231
Williams, *Lieut.* D. E., 21
Williams, *Sgt* R., 11
Williams, *Sgt* W. H., 176
Willison, *Brig.* A. C., 174, **236**
Wilson, *Capt* C. H., 99, 106
Windeyer, *Capt.* Frank, 238
Windeyer, *Lieut.-Col.* W. J. V., 141-2
"Wolf" (German strongpost), 291; falls to British, 305
Woods, *Capt.* H. A., 144
Wootten, *Brig.* G. F., 148, **149**; sketch of, 148